Architect's Studio Handbook

Architect's Studio Handbook

Terry L. Patterson, NCARB

McGraw-Hill

New York   Chicago   San Francisco
Lisbon   London   Madrid   Mexico City
Milan   New Delhi   San Juan   Seoul
Singapore   Sydney   Toronto

Cataloging-in-Publication Data is on file with the Library of Congress

McGraw-Hill

A Division of The McGraw-Hill Companies

1234567890   DOC/DOC   0987654321

ISBN 0-07-049446-0

The sponsoring editor for this book was Scott Grillo, the editing supervisor was Daina Penikas, and the production supervisor was Sherri Souffrance. It was set in Bookman, Graphite MM, Helvetica, Lucida Math, and Times by Jennie M. Patterson.

Printed and bound by R. R. Donnelley & Sons Company.

 This book is printed on recycled, acid-free paper containing a minimum of 50% recycled, de-inked fiber.

McGraw-Hill books are available at special quantity discounts to use as premiums and sales promotions, or for use in corporate training programs. For more information, please write to the Director of Special Sales, McGraw-Hill, Two Penn Plaza, New York, NY 10121-2298.

To my brother, Randy B. Patterson

Contents

Preface

Differing from typical reference manuals for those in the field or study of architecture, the *Architect's Studio Handbook* is based on practices now common in the field, and provides advice and guidelines from persons working in the building industry. (More than 150 architects, engineers, clients, contractors, construction managers, building officials, code consultants, and other professionals from all 50 states contributed their expertise to this handbook.) Rather than presenting theoretical formats and procedures, this handbook illustrates the methods *actually* being used in offices, today. It focuses on building types other than one- and two-family detached housing.

The handbook is designed to be useful in the studio work typical of architectural offices, including design, design development, and the production of working drawings. It will also be useful to students of architecture in their studio work.

The handbook is divided into parts, corresponding to the phases of studio work. Part I provides technical data for the schematic and design development phases. Space allocation tables, structural data, HVAC guidelines, and materials information are provided for designers so that they may plan space in their sketches for the building technology which will be sized by others and, thus, can be integrated into the scheme with a minimum of redesign. Also included to assist designers are engineers' summaries of key issues in selecting and integrating structural systems into architecture. Another feature which aids the designer is the way in which information in this handbook is conveyed visually, as well as being quickly accessible. For instance, instead of cumbersome tables, charts have been used to provide span limits, and graphics have been included to illustrate building materials data.

Part II of the handbook focuses on working drawings and includes other material that is also of interest to designers. CAD production guidelines are provided in the form of an office manual currently in use by a major architectural firm. Formats from working drawings produced by award-winning architects from New York to California are illustrated. Advice from contractors and construction managers on improving working drawings is provided. Comments from building officials and code experts on the successful submission of documents for building permits are included. Specifications are addressed where the issues are similar to those of working drawings. Design-build professionals and architects having practiced in foreign countries comment on the technical and other aspects of their respective specialties.

The handbook is a reference for state-of-the-art practices in architectural studio production.

Terry L. Patterson
Norman, Oklahoma

Part I

Technical Data
for
Schematic Design

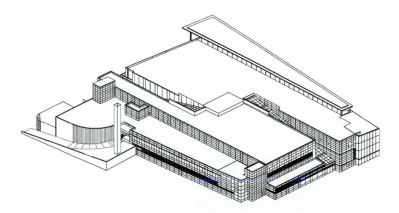

A university administration and classroom center.
Perkins Eastman Architects, P.C. New York, New York.

This section includes information that will help designers provide adequate space in the plan and section for the building technology and function. It begins with space allocation data from existing buildings, which helps shape realistic plan layouts. Next, structural guidelines help designers tentatively select structural systems and understand the elements and sizes necessary which affect the nature of space.

The associated span information aids in the initial selection of structural member sizes, thus, vertical clearances can be provided early in the process. This span data is presented in a user-friendly bar chart format, wherein the longest span capabilities can be readily identified by the relative lengths of the bars.

In addition, structure load-bearing capability is presented in small tables rather than large ones, therefore reducing the number of variables that must be reconciled in order to identify the member of choice. Structural data is followed by guidelines for selecting tentative HVAC systems. The system components are identified so that accommodations can be made for them in schematic sketches.

The section concludes with shape and size limits of selected building components provided in graphic format to help the designer propose realistic building configurations and compositions. The component data illustrated are based on those manufactured at the time of publication, as depicted in manufacturers' literature. (Manufacturers are not responsible for the interpretation and reorganization of their product information presented here.)

Space Allocation Case Studies

This chapter may be used to assign tentative square footage to circulation, mechanical/electrical rooms, and toilets in the schematic design of buildings of similar type and size to those listed. The data provided is derived from surveys of working drawings for existing buildings. Building types that were common and represented a variety of types were selected for the study. Storage was omitted from the survey since a sense of storage required is usually available in the building design program. Janitors' closets were omitted due to their very small impact on space allocation.

Net square footage (not including wall thicknesses) was calculated for circulation space, mechanical/electrical room space, and toilet room space in several common building types. This square footage was then converted to a percentage of the total building area. Designers can use these statistics as a guide to providing adequate space in the schematic phase for these service functions.

Elevators are included in the circulation study. Often, the space provided for elevators in the design phase is too small and must be enlarged after the elevator suppliers are brought into the process. When it is learned that more space is needed for elevators in the late stages of the design development phase, difficulties arise because the elevators are typically in a central location, and the expansion or addition of elevator shafts affects all the spaces around them. Securing the input of elevator professionals is a must very early in the schematic phase but until they arrive, the percentages of floor area occupied by elevators in the case studies can provide a guide for sketching purposes.

Codes require minimum toilet facilities as well as minimum clearances in toilet rooms. In order to determine how much space must be provided for toilet rooms, the toilet layouts would have to be developed near the beginning of the design process. At that stage, larger issues usually occupy the designer. So, the following percentages of building area occupied by toilet rooms in the case studies can provide a general guide for space to include in the early sketches of the building plan.

Codes also require minimum widths and maximum travel distance for means of egress which include corridors and stairways. Because many circulation elements in a building typically far exceed the code minimums and fall significantly short of the maximums, code guidelines are not convenient to use for circulation in the earliest stages of design. The case study statistics provided here (which include lobbies) can be used to learn if a schematic plan conforms to the square footage of circulation for several existing buildings. Failure to match the case study areas does not mean that the design is inadequate. A large degree of variation may warrant a restudy of the circulation before proceeding to the next step in the design process.

Tentative space can be assigned to mechanical and electrical rooms in schematic plan studies based on the percentages that these areas occupy in the existing buildings of the case studies.

Circulation Space Allocation

Building: **A MULTISTORY RESIDENTIAL BUILDING**[1]	
Area of building	229,660 sf
% of building area occupied by corridors and foyers	6.91%
% of building area occupied by stairways	1.60%
Number of passenger elevators	4
% of building area occupied by all elevator shafts	0.16%
% of building area occupied by elevator machine rooms	0.10%
Building: **A MULTISTORY RESIDENTIAL BUILDING**[1]	
Area of building	135,000 sf
% of building area occupied by corridors and foyers	4.60%
% of building area occupied by stairways	1.61%
Number of passenger elevators	2
% of building area occupied by all elevator shafts	0.13%
% of building area occupied by elevator machine rooms	0.10%

Fig. 1–1.

Building: **AN OFFICE BUILDING**[1]

Area of building	64,324 sf
% of building area occupied by corridors and foyers	7.42%
% of building area occupied by stairways	1.77%
Number of passenger elevators	1
% of building area occupied by all elevator shafts	0.19%
% of building area occupied by elevator machine rooms	0.07%

Building: **AN OFFICE BUILDING**[2]

Area of building	45,956 sf
% of building area occupied by corridors and foyers	17.69%
% of building area occupied by stairways	3.78%
Number of passenger elevators	1
% of building area occupied by all elevator shafts	0.14%
% of building area occupied by elevator machine rooms	0.13%

Building: **A POLICE DEPARTMENT**[3]

Area of building	30,000 sf
% of building area occupied by corridors and foyers	15.33%
% of building area occupied by stairways	3.0%
Number of passenger elevators	1
% of building area occupied by all elevator shafts	0.34%
% of building area occupied by elevator machine rooms	0.24%

Fig. 1–1 (continued).

Building: **A UNIVERSITY SPORTS AND FINE ARTS COMPLEX**[2]	
Area of building	91,289 sf
% of building area occupied by corridors and foyers	23.22%
% of building area occupied by stairways	2.75%
Number of passenger elevators	2
% of building area occupied by all elevator shafts	0.11%
% of building area occupied by elevator machine rooms	0.04%

Building: **A UNIVERSITY ADMINISTRATION AND CLASSROOM CENTER**[4]	
Area of building	274,806 sf
% of building area occupied by corridors and foyers	18.45%
% of building area occupied by stairways	3.12%
Number of passenger elevators	3
Number of service elevators	1
% of building area occupied by all elevator shafts	0.26%
% of building area occupied by elevator machine rooms	0.07%

Building: **A HIGH SCHOOL**[5]	
Area of building	464,557 sf
% of building area occupied by corridors and foyers	19.8%
% of building area occupied by stairways	2.5%
Number of passenger elevators	1
% of building area occupied by all elevator shafts	0.01%
% of building area occupied by elevator machine rooms	0.01%

Fig. 1–1 (continued).

Building: **AN ELEMENTARY SCHOOL**[6]

Area of building	122,670 sf
% of building area occupied by corridors and foyers	15.8%
% of building area occupied by stairways	2.05%
Number of passenger elevators	2
% of building area occupied by all elevator shafts	0.17%

Building: **A HEALTH CARE CENTER**[7]

Area of building	498,312 sf
% of building area occupied by corridors and foyers	22.38%
% of building area occupied by stairways	1.26%
Number of passenger elevators	11
Number of service elevators	2
% of building area occupied by all elevator shafts	0.98%
% of building area occupied by elevator machine rooms	0.21%

Building: **A CHURCH**[8]

Area of building	11,680 sf
% of building area occupied by corridors and foyers	14.02%
% of building area occupied by stairways	4.25%

Fig. 1–1 (concluded).

Building Service Space Allocation

Building: A MULTISTORY RESIDENTIAL BUILDING[1]	
Area of building	229,660 sf
Area of largest electrical room	105 sf
% of building area occupied by all electrical rooms	0.25%

Building: A MULTISTORY RESIDENTIAL BUILDING[1]	
Area of building	135,000 sf
Area of largest electrical room	156 sf
% of building area occupied by all electrical rooms	0.23%

Building: AN OFFICE BUILDING[1]	
Area of building	66,324 sf
Area of largest electrical room	287 sf
% of building area occupied by all electrical rooms	0.50%
Area of largest telephone equipment space	45 sf
% of building area occupied by all telephone equipment spaces	0.07%

Fig. 1–2.

Building: AN OFFICE BUILDING[2]	
Area of building	45,956 sf
Area of largest mechanical room	131 sf
% of building area occupied by all mechanical rooms	0.38%
Area of largest mechanical/electrical room combination	650 sf
% of building area occupied by all mechanical/electrical room combinations	1.41%
% of building area occupied by all mechanical rooms, and electrical rooms	1.79%
Area of largest telephone equipment space	71 sf
% of building area occupied by all telephone equipment spaces	0.15%

Building: AN OFFICE, STORAGE, AND MAINTENANCE FACILITY[9]	
Area of building	66,566 sf
Area of largest mechanical room	1,433 sf
% of building area occupied by all mechanical rooms	2.15%
Area of largest electrical room	243 sf
% of building area occupied by all electrical rooms	0.36%
% of building area occupied by all mechanical rooms and electrical rooms	2.52%
Area of largest telephone equipment space	115 sf
% of building area occupied by all telephone equipment spaces	0.17%

Fig. 1–2 (continued).

Building: A POLICE AND COURT FACILITY[10]

Area of building	35,298 sf
Area of largest mechanical room	1,579 sf
% of building area occupied by all mechanical rooms	4.47%
Area of largest electrical room	219 sf
% of building area occupied by all electrical rooms	0.62%
% of building area occupied by all mechanical rooms and electrical rooms	5.09%
Area of largest telephone equipment space	420 sf
% of building area occupied by all telephone equipment spaces	1.19%

Building: A POLICE DEPARTMENT[3]

Area of building	30,000 sf
Area of largest mechanical room	280 sf
% of building area occupied by all mechanical rooms	1.87%
Area of largest electrical room	155 sf
% of building area occupied by all electrical rooms	0.52%
Area of largest mechanical/electrical room combination	635.5 sf
% of building area occupied by all mechanical/electrical room combinations	2.12%
% of building area occupied by all mechanical rooms, electrical rooms and mechanical/electrical room combinations	4.50%
Area of largest telephone equipment space	96.6 sf
% of building area occupied by all telephone equipment spaces	0.32%

Fig. 1–2 (continued).

Building: A UNIVERSITY SPORTS AND FINE ARTS COMPLEX[2]	
Area of building	91,289 sf
Area of largest mechanical room	1,873 sf
% of building area occupied by all mechanical rooms	4.34%
Area of largest electrical room	282 sf
% of building area occupied by all electrical rooms	0.31%
% of building area occupied by all mechanical rooms and electrical rooms	4.65%
Area of boiler room	594 sf
% of building area occupied by boiler room	0.65%

Building: A UNIVERSITY ADMINISTRATION AND CLASSROOM CENTER[4]	
Area of building	274,806 sf
Area of largest mechanical room	2,720 sf
% of building area occupied by all mechanical rooms	5.54%
Area of largest electrical room	135
% of building area occupied by all electrical rooms	0.13%
% of building area occupied by all mechanical rooms and electrical rooms	5.67%
Area of largest telephone equipment space	299 sf
% of building area occupied by all telephone equipment spaces	0.24%

Fig. 1–2 (continued).

Building: **A HIGH SCHOOL**[5]	
Area of building	464,557 sf
Area of largest mechanical room	3,062 sf
% of building area occupied by all mechanical rooms	4.01%
Area of largest electrical room	750.4 sf
% of building area occupied by all electrical rooms	0.30%
% of building area occupied by all mechanical rooms and electrical rooms	4.31%
Area of largest telephone equipment space	155 sf
% of building area occupied by all telephone equipment spaces	0.06%

Building: **AN ELEMENTARY SCHOOL**[6]	
Area of building	122,670 sf
Area of largest mechanical room	532 sf
% of building area occupied by all mechanical rooms	1.35%
Area of largest electrical room	233 sf
% of building area occupied by all electrical rooms	0.29%
% of building area occupied by all mechanical rooms and electrical rooms	1.63%
Area of boiler room	1,815 sf
% of building area occupied by boiler room	1.48%

Fig. 1–2 (continued).

Building: AN ELEMENTARY SCHOOL[5]	
Area of building	111,015 sf
Area of largest mechanical room	1,239 sf
% of building area occupied by all mechanical rooms	3.70%
% of building area occupied by all electrical rooms	0.19%
% of building area occupied by all mechanical rooms and electrical rooms	3.89%
Area of boiler room	333 sf
% of building area occupied by boiler room	0.30%
Area of largest telephone equipment space	30 sf
% of building area occupied by all telephone equipment spaces	0.03%

Building: AN ELEMENTARY SCHOOL MULTIPURPOSE BUILDING[11]	
Area of building	3,351 sf
Area of largest mechanical room	76 sf
% of building area occupied by all mechanical rooms	2.27%

Building: A SCHOOL DISTRICT KITCHEN[11]	
Area of building	7,396 sf
Area of largest mechanical room	127 sf
% of building area occupied by all mechanical rooms	2.20%
Area of largest electrical room	181 sf
% of building area occupied by all electrical rooms	2.45%
% of building area occupied by all mechanical rooms and electrical rooms	4.65%

Fig. 1–2 (continued).

Building: **A CHURCH**[8]	
Area of building	11,680 sf
Area of largest mechanical room	87 sf
% of building area occupied by all mechanical rooms	1.36%

Building: **A WAREHOUSE ADDITION**[12]	
Area of building	41,235 sf
Area of largest mechanical room	397 sf
% of building area occupied by all mechanical rooms	0.96%
Area of largest electrical room	159 sf
% of building area occupied by all electrical rooms	0.38%
% of building area occupied by all mechanical rooms and electrical rooms	1.35%

Fig. 1–2 (concluded).

Toilet Room Space Allocation

Building: AN OFFICE BUILDING[1]	
Area of building	66,324 sf
% of building area occupied by men's toilet rooms	1.02%
% of building area occupied by women's toilet rooms	0.09%
% of building area occupied by all toilet rooms	1.09%

Building: AN OFFICE BUILDING[2]	
Area of building	45,956 sf
% of building area occupied by men's toilet rooms	1.10%
% of building area occupied by women's toilet rooms	1.10%
% of building area occupied by unisex toilet rooms	0.56%
% of building area occupied by all toilet rooms	2.77%

Building: A POLICE DEPARTMENT[3]	
Area of building	30,000 sf
% of building area occupied by men's toilet rooms	0.98%
% of building area occupied by women's toilet rooms	0.98%
% of building area occupied by unisex toilet rooms	0.13%
% of building area occupied by all toilet rooms	2.10%

Fig. 1–3.

Building: **A** UNIVERSITY SPORTS AND FINE ARTS COMPLEX[2]	
Area of building	91,289 sf
% of building area occupied by men's toilet rooms	1.15%
% of building area occupied by women's toilet rooms	1.15%
% of building area occupied by all toilet rooms	2.31%

Building: **A** UNIVERSTIY ADMINISTRATION AND CLASSROOM CENTER[4]	
Area of building	274,806 sf
% of building area occupied by men's toilet rooms	0.73%
% of building area occupied by women's toilet rooms	0.73%
% of building area occupied by all toilet rooms	1.45%

Building: **A** HIGH SCHOOL[5]	
Area of building	464,557 sf
% of building area occupied by men's toilet rooms	0.38%
% of building area occupied by women's toilet rooms	0.38%
% of building area occupied by unisex toilet rooms	0.01%
% of building area occupied by all toilet rooms	0.77%

Building: **A**N ELEMENTARY SCHOOL[6]	
Area of building	122,670 sf
% of building area occupied by men's toilet rooms	0.84%
% of building area occupied by women's toilet rooms	0.84%
% of building area occupied by unisex toilet rooms	0.61%
% of building area occupied by all toilet rooms	2.28%

Fig. 1–3 (continued).

Building: AN ELEMENTARY SCHOOL[5]	
Area of building	111,015 sf
% of building area occupied by men's toilet rooms	1.63%
% of building area occupied by women's toilet rooms	1.93%
% of building area occupied by unisex toilet rooms	0.44%
% of building area occupied by all toilet rooms	4.00%

Building: A CHURCH[8]	
Area of building	11,680 sf
% of building area occupied by men's toilet rooms	1.83%
% of building area occupied by women's toilet rooms	1.83%
% of building area occupied by all toilet rooms	3.66%

Fig. 1–3 (concluded).

Firms contributing drawings to this study include: [1]Ankrom Moisan Associated Architects, Portland, Oregon; [2]Gossen Livingston Associates, Inc., Architecutre, Wichita, Kansas; [3]Cromwell Architects Engineers, Little Rock, Arkansas; [4]Perkins Eastman Architects, P.C., New York, New York; [5]PBK Architects, Inc., Houston, Dallas/Fort Worth, San Antonio, Austin, League City, Texas; [6]HKT Architects, Inc., Somerville, Massachusetts; [7]Watkins Hamilton Ross Architects, Houston, Texas; [8]Mullins and Weida, Architect and Associate, Bear Creek, Pennsylvania; [9]Wilson Darnell Mann P.A., Architects, Wichita, Kansas; [10]The Hollis and Miller Group, Inc., Lee's Summit, Missouri; [11]Phillips Metsch Sweeney Moore Architects, Santa Barbara, California; [12]Stephen Wen + Associates, Architects, Inc., Pasadena, California.

Structure

This chapter begins with general guidelines for structural design provided by two engineering firms. The systems addressed are wood, steel, concrete, and post-tensioned concrete. The comments regarding these systems are intended to help architectural designers provide for a more economical and efficient structure by accommodating the nature of the system in the configuration of the building design. Notes helpful for choosing a structural system, for facilitating economy in the system selected, and for key detailing in the system are provided.

Following the general guidelines are three sections of wood and light-gage steel data, provided to assist the architectural detailer in accommodating the structure. Where actual structural sizes are not yet determined by the engineer, the architect can refer to the span and load data to estimate member sizes for purposes of architectural detailing. This makes the common reference note "see structural for size" on the architectural working drawings meaningful, as it is more likely that the members designed by the engineer will fit into the detail provided by the architect.

The span data are provided in the form of charts, which are more easily read than are tables and which provide a visual comparison of members. For instance, the spans of joists and beams are proportionately represented by bar charts which extend *across* the page. Similarly, studs are proportionately represented by bar charts which extend *up* the page. Using this system, which permits a quick visual comparison of the options, it is easy to find the member able to make the necessary span. Likewise, wood members can be quickly compared to light-gage steel members to determine relative abilities.

For structural member load capability, the range of data is too large to convert to a meaningful bar chart. In these cases tables are provided that are easier to read than those typical of manufacturers' literature. The tables are smaller with more white space than in the typical industry table. Also, the format of titles and property variables are simplified, thus the applicable table is easy to locate.

Guidelines for Structural Wood, Steel, and Concrete Design

Cheri J. Leigh, P.E.
Leigh & O'Kane LLC
Structural Engineers
Kansas City, Missouri

Wood

Wood is a commonly used framing material for residential and light commercial buildings.

A. Its best features are
1. Economical material.
2. Readily available.
3. Renewable source of building material (environmental concern).
4. Does not required highly skilled labor.
5. Can be modified in the field.
6. Easily frames pitched roofs.

B. It performs best structurally when
1. Spans for joists and rafters are under 16'.
2. Load-bearing walls and shear walls have a minimum of openings.
3. Load-bearing walls line up (stack) from one level to another.
4. Exterior shear walls are available for lateral loads.

C. Guidelines for roof rafters
1. Roof rafters are generally 24" o.c., with 1/2" or 5/8" plywood or APA-rated material.
2. Ceiling joists must run parallel to the rafters, when the rafters are pitched, to act as tension members to take the horizontal thrust at the top of the wall. (Fig. 2–1.)
3. Rafter span (feet) to depth (inches) ratio for 24" o.c. = 1.3:1 to 1.4:1.
4. Rafter span (feet) to depth (inches) ratio for 16" o.c. = 1.6:1 to 1.7:1.

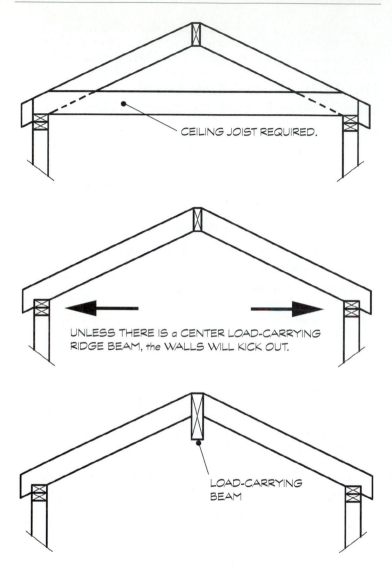

Fig. 2–1. Sections at roofs. Pitched rafters must have parallel ceiling joists to act as tension members to take the horizontal thrust at the top of the wall.

5. Species grades vary across the nation. A standard material for the Midwest is Douglas Fir Larch #2. In general, allowable material strengths have been reduced over the years as lumber is now being harvested from newer growth forests.

6. When spans exceed 16' to 18', roof trusses are an economical option.

7. Only pre-engineered trusses with pressure-applied metal plate connectors should be considered. The nailing pattern for do-it-yourself trusses is not practical. (Fig. 2–2.)

D. Guidelines for floor joists

1. Joists are generally at 16" o.c. with 5/8" or 3/4" plywood. This is less of a structural criterion than a performance criterion for deflection and "springyness."

2. Joist span (feet) to depth (inches) ratio for 24" o.c. = 1.1:1.

3. Joist span (feet) to depth (inches) ratio for 16" o.c. = 1.3:1 to 1.4:1.

4. When spans exceed 17', pre-engineered I-joists are an economical option. Some contractors say they are cheaper than dimensional lumber. There is less warpage and shrinkage with these members and they can be cut to length in the field. (Fig. 2–3.)

5. Joists framing into a beam or header should be attached with metal joist hangers, rather than "toe-nailed" into the header.

E. Guidelines for headers

1. Multiple joists are usually used for headers. Shear will often control over flexure.

2. If the capacity of dimensional lumber is exceeded, engineered products known generically as "laminated veneer lumber" (LVL) are an economical option. They have higher strengths and less warpage and shrinkage. They are a glued wood product and are similar to multiple vertical widths of plywood (unlike a glued laminated beam which is multiple horizontal pieces of 2x material). (Fig. 2–4.)

3. If the capacity of the LVL is exceeded, a steel "flitch plate" can be used. This steel plate is approximately 1/4" thick and the same depth as the lumber. It is sandwiched between the lumber and bolted through at 12" o.c., staggered. (Fig. 2–5.)

4. If the load is such that a steel beam is required, it will probably exceed the capacity of the studs at the end, and a steel pipe column should be considered for bearing.

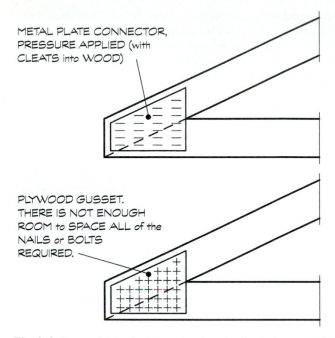

METAL PLATE CONNECTOR,
PRESSURE APPLIED (with
CLEATS into WOOD)

PLYWOOD GUSSET.
THERE IS NOT ENOUGH
ROOM to SPACE ALL of the
NAILS or BOLTS
REQUIRED.

Fig. 2–2. Pre-engineered truss connection details. Only pre-engineered trusses with pressure-applied metal plate connectors should be considered. The nailing pattern for do-it-yourself trusses is not practical.

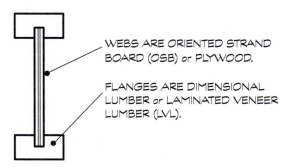

WEBS ARE ORIENTED STRAND
BOARD (OSB) or PLYWOOD.

FLANGES ARE DIMENSIONAL
LUMBER or LAMINATED VENEER
LUMBER (LVL).

Fig. 2–3. I-joist section. When spans exceed 17', pre-engineered I-joists are an economical option. These members have less warpage and shrinkage and can be cut to length in the field.

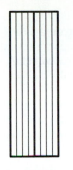

Fig. 2–4. Section, laminated veneer lumber. Where the capacity of dimensional lumber is exceeded, laminated veneer lumber (LVL) is an economical option.

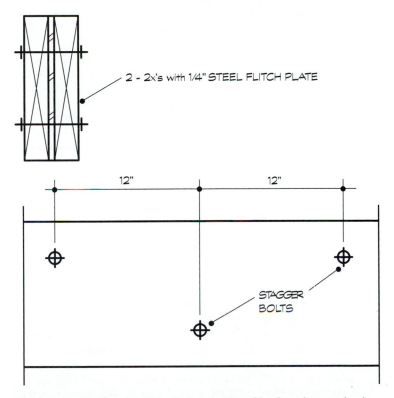

2 - 2x's with 1/4" STEEL FLITCH PLATE

12"   12"

STAGGER
BOLTS

Fig. 2–5. Section and elevation. If the capacity of laminated veneer lumber is exceeded, a steel "flitch plate" can be used.

F. Lateral systems

1. Wood buildings usually rely on a wood diaphragm on the roof, floors, and walls. Because wood is a "flexible" diaphragm, and cannot transfer torsional loads, all four walls in a rectangular building must have a resisting lateral element, usually a shear wall.

2. The roof diaphragm usually requires a nailing pattern of at least 6" o.c. at the perimeter of each sheet of plywood, and 12" o.c. at each intermediate member it crosses. More nailing may be required if the lateral loads are high or if the walls are far apart. In addition, the diaphragm may need to be "blocked," that is, an additional member is added under each joint of the plywood. "H-clips" are not equivalent to blocking. (Fig. 2–6.)

3. The lateral loads from the roof diaphragm must be transferred to the resisting wall elements. If the rafters overhang the walls, there must be a continuous blocking piece that nails the roof deck to the wall to make the load transfer. (Fig. 2–7.)

4. Overturning on the wall must also be considered. This becomes very important in a multistory building. If the shear panels are narrow, more than 2:1 height to width, the resulting tension and compression forces become very large. The compression forces may be resisted by multiple studs, however, the connections for the tension forces become critical. Various manufacturers make products for this purpose, known as "hold downs" or "tie downs" at the foundation and "strap ties" at the floors. (Fig. 2–8 and Fig. 2–9.)

5. Shear walls are useless if they do not continue to the foundation. Stopping a shear wall because of open space on the first floor essentially eliminates that shear wall from taking load.

G. Miscellaneous comments

1. Structural engineers usually draw the second floor framing with the walls and headers of the first floor below, because they are indicating what the members are framing to. When architects draw the second floor, they are indicating the walls and openings above the floor.

2. If the load-bearing walls do not stack directly over each other from one level to another, the floor joists will need to be increased or doubled to account for the additional loads. In addition, vertically misaligned load-bearing walls make the construction more difficult and increase the likelihood that the floors will later sag. In general, the most simple load path is

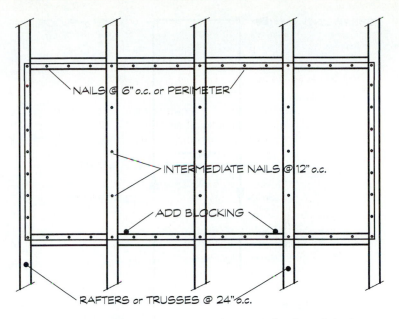

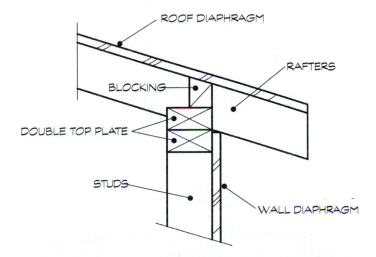

Fig. 2–6. Roof diaphragm. The usual maximum spacing for nails is shown.

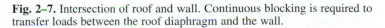

Fig. 2–7. Intersection of roof and wall. Continuous blocking is required to transfer loads between the roof diaphragm and the wall.

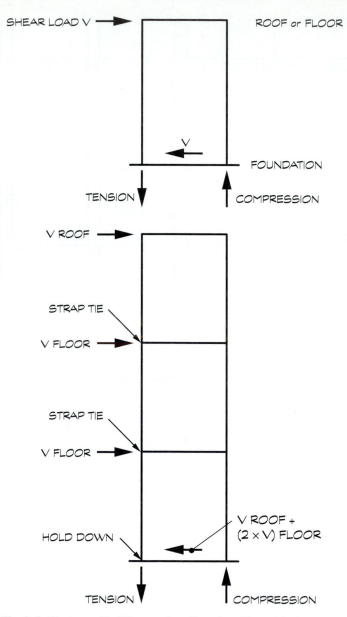

Fig. 2–8. Diagram of building section. Transfer of lateral loads to the foundation requires hold-down devices and strap ties, floor-to-floor, to resist tension.

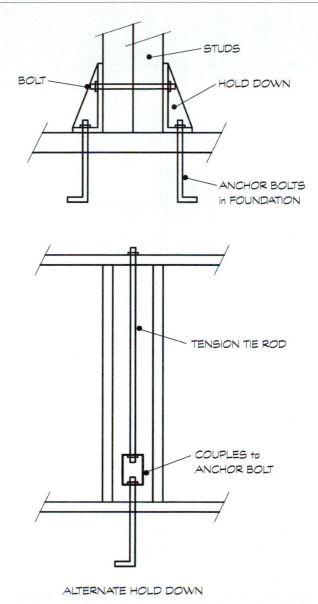

Fig. 2–9. Hold-down devices. Various manufacturers make "hold downs" or "tie downs" to take the tensile load at the foundation generated by lateral loads.

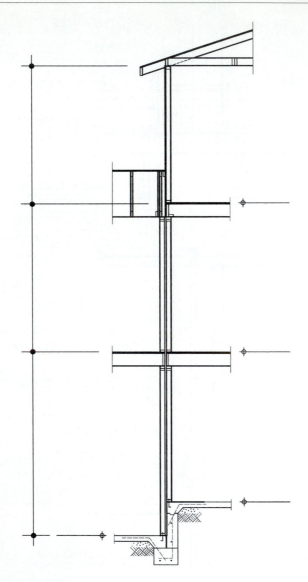

Fig. 2–10. Typical wood wall section format. Key height dimension lines shown. Vertical member sizes, steel sizes, and elevations to be added. For horizontal framing sizes, reference is made to framing plans.

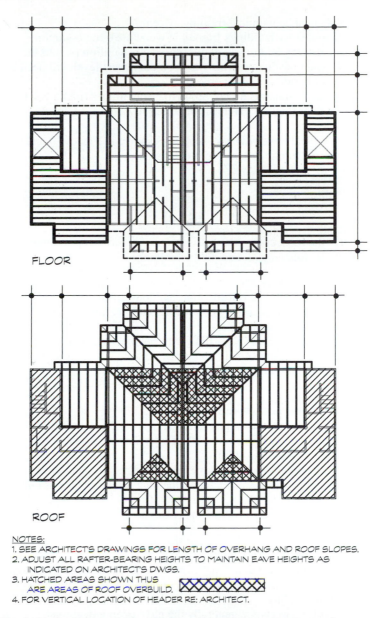

FLOOR

ROOF

NOTES:
1. SEE ARCHITECT'S DRAWINGS FOR LENGTH OF OVERHANG AND ROOF SLOPES.
2. ADJUST ALL RAFTER-BEARING HEIGHTS TO MAINTAIN EAVE HEIGHTS AS
   INDICATED ON ARCHITECT'S DWGS.
3. HATCHED AREAS SHOWN THUS
   ARE AREAS OF ROOF OVERBUILD.
4. FOR VERTICAL LOCATION OF HEADER RE: ARCHITECT.

Fig. 2–11. Typical wood framing plans. Overall dimension lines and notes
are shown. Dimensions, member size and spacing, and section cuts to be
added.

the most economical framing system.

3. Three-story buildings framed in wood are quite common. Four-story buildings are possible, with attention paid to the lateral resisting system. Studs on the lowest level will need to be either double 2x4s or 2x6s.

4. These comments do not apply to heavy timber (members 4" thick or thicker). Heavy timber has its own set of design criteria.

5. A typical structrual wall section is shown in Fig. 2–10 and typical framing plans are illustrated in Fig. 2–11.

Steel

Steel is the most commonly used framing material for commercial, industrial, educational, and public buildings.

A. Its best features are

1. Economical material for short and long spans of all loadings.
2. High degree of quality control with fabrication in a steel fabrication shop.
3. Can be modified in the field with certified welders.
4. Connections are easily welded or bolted.
5. Can build multiple stories with low dead load.
6. Fast erection.

B. It performs best structurally when

1. Bays are laid out so that the joists span 30' or less for a floor or, if there is a roof only, 40' or less. Supporting beams are most economical at 30'.
2. Generally, if the bay is longer in one direction than in the other, the joists are framed in the long direction because they are the more economical material. Otherwise, the supporting beam depth gets proportionally too deep. (Fig. 2–12 and Fig. 2–13.)

C. Guidelines for roof joists

1. Roof joist placed at 5' o.c. with a 1-1/2" metal deck is standard for the Midwest. This depends on local snow loading or wind uplift loading.
2. Steel bar joists are generally the most economical joist material. They are both lighter weight and cheaper per pound than rolled beam shapes. The disadvantage is that they are

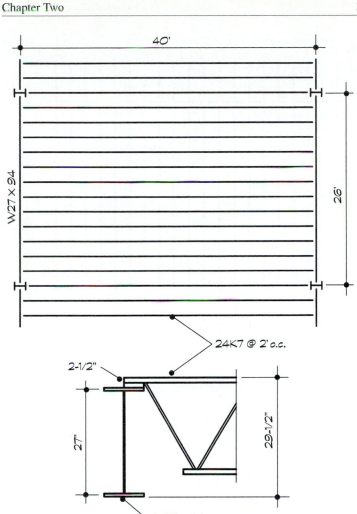

Joists: 4628 lb × $0.80/lb = $3702

Beam: 2444 lb × $1.00/lb = $2444

Total: $3702 + $2444 = $6146 per bay at 29-1/2" depth

Fig. 2–12. Cost comparison. For a 26' × 40' bay, joists framed in the long direction ($6146) is a less expensive system than is a system of joists running the short direction ($7174).

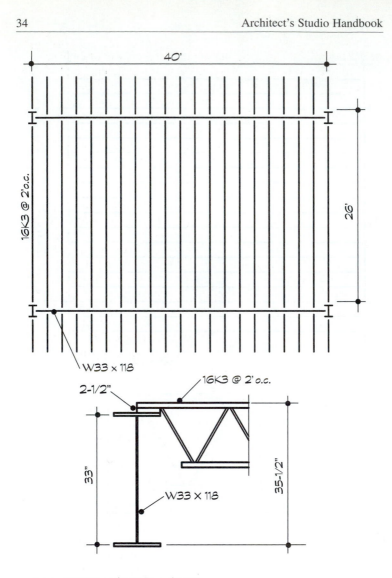

Joists: 3068 lb × $0.80/lb = $2454

Beam: 4720 lb × $1.00/lb = $4720

Total: $2454 + $4720 = $7174 per bay at 35-1/2" depth

Fig. 2–13. Cost comparison. For a 26' × 40' bay, joists framed in the short direction ($7174) is a more expensive system than is a system of joists running the long direction ($6146).

fabricated at a limited number of locations and often have a
long lead time for delivery. Because the individual members of
the bar joists are small angles or steel rods, they must be
specifically designed for concentrated loads from mechanical
units, screen walls, or additional snow drift or wind uplift.
They are difficult to modify in the field.

3. The openings in the joists are sometimes large enough to
   accommodate the mechanical ducting or piping.

4. Joist span (feet) to depth (inches) ratio for 5' o.c. = 1.5:1 to
   1.7:1. Ratios for joist spans more than 50' would be greater.

5. Deflection of roofs is restricted to L/360 for live loads with a
   finished ceiling, such as gypboard, and L/240 for total loads.
   (L is span in inches.)

6. Rolled steel beams can also be used. Deflection will start to
   control the section sooner. In order to get the most benefit of
   the steel shape, the joists are often moved to 7' to 10' o.c.,
   requiring a heavier and deeper 3" metal deck.

7. The roof is usually sloped to drain. This is easy to accomplish
   by sloping the joists and beams at least 1/4" per foot, and costs
   almost nothing additional. More detailed sloping to the drains
   can be accomplished with rigid insulation. If the entire roof
   structure is flat, using rigid insulation to create the entire
   slope is very expensive, especially for a large roof.

D. Guidelines for floor joists

1. Generally bar joists are the most economical at 24" o.c., with a
   1/2" metal deck and 3" of concrete. The metal deck is a form
   only until the concrete sets up.

2. Joist span (feet) to depth (inches) ratio for 24" o.c. = 1.5:1 to
   1.7:1 for typical office loading of 50 psf live load, 20 psf
   partition load, and 50 psf dead load.

3. Vibration can be a problem for bar joists with a thin concrete
   deck in the 28' span length range. This can occur in open floor
   areas in a shopping center, for example. Partitions and
   furnishings can dampen the vibration. A thicker floor deck,
   such as the 3" concrete suggested above, can also dampen the
   vibration.

4. Rolled steel shapes can also be used for floor joists, however,
   to get the full benefit from the steel shape, they are usually
   spaced farther apart, 5' to 7'. This requires a deeper and thicker
   metal deck with more concrete. This option is sometimes
   chosen to get a fire rating out of the deck so that the deck does
   not have to be fireproofed. It also makes a stiffer floor. It is

more often used when the floor loads are higher and vibration
is a consideration.

5. Rolled shapes do not easily accommodate openings for
ductwork or piping. Some portions of the web can be
penetrated, but almost never the flanges. Review with the
structural engineer.

6. Composite action with both the deck and joists can reduce
steel costs and provide a stiffer floor. A composite metal deck
has small dimples in the sides of the flutes which cause the
deck and concrete to act together for a more efficient section.
The deck costs more, but reduces the amount of concrete
thickness. Joists can be spaced farther apart, 7' to 10'.
(Fig. 2–14.)

7. Composite joists can also be used to further increase the
efficiency of the joist. This requires welding studs onto the
joist, usually a pair of studs every 12" or so, depending on the
loads. However, the size of the joist can be reduced. Both
rolled beams and bar joists can be made as composites. These
joists can be spaced even farther apart. (Fig. 2–15.)

8. It is best to space the floor joists so that one frames into the
column. This effectively braces the column at the floor level in
the direction of the joist.

E. Guidelines for beams

1. Beams are usually rolled shapes and vary from 4" deep to 36"
deep. Deeper sections are available from some mills. Beams
can also be welded out of plates to any depth, but would
generally be more expensive than common rolled shapes.

2. Wide flange beams, or W shapes, are the most commonly used
section. W8×24 indicates a nominal 8" deep section that
weighs 24 pounds per lineal foot along the beam length. The
use of S shapes, which have narrower flanges, is less common,
and they are used for particular applications such as underhung
crane beams. The term "I-beam" is archaic.

3. Floor beams are typically simple span beams, since they must
frame into columns. Span (feet) to depth (inches) ratio = 1.0:1
to 1.08:1 with typical office loading of 50 psf live load, 20 psf
partition load, and 50 psf dead load.

4. Roof beams can run over the tops of columns and utilize
continuous beam action. This is done with cantilever beams
and drop beams, and saves beam costs. Span (feet) to depth
(inches) ratio = 1.4:1 with typical loading of 50 psf dead plus
live load. (Fig. 2–16.)

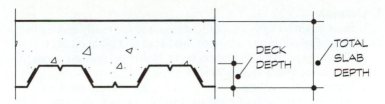

Fig. 2–14. Composite slab. A composite metal deck has small dimples in the sides of the flutes that cause the deck and concrete to act together for a more efficient section.

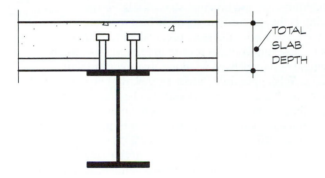

Fig. 2–15. Composite beams and joists. Both rolled beams and bar joists can be made composite by welding studs to the top at about 12" o.c. depending on loads.

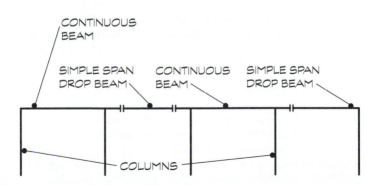

Fig. 2–16. Cantilevered and "drop beams." Drop beams are "dropped" into place after the continuous beams are set.

F. Columns

1. Steel columns have a small footprint and are easily hidden in walls. For columns with pure axial load and no bending, tubes (TS) or pipes are efficient sections. However, they are more difficult to frame than a W-section.
2. For W-section columns with bending, the column must be oriented in the axis of bending. For W-columns without bending, the beams should frame into the web of the column to avoid adding eccentric loads to the columns. (Fig. 2–17.)

G. Lateral systems

1. Steel buildings can use bracing, shear walls, or frame action. X-bracing is the most efficient and stiffest method. It uses tension to resist loads, and steel is excellent in tension. Its members must run from the roof to the foundation. Many commercial buildings have windows that interfere with X-bracing. Where possible, however, it should be considered. K-bracing and Chevron bracing can also be considered although they are not as efficient, as some members are in compression and their loads are induced into the column or beam. (Fig. 2–18.)
2. Shear walls are usually reinforced masonry or concrete. They are most efficient if they are placed in a symmetrical manner around the perimeter of the building and do not contain large openings. A stairwell on one end of the building will cause additional torsion in the diaphragm and will result in excessive forces and deflections.
3. Frame action means connecting the beams and columns with rigid connections that do not allow rotation of the joints. This induces additional moment into the members and increases their weights and depths. In addition, the frame will still sway at the top. Frame action should be considered as a last resort for lateral resistance. (Fig. 2–19 and Fig. 2–20.)

H. Miscellaneous comments

1. Pre-engineered metal buildings are an efficient use of steel framing if the building has some repetition and uses some standard components, such as roof joists and wall purlins, and roof or wall metal panels. Manufacturers' products vary. Some use completely conventional rolled shapes, others use tapered welded beams and columns.
2. Steel framing is not a fire-rated material and may require extensive sprayed-on fireproofing material or boxing-in with

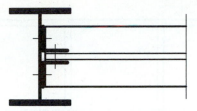

NEGLIGIBLE MOMENT in COLUMN

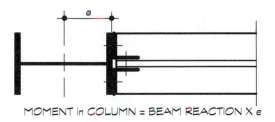

MOMENT in COLUMN = BEAM REACTION X e

Fig. 2–17. Plan views of beam-to-column connections.

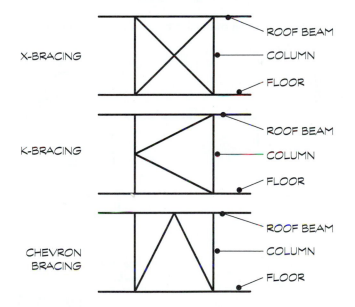

Fig. 2–18. Elevation diagrams of steel bracing configurations for lateral loads.

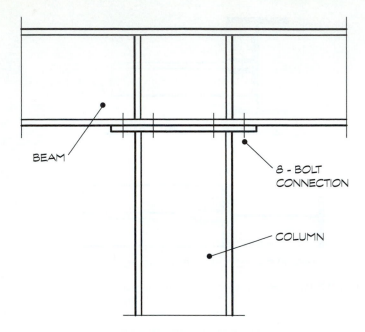

Fig. 2–19. Moment-resisting connection between beam and column.

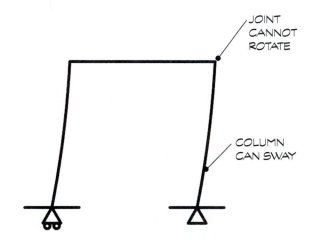

Fig. 2–20. Elevation diagram of steel framing with moment-resisting connections between columns and beams.

fire-rated gypsum board to accomplish the appropriate fire rating. All elements in the roof or floor assembly need to be reviewed by the structural engineer for each specific Underwriters Laboratory rating. Sometimes there are minimum joist or beam sizes for the assembly that exceed the engineer's design.

Concrete

Concrete is the material for a multitude of monolithic structural systems. Depending on the location and workforce, it can compete with steel for some building types.

A. Its best features are
1. Flexibility in form and shape.
2. Exposed structure can be architecturally aesthetic.
3. Material is readily available worldwide.
4. Environmental advantages.
5. Provides fireproofing.
6. Mass reduces vibration and sound transmission.
7. Long-term durability.

B. It performs best when
1. Bays are in the 30' to 40' range and are repetitious.

C. One-way beam and slab system
1. Flat slab spans one-way to beams.
2. Bays must be shorter (20' or less) to keep the thickness of the slab reasonable. Likewise, the bay spacing in the beam direction must be shorter (25' to 35') to keep the beam depth reasonable. (Fig. 2–21.)
3. This system has low forming cost.
4. This system is most often used in transition areas in a building where the regular module for joists is compromised, or used for shorter spans around openings for elevators and stairs.
5. A variation on this system is a cast-in-place, post-tensioned beam and slab. This system is used for parking garages, where a 9" slab spans 20' with stressing tendons, and the beams span 60' to the columns. This unusually long span for concrete is possible because of the high strength of the stressing tendons.

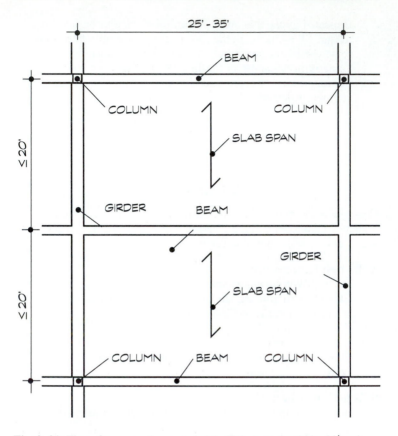

Fig. 2–21. Plan of one-way beam and slab. Slab span should be 20' or less and beam span should be between 25' and 35'.

D. One-way joist slab system

1. A one-way slab, usually 4" thick, spans to narrow rib joists which span to deeper beams. The joists are usually not more than 24" deep and are spaced 24" to 36" o.c.

2. Bays must be regular to use the repetitious pan form. Spans are typically less than 35', unless post-tensioning is used. (Fig. 2–22.)

3. Slab thickness can be adjusted to increase fire rating.

4. A more economical version of this is the one-way wide

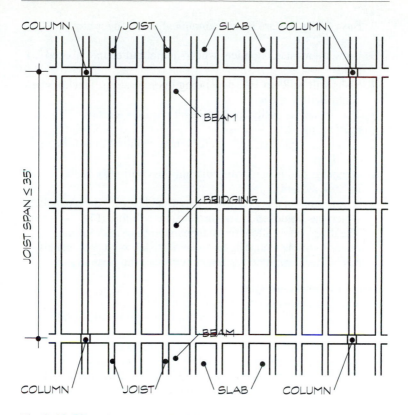

Fig. 2–22. Plan of one-way joist slab system. Spans are typically less than 35' unless using post-tensioning.

module system, also called skip-joist system. The joists are spaced at double the spacing of the traditional system, to reduce the forming costs. It also reduces the dead load of the system. The increased slab thickness provides a better fire rating. With this system, a wider supporting beam is also used. It is usually sized so that the depth is flush with the joists, and is made as wide as it needs to be to work, up to 48". Keeping the beam flush also reduces the forming costs.

E. Two-way flat plate
1. This is a flat slab with two-way action.

2. Bays 25' or less are more economical than longer bays.
   (Fig. 2–23.)
3. Bays are most economical when square, but cannot exceed 2:1
   ratio.
4. Slabs will be 8" to 10", depending upon loading. Thickness is
   controlled by shear.
5. This system is easily formed, but it requires a lot of
   reinforcing.
6. A more complex structural analysis is required than for a one-
   way slab.
7. Openings and irregularities disrupt the continuity of the
   integral system.
8. A variation on this is the two-way flat slab with drop panels,
   which has a thickened slab around the column. (Fig. 2–24.)
   The drop panels allow for reduced slab thickness for the
   majority of the slab. The two-way flat slab with drop panels
   has higher forming costs than a two-way flat plate system.

F. Two-way joist slab system
1. This system is also called waffle slab.
2. This system has joist action in both directions with solid
   panels at the columns. (Fig. 2–25.)
3. This system has higher forming costs than other systems.
4. This system is more shallow than the one-way joist system.
5. This system can span 35'-40', farther than a two-way flat slab.
6. This system requires a more complex structural analysis than
   other systems.
7. Openings and irregularities disrupt the continuity of the
   integral system.

G. Columns
1. Because of the integral nature of concrete, the columns are
   most often designed with frame action to resist lateral loads.
   The size and detailing requirements for the columns are
   critical, especially in high seismic areas.
2. A minimum column size is 12". In a multistory building
   the size of the columns may increase to 24" or more. The
   columns might also require higher strength concrete than the
   rest of the structure.
3. Several factors can require columns to be large. First, since the
   columns are doing double duty by carrying both vertical
   (axial) and lateral loads (bending), the size and spacing of the
   reinforcing bars can be a significant element in column sizing.

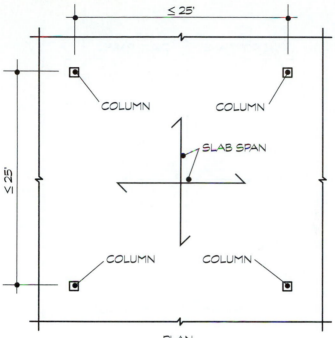

PLAN

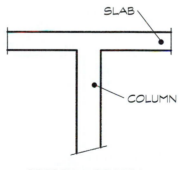

SECTION at COLUMN

Fig. 2–23. Two-way flat plate concrete slab. Formwork is relatively economical without drop panels at columns.

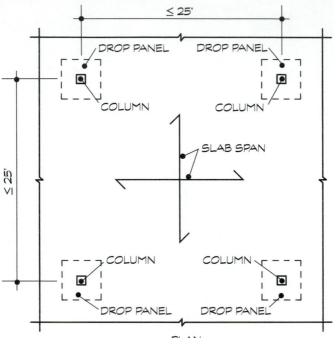

PLAN

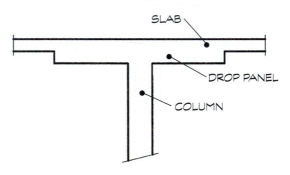

SECTION at COLUMN

Fig. 2–24. Two-way flat slab with drop panels. Drop panels permit the slab to be thinner.

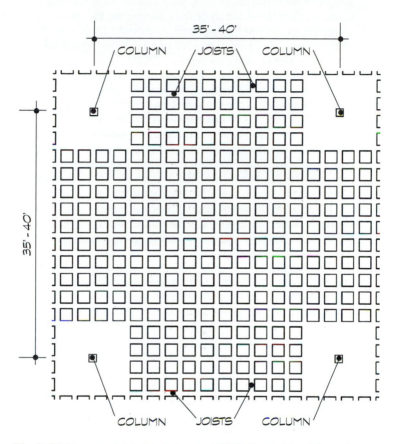

Fig. 2–25. Two-way joist slab. Joists span both ways with solid panels at the columns.

Second, the splicing of the reinforcing bars, and the minimum spacing and cover on the bars, affect column size. And third, code provisions can magnify moments in slender columns.

H. Construction issues

1. No other structural system is as dependent on quality control in the field as is concrete. The quality of concrete depends on the accuracy of the mix used that day, on the

weather both at the time of the pour and on the days until it cures, on the consolidation of the concrete, on the exact placement of the reinforcing steel, and on the formwork. If any of these items is not up to quality standards, the structural integrity of the system is at risk.

It should also be noted that although the materials for concrete construction are available almost anywhere in the world, the quality of the construction crew has more of an effect on the structure's integrity than do the materials themselves. For instance, it is not always possible to see the deficiencies of the workmanship once the concrete has been poured. In particular, although the strength of the cured concrete mix can be verified, the placement of the reinforcing steel is impossible to visually verify after the fact.

For the reasons noted above, concrete systems are the most intensely inspected structural systems by testing and design professionals. Therefore, quality control inspections need to be factored into the total construction cost of the system.

2. This system doesn't go up as quickly as structural steel, but it can start sooner, as the reinforcing steel fabrication takes less time than the structural steel fabrication.

3. The construction schedule depends on weather in some regions of the country. Cold weather construction is possible, but additional provisions must be made for the concrete mix and the protection after placement. Hot weather construction is also possible, but again additional provisions must be made for the mix and its protection after placement.

4. Openings in the systems must be planned and provided for during forming. Holes cannot be randomly drilled after the construction is in place because of the reinforcing steel. Likewise, field modifications after construction is complete are difficult.

Leigh & O'Kane LLC is a structural engineering firm in Kansas City, Missouri. Principals are Cheri Leigh, P.E. and Ronald O'Kane, P.E. They work in the commercial and public areas as consultants to architects. Typical projects are offices, retail, multiple-family housing, medical facilities, schools, and public buildings such as community centers and fire stations.

The engineers at Leigh & O'Kane have worked in all materials. Each project is unique and demands a unique structural solution. They have framed buildings in wood, steel, masonry, and concrete, each according to the requirements of the project. They are responsive to issues of durability, aesthetics, and economy, as well as the requirements of good structural design.

Leigh & O'Kane recently won an Engineering Excellence award from the Consulting Engineering Council of Missouri for their work on the Starlight Theatre Stagehouse. Other key projects are the buildings for the new Kansas International Speedway Corporation, Bartle Hall Conference Center, and the American Jazz Museum.

Post-tensioned Concrete Systems

Martin Cuadra, P.E.
Uzun & Case Engineers
Atlanta, Georgia
www.uzuncase.com

Cost, architectural limitations, and construction limitations are what decide which structural system will be used for a given project. Included in a preliminary pricing package are proposed schematic plans for framing alternatives. Based on these plans the contractor prices the most cost-effective system. The structural engineer proceeds to design the chosen system and submits plans for construction. History of development in the southeastern United States shows that post-tensioned (P.T.) concrete systems prove to be one of the most desirable structural concrete systems for commercial construction. The bay size, availability of concrete construction materials, and locale have a significant impact on the selection of the system.

The typical bay size for structures varies depending on the structure's intended use; office buildings normally range from 35 feet to 50 feet, high-rise condominiums from 20 feet to 30 feet, and parking structures from 24 feet to 60 feet. When columns are spaced at no more than 30 feet apart, a standard reinforced concrete (R.C.) system is typically used. When structural depth is also limited, a two-way P.T. slab system is usually the best or only system available. When bay size exceeds 30 feet, the most cost-effective scheme is a combination P.T. beam and skip joist/beams (narrow beams at 6 feet on center or more) system. Cleaner and more desirable for other trades, yet slightly more expensive, is the P.T. beam and one-way slab design. Since the vast majority of concrete commercial construction is multistory office and parking structures, P.T. systems are almost exclusively used now, although precast decks are also considered.

The advantages of P.T. design are numerous. Because of the maximum span to beam depth ratio, P.T. frames support the trend for more open floor plans by confining the columns to skin and core locations while controlling deflections for longer spans. Cantilevered P.T. beams also allow for more valuable office views by pulling the columns away from the corners. P.T. beams can be designed to accommodate smaller column sizes than R.C. structures by absorbing much of the moment formerly resisted by the columns.

But the benefits of P.T. designs go beyond the aesthetic realm. Typically, P.T. construction fits within the 19-inch to 25-inch structural depth favored by architects. A 21-inch system generally consists of 16-inch, readily available, standard metal pan forms plus a 5-inch slab (minimum slab thickness for a 2-hour fire rating). If shallower sections are needed, a 14-inch standard pan plus a 5-inch slab may be used. If long spans necessitate a deeper section, a 20-inch standard pan plus a 5-inch slab may be used. Depths greater than 25 inches would be required with an R.C. system and are considered nonstandard, requiring more expensive forming. Finally, since exterior spans usually control the post-tensioning design, the center spans (ranging from 18 feet to 30 feet) inherently have the extra capacity required for mechanical room loads.

P.T. and precast systems are almost always the only systems used for multilevel parking structures. If the architect designs a deck with architectural precast spandrel beams, a precast deck might be most cost-effective because the structural spandrel may be cast with the desired architectural finish. With a cast-in-place P.T. deck, the architectural spandrel must be a secondary piece attached to the structure effectively adding cost to the structure. Aside from this exception, a P.T. deck is generally less expensive to construct. Structural cost considerations are not limited to construction materials and labor but also include durability and long-term maintenance. As is well known, concrete cracks due to shrinkage during curing no matter what is done. In a P.T. system the stressing tendons effectively subject the entire horizontal surface to compressive forces which hold cracks together limiting water leakage and efflorescence problems. All in all, a P.T. deck, when properly designed and built, results in a superior structure with low maintenance requirements.

Post-tensioned concrete building systems do have their disadvantages. P.T. construction adds a level of complication, and placement mistakes could be costly. From time to time, a cable might break during the stressing operation, but there are rehabilitative methods, such as pulling out the broken strand and pushing through another high-strength strand of smaller diameter.

Because of high tension in unbonded prestressing tendons (usually around 33,000 pounds), it is critical that the strands are not kinked, corroded, or otherwise damaged in any way before or after concrete placement. The presence of cables limits coring or drilling into the P.T. beams or slabs, and such operations are usually discouraged. In limited cases, however, with the structural engineer's approval, coring may be performed in specific areas. With the use of x-ray or other nondestructive testing, the contractor might have a good idea where the tendons lie and might be able to avoid them. The fact that tendons can be slightly curved makes knowing their exact location even more difficult. (Fig. 2–26.) Any member that is directly attached to the P.T. system must attach to embedded steel plates that are placed prior to concrete placement requiring a greater amount of coordination among the disciplines.

P.T. structures experience increased creep (irreversible shrinkage due to sustained compressive forces) that must be accounted for by the engineer. This means that additional expansion joints might be necessary, but with temporary pour joints, structures up to 400 feet long can be designed without the need for expansion joints.

Summary

P.T. structural systems are good for:
- Long spans and controlled deflections.
- High span to system depth ratio.
- Increased efficiency of concrete use.
- Induced state of compression which adds durability to any cast-in-place project.

Uzun & Case Engineers is staffed by experienced professionals, ensuring clients of designs that are appropriate, practical, and economical. Experienced in a broad range of building types and technologies, Uzun & Case Engineers is capable of handling our clients' most challenging engineering problems. Having completed projects ranging in size and diversity from tensile fabric canopies to high-rise office buildings, hotels, and casinos with construction costs in excess of $250,000,000, our organization is capable of handling the full range of our clients' structural engineering needs. Uzun & Case Engineers is a firm located in Atlanta, Georgia.

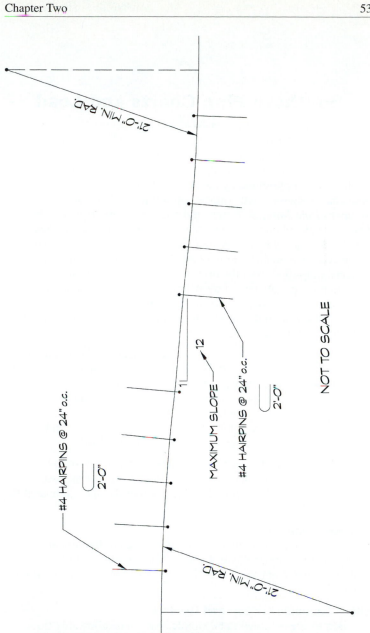

Fig. 2–26. Tendon detail at horizontal curvature. Post-tensioning tendons can curve in a horizontal plane within the limits shown.

Southern Pine Charts and Load Tables

The charts and tables in this section were derived from two publications copyrighted by the Southern Forest Products Association <www.southernpine.com> titled *Maximum Spans: Southern Pine Joists & Rafters* and *Southern Pine: Headers & Beams*. They are intended for use in estimating structural sizes suitable for the schematic design. Selection of final sizes should be made according to engineering calculations. For quick use, these data are simplified from the original publications. For more detail regarding the parameters, restrictions, and variations applicable to the data, it is necessary to review the source documents. Abbreviated guidelines for the charts and tables are provided in the following summaries.

Structural members are assumed to be adequately anchored and braced, to have the necessary bearing length, to be within moisture content limits, and to be used within certain temperature limits. Only uniform gravity loads are considered. The data address common applications in general and do not account for extreme, unusual, or special conditions. Chart headings use the pound symbol (#) to indicate pounds per square foot for loads.

Floor Joist Spans, Ceiling Joist Spans, and Rafter Spans

The joists are assumed to be used in multiples of at least 3. Live-load deflection is limited to a fraction of the span indicated by L/360 or L/240.

Built-up Beams and Headers

Allowable loads limited by both total-load deflection and live-load deflection are provided. Loads must be within both limits for a particular span and beam size. The allowable loads are in addition to beam weight.

Glued Laminated Beams and Headers

Beams are assumed to be simple spans. The allowable floor loads listed under the deflection limit of L/240 are total loads and those listed under the deflection limit of L/360 are live loads. The allowable roof loads listed under the deflection limit of L/180 are dead loads plus snow loads, and those listed under the deflection limit of L/240 are snow loads. Loads must be within *both* limits for a particular span and beam size.

Floor Beams

The charts indicate the length of floor (measured perpendicular to the beam) that can be carried by the beam for the given loads. The supported floor extends across the beam and spans to walls on both sides of the beam. The length of floor is the total length from the supporting wall on one side of the beam to the supporting wall on the other side of the beam. It is assumed that the beam is centered in the span of the floor. The single members with fractions in their dimensions are glued laminated beams.

Floor Edge Beams

The charts indicate the length of floor (measured perpendicular to the beam) that can be carried by the beam for the given loads. The supported floor is on only one side of the beam and extends to a wall. The length of floor is measured from the beam to the supporting wall. The beam is at the edge of the span of the floor. The single members in the charts with fractions in their dimensions are glued laminated beams.

Roof Ridge Beams

The charts indicate the (projected) length of roof supported by a beam at the ridge for the given loads. The roof extends from the beam to walls on both sides of the beam. The length of the roof is measured in a horizontal plane from the supporting wall on one side of the ridge to the supporting wall on the other side of the ridge. The single members in the charts with fractions in their dimensions are glued laminated beams.

Door and Window Lintels

The charts indicate allowable lintel spans in exterior load-bearing walls. In the one-story charts, the lintels support only the roof. In the two-story charts, the lintels support the second floor, the second story wall, and the roof above it. The roof load includes a 2' overhang. The single members in the charts with fractions in their dimensions are glued laminated beams in simple span conditions.

Interpretation of the data in the source publications and its conversion to the new format in this chapter is solely the work of the author, who is responsible for any errors therein. The Southern Forest Products Association did not participate in this project and has not reviewed the results.

Floor Joist Spans (ft.) (Southern Pine)

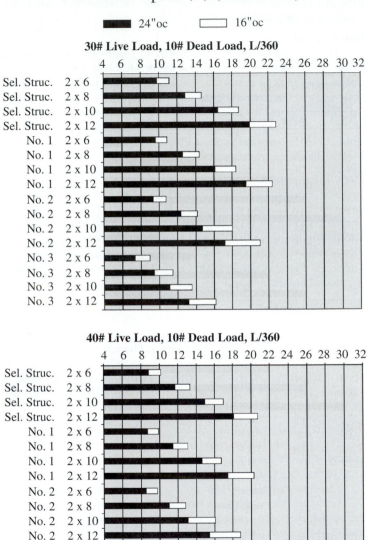

Fig. 2–27.

Floor Joist Spans (ft.) (Southern Pine)

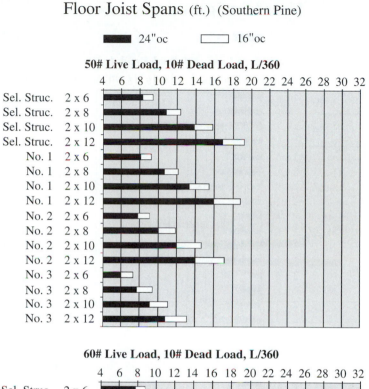

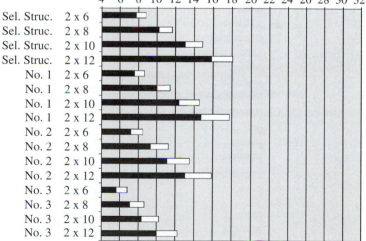

Fig. 2–27 (continued).

Floor Joist Spans (ft.) (Southern Pine)

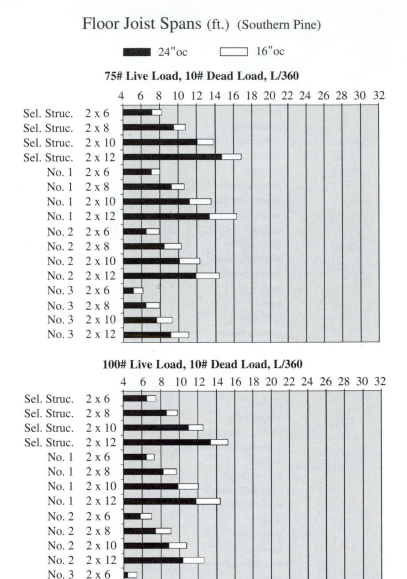

Fig. 2–27 (continued).

Floor Joist Spans (ft.) (Southern Pine)

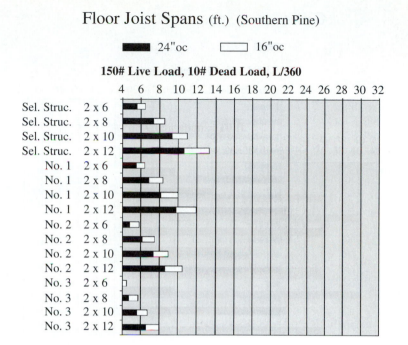

Fig. 2–27 (concluded).

Ceiling Joist Spans (ft.) (Southern Pine)

■■■ 24"oc   ☐ 16"oc

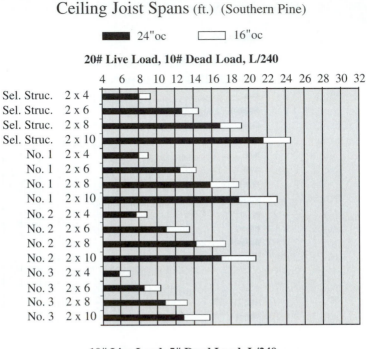

20# Live Load, 10# Dead Load, L/240

10# Live Load, 5# Dead Load, L/240

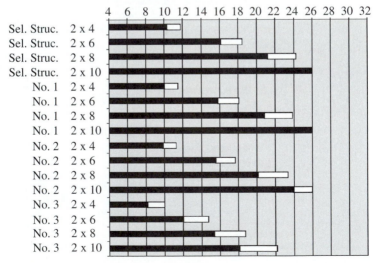

Fig. 2–28.

Roof Rafter Spans (ft.) (Southern Pine)

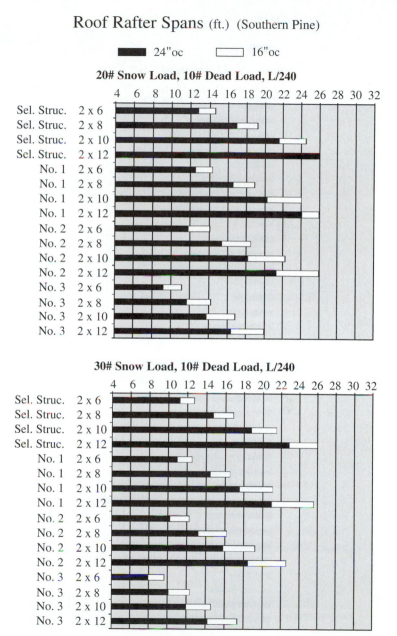

20# Snow Load, 10# Dead Load, L/240

30# Snow Load, 10# Dead Load, L/240

Fig. 2–29.

Roof Rafter Spans (ft.) (Southern Pine)

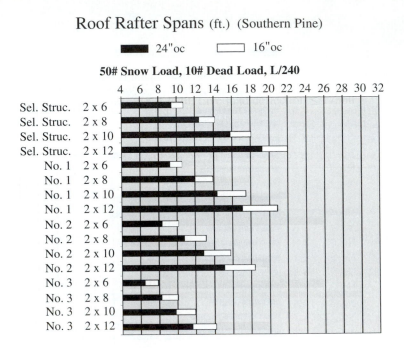

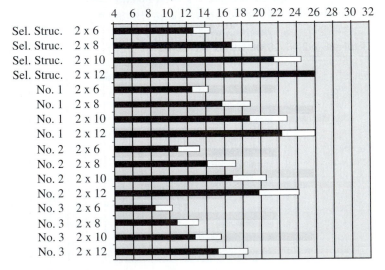

Fig. 2–29 (continued).

Roof Rafter Spans (ft.) (Southern Pine)

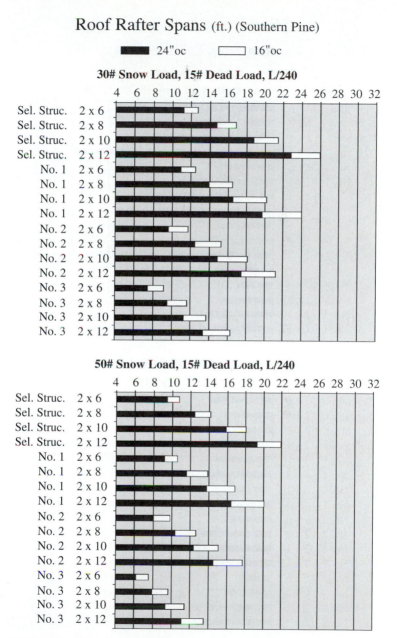

■ 24"oc   □ 16"oc

30# Snow Load, 15# Dead Load, L/240

50# Snow Load, 15# Dead Load, L/240

Fig. 2–29 (continued).

Roof Rafter Spans (ft.) (Southern Pine)

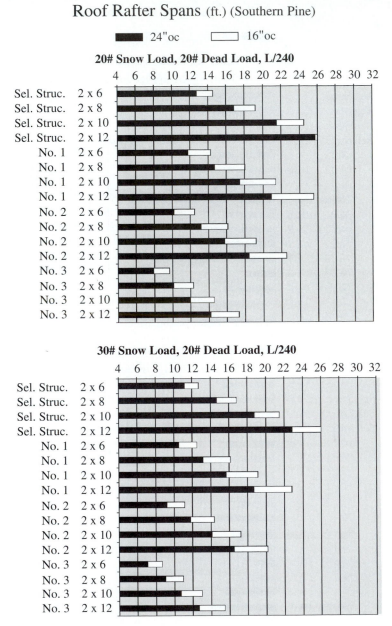

Fig. 2–29 (continued).

Roof Rafter Spans (ft.) (Southern Pine)

■ 24"oc   □ 16"oc

50# Snow Load, 20# Dead Load, L/240

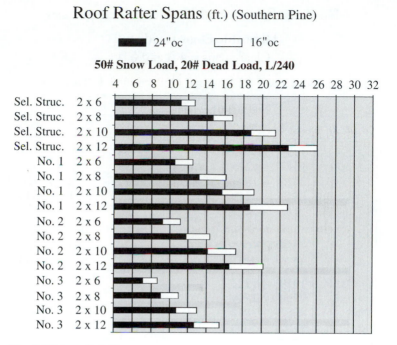

Fig. 2–29 (concluded).

Built-up Beams and Headers (Southern Pine)

Allowable Floor Loads (plf)

Clear spans = **4 ft** and **6 ft**

Dead Load + Live Load (deflection ≤ **L/240**)

Size	Clear span = 4 ft			Clear span = 6 ft		
	No.1	No.2	No.3	No.1	No.2	No.3
2-2x6	959	754	458	448	340	204
2-2x8	1397	1225	733	699	562	330
2-2x10	2025	1697	1007	972	792	458
2-2x12	2843	2249	1397	1353	1071	644
3-2x6	1439	1293	788	771	586	352
3-2x8	2096	2096	1258	1201	967	569
3-2x10	3038	2905	1725	1670	1358	788
3-2x12	4276	3824	2384	2197	1834	1106
4-2x6	1919	1724	1050	1027	782	470
4-2x8	2794	2794	1677	1602	1289	758
4-2x10	4051	3873	2300	2227	1811	1051
4-2x12	5702	5098	3179	2929	2445	1475

Live Load (deflection ≤ **L/360**)

Size	Clear span = 4 ft			Clear span = 6 ft		
	No.1	No.2	No.3	No.1	No.2	No.3
2-2x6	959	754	458	448	340	204
2-2x8	1397	1225	733	699	562	330
2-2x10	2025	1697	1007	972	792	458
2-2x12	2843	2249	1397	1353	1071	644
3-2x6	1439	1293	788	699	586	352
3-2x8	2096	2096	1258	1201	967	569
3-2x10	3038	2905	1725	1670	1358	788
3-2x12	4276	3824	2384	2197	1834	1106
4-2x6	1919	1724	1050	932	782	470
4-2x8	2794	2794	1677	1602	1289	758
4-2x10	4051	3873	2300	2227	1811	1051
4-2x12	5702	5098	3179	2929	2445	1475

Fig. 2–30.

Built-up Beams and Headers (Southern Pine)

Allowable Floor Loads (plf)

Clear spans = **8 ft** and **10 ft**

Dead Load + Live Load (deflection ≤ **L/240**)

Size	Clear span = 8 ft			Clear span = 10 ft		
	No.1	No.2	No.3	No.1	No.2	No.3
2-2x6	253	191	114	151	121	71
2-2x8	397	318	185	254	203	117
2-2x10	556	451	257	357	288	163
2-2x12	783	615	364	506	395	232
3-2x6	436	330	197	227	210	124
3-2x8	684	548	319	439	351	202
3-2x10	957	776	444	616	498	282
3-2x12	1344	1057	628	871	681	401
4-2x6	581	440	262	303	280	165
4-2x8	912	731	426	585	467	270
4-2x10	1276	1035	592	822	664	377
4-2x12	1792	1409	837	1161	908	534

Live Load (deflection ≤ **L/360**)

Size	Clear span = 8 ft			Clear span = 10 ft		
	No.1	No.2	No.3	No.1	No.2	No.3
2-2x6	201	190	114	104	98	71
2-2x8	397	318	185	235	203	117
2-2x10	556	451	257	357	288	163
2-2x12	783	615	364	506	395	232
3-2x6	300	284	197	155	146	124
3-2x8	679	548	319	352	333	202
3-2x10	957	776	444	616	498	282
3-2x12	1344	1057	628	871	681	401
4-2x6	400	379	262	207	195	165
4-2x8	905	731	426	469	444	270
4-2x10	1276	1035	592	822	664	377
4-2x12	1792	1409	837	1161	908	534

Fig. 2–30 (continued).

Built-up Beams and Headers (Southern Pine)

Allowable Floor Loads (plf)

Clear spans = **12 ft** and **14 ft**

Dead Load + Live Load (deflection ≤ **L/240**)

	Clear span = 12 ft			Clear span = 14 ft		
Size	No.1	No.2	No.3	No.1	No.2	No.3
2-2x6	86	81	48	53	50	35
2-2x8	176	140	80	125	102	57
2-2x10	248	199	112	181	145	80
2-2x12	352	274	159	257	200	115
3-2x6	130	122	84	80	75	61
3-2x8	300	242	138	187	176	100
3-2x10	428	345	194	313	251	140
3-2x12	607	473	276	445	346	200
4-2x6	173	162	113	106	99	81
4-2x8	400	323	185	249	234	133
4-2x10	570	459	258	417	335	187
4-2x12	809	630	368	593	461	267

Live Load (deflection ≤ **L/360**)

	Clear span = 12 ft			Clear span = 14 ft		
Size	No.1	No.2	No.3	No.1	No.2	No.3
2-2x6	60	57	48	38	36	31
2-2x8	137	129	80	87	82	57
2-2x10	248	199	112	179	145	80
2-2x12	352	274	159	257	200	115
3-2x6	90	85	75	57	54	47
3-2x8	205	194	138	130	122	100
3-2x10	423	345	194	268	251	140
3-2x12	607	473	276	445	346	200
4-2x6	120	113	99	76	72	63
4-2x8	273	258	185	173	163	133
4-2x10	564	459	258	357	335	187
4-2x12	809	630	368	593	461	267

Fig. 2–30 (continued).

Built-up Beams and Headers (Southern Pine)

Allowable Floor Loads (plf)

Clear spans = **16 ft** and **18 ft**

Dead Load + Live Load (deflection ≤ L/240)

Size	Clear span = 16 ft			Clear span = 18 ft		
	No.1	No.2	No.3	No.1	No.2	No.3
2-2x6	34	32	26	23	21	18
2-2x8	82	77	43	56	53	33
2-2x10	137	110	60	107	85	46
2-2x12	196	151	86	153	118	67
3-2x6	51	48	41	34	32	27
3-2x8	123	116	75	84	79	57
3-2x10	238	191	105	181	149	81
3-2x12	339	263	151	266	205	117
4-2x6	69	64	55	46	43	36
4-2x8	164	154	100	112	105	77
4-2x10	317	254	140	241	198	108
4-2x12	452	350	201	355	274	155

Live Load (deflection ≤ L/360)

Size	Clear span = 16 ft			Clear span = 18 ft		
	No.1	No.2	No.3	No.1	No.2	No.3
2-2x6	26	24	21	18	17	15
2-2x8	58	55	43	41	39	3
2-2x10	120	110	60	85	80	46
2-2x12	196	151	86	152	118	67
3-2x6	38	36	32	27	25	22
3-2x8	87	82	72	61	58	51
3-2x10	180	170	105	127	120	81
3-2x12	323	263	151	227	205	117
4-2x6	51	48	42	36	34	30
4-2x8	116	110	96	82	77	68
4-2x10	240	227	140	169	160	108
4-2x12	430	350	201	303	274	155

Fig. 2–30 (continued).

Built-up Beams and Headers (Southern Pine)

Allowable Roof Loads (plf)

Clear spans = **4 ft** and **6 ft**

Dead Load + Live Load (deflection ≤ **L/180**)

Size	Clear span = 4 ft			Clear span = 6 ft		
	No.1	No.2	No.3	No.1	No.2	No.3
2-2x6	1104	862	525	514	391	235
2-2x8	1608	1396	839	800	644	379
2-2x10	2330	1925	1150	1110	906	525
2-2x12	3198	2536	1589	1540	1222	738
3-2x6	1656	1478	903	884	673	405
3-2x8	2411	2397	1438	1374	1107	653
3-2x10	3495	3290	1967	1906	1552	904
3-2x12	4919	4301	2707	2528	2089	1267
4-2x6	2208	1970	1204	1178	897	540
4-2x8	3215	3196	1917	1832	1476	871
4-2x10	4660	4387	2623	2541	2070	1206
4-2x12	6559	5735	3609	3371	2786	1689

Live Load (deflection ≤ **L/240**)

Size	Clear span = 4 ft			Clear span = 6 ft		
	No.1	No.2	No.3	No.1	No.2	No.3
2-2x6	1104	862	525	514	319	235
2-2x8	1608	1396	839	800	644	379
2-2x10	2330	1925	1150	1110	906	525
2-2x12	3198	2536	1589	1540	1222	738
3-2x6	1656	1478	903	884	673	405
3-2x8	2411	2397	1438	1374	1107	653
3-2x10	3495	3290	1967	1906	1552	904
3-2x12	4919	4301	2707	2528	2089	1267
4-2x6	2208	1970	1204	1178	897	540
4-2x8	3215	3196	1917	1832	1476	871
4-2x10	4660	4387	2623	2541	2070	1206
4-2x12	6559	5735	3609	3371	2786	1689

Fig. 2–30 (continued).

Built-up Beams and Headers (Southern Pine)

Allowable Roof Loads (plf)

Clear spans = **8 ft** and **10 ft**

Dead Load + Live Load (deflection ≤ **L/180**)

Size	Clear span = 8 ft			Clear span = 10 ft		
	No.1	No.2	No.3	No.1	No.2	No.3
2-2x6	291	220	131	186	140	83
2-2x8	456	366	213	293	234	135
2-2x10	638	517	296	411	332	188
2-2x12	896	704	419	580	454	267
3-2x6	501	380	227	304	242	143
3-2x8	785	630	368	505	404	234
3-2x10	1096	890	511	708	573	326
3-2x12	1536	1210	721	999	782	462
4-2x6	668	506	302	406	323	191
4-2x8	1047	840	490	673	538	311
4-2x10	1462	1187	682	944	764	434
4-2x12	2048	1614	962	1331	1043	615

Live Load (deflection ≤ **L/240**)

Size	Clear span = 8 ft			Clear span = 10 ft		
	No.1	No.2	No.3	No.1	No.2	No.3
2-2x6	291	220	131	155	140	83
2-2x8	456	366	213	293	234	135
2-2x10	638	517	296	411	332	188
2-2x12	896	704	419	580	454	267
3-2x6	449	380	227	232	219	143
3-2x8	785	630	368	505	404	234
3-2x10	1096	890	511	708	573	326
3-2x12	1536	1210	721	999	782	462
4-2x6	598	506	302	309	292	191
4-2x8	1047	840	490	673	538	311
4-2x10	1462	1187	682	944	764	434
4-2x12	2048	1614	962	1331	1043	615

Fig. 2–30 (continued).

Built-up Beams and Headers (Southern Pine)

Allowable Roof Loads (plf)
Clear spans = **12 ft** and **14 ft**

Dead Load + Live Load (deflection ≤ **L/180**)

Size	Clear span = 12 ft			Clear span = 14 ft		
	No.1	No.2	No.3	No.1	No.2	No.3
2-2x6	116	96	56	72	68	40
2-2x8	203	161	92	148	117	67
2-2x10	285	230	129	209	168	93
2-2x12	404	315	184	297	230	133
3-2x6	174	164	98	108	101	70
3-2x8	350	279	160	251	204	116
3-2x10	492	397	224	361	290	162
3-2x12	697	544	318	512	399	231
4-2x6	232	218	131	144	135	94
4-2x8	467	372	214	335	271	154
4-2x10	656	529	299	481	387	216
4-2x12	930	725	425	683	531	309

Live Load (deflection ≤ **L/240**)

Size	Clear span = 12 ft			Clear span = 14 ft		
	No.1	No.2	No.3	No.1	No.2	No.3
2-2x6	90	85	56	57	54	40
2-2x8	203	161	92	130	117	67
2-2x10	285	230	129	209	168	93
2-2x12	404	315	184	297	230	133
3-2x6	135	127	98	85	80	70
3-2x8	307	279	160	194	183	116
3-2x10	492	397	224	361	290	162
3-2x12	697	544	318	512	399	231
4-2x6	180	170	131	114	107	94
4-2x8	409	372	214	259	244	154
4-2x10	656	529	299	481	387	216
4-2x12	930	725	425	683	531	309

Fig. 2–30 (continued).

Built-up Beams and Headers (Southern Pine)

Allowable Roof Loads (plf)
Clear spans = **16 ft** and **18 ft**

Dead Load + Live Load (deflection ≤ **L/180**)

Size	Clear span = 16 ft			Clear span = 18 ft		
	No.1	No.2	No.3	No.1	No.2	No.3
2-2x6	47	44	30	32	30	23
2-2x8	111	89	50	77	69	38
2-2x10	159	127	70	124	99	54
2-2x12	226	175	100	177	137	78
3-2x6	71	66	53	48	45	38
3-2x8	166	154	87	115	108	67
3-2x10	275	220	122	215	172	94
3-2x12	391	303	175	307	238	136
4-2x6	94	88	70	64	60	51
4-2x8	222	206	116	153	144	90
4-2x10	366	294	163	287	230	126
4-2x12	521	404	233	410	317	181

Live Load (deflection ≤ **L/240**)

Size	Clear span = 16 ft			Clear span = 18 ft		
	No.1	No.2	No.3	No.1	No.2	No.3
2-2x6	38	36	30	27	25	22
2-2x8	87	82	50	61	58	38
2-2x10	159	127	70	124	99	54
2-2x12	226	175	100	177	137	78
3-2x6	57	54	47	40	38	33
3-2x8	131	123	87	92	87	67
3-2x10	270	220	122	190	172	94
3-2x12	391	303	175	307	238	136
4-2x6	76	72	63	54	51	44
4-2x8	174	164	116	123	116	90
4-2x10	360	294	163	253	230	126
4-2x12	521	404	233	410	317	181

Fig. 2–30 (concluded).

Glued Laminated Beams and Headers
(Southern Pine)

Allowable Floor Loads (plf)

Beam clear span = **6 ft**

Depth	Width = 3-1/2"			Width = 5-1/2"		
	Bearing required	Allowable load		Bearing required	Allowable load	
		L/240	L/360		L/240	L/360
8-1/4"	3.0"	1659	1659	—	—	—
9-5/8"	3.0"	2212	2212	—	—	—
11"	4.5"	2819	2819	4.5"	4431	4431
12-3/8"	—	—	—	4.5"	5455	5455

Beam clear span = **8 ft**

Depth	Width = 3-1/2"			Width = 5-1/2"		
	Bearing required	Allowable load		Bearing required	Allowable load	
		L/240	L/360		L/240	L/360
8-1/4"	1.5"	954	813	—	—	—
9-5/8"	3.0"	1284	1268	—	—	—
11"	3.0"	1656	1656	3.0"	2603	2603
12-3/8"	4.5"	2065	2065	4.5"	3245	3245
13-3/4"	4.5"	2506	2506	4.5"	3938	3938
15-1/8"	6.0"	2975	2975	6.0"	4675	4675
16-1/2"	—	—	—	6.0"	5449	5449

Beam clear span = **10 ft**

Depth	Width = 3-1/2"			Width = 5-1/2"		
	Bearing required	Allowable load		Bearing required	Allowable load	
		L/240	L/360		L/240	L/360
8-1/4"	1.5"	615	423	—	—	—
9-5/8"	3.0"	832	665	—	—	—
11"	3.0"	1079	980	3.0"	1696	1540
12-3/8"	3.0"	1353	1353	3.0"	2127	2127
13-3/4"	4.5"	1654	1654	4.5"	2599	2599
15-1/8"	4.5"	1978	1978	4.5"	3108	3108
16-1/2"	6.0"	2323	2323	6.0"	3651	3651
17-7/8"	6.0"	2688	2688	6.0"	4224	4224
19-1/4"	—	—	—	7.5"	4822	4822
20-5/8"	—	—	—	7.5"	5444	5444

Fig. 2–31.

Glued Laminated Beams and Headers
(Southern Pine)
Allowable Floor Loads (plf)

Beam clear span = **12 ft**

Depth	Width = 3-1/2"			Width = 5-1/2"		
	Bearing required	Allowable load		Bearing required	Allowable load	
		L/240	L/360		L/240	L/360
8-1/4"	1.5"	365	248	—	—	—
9-5/8"	1.5"	576	390	—	—	—
11"	3.0"	755	577	3.0"	1186	906
12-3/8"	3.0"	950	813	3.0"	1493	1277
13-3/4"	3.0"	1165	1102	3.0"	1831	1732
15-1/8"	4.5"	1400	1400	4.5"	2199	2199
16-1/2"	4.5"	1651	1651	4.5"	2595	2595
17-7/8"	6.0"	1920	1920	6.0"	3017	3017
19-1/4"	—	—	—	6.0"	3462	3462
20-5/8"	—	—	—	7.5"	3920	3920
22"	—	—	—	7.5"	4392	4392
23-3/8"	—	—	—	9.0"	4880	4880

Beam clear span = **14 ft**

Depth	Width = 3-1/2"			Width = 5-1/2"		
	Bearing required	Allowable load		Bearing required	Allowable load	
		L/240	L/360		L/240	L/360
8-1/4"	1.5"	229	157	—	—	—
9-5/8"	1.5"	364	248	—	—	—
11"	1.5"	541	367	1.5"	850	577
12-3/8"	3.0"	701	518	3.0"	1102	815
13-3/4"	3.0"	862	705	3.0"	1355	1108
15-1/8"	3.0"	1038	930	3.0"	1631	1462
16-1/2"	4.5"	1228	1195	4.5"	1930	1878
17-7/8"	4.5"	1432	1432	4.5"	2244	2244
19-1/4"	—	—	—	6.0"	2574	2574
20-5/8"	—	—	—	6.0"	2922	2922
22"	—	—	—	6.0"	3286	3286
23-3/8"	—	—	—	7.5"	3665	3665

Fig. 2–31 (continued).

Glued Laminated Beams and Headers
(Southern Pine)
Allowable Floor Loads (plf)

Beam clear span = **16 ft**

Depth	Width = 3-1/2"			Width = 5-1/2"		
	Bearing required	Allowable load		Bearing required	Allowable load	
		L/240	L/360		L/240	L/360
8-1/4"	1.5"	151	106	—	—	—
9-5/8"	1.5"	242	167	—	—	—
11"	1.5"	363	248	1.5"	570	390
12-3/8"	3.0"	515	351	3.0"	809	551
13-3/4"	3.0"	662	477	3.0"	1040	750
15-1/8"	3.0"	798	631	3.0"	1253	992
16-1/2"	3.0"	947	813	3.0"	1479	1278
17-7/8"	4.5"	1106	1025	4.5"	1721	1611
19-1/4"	—	—	—	4.5"	1979	1979
20-5/8"	—	—	—	6.0"	2251	2251
22"	—	—	—	6.0"	2538	2538
23-3/8"	—	—	—	6.0"	2838	2838

Beam clear span = **18 ft**

Depth	Width = 3-1/2"			Width = 5-1/2"		
	Bearing required	Allowable load		Bearing required	Allowable load	
		L/240	L/360		L/240	L/360
8-1/4"	1.5"	104	74	—	—	—
9-5/8"	1.5"	168	118	—	—	—
11"	1.5"	253	175	1.5"	398	275
12-3/8"	1.5"	361	248	1.5"	568	390
13-3/4"	3.0"	495	338	3.0"	778	531
15-1/8"	3.0"	632	447	3.0"	985	702
16-1/2"	3.0"	750	577	3.0"	1165	907
17-7/8"	4.5"	878	728	4.5"	1358	1145
19-1/4"	—	—	—	4.5"	1564	1421
20-5/8"	—	—	—	4.5"	1782	1735
22"	—	—	—	6.0"	2012	2012
23-3/8"	—	—	—	6.0"	2253	2253

Fig. 2–31 (continued).

Glued Laminated Beams and Headers
(Southern Pine)
Allowable Floor Loads (plf)

Beam clear span = **20 ft**

Depth	Width = 3-1/2"			Width = 5-1/2"		
	Bearing required	Allowable load		Bearing required	Allowable load	
		L/240	L/360		L/240	L/360
8-1/4"	1.5"	74	54	—	—	—
9-5/8"	1.5"	121	86	—	—	—
11"	1.5"	183	128	1.5"	287	201
12-3/8"	1.5"	262	182	1.5"	411	286
13-3/4"	1.5"	360	248	1.5"	566	390
15-1/8"	3.0"	479	328	3.0"	753	516
16-1/2"	3.0"	608	423	3.0"	939	666
17-7/8"	3.0"	712	536	3.0"	1096	842
19-1/4"	—	—	—	4.5"	1263	1046
20-5/8"	—	—	—	4.5"	1441	1279
22"	—	—	—	4.5"	1629	1542
23-3/8"	—	—	—	6.0"	1827	1827

Beam clear span = **22 ft**

Depth	Width = 3-1/2"			Width = 5-1/2"		
	Bearing required	Allowable load		Bearing required	Allowable load	
		L/240	L/360		L/240	L/360
9-5/8"	1.5"	89	65	—	—	—
11"	1.5"	135	97	1.5"	212	152
12-3/8"	1.5"	195	137	1.5"	306	215
13-3/4"	1.5"	269	187	1.5"	422	294
15-1/8"	3.0"	359	248	3.0"	564	390
16-1/2"	3.0"	466	320	3.0"	732	503
17-7/8"	3.0"	586	405	3.0"	901	637
19-1/4"	—	—	—	3.0"	1039	792
20-5/8"	—	—	—	4.5"	1187	969
22"	—	—	—	4.5"	1343	1170
23-3/8"	—	—	—	4.5"	1508	1396

Fig. 2–31 (continued).

Glued Laminated Beams and Headers
(Southern Pine)

Allowable Floor Loads (plf)

Beam clear span = **24 ft**

Depth	Width = 3-1/2"			Width = 5-1/2"		
	Bearing required	Allowable load L/240	L/360	Bearing required	Allowable load L/240	L/360
9-5/8"	1.5"	66	50	—	—	—
11"	1.5"	102	74	1.5"	160	117
12-3/8"	1.5"	148	106	1.5"	232	166
13-3/4"	1.5"	205	145	1.5"	322	227
15-1/8"	1.5"	275	192	1.5"	431	302
16-1/2"	3.0"	358	248	3.0"	562	390
17-7/8"	3.0"	455	314	3.0"	715	493
19-1/4"	—	—	—	3.0"	869	613
20-5/8"	—	—	—	3.0"	993	751
22"	—	—	—	4.5"	1124	908
23-3/8"	—	—	—	4.5"	1264	1084

Beam clear span = **26 ft**

Depth	Width = 3-1/2"			Width = 5-1/2"		
	Bearing required	Allowable load L/240	L/360	Bearing required	Allowable load L/240	L/360
11"	1.5"	78	59	1.5"	123	92
12-3/8"	1.5"	114	83	1.5"	179	131
13-3/4"	1.5"	159	114	1.5"	250	179
15-1/8"	1.5"	214	151	1.5"	336	238
16-1/2"	1.5"	279	196	1.5"	439	308
17-7/8"	3.0"	356	248	3.0"	560	390
19-1/4"	—	—	—	3.0"	701	485
20-5/8"	—	—	—	3.0"	841	594
22"	—	—	—	4.5"	953	718
23-3/8"	—	—	—	4.5"	1072	858

Fig. 2–31 (continued).

Glued Laminated Beams and Headers
(Southern Pine)
Allowable Floor Loads (plf)

Beam clear span = **28 ft**

Depth	Width = 3-1/2"			Width = 5-1/2"		
	Bearing required	Allowable load		Bearing required	Allowable load	
		L/240	L/360		L/240	L/360
12-3/8"	1.5"	89	67	1.5"	140	105
13-3/4"	1.5"	125	91	1.5"	197	144
15-1/8"	1.5"	169	122	1.5"	265	191
16-1/2"	1.5"	221	157	1.5"	348	247
17-7/8"	3.0"	283	199	3.0"	445	313
19-1/4"	—	—	—	3.0"	558	390
20-5/8"	—	—	—	3.0"	688	478
22"	—	—	—	3.0"	817	577
23-3/8"	—	—	—	4.5"	919	690

Beam clear span = **30 ft**

Depth	Width = 3-1/2"			Width = 5-1/2"		
	Bearing required	Allowable load		Bearing required	Allowable load	
		L/240	L/360		L/240	L/360
12-3/8"	1.5"	71	54	1.5"	111	85
13-3/4"	1.5"	100	74	1.5"	157	117
15-1/8"	1.5"	135	99	1.5"	212	156
16-1/2"	1.5"	178	128	1.5"	279	201
17-7/8"	1.5"	228	163	1.5"	358	255
19-1/4"	—	—	—	3.0"	451	318
20-5/8"	—	—	—	3.0"	556	390
22"	—	—	—	3.0"	677	471
23-3/8"	—	—	—	3.0"	796	563

Fig. 2–31 (continued).

Glued Laminated Beams and Headers
(Southern Pine)
Allowable Floor Loads (plf)
Beam clear span = **32 ft**

Depth	Width = 3-1/2"			Width = 5-1/2"		
	Bearing required	Allowable load		Bearing required	Allowable load	
		L/240	L/360		L/240	L/360
13-3/4"	1.5"	80	61	1.5"	126	97
15-1/8"	1.5"	109	82	1.5"	171	128
16-1/2"	1.5"	144	106	1.5"	227	166
17-7/8"	1.5"	186	134	1.5"	292	211
19-1/4"	—	—	—	1.5"	368	263
20-5/8"	—	—	—	3.0"	455	322
22"	—	—	—	3.0"	554	390
23-3/8"	—	—	—	3.0"	667	466

Beam clear span = **34 ft**

Depth	Width = 3-1/2"			Width = 5-1/2"		
	Bearing required	Allowable load		Bearing required	Allowable load	
		L/240	L/360		L/240	L/360
13-3/4"	1.5"	65	51	1.5"	102	81
15-1/8"	1.5"	89	68	1.5"	140	107
16-1/2"	1.5"	118	88	1.5"	185	139
17-7/8"	1.5"	152	112	1.5"	239	176
19-1/4"	—	—	—	1.5"	303	220
20-5/8"	—	—	—	3.0"	376	269
22"	—	—	—	3.0"	459	326
23-3/8"	—	—	—	3.0"	553	390

Fig. 2–31 (continued).

Glued Laminated Beams and Headers
(Southern Pine)
Allowable Floor Loads (plf)

Beam clear span = **36 ft**

Depth	Width = 3-1/2"			Width = 5-1/2"		
	Bearing required	Allowable load		Bearing required	Allowable load	
		L/240	L/360		L/240	L/360
15-1/8"	1.5"	73	57	1.5"	114	90
16-1/2"	1.5"	97	74	1.5"	153	117
17-7/8"	1.5"	126	95	1.5"	198	149
19-1/4"	—	—	—	1.5"	251	185
20-5/8"	—	—	—	1.5"	313	227
22"	—	—	—	3.0"	383	275
23-3/8"	—	—	—	3.0"	462	329

Beam clear span = **38 ft**

Depth	Width = 3-1/2"			Width = 5-1/2"		
	Bearing required	Allowable load		Bearing required	Allowable load	
		L/240	L/360		L/240	L/360
16-1/2"	1.5"	81	63	1.5"	127	100
17-7/8"	1.5"	105	80	1.5"	165	126
19-1/4"	—	—	—	1.5"	210	158
20-5/8"	—	—	—	1.5"	262	194
22"	—	—	—	3.0"	321	235
23-3/8"	—	—	—	3.0"	389	281

Fig. 2–31 (continued).

Glued Laminated Beams and Headers
(Southern Pine)
Allowable Roof Loads (plf)

Beam clear span = **6 ft**

Depth	Width = 3-1/2"			Width = 5-1/2"		
	Bearing required	Allowable load		Bearing required	Allowable load	
		L/240	L/360		L/240	L/360
8-1/4"	3.0"	1892	1892	—	—	—
9-5/8"	4.5"	2514	2514	—	—	—
11"	—	—	—	4.5"	5017	5017

Beam clear span = **8 ft**

Depth	Width = 3-1/2"			Width = 5-1/2"		
	Bearing required	Allowable load		Bearing required	Allowable load	
		L/240	L/360		L/240	L/360
8-1/4"	3.0"	1093	1093	—	—	—
9-5/8"	3.0"	1469	1469	—	—	—
11"	4.5"	1889	1889	4.5"	2969	2969
12-3/8"	4.5"	2350	2350	4.5"	3693	3693
13-3/4"	6.0"	2844	2844	6.0"	4469	4469
15-1/8"	—	—	—	6.0"	5289	5289

Beam clear span = **10 ft**

Depth	Width = 3-1/2"			Width = 5-1/2"		
	Bearing required	Allowable load		Bearing required	Allowable load	
		L/240	L/360		L/240	L/360
8-1/4"	1.5"	706	632	—	—	—
9-5/8"	3.0"	954	954	—	—	—
11"	3.0"	1235	1235	3.0"	1941	1941
12-3/8"	4.5"	1547	1547	4.5"	2431	2431
13-3/4"	4.5"	1887	1887	4.5"	2965	2965
15-1/8"	6.0"	2252	2252	6.0"	3539	3539
16-1/2"	6.0"	2640	2640	6.0"	4148	4148
17-7/8"	—	—	—	7.5"	4788	4788
19-1/4"	—	—	—	7.5"	5452	5452

Fig. 2–31 (continued).

Glued Laminated Beams and Headers
(Southern Pine)
Allowable Roof Loads (plf)

Beam clear span = **12 ft**

Depth	Width = 3-1/2"			Width = 5-1/2"		
	Bearing required	Allowable load		Bearing required	Allowable load	
		L/240	L/360		L/240	L/360
8-1/4"	1.5"	486	370	—	—	—
9-5/8"	3.0"	667	582	—	—	—
11"	3.0"	866	860	3.0"	1361	1352
12-3/8"	3.0"	1089	1089	3.0"	1711	1711
13-3/4"	4.5"	1334	1334	4.5"	2096	2096
15-1/8"	4.5"	1600	1600	4.5"	2514	2514
16-1/2"	6.0"	1885	1885	6.0"	2961	2961
17-7/8"	6.0"	2187	2187	6.0"	3437	3437
19-1/4"	—	—	—	7.5"	3937	3937
20-5/8"	—	—	—	7.5"	4449	4449
22"	—	—	—	9.0"	4976	4976
23-3/8"	—	—	—	9.0"	5517	5517

Beam clear span = **14 ft**

Depth	Width = 3-1/2"			Width = 5-1/2"		
	Bearing required	Allowable load		Bearing required	Allowable load	
		L/240	L/360		L/240	L/360
8-1/4"	1.5"	229	157	—	—	—
9-5/8"	1.5"	364	248	—	—	—
11"	3.0"	541	367	3.0"	1004	861
12-3/8"	3.0"	701	518	3.0"	1265	1216
13-3/4"	3.0"	862	705	3.0"	1554	1554
15-1/8"	4.5"	1038	930	4.5"	1869	1869
16-1/2"	4.5"	1228	1195	4.5"	2209	2209
17-7/8"	6.0"	1432	1432	6.0"	2565	2565
19-1/4"	—	—	—	6.0"	2938	2938
20-5/8"	—	—	—	6.0"	3331	3331
22"	—	—	—	7.5"	3741	3741
23-3/8"	—	—	—	9.0"	4166	4166

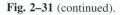

Fig. 2–31 (continued).

Glued Laminated Beams and Headers
(Southern Pine)
Allowable Roof Loads (plf)

Beam clear span = **16 ft**

	Width = 3-1/2"			Width = 5-1/2"		
	Bearing	Allowable load		Bearing	Allowable load	
Depth	required	L/240	L/360	required	L/240	L/360
8-1/4"	1.5"	204	158	—	—	—
9-5/8"	1.5"	325	250	—	—	—
11"	3.0"	484	370	3.0"	760	581
12-3/8"	3.0"	618	523	3.0"	971	822
13-3/4"	3.0"	760	712	3.0"	1195	1120
15-1/8"	3.0"	916	916	3.0"	1438	1438
16-1/2"	4.5"	1085	1085	4.5"	1696	1696
17-7/8"	4.5"	1267	1267	4.5"	1972	1972
19-1/4"	—	—	—	6.0"	2265	2265
20-5/8"	—	—	—	6.0"	2574	2574
22"	—	—	—	6.0"	2898	2898
23-3/8"	—	—	—	7.5"	3236	3236

Beam clear span = **18 ft**

	Width = 3-1/2"			Width = 5-1/2"		
	Bearing	Allowable load		Bearing	Allowable load	
Depth	required	L/240	L/360	required	L/240	L/360
8-1/4"	1.5"	141	112	—	—	—
9-5/8"	1.5"	227	176	—	—	—
11"	1.5"	229	262	1.5"	533	411
12-3/8"	3.0"	482	370	3.0"	758	581
13-3/4"	3.0"	602	504	3.0"	943	793
15-1/8"	3.0"	726	667	3.0"	1133	1049
16-1/2"	4.5"	861	860	4.5"	1338	1338
17-7/8"	4.5"	1007	1007	4.5"	1558	1558
19-1/4"	—	—	—	4.5"	1793	1793
20-5/8"	—	—	—	6.0"	2041	2041
22"	—	—	—	6.0"	2302	2302
23-3/8"	—	—	—	6.0"	2576	2576

Fig. 2–31 (continued).

Glued Laminated Beams and Headers
(Southern Pine)
Allowable Roof Loads (plf)

Beam clear span = **20 ft**

Depth	Width = 3-1/2"			Width = 5-1/2"		
	Bearing required	Allowable load		Bearing required	Allowable load	
		L/240	L/360		L/240	L/360
8-1/4"	1.5"	101	81	—	—	—
9-5/8"	1.5"	163	129	—	—	—
11"	1.5"	246	192	1.5"	386	301
12-3/8"	1.5"	351	271	1.5"	552	427
13-3/4"	3.0"	481	370	3.0"	756	581
15-1/8"	3.0"	588	490	3.0"	913	770
16-1/2"	3.0"	699	632	3.0"	1080	994
17-7/8"	4.5"	818	799	4.5"	1259	1257
19-1/4"	—	—	—	4.5"	1451	1451
20-5/8"	—	—	—	4.5"	1654	1654
22"	—	—	—	6.0"	1868	1868
23-3/8"	—	—	—	6.0"	2093	2093

Beam clear span = **22 ft**

Depth	Width = 3-1/2"			Width = 5-1/2"		
	Bearing required	Allowable load		Bearing required	Allowable load	
		L/240	L/360		L/240	L/360
9-5/8"	1.5"	121	97	—	—	—
11"	1.5"	183	144	1.5"	287	227
12-3/8"	1.5"	262	205	1.5"	412	322
13-3/4"	3.0"	361	280	3.0"	567	439
15-1/8"	3.0"	480	370	3.0"	750	582
16-1/2"	3.0"	578	478	3.0"	888	752
17-7/8"	3.0"	675	605	3.0"	1036	951
19-1/4"	—	—	—	4.5"	1195	1182
20-5/8"	—	—	—	4.5"	1364	1364
22"	—	—	—	4.5"	1543	1543
23-3/8"	—	—	—	6.0"	1731	1731

Fig. 2–31 (continued).

Glued Laminated Beams and Headers
(Southern Pine)
Allowable Roof Loads (plf)

Beam clear span = **24 ft**

	Width = 3-1/2"			Width = 5-1/2"		
	Bearing	Allowable load		Bearing	Allowable load	
Depth	required	L/240	L/360	required	L/240	L/360
9-5/8"	1.5"	91	75	—	—	—
11"	1.5"	139	112	1.5"	218	175
12-3/8"	1.5"	200	158	1.5"	315	249
13-3/4"	1.5"	276	216	1.5"	434	340
15-1/8"	3.0"	369	287	3.0"	579	450
16-1/2"	3.0"	479	370	3.0"	741	582
17-7/8"	3.0"	564	468	3.0"	866	737
19-1/4"	—	—	—	3.0"	1000	916
20-5/8"	—	—	—	4.5"	1142	1121
22"	—	—	—	4.5"	1293	1293
23-3/8"	—	—	—	4.5"	1452	1452

Beam clear span = **26 ft**

	Width = 3-1/2"			Width = 5-1/2"		
	Bearing	Allowable load		Bearing	Allowable load	
Depth	required	L/240	L/360	required	L/240	L/360
11"	1.5"	107	88	1.5"	169	138
12-3/8"	1.5"	155	125	1.5"	244	196
13-3/4"	1.5"	215	171	1.5"	338	268
15-1/8"	1.5"	288	226	1.5"	453	356
16-1/2"	3.0"	375	292	3.0"	590	460
17-7/8"	3.0"	478	370	3.0"	734	582
19-1/4"	—	—	—	3.0"	847	724
20-5/8"	—	—	—	4.5"	969	887
22"	—	—	—	4.5"	1097	1072
23-3/8"	—	—	—	4.5"	1233	1233

Fig. 2–31 (continued).

Glued Laminated Beams and Headers
(Southern Pine)
Allowable Roof Loads (plf)

Beam clear span = **28 ft**

Depth	Width = 3-1/2"			Width = 5-1/2"		
	Bearing required	Allowable load		Bearing required	Allowable load	
		L/240	L/360		L/240	L/360
12-3/8"	1.5"	123	100	1.5"	193	157
13-3/4"	1.5"	170	137	1.5"	268	215
15-1/8"	1.5"	229	182	1.5"	360	286
16-1/2"	3.0"	299	235	3.0"	470	369
17-7/8"	3.0"	381	298	3.0"	599	468
19-1/4"	—	—	—	3.0"	726	582
20-5/8"	—	—	—	3.0"	831	713
22"	—	—	—	4.5"	942	862
23-3/8"	—	—	—	4.5"	1059	1030

Beam clear span = **30 ft**

Depth	Width = 3-1/2"			Width = 5-1/2"		
	Bearing required	Allowable load		Bearing required	Allowable load	
		L/240	L/360		L/240	L/360
12-3/8"	1.5"	98	81	1.5"	154	128
13-3/4"	1.5"	137	112	1.5"	215	175
15-1/8"	1.5"	184	148	1.5"	289	233
16-1/2"	1.5"	241	192	1.5"	379	301
17-7/8"	3.0"	308	243	3.0"	484	382
19-1/4"	—	—	—	3.0"	606	475
20-5/8"	—	—	—	3.0"	719	582
22"	—	—	—	4.5"	816	704
23-3/8"	—	—	—	4.5"	918	842

Fig. 2–31 (continued).

Glued Laminated Beams and Headers
(Southern Pine)
Allowable Roof Loads (plf)

Beam clear span = **32 ft**

Depth	Width = 3-1/2"			Width = 5-1/2"		
	Bearing required	Allowable load L/240	L/360	Bearing required	Allowable load L/240	L/360
13-3/4"	1.5"	111	92	1.5"	714	145
15-1/8"	1.5"	150	122	1.5"	235	192
16-1/2"	1.5"	197	158	1.5"	309	249
17-7/8"	3.0"	252	201	3.0"	396	315
19-1/4"	—	—	—	3.0"	497	393
20-5/8"	—	—	—	3.0"	613	481
22"	—	—	—	3.0"	713	582
23-3/8"	—	—	—	4.5"	802	696

Beam clear span = **34 ft**

Depth	Width = 3-1/2"			Width = 5-1/2"		
	Bearing required	Allowable load L/240	L/360	Bearing required	Allowable load L/240	L/360
13-3/4"	1.5"	90	77	1.5"	142	121
15-1/8"	1.5"	123	102	1.5"	193	160
16-1/2"	1.5"	162	132	1.5"	254	208
17-7/8"	1.5"	208	168	1.5"	327	264
19-1/4"	—	—	—	1.5"	411	328
20-5/8"	—	—	—	3.0"	508	402
22"	—	—	—	3.0"	618	487
23-3/8"	—	—	—	3.0"	706	582

Fig. 2–31 (continued).

Glued Laminated Beams and Headers
(Southern Pine)
Allowable Roof Loads (plf)

Beam clear span = **36 ft**

Depth	Width = 3-1/2"			Width = 5-1/2"		
	Bearing required	Allowable load		Bearing required	Allowable load	
		L/240	L/360		L/240	L/360
15-1/8"	1.5"	101	86	1.5"	159	135
16-1/2"	1.5"	134	112	1.5"	211	175
17-7/8"	1.5"	173	142	1.5"	272	222
19-1/4"	—	—	—	3.0"	343	277
20-5/8"	—	—	—	3.0"	425	340
22"	—	—	—	3.0"	518	411
23-3/8"	—	—	—	3.0"	623	492

Beam clear span = **38 ft**

Depth	Width = 3-1/2"			Width = 5-1/2"		
	Bearing required	Allowable load		Bearing required	Allowable load	
		L/240	L/360		L/240	L/360
16-1/2"	1.5"	112	95	1.5"	176	149
17-7/8"	1.5"	145	120	1.5"	228	189
19-1/4"	—	—	—	1.5"	288	236
20-5/8"	—	—	—	1.5"	358	290
22"	—	—	—	3.0"	437	351
23-3/8"	—	—	—	3.0"	527	419

Fig. 2–31 (concluded).

Floor Beams (Southern Pine)

Total length of floor supported on both sides of the beam
measured ⊥ to the beam.

40# Live load, 10# Dead load
Total load deflection ≤ **L/240,** Live load deflection ≤ **L/360**

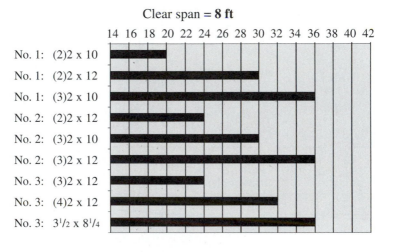

Clear span = **8 ft**

No. 1:	(2)2 x 10
No. 1:	(2)2 x 12
No. 1:	(3)2 x 10
No. 2:	(2)2 x 12
No. 2:	(3)2 x 10
No. 2:	(3)2 x 12
No. 3:	(3)2 x 12
No. 3:	(4)2 x 12
No. 3:	3¹/₂ x 8¹/₄

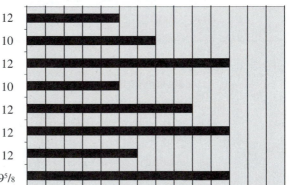

Clear span = **9 ft**

No. 1:	(2)2 x 12
No. 1:	(3)2 x 10
No. 1:	(3)2 x 12
No. 2:	(3)2 x 10
No. 2:	(3)2 x 12
No. 2:	(4)2 x 12
No. 3:	(4)2 x 12
No. 3:	3¹/₂ x 9⁵/₈

Fig. 2–32.

Floor Beams (Southern Pine)

Total length of floor supported on both sides of the beam
measured ⊥ to the beam.

40# Live load, **10#** Dead load
Total load deflection ≤ **L/240,** Live load deflection ≤ **L/360**

Clear span = **10 ft**

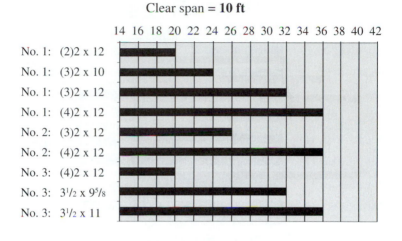

Clear span = **11 ft**

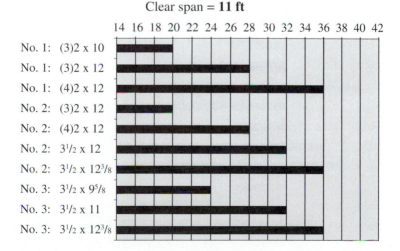

Fig. 2–32 (continued).

Floor Beams (Southern Pine)

Total length of floor supported on both sides of the beam
measured ⊥ to the beam.

40# Live load, **10#** Dead load
Total load deflection ≤ **L/240,** Live load deflection ≤ **L/360**

Clear span = **12 ft**

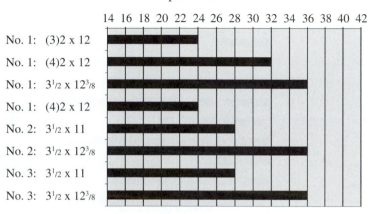

Clear span = **13 ft**

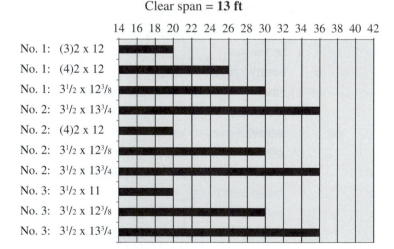

Fig. 2–32 (continued).

Floor Beams (Southern Pine)

Total length of floor supported on both sides of the beam
measured ⊥ to the beam.

40# Live load, **10#** Dead load
Total load deflection **≤ L/240,** Live load deflection **≤ L/360**

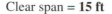

Clear span = **14 ft**

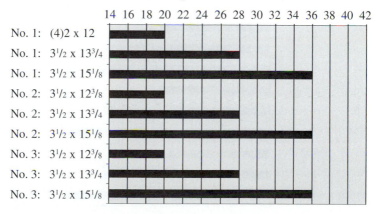

Clear span = **15 ft**

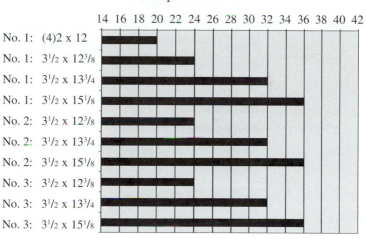

Fig. 2–32 (continued).

Floor Beams (Southern Pine)

Total length of floor supported on both sides of the beam
measured ⊥ to the beam.

40# Live load, **10#** Dead load
Total load deflection ≤ **L/240,** Live load deflection ≤ **L/360**

Clear span = **16 ft**

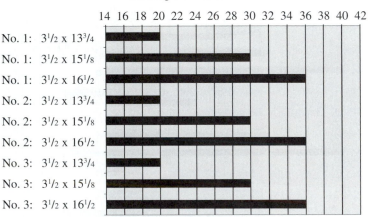

Clear span = **17 ft**

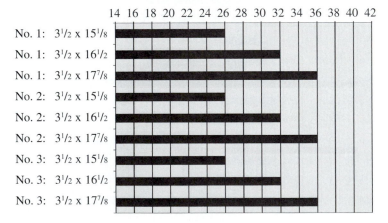

Fig. 2–32 (continued).

Floor Beams (Southern Pine)

Total length of floor supported on both sides of the beam
measured ⊥ to the beam.

40# Live load, **10#** Dead load
Total load deflection ≤ **L/240,** Live load deflection ≤ **L/360**

Clear span = **18 ft**

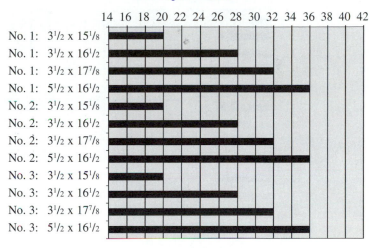

Fig. 2–32 (concluded).

Floor Edge Beams (Southern Pine)

Length of floor supported on only one side of the beam
measured ⊥ to the beam.

40# Live load, **10#** Dead load
Total load deflection **≤ L/240,** Live load deflection **≤ L/360**

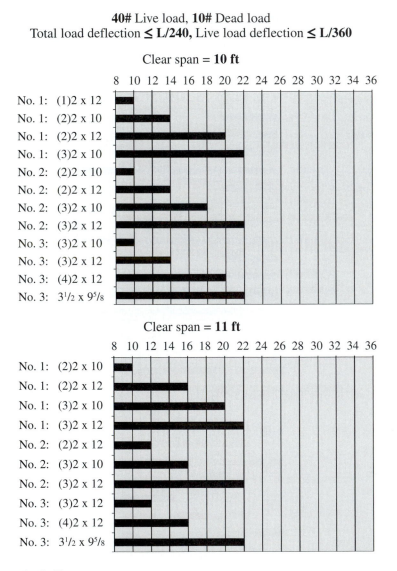

Fig. 2–33.

Floor Edge Beams (Southern Pine)

Length of floor supported on only one side of the beam
measured ⊥ to the beam.

40# Live load, **10#** Dead load
Total load deflection ≤ **L/240,** Live load deflection ≤ **L/360**

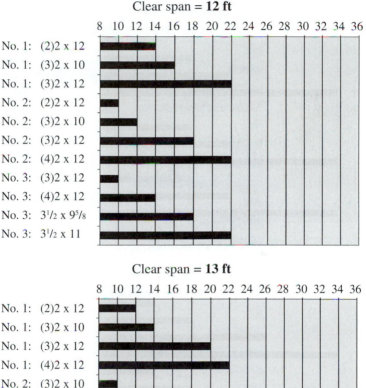

Clear span = **12 ft**

	8 10 12 14 16 18 20 22 24 26 28 30 32 34 36
No. 1: (2)2 x 12	
No. 1: (3)2 x 10	
No. 1: (3)2 x 12	
No. 2: (2)2 x 12	
No. 2: (3)2 x 10	
No. 2: (3)2 x 12	
No. 2: (4)2 x 12	
No. 3: (3)2 x 12	
No. 3: (4)2 x 12	
No. 3: 3^1/$_2$ x 9^5/$_8$	
No. 3: 3^1/$_2$ x 11	

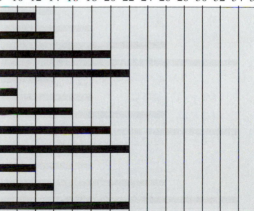

Clear span = **13 ft**

	8 10 12 14 16 18 20 22 24 26 28 30 32 34 36
No. 1: (2)2 x 12	
No. 1: (3)2 x 10	
No. 1: (3)2 x 12	
No. 1: (4)2 x 12	
No. 2: (3)2 x 10	
No. 2: (3)2 x 12	
No. 2: (4)2 x 12	
No. 2: 3^1/$_2$ x 11	
No. 3: (4)2 x 12	
No. 3: 3^1/$_2$ x 9^5/$_8$	
No. 3: 3^1/$_2$ x 11	

Fig. 2–33 (continued).

Floor Edge Beams (Southern Pine)

Length of floor supported on only one side of the beam
measured ⊥ to the beam.

40# Live load, **10#** Dead load
Total load deflection **≤ L/240,** Live load deflection **≤ L/360**

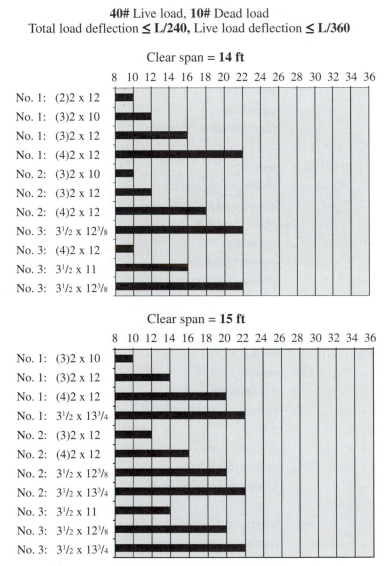

Fig. 2–33 (continued).

Floor Edge Beams (Southern Pine)

Length of floor supported on only one side of the beam
measured ⊥ to the beam.

40# Live load, **10#** Dead load
Total load deflection ≤ **L/240,** Live load deflection ≤ **L/360**

Clear span = **16 ft**

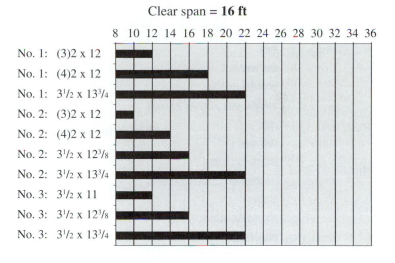

	8 10 12 14 16 18 20 22 24 26 28 30 32 34 36
No. 1:	(3)2 x 12
No. 1:	(4)2 x 12
No. 1:	3¹/₂ x 13³/₄
No. 2:	(3)2 x 12
No. 2:	(4)2 x 12
No. 2:	3¹/₂ x 12³/₈
No. 2:	3¹/₂ x 13³/₄
No. 3:	3¹/₂ x 11
No. 3:	3¹/₂ x 12³/₈
No. 3:	3¹/₂ x 13³/₄

Clear span = **17 ft**

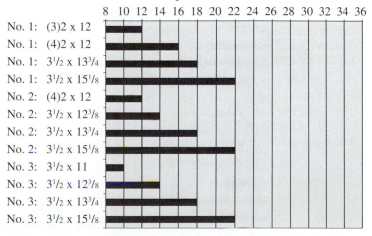

	8 10 12 14 16 18 20 22 24 26 28 30 32 34 36
No. 1:	(3)2 x 12
No. 1:	(4)2 x 12
No. 1:	3¹/₂ x 13³/₄
No. 1:	3¹/₂ x 15¹/₈
No. 2:	(4)2 x 12
No. 2:	3¹/₂ x 12³/₈
No. 2:	3¹/₂ x 13³/₄
No. 2:	3¹/₂ x 15¹/₈
No. 3:	3¹/₂ x 11
No. 3:	3¹/₂ x 12³/₈
No. 3:	3¹/₂ x 13³/₄
No. 3:	3¹/₂ x 15¹/₈

Fig. 2–33 (continued).

Floor Edge Beams (Southern Pine)

Length of floor supported on only one side of the beam
measured ⊥ to the beam.

40# Live load, **10#** Dead load
Total load deflection ≤ **L/240,** Live load deflection ≤ **L/360**

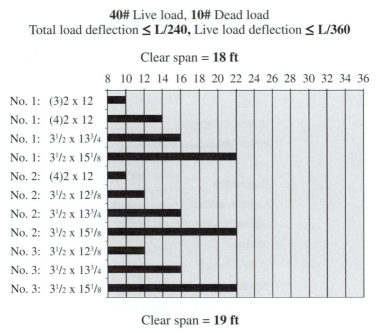

Clear span = **18 ft**

| | 8 | 10 | 12 | 14 | 16 | 18 | 20 | 22 | 24 | 26 | 28 | 30 | 32 | 34 | 36 |

No. 1: (3)2 x 12
No. 1: (4)2 x 12
No. 1: $3^1/_2$ x $13^3/_4$
No. 1: $3^1/_2$ x $15^1/_8$
No. 2: (4)2 x 12
No. 2: $3^1/_2$ x $12^3/_8$
No. 2: $3^1/_2$ x $13^3/_4$
No. 2: $3^1/_2$ x $15^1/_8$
No. 3: $3^1/_2$ x $12^3/_8$
No. 3: $3^1/_2$ x $13^3/_4$
No. 3: $3^1/_2$ x $15^1/_8$

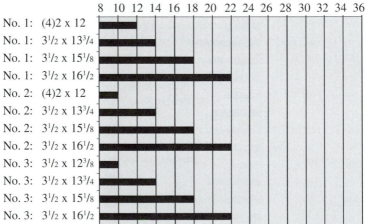

Clear span = **19 ft**

| | 8 | 10 | 12 | 14 | 16 | 18 | 20 | 22 | 24 | 26 | 28 | 30 | 32 | 34 | 36 |

No. 1: (4)2 x 12
No. 1: $3^1/_2$ x $13^3/_4$
No. 1: $3^1/_2$ x $15^1/_8$
No. 1: $3^1/_2$ x $16^1/_2$
No. 2: (4)2 x 12
No. 2: $3^1/_2$ x $13^3/_4$
No. 2: $3^1/_2$ x $15^1/_8$
No. 2: $3^1/_2$ x $16^1/_2$
No. 3: $3^1/_2$ x $12^3/_8$
No. 3: $3^1/_2$ x $13^3/_4$
No. 3: $3^1/_2$ x $15^1/_8$
No. 3: $3^1/_2$ x $16^1/_2$

Fig. 2–33 (continued).

Floor Edge Beams (Southern Pine)

Length of floor supported on only one side of the beam
measured ⊥ to the beam.

40# Live load, **10#** Dead load
Total load deflection ≤ **L/240,** Live load deflection ≤ **L/360**

Clear span = **20 ft**

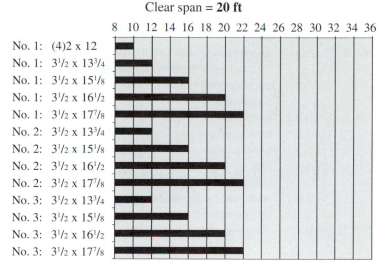

Fig. 2–33 (concluded).

Roof Ridge Beams (Southern Pine)

Total length of roof supported on both sides of the beam measured
on a horizontal plane and ⊥ to the beam.

21# Live load, **10#** Dead load
Total load deflection ≤ **L/180,** Live load deflection ≤ **L/240**

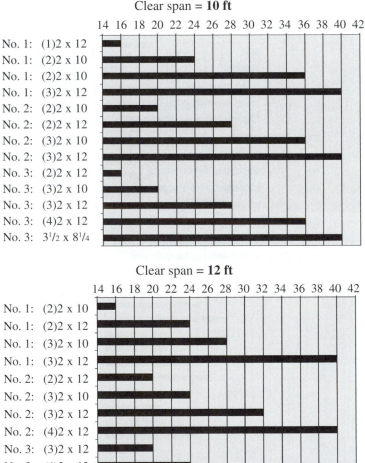

Fig. 2–34.

Roof Ridge Beams (Southern Pine)

Total length of roof supported on both sides of the beam measured
on a horizontal plane and ⊥ to the beam.

21# Live load, **10#** Dead load
Total load deflection **≤ L/180,** Live load deflection **≤ L/240**

Clear span = **14 ft**

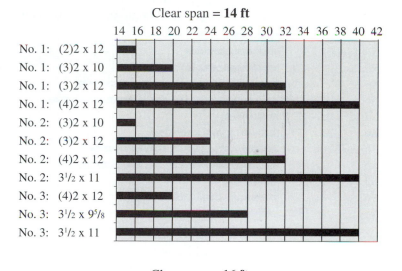

Clear span = **16 ft**

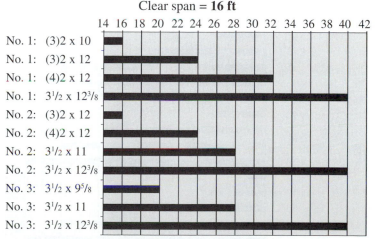

Fig. 2–34 (continued).

Roof Ridge Beams (Southern Pine)

Total length of roof supported on both sides of the beam measured
on a horizontal plane and ⊥ to the beam.

21# Live load, **10#** Dead load
Total load deflection **≤ L/180,** Live load deflection **≤ L/240**

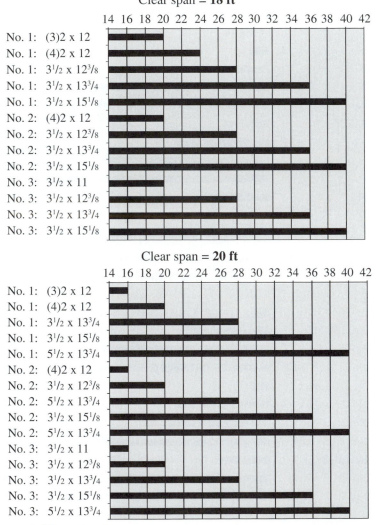

Clear span = **18 ft**

	14 16 18 20 22 24 26 28 30 32 34 36 38 40 42
No. 1: (3)2 x 12	
No. 1: (4)2 x 12	
No. 1: $3^1/_2$ x $12^3/_8$	
No. 1: $3^1/_2$ x $13^3/_4$	
No. 1: $3^1/_2$ x $15^1/_8$	
No. 2: (4)2 x 12	
No. 2: $3^1/_2$ x $12^3/_8$	
No. 2: $3^1/_2$ x $13^3/_4$	
No. 2: $3^1/_2$ x $15^1/_8$	
No. 3: $3^1/_2$ x 11	
No. 3: $3^1/_2$ x $12^3/_8$	
No. 3: $3^1/_2$ x $13^3/_4$	
No. 3: $3^1/_2$ x $15^1/_8$	

Clear span = **20 ft**

	14 16 18 20 22 24 26 28 30 32 34 36 38 40 42
No. 1: (3)2 x 12	
No. 1: (4)2 x 12	
No. 1: $3^1/_2$ x $13^3/_4$	
No. 1: $3^1/_2$ x $15^1/_8$	
No. 1: $5^1/_2$ x $13^3/_4$	
No. 2: (4)2 x 12	
No. 2: $3^1/_2$ x $12^3/_8$	
No. 2: $5^1/_2$ x $13^3/_4$	
No. 2: $3^1/_2$ x $15^1/_8$	
No. 2: $5^1/_2$ x $13^3/_4$	
No. 3: $3^1/_2$ x 11	
No. 3: $3^1/_2$ x $12^3/_8$	
No. 3: $3^1/_2$ x $13^3/_4$	
No. 3: $3^1/_2$ x $15^1/_8$	
No. 3: $5^1/_2$ x $13^3/_4$	

Fig. 2–34 (continued).

Roof Ridge Beams (Southern Pine)

Total length of roof supported on both sides of the beam measured
on a horizontal plane and ⊥ to the beam.

21# Live load, **10#** Dead load
Total load deflection ≤ **L/180,** Live load deflection ≤ **L/240**

Clear span = **22 ft**

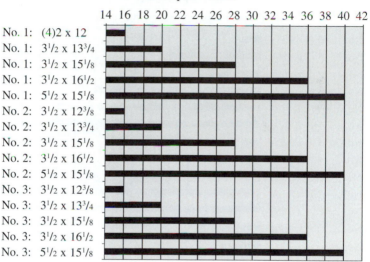

Fig. 2–34 (continued).

Roof Ridge Beams (Southern Pine)

Total length of roof supported on both sides of the beam measured
on a horizontal plane and ⊥ to the beam.

21# Live load, **10#** Dead load
Total load deflection ≤ **L/180,** Live load deflection ≤ **L/240**

Clear span = **24 ft**

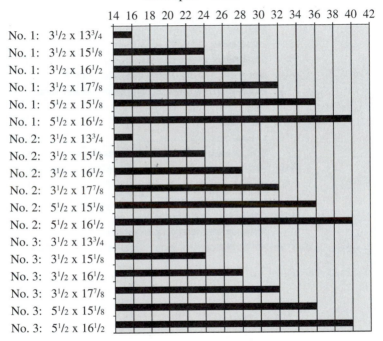

Fig. 2–34 (continued).

Roof Ridge Beams (Southern Pine)

Total length of roof supported on both sides of the beam measured
on a horizontal plane and ⊥ to the beam.

49# Live load, **10#** Dead load
Total load deflection **≤ L/180,** Live load deflection **≤ L/240**

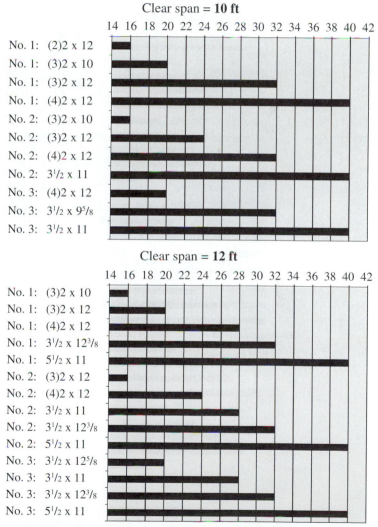

Clear span = **10 ft**

14 16 18 20 22 24 26 28 30 32 34 36 38 40 42

No. 1: (2)2 x 12
No. 1: (3)2 x 10
No. 1: (3)2 x 12
No. 1: (4)2 x 12
No. 2: (3)2 x 10
No. 2: (3)2 x 12
No. 2: (4)2 x 12
No. 2: $3^1/_2$ x 11
No. 3: (4)2 x 12
No. 3: $3^1/_2$ x $9^5/_8$
No. 3: $3^1/_2$ x 11

Clear span = **12 ft**

14 16 18 20 22 24 26 28 30 32 34 36 38 40 42

No. 1: (3)2 x 10
No. 1: (3)2 x 12
No. 1: (4)2 x 12
No. 1: $3^1/_2$ x $12^3/_8$
No. 1: $5^1/_2$ x 11
No. 2: (3)2 x 12
No. 2: (4)2 x 12
No. 2: $3^1/_2$ x 11
No. 2: $3^1/_2$ x $12^3/_8$
No. 2: $5^1/_2$ x 11
No. 3: $3^1/_2$ x $12^5/_8$
No. 3: $3^1/_2$ x 11
No. 3: $3^1/_2$ x $12^3/_8$
No. 3: $5^1/_2$ x 11

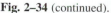

Fig. 2–34 (continued).

Roof Ridge Beams (Southern Pine)

Total length of roof supported on both sides of the beam measured
on a horizontal plane and ⊥ to the beam.

49# Live load, **10#** Dead load
Total load deflection ≤ **L/180,** Live load deflection ≤ **L/240**

Clear span = **14 ft**

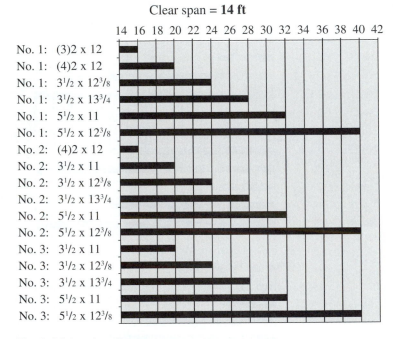

| | 14 16 18 20 22 24 26 28 30 32 34 36 38 40 42 |

No. 1: (3)2 x 12
No. 1: (4)2 x 12
No. 1: $3^1/_2$ x $12^3/_8$
No. 1: $3^1/_2$ x $13^3/_4$
No. 1: $5^1/_2$ x 11
No. 1: $5^1/_2$ x $12^3/_8$
No. 2: (4)2 x 12
No. 2: $3^1/_2$ x 11
No. 2: $3^1/_2$ x $12^3/_8$
No. 2: $3^1/_2$ x $13^3/_4$
No. 2: $5^1/_2$ x 11
No. 2: $5^1/_2$ x $12^3/_8$
No. 3: $3^1/_2$ x 11
No. 3: $3^1/_2$ x $12^3/_8$
No. 3: $3^1/_2$ x $13^3/_4$
No. 3: $5^1/_2$ x 11
No. 3: $5^1/_2$ x $12^3/_8$

Fig. 2–34 (continued).

Roof Ridge Beams (Southern Pine)

Total length of roof supported on both sides of the beam measured
on a horizontal plane and ⊥ to the beam.

49# Live load, **10#** Dead load
Total load deflection **≤ L/180,** Live load deflection **≤ L/240**

Clear span = **16 ft**

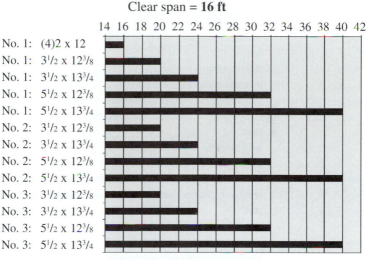

Clear span = **18 ft**

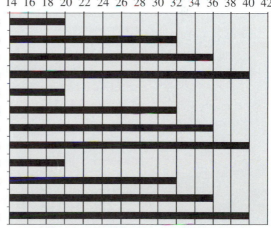

Fig. 2–34 (continued).

Roof Ridge Beams (Southern Pine)

Total length of roof supported on both sides of the beam measured
on a horizontal plane and $\perp$ to the beam.

49 # Live load, 10# Dead load
Total load deflection $\leq$ **L/180,** Live load deflection $\leq$ **L/240**

Clear span = **20 ft**

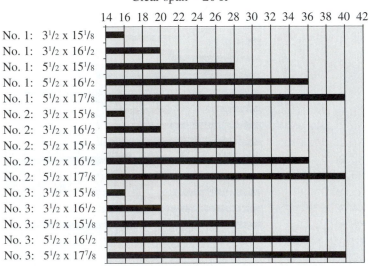

Fig. 2–34 (continued).

Roof Ridge Beams (Southern Pine)

Total length of roof supported on both sides of the beam measured
on a horizontal plane and ⊥ to the beam.

49 # Live load, **10#** Dead load
Total load deflection **≤ L/180,** Live load deflection **≤ L/240**

Clear span = **22 ft**

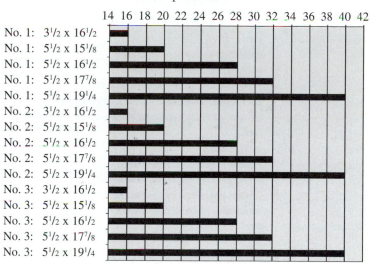

Fig. 2–34 (continued).

Roof Ridge Beams (Southern Pine)

Total length of roof supported on both sides of the beam measured
on a horizontal plane and ⊥ to the beam.

49 # Live load, **10#** Dead load
Total load deflection **≤ L/180,** Live load deflection **≤ L/240**

Clear span = **24 ft**

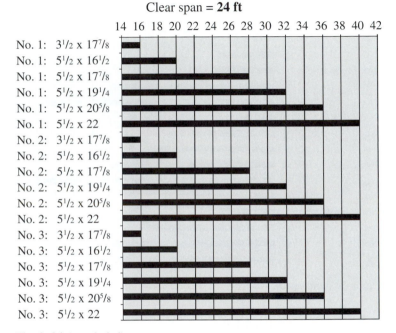

	14 16 18 20 22 24 26 28 30 32 34 36 38 40 42
No. 1:	$3^1/_2$ x $17^7/_8$
No. 1:	$5^1/_2$ x $16^1/_2$
No. 1:	$5^1/_2$ x $17^7/_8$
No. 1:	$5^1/_2$ x $19^1/_4$
No. 1:	$5^1/_2$ x $20^5/_8$
No. 1:	$5^1/_2$ x 22
No. 2:	$3^1/_2$ x $17^7/_8$
No. 2:	$5^1/_2$ x $16^1/_2$
No. 2:	$5^1/_2$ x $17^7/_8$
No. 2:	$5^1/_2$ x $19^1/_4$
No. 2:	$5^1/_2$ x $20^5/_8$
No. 2:	$5^1/_2$ x 22
No. 3:	$3^1/_2$ x $17^7/_8$
No. 3:	$5^1/_2$ x $16^1/_2$
No. 3:	$5^1/_2$ x $17^7/_8$
No. 3:	$5^1/_2$ x $19^1/_4$
No. 3:	$5^1/_2$ x $20^5/_8$
No. 3:	$5^1/_2$ x 22

Fig. 2–34 (concluded).

Door and Window Lintels (Southern Pine)

Chart indicates the length (ft) of roof framing resting on the lintel.

21# Snow load, **10#** Dead load

Total load deflection $\leq$ **L/180**, Live deflection $\leq$ **L/240**

One-story Buildings

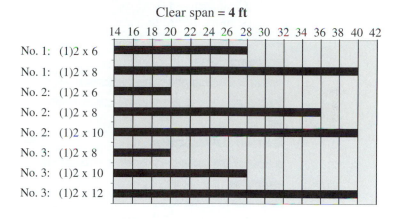

Clear span = **4 ft**

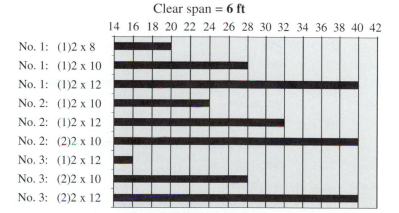

Clear span = **6 ft**

Fig. 2–35.

Door and Window Lintels (Southern Pine)

Chart indicates the length (ft) of roof framing resting on the lintel.

21# Snow load, **10#** Dead load
Total load deflection ≤ **L/180**, Live deflection ≤ **L/240**

One-story Buildings

Clear span = **8 ft**

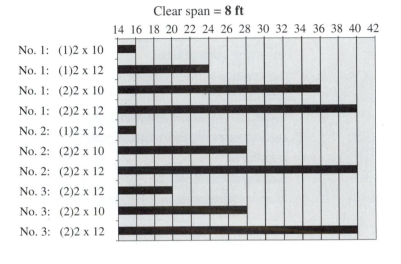

Clear span = **9 ft**

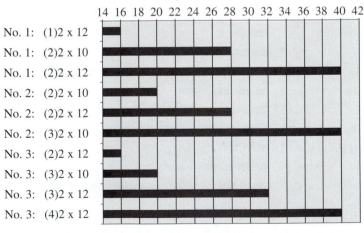

Fig. 2–35 (continued).

Door and Window Lintels (Southern Pine)

Chart indicates the length (ft) of roof framing resting on the lintel.

21# Snow load, **10#** Dead load
Total load deflection ≤ **L/180**, Live deflection ≤ **L/240**

One-story Buildings

Clear span = **10 ft**

14 16 18 20 22 24 26 28 30 32 34 36 38 40 42

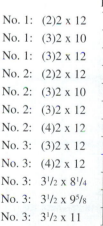
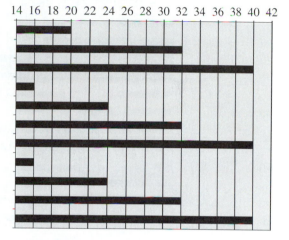

No. 1: (2)2 x 10
No. 1: (2)2 x 12
No. 1: (3)2 x 10
No. 2: (2)2 x 10
No. 2: (2)2 x 12
No. 2: (3)2 x 10
No. 2: (3)2 x 12
No. 3: (3)2 x 10
No. 3: (3)2 x 12
No. 3: (4)2 x 12
No. 3: 3¹/₂ x 8¹/₄

Clear span = **12 ft**

14 16 18 20 22 24 26 28 30 32 34 36 38 40 42

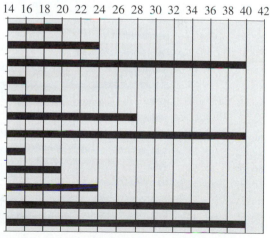
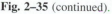

No. 1: (2)2 x 12
No. 1: (3)2 x 10
No. 1: (3)2 x 12
No. 2: (2)2 x 12
No. 2: (3)2 x 10
No. 2: (3)2 x 12
No. 2: (4)2 x 12
No. 3: (3)2 x 12
No. 3: (4)2 x 12
No. 3: 3¹/₂ x 8¹/₄
No. 3: 3¹/₂ x 9⁵/₈
No. 3: 3¹/₂ x 11

Fig. 2–35 (continued).

Door and Window Lintels (Southern Pine)

Chart indicates the length (ft) of roof framing resting on the lintel.

21# Snow load, **10#** Dead load
Total load deflection ≤ **L/180**, Live deflection ≤ **L/240**

One-story Buildings

Clear span = **16 ft**

14 16 18 20 22 24 26 28 30 32 34 36 38 40 42

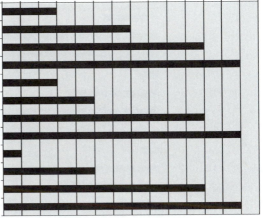

No. 1: (3)2 x 12
No. 1: (4)2 x 12
No. 1: 3¹/₂ x 12³/₈
No. 1: 3¹/₂ x 13³/₄
No. 2: (4)2 x 12
No. 2: 3¹/₂ x 11
No. 2: 3¹/₂ x 12³/₈
No. 2: 3¹/₂ x 13³/₄
No. 3: 3¹/₂ x 9⁵/₈
No. 3: 3¹/₂ x 11
No. 3: 3¹/₂ x 12³/₈
No. 3: 3¹/₂ x 13³/₄

Clear span = **18 ft**

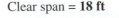

14 16 18 20 22 24 26 28 30 32 34 36 38 40 42

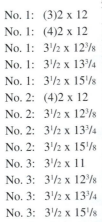
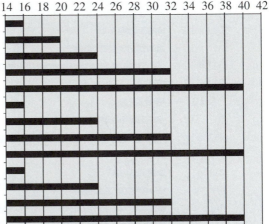

No. 1: (3)2 x 12
No. 1: (4)2 x 12
No. 1: 3¹/₂ x 12³/₈
No. 1: 3¹/₂ x 13³/₄
No. 1: 3¹/₂ x 15¹/₈
No. 2: (4)2 x 12
No. 2: 3¹/₂ x 12³/₈
No. 2: 3¹/₂ x 13³/₄
No. 2: 3¹/₂ x 15¹/₈
No. 3: 3¹/₂ x 11
No. 3: 3¹/₂ x 12³/₈
No. 3: 3¹/₂ x 13³/₄
No. 3: 3¹/₂ x 15¹/₈

Fig. 2–35 (continued).

Door and Window Lintels (Southern Pine)

Chart indicates the length (ft) of roof framing resting on the lintel.

49# Snow load, 10# Dead load
Total load deflection ≤ **L/180**, Live deflection ≤ **L/240**

One-story Buildings

Clear span = **4 ft**

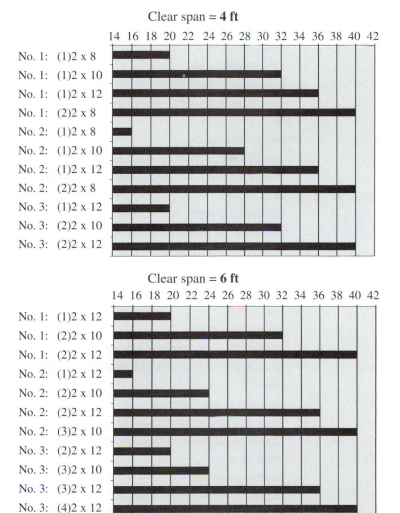

Fig. 2–35 (continued).

Door and Window Lintels (Southern Pine)

Chart indicates the length (ft) of roof framing resting on the lintel.
49# Snow load, **10#** Dead load
Total load deflection $\leq$ **L/180**, Live deflection $\leq$ **L/240**

One-story Buildings

Clear span = **8 ft**

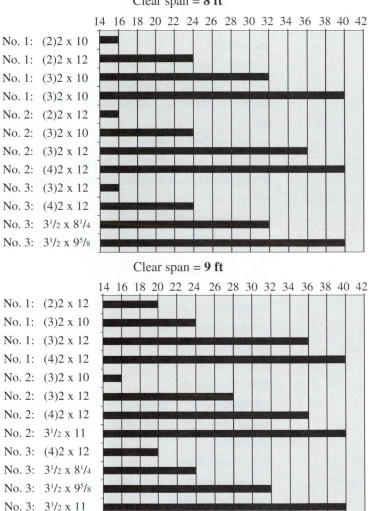

Clear span = **9 ft**

Fig. 2–35 (continued).

Door and Window Lintels (Southern Pine)

Chart indicates the length (ft) of roof framing resting on the lintel.

49# Snow load, **10#** Dead load
Total load deflection ≤ **L/180**, Live deflection ≤ **L/240**

One-story Buildings

Clear span = **10 ft**

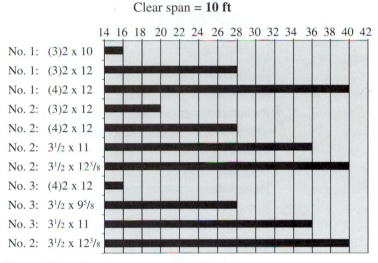

Fig. 2–35 (continued).

Door and Window Lintels (Southern Pine)

Chart indicates the length (ft) of roof framing resting on the lintel.

49# Snow load, **10#** Dead load
Total load deflection ≤ **L/180**, Live deflection ≤ **L/240**

One-story Buildings

Clear span = **12 ft**

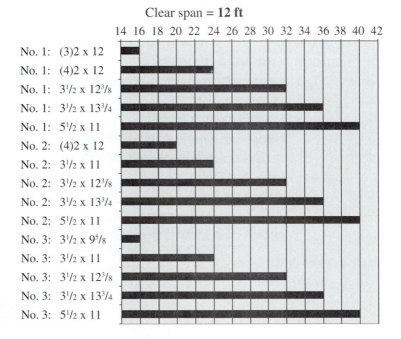

	14 16 18 20 22 24 26 28 30 32 34 36 38 40 42
No. 1: (3)2 x 12	
No. 1: (4)2 x 12	
No. 1: $3^1/_2$ x $12^3/_8$	
No. 1: $3^1/_2$ x $13^3/_4$	
No. 1: $5^1/_2$ x 11	
No. 2: (4)2 x 12	
No. 2: $3^1/_2$ x 11	
No. 2: $3^1/_2$ x $12^3/_8$	
No. 2: $3^1/_2$ x $13^3/_4$	
No. 2: $5^1/_2$ x 11	
No. 3: $3^1/_2$ x $9^5/_8$	
No. 3: $3^1/_2$ x 11	
No. 3: $3^1/_2$ x $12^3/_8$	
No. 3: $3^1/_2$ x $13^3/_4$	
No. 3: $5^1/_2$ x 11	

Fig. 2–35 (continued).

Door and Window Lintels (Southern Pine)

Chart indicates the length (ft) of roof framing resting on the lintel.

49# Snow load, **10#** Dead load
Total load deflection ≤ **L/180**, Live deflection ≤ **L/240**

One-story Buildings

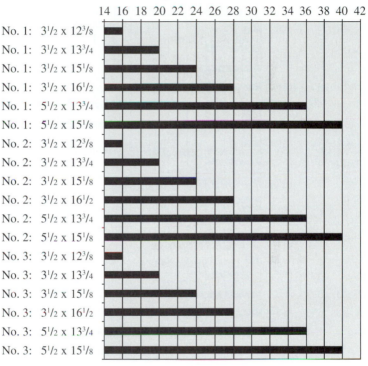

Clear span = **16 ft**

Fig. 2–35 (continued).

Door and Window Lintels (Southern Pine)

Chart indicates the length (ft) of roof framing resting on the lintel.

49# Snow load, **10#** Dead load
Total load deflection ≤ **L/180**, Live deflection ≤ **L/240**

One-story Buildings

Clear span = **18 ft**

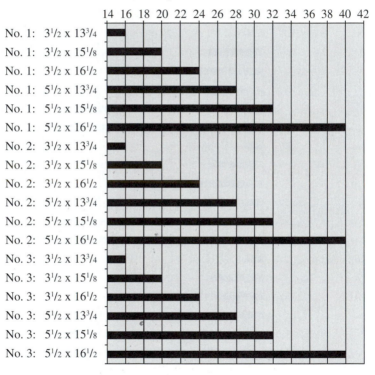

	14	16	18	20	22	24	26	28	30	32	34	36	38	40	42

No. 1: $3^{1}/_{2}$ x $13^{3}/_{4}$
No. 1: $3^{1}/_{2}$ x $15^{1}/_{8}$
No. 1: $3^{1}/_{2}$ x $16^{1}/_{2}$
No. 1: $5^{1}/_{2}$ x $13^{3}/_{4}$
No. 1: $5^{1}/_{2}$ x $15^{1}/_{8}$
No. 1: $5^{1}/_{2}$ x $16^{1}/_{2}$
No. 2: $3^{1}/_{2}$ x $13^{3}/_{4}$
No. 2: $3^{1}/_{2}$ x $15^{1}/_{8}$
No. 2: $3^{1}/_{2}$ x $16^{1}/_{2}$
No. 2: $5^{1}/_{2}$ x $13^{3}/_{4}$
No. 2: $5^{1}/_{2}$ x $15^{1}/_{8}$
No. 2: $5^{1}/_{2}$ x $16^{1}/_{2}$
No. 3: $3^{1}/_{2}$ x $13^{3}/_{4}$
No. 3: $3^{1}/_{2}$ x $15^{1}/_{8}$
No. 3: $3^{1}/_{2}$ x $16^{1}/_{2}$
No. 3: $5^{1}/_{2}$ x $13^{3}/_{4}$
No. 3: $5^{1}/_{2}$ x $15^{1}/_{8}$
No. 3: $5^{1}/_{2}$ x $16^{1}/_{2}$

Fig. 2–35 (concluded).

1st-Floor Door and Window Lintels (Southern Pine)

Chart indicates the length (ft) of roof framing supported by the lintel.

21# Snow load, **10#** Dead load
Total load deflection ≤ **L/240**, Live deflection ≤ **L/360**

Two-story Buildings

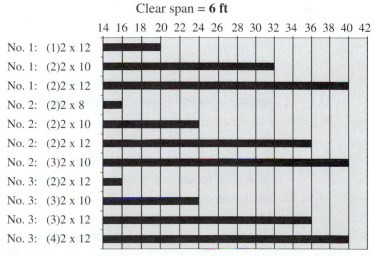

Clear span = **4 ft**

Clear span = **6 ft**

Fig. 2–36.

1st-Floor Door and Window Lintels (Southern Pine)

Chart indicates the length (ft) of roof framing supported by the lintel.

21# Snow load, **10#** Dead load
Total load deflection ≤ **L/240**, Live deflection ≤ **L/360**

Two-story Buildings

Clear span = **8 ft**

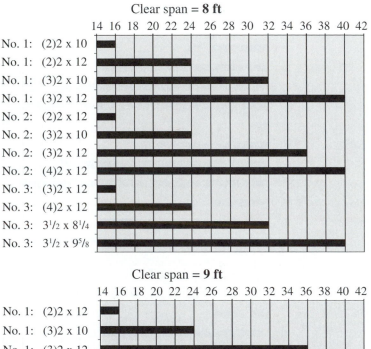

Clear span = **9 ft**

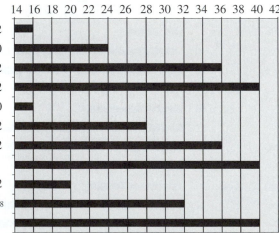

Fig. 2–36 (continued).

1st-Floor Door and Window Lintels (Southern Pine)
Chart indicates the length (ft) of roof framing supported by the lintel.

21# Snow load, **10#** Dead load
Total load deflection ≤ **L/240**, Live deflection ≤ **L/360**

Two-story Buildings

Clear span = **10 ft**

14 16 18 20 22 24 26 28 30 32 34 36 38 40 42

No. 1: (3)2 x 10
No. 1: (3)2 x 12
No. 1: (4)2 x 12
No. 2: (3)2 x 12
No. 2: (4)2 x 12
No. 2: $3^1/_2$ x 11
No. 2: $3^1/_2$ x $12^3/_8$
No. 3: (4)2 x 12
No. 3: $3^1/_2$ x $9^5/_8$
No. 3: $3^1/_2$ x 11
No. 2: $3^1/_2$ x $12^3/_8$

Clear span = **12 ft**

14 16 18 20 22 24 26 28 30 32 34 36 38 40 42

No. 1: (3)2 x 12
No. 1: (4)2 x 12
No. 1: $3^1/_2$ x $12^3/_8$
No. 1: $3^1/_2$ x $13^3/_4$
No. 1: $5^1/_2$ x 11
No. 2: (4)2 x 12
No. 2: $3^1/_2$ x 11
No. 2: $3^1/_2$ x $12^3/_8$
No. 2: $3^1/_2$ x $13^3/_4$
No. 2: $5^1/_2$ x 11
No. 3: $3^1/_2$ x 11
No. 3: $3^1/_2$ x $12^3/_8$
No. 3: $3^1/_2$ x $13^3/_4$
No. 3: $5^1/_2$ x 11

Fig. 2–36 (continued).

1st-Floor Door and Window Lintels (Southern Pine)

Chart indicates the length (ft) of roof framing supported by the lintel.

21# Snow load, **10#** Dead load

Total load deflection ≤ **L/240**, Live deflection ≤ **L/360**

Two-story Buildings

Clear span = **16 ft**

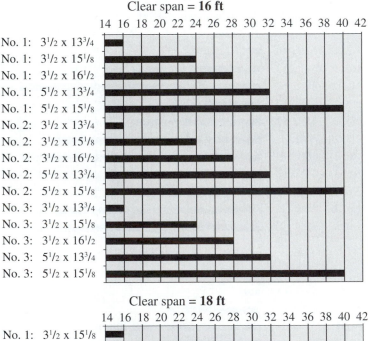

	14 16 18 20 22 24 26 28 30 32 34 36 38 40 42
No. 1: $3^1/_2$ x $13^3/_4$	
No. 1: $3^1/_2$ x $15^1/_8$	
No. 1: $3^1/_2$ x $16^1/_2$	
No. 1: $5^1/_2$ x $13^3/_4$	
No. 1: $5^1/_2$ x $15^1/_8$	
No. 2: $3^1/_2$ x $13^3/_4$	
No. 2: $3^1/_2$ x $15^1/_8$	
No. 2: $3^1/_2$ x $16^1/_2$	
No. 2: $5^1/_2$ x $13^3/_4$	
No. 2: $5^1/_2$ x $15^1/_8$	
No. 3: $3^1/_2$ x $13^3/_4$	
No. 3: $3^1/_2$ x $15^1/_8$	
No. 3: $3^1/_2$ x $16^1/_2$	
No. 3: $5^1/_2$ x $13^3/_4$	
No. 3: $5^1/_2$ x $15^1/_8$	

Clear span = **18 ft**

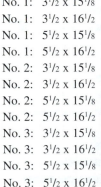
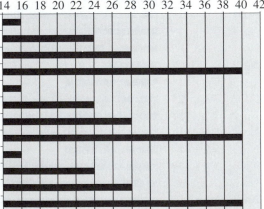

	14 16 18 20 22 24 26 28 30 32 34 36 38 40 42
No. 1: $3^1/_2$ x $15^1/_8$	
No. 1: $3^1/_2$ x $16^1/_2$	
No. 1: $5^1/_2$ x $15^1/_8$	
No. 1: $5^1/_2$ x $16^1/_2$	
No. 2: $3^1/_2$ x $15^1/_8$	
No. 2: $3^1/_2$ x $16^1/_2$	
No. 2: $5^1/_2$ x $15^1/_8$	
No. 2: $5^1/_2$ x $16^1/_2$	
No. 3: $3^1/_2$ x $15^1/_8$	
No. 3: $3^1/_2$ x $16^1/_2$	
No. 3: $5^1/_2$ x $15^1/_8$	
No. 3: $5^1/_2$ x $16^1/_2$	

Fig. 2–36 (continued).

1st-Floor Door and Window Lintels (Southern Pine)

Chart indicates the length (ft) of roof framing supported by the lintel.

49# Snow load, **10#** Dead load
Total load deflection ≤ **L/240**, Live deflection ≤ **L/360**

Two-story Buildings

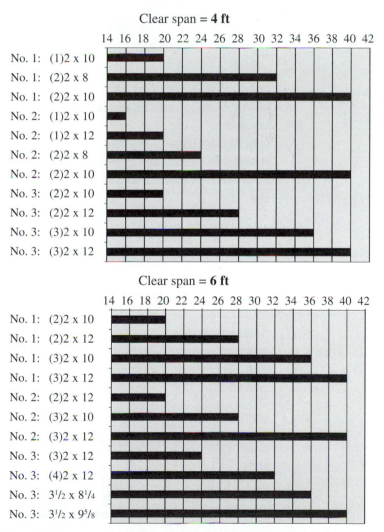

Fig. 2–36 (continued).

1st-Floor Door and Window Lintels (Southern Pine)

Chart indicates the length (ft) of roof framing supported by the lintel.

49# Snow load, **10#** Dead load
Total load deflection $\leq$ **L/240**, Live deflection $\leq$ **L/360**

Two-story Buildings

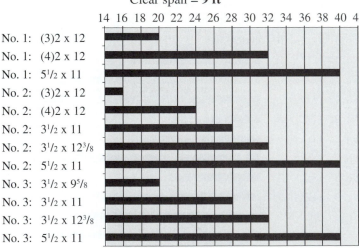

Clear span = **8 ft**

14 16 18 20 22 24 26 28 30 32 34 36 38 40 42

No. 1: (2)2 x 12
No. 1: (3)2 x 10
No. 1: (3)2 x 12
No. 1: (4)2 x 12
No. 2: (3)2 x 12
No. 2: (4)2 x 12
No. 2: 3¹/₂ x 11
No. 2: 5¹/₂ x 11
No. 3: (4)2 x 12
No. 3: 3¹/₂ x 9⁵/₈
No. 3: 3¹/₂ x 11
No. 3: 5¹/₂ x 11

Clear span = **9 ft**

14 16 18 20 22 24 26 28 30 32 34 36 38 40 42

No. 1: (3)2 x 12
No. 1: (4)2 x 12
No. 1: 5¹/₂ x 11
No. 2: (3)2 x 12
No. 2: (4)2 x 12
No. 2: 3¹/₂ x 11
No. 2: 3¹/₂ x 12³/₈
No. 2: 5¹/₂ x 11
No. 3: 3¹/₂ x 9⁵/₈
No. 3: 3¹/₂ x 11
No. 3: 3¹/₂ x 12³/₈
No. 3: 5¹/₂ x 11

Fig. 2–36 (continued).

1st-Floor Door and Window Lintels (Southern Pine)

Chart indicates the length (ft) of roof framing supported by the lintel.

49# Snow load, **10#** Dead load
Total load deflection ≤ **L/240**, Live deflection ≤ **L/360**

Two-story Buildings

Clear span = **10 ft**

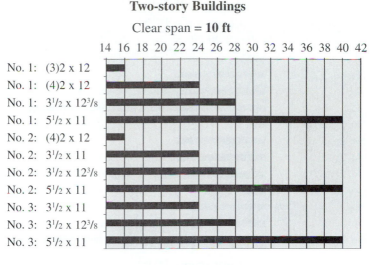

Clear span = **12 ft**

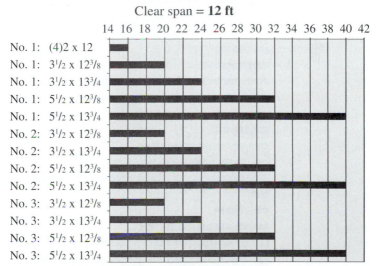

Fig. 2–36 (continued).

1st-Floor Door and Window Lintels (Southern Pine)

Chart indicates the length (ft) of roof framing supported by the lintel.

49# Snow load, **10#** Dead load

Total load deflection ≤ **L/240**, Live deflection ≤ **L/360**

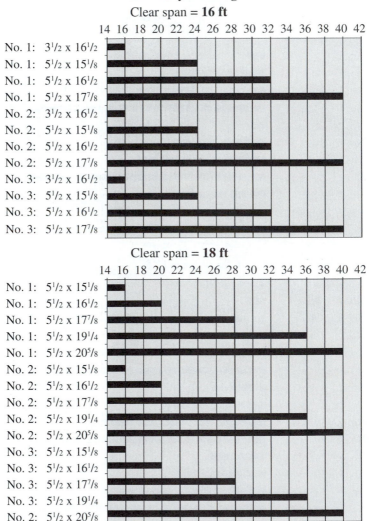

Two-story Buildings

Clear span = **16 ft**

	14 16 18 20 22 24 26 28 30 32 34 36 38 40 42
No. 1: $3^1/_2$ x $16^1/_2$	
No. 1: $5^1/_2$ x $15^1/_8$	
No. 1: $5^1/_2$ x $16^1/_2$	
No. 1: $5^1/_2$ x $17^7/_8$	
No. 2: $3^1/_2$ x $16^1/_2$	
No. 2: $5^1/_2$ x $15^1/_8$	
No. 2: $5^1/_2$ x $16^1/_2$	
No. 2: $5^1/_2$ x $17^7/_8$	
No. 3: $3^1/_2$ x $16^1/_2$	
No. 3: $5^1/_2$ x $15^1/_8$	
No. 3: $5^1/_2$ x $16^1/_2$	
No. 3: $5^1/_2$ x $17^7/_8$	

Clear span = **18 ft**

	14 16 18 20 22 24 26 28 30 32 34 36 38 40 42
No. 1: $5^1/_2$ x $15^1/_8$	
No. 1: $5^1/_2$ x $16^1/_2$	
No. 1: $5^1/_2$ x $17^7/_8$	
No. 1: $5^1/_2$ x $19^1/_4$	
No. 1: $5^1/_2$ x $20^5/_8$	
No. 2: $5^1/_2$ x $15^1/_8$	
No. 2: $5^1/_2$ x $16^1/_2$	
No. 2: $5^1/_2$ x $17^7/_8$	
No. 2: $5^1/_2$ x $19^1/_4$	
No. 2: $5^1/_2$ x $20^5/_8$	
No. 3: $5^1/_2$ x $15^1/_8$	
No. 3: $5^1/_2$ x $16^1/_2$	
No. 3: $5^1/_2$ x $17^7/_8$	
No. 3: $5^1/_2$ x $19^1/_4$	
No. 2: $5^1/_2$ x $20^5/_8$	

Fig. 2–36 (concluded).

Western Lumber Span Charts

The charts in the following section were derived from two publications copyrighted by the Western Wood Products Association <www.wwpa.org> titled *Western Lumber Span Tables* and *Western Lumber Product Use Manual.* These charts are intended for use in estimating structural sizes suitable for the schematic design and detailing phases of a project only. They are not appropriate for the selection of final sizes, which should be made according to engineering calculations. For quick use, these data are simplified from the original publications. For more detail regarding the parameters, restrictions, and variations applicable to the data, it is necessary to review the source documents. Abbreviated guidelines for the charts are provided in the following summary.

Structural members are assumed to be adequately anchored and braced, in order to have the necessary bearing length. They are assumed to be within moisture content limits, and they are assumed to be used within certain temperature limits. Only uniform gravity loads are considered. The data address common applications in general and do not account for extreme, unusual, or special conditions. Chart headings use the pound symbol (#) to indicate pounds per square foot for loads. The floor and roof decking charts include two grades of wood: selected decking (Sel) and commercial decking (Com). The entries titled "random lay-up" refer to random controlled lay-up.

Interpretation of the data in the source publications and its conversion to the new format in this chapter is solely the work of the author, who is responsible for any errors therein. The Western Wood Products Association did not participate in this project and has not reviewed the results.

Floor Joist Spans (ft.) (Douglas Fir-Larch)

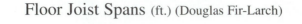
■■■ 24"oc   ☐ 16"oc

30# Live load, **10#** Dead load, Live load deflection ≤ **L/360**

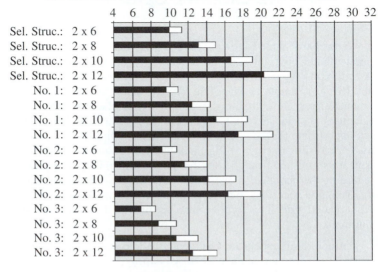

40# Live load, **10#** Dead load, Live load deflection ≤ **L/360**

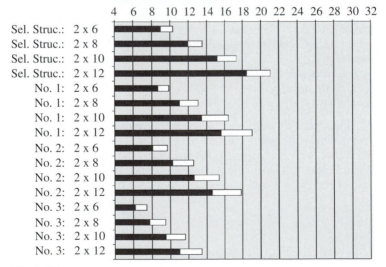

Fig. 2–37.

Floor Joist Spans (ft.) (Douglas Fir-Larch)

■ 24"oc   ☐ 16"oc

50# Live load, **10#** Dead load, Live load deflection ≤ **L/360**

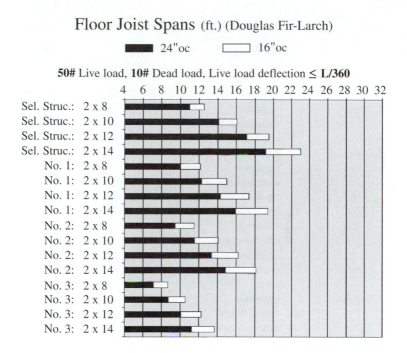

60# Live load, **10#** Dead load, Live load deflection ≤ **L/360**

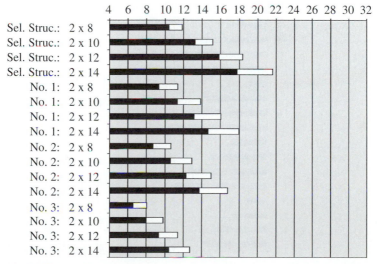

Fig. 2–37 (concluded).

Floor Joist Spans (ft.) (Hem-Fir)

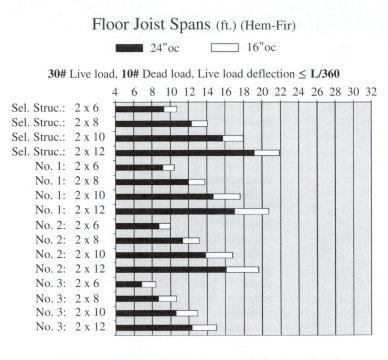

30# Live load, **10#** Dead load, Live load deflection ≤ **L/360**

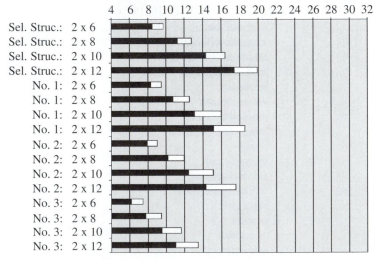

40# Live load, **10#** Dead load, Live load deflection ≤ **L/360**

Fig. 2–38.

Floor Joist Spans (ft.) (Hem-Fir)

■ 24"oc   □ 16"oc

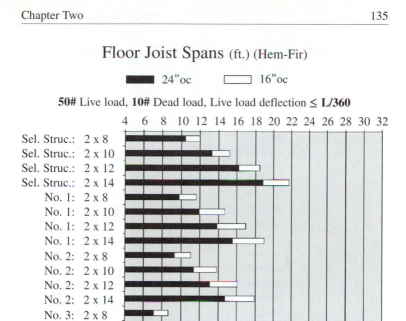

50# Live load, **10#** Dead load, Live load deflection ≤ **L/360**

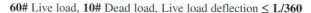

60# Live load, **10#** Dead load, Live load deflection ≤ **L/360**

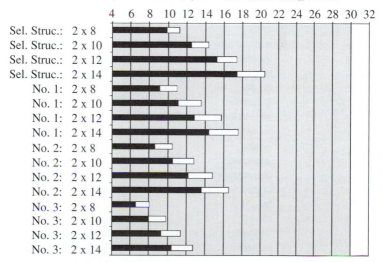

Fig. 2–38 (concluded).

Floor Joist Spans (ft.) (Western Woods)

■ 24"oc   □ 16"oc

30# Live load, **10#** Dead load, Live load deflection ≤ **L/360**

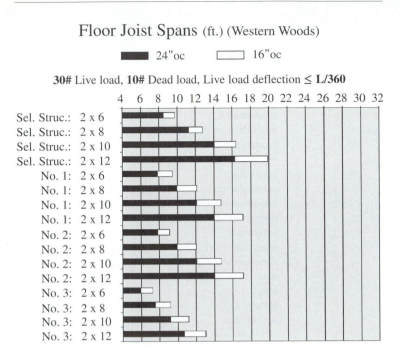

40# Live load, **10#** Dead load, Live load deflection ≤ **L/360**

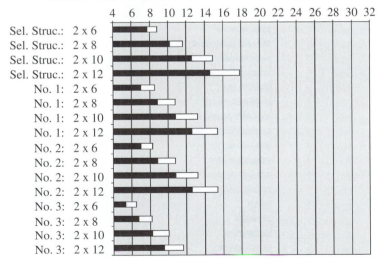

Fig. 2–39.

Floor Joist Spans (ft.) (Western Woods)

50# Live load, **10#** Dead load, Live load deflection ≤ **L/360**

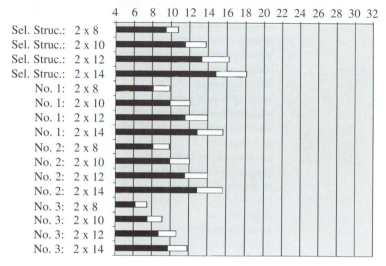

60# Live load, **10#** Dead load, Live load deflection ≤ **L/360**

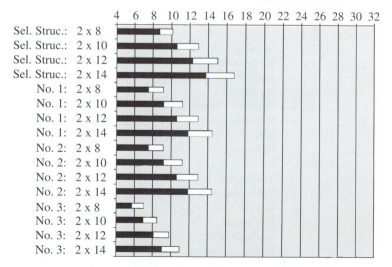

Fig. 2–39 (concluded).

Roof Rafter Spans (ft.) (Douglas Fir-Larch)

■■■ 24"oc   ☐ 16"oc

20# Snow load, **10#** Dead load, Live load deflection ≤ **L/240**

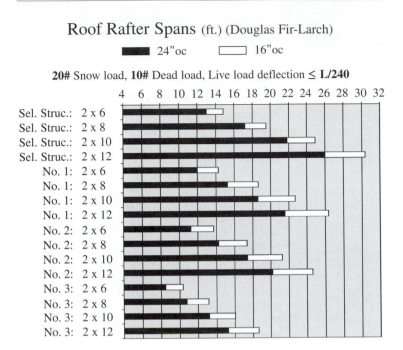

30# Snow load, **10#** Dead load, Live load deflection ≤ **L/240**

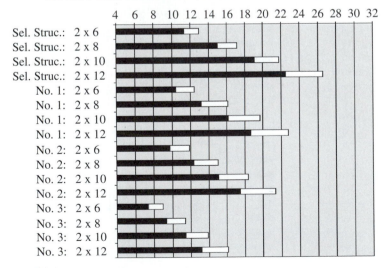

Fig. 2–40.

Roof Rafter Spans (ft.) (Douglas Fir-Larch)

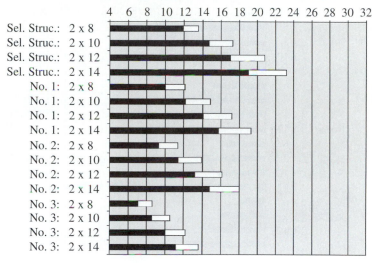

60# Snow load, **10#** Dead load, Live load deflection ≤ **L/240**

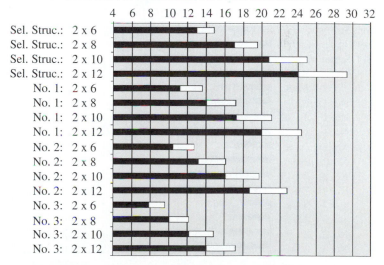

20# Snow load, **15#** Dead load, Live load deflection ≤ **L/240**

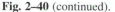

Fig. 2–40 (continued).

Roof Rafter Spans (ft.) (Douglas Fir-Larch)

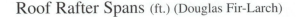 ■■■ 24"oc   ☐ 16"oc

30# Snow load, **15#** Dead load, Live load deflection ≤ **L/240**

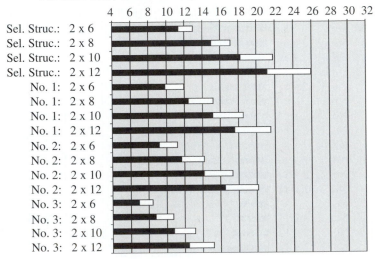

60# Snow load, **15#** Dead load, Live load deflection ≤ **L/240**

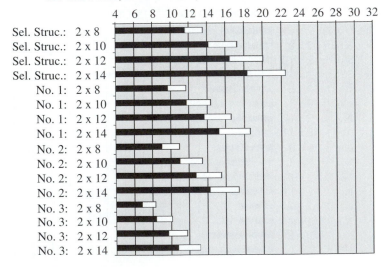

Fig. 2–40 (concluded).

Roof Rafter Spans (ft.) (Hem-Fir)

■ 24"oc   □ 16"oc

20# Snow load, **10#** Dead load, Live load deflection ≤ **L/240**

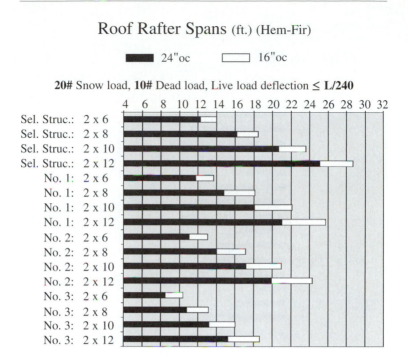

30# Snow load, **10#** Dead load, Live load deflection ≤ **L/240**

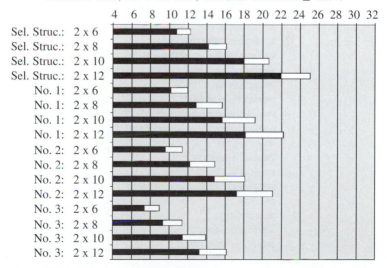

Fig. 2–41.

Roof Rafter Spans (ft.) (Hem-Fir)

■ 24"oc   □ 16"oc

60# Snow load, **10#** Dead load, Live load deflection ≤ **L/240**

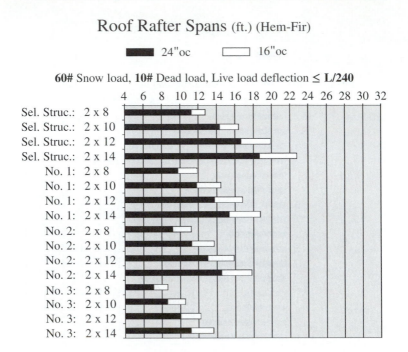

20# Snow load, **15#** Dead load, Live load deflection ≤ **L/240**

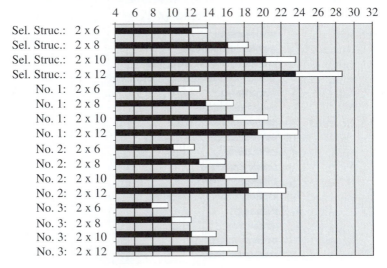

Fig. 2–41 (continued).

Roof Rafter Spans (ft.) (Hem-Fir)

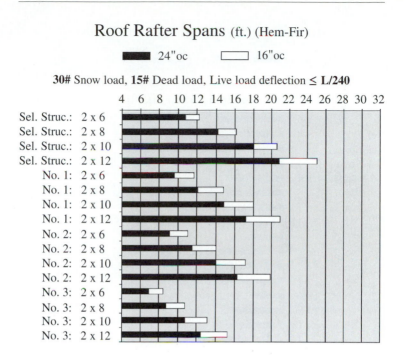

30# Snow load, **15#** Dead load, Live load deflection ≤ **L/240**

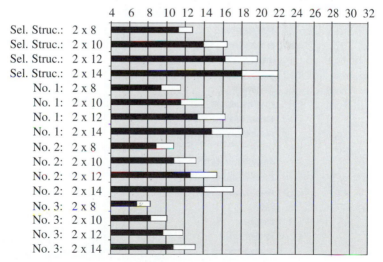

60# Snow load, **15#** Dead load, Live load deflection ≤ **L/240**

Fig. 2–41 (concluded).

Roof Rafter Spans (ft.) (Western Woods)

■■■ 24"oc   ☐ 16"oc

20# Snow load, **10#** Dead load, Live load deflection ≤ **L/240**

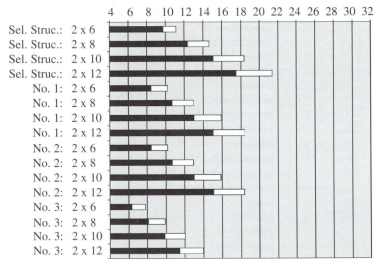

30# Snow load, **10#** Dead load, Live load deflection ≤ **L/240**

Fig. 2–42.

Roof Rafter Spans (ft.) (Western Woods)

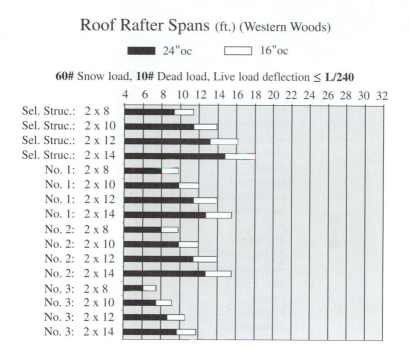

60# Snow load, **10#** Dead load, Live load deflection ≤ **L/240**

20# Snow load, **15#** Dead load, Live load deflection ≤ **L/240**

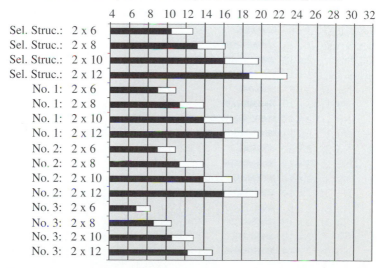

Fig. 2–42 (continued).

Roof Rafter Spans (ft.) (Western Woods)

■ 24"oc   □ 16"oc

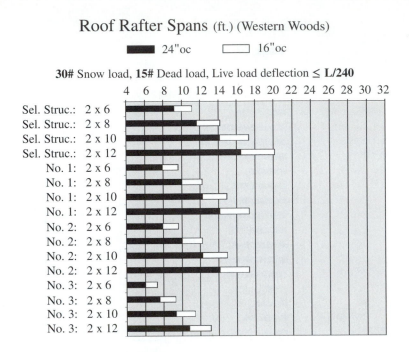

30# Snow load, **15#** Dead load, Live load deflection ≤ **L/240**

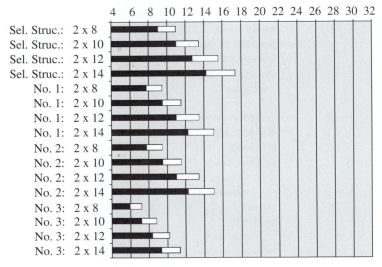

60# Snow load, **15#** Dead load, Live load deflection ≤ **L/240**

Fig. 2–42 (concluded).

Ceiling Joist Spans (ft.) (Douglas Fir-Larch)

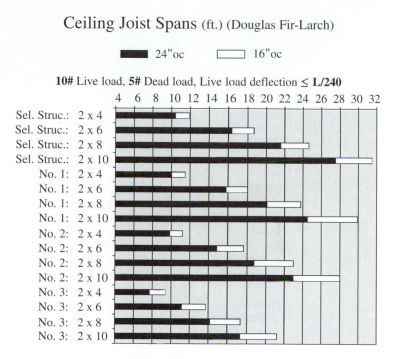

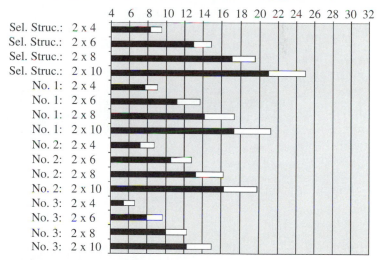

Fig. 2–43.

Ceiling Joist Spans (ft.) (Douglas Fir-Larch)

■■■ 24"oc   ☐ 16"oc

20# Live load, **10#** Dead load, Live load deflection ≤ **L/360**

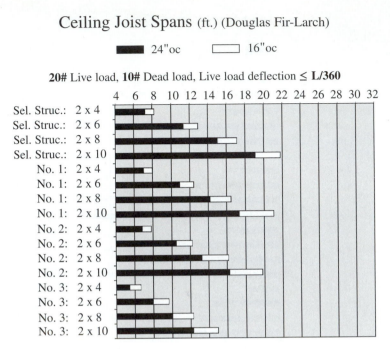

Fig. 2–43 (concluded).

Ceiling Joist Spans (ft.) (Hem-Fir)

■ 24"oc   □ 16"oc

10# Live load, **5#** Dead load, Live load deflection ≤ **L/240**

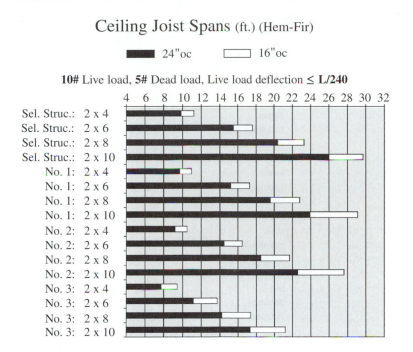

20# Live load, **10#** Dead load, Live load deflection ≤ **L/240**

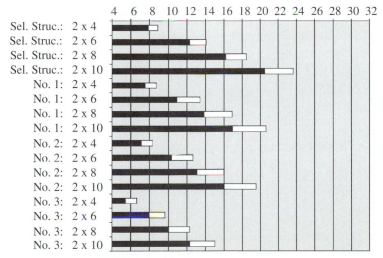

Fig. 2–44.

Ceiling Joist Spans (ft.) (Hem-Fir)

■■■ 24"oc   ☐ 16"oc

20# Live load, **10#** Dead load, Live load deflection ≤ **L/360**

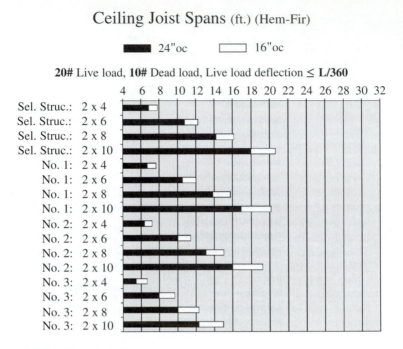

Fig. 2–44 (concluded).

Ceiling Joist Spans (ft.) (Western Woods)

■ 24"oc   □ 16"oc

10# Live load, **5#** Dead load, Live load deflection ≤ **L/240**

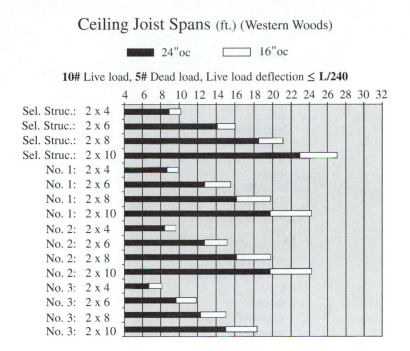

20# Live load, **10#** Dead load, Live load deflection ≤ **L/240**

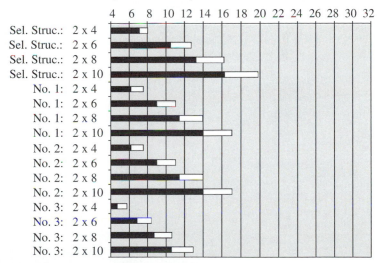

Fig. 2–45.

Ceiling Joist Spans (ft.) (Western Woods)

■■■ 24"oc   ☐ 16"oc

20# Live load, **10#** Dead load, Live load deflection ≤ **L/360**

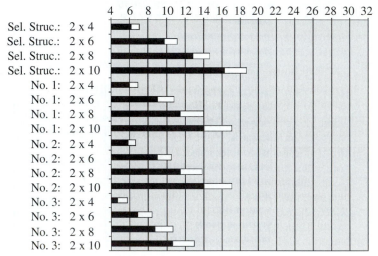

Fig. 2–45 (concluded).

Wood Floor Decking Spans (ft.)

2" thick, 4" to 12" widths

Maximum moisture content 19%
40# Live load, **10#** Dead load
Live load deflection ≤ **L/480**

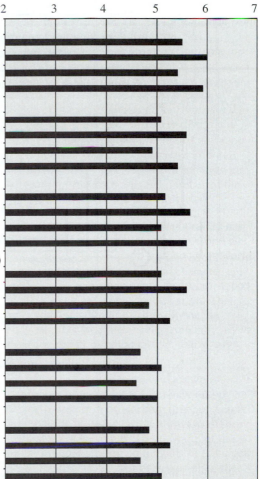

Fig. 2–46.

Wood Floor Decking Spans (ft.)

3" thick, **4"** to **12"** widths

Maximum moisture content 19%
40# Live load, **10#** Dead load
Live load deflection **≤ L/480**

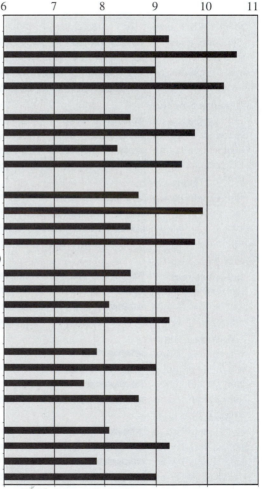

Fig. 2–46 (concluded).

Wood Roof Decking Spans (ft.)

2" thick, 4" to 12" widths

Maximum moisture content 19%
30# Snow load, **10#** Dead load
Live load deflection ≤ **L/240**

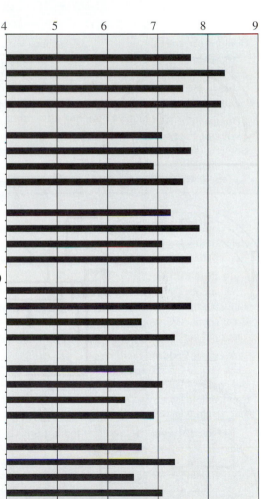

Fig. 2–47.

Wood Roof Decking Spans (ft.)

3" thick, 4" to 12" widths

Maximum moisture content 19%
30# Live load, **10#** Dead load
Live load deflection $\leq$ **L/240**

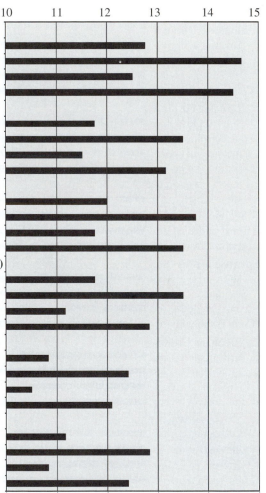

Fig. 2–47 (concluded).

Cold-Formed Steel Span Charts and Load Tables

The charts and tables in the following section were derived from a publication produced by Clark Steel Framing Systems <www.clarksteel.com> titled *Product Technical Data & Tables*, and are intended for use in estimating structural sizes of cold-formed steel members suitable for the schematic design and detailing phases of a project. They are not appropriate for the selection of final sizes, which should be made according to engineering calculations. For quick use, these data are simplfied from the original publication. For more detail regarding the parameters, restrictions, and variations applicable to the date, it is necessary to review the source document. Abbreviated guidelines for the charts and tables are provided in the following summaries.

Structural members are assumed to be adequately anchored and braced (unless otherwise noted). They are assumed to have the necessary bearing length, and to have webs stiffened where necesary. Web stiffeners do not affect spatial decisions so their requirements are omitted here. They are, however, often necessary and guidelines for their use may be found in the source document in a printed version or on the Web site. The data address common applications in general and do not account for extreme, unusual, or special conditions.

Steel Joist Spans

The charts are based on joists assumed to have continuous lateral support at the compression flange. The spans for charts based on two equal spans are measured from the center support to either end support. In this case, the joist must be continuous across the center support. A 3.5" bearing length is assumed at all supports. Joists must be braced at all supports by track or blocking to prevent rotation.

Double Member Beams

Beams in these load tables are assembled from two members in either a "box" configuration or back-to-back. A minimum bearing

length of 1" is required. Members are assumed to be without holes.
Beams are simply supported and must be adequately braced for
bending purposes. Loads are uniform bending loads only.

Structural and Nonstructural Studs

The tables list allowable heights for studs. Studs are assumed to
have continuous support at both flanges for the full length of the
stud.

Structural Studs Combined Loads

Allowable loads in these tables are based on the weak axis of
the stud. Bracing for torsion is assumed to be provided 4' o.c.
Continuous support of both flanges is assumed.

Structural Studs Pure Axial Load

The allowable loads in the table are assumed to be concentric
on a single stud. Stud lengths are unbraced.

Interpretation of the data in the source publication and its
conversion to the new format in this chapter is solely the work of
the author, who is responsible for any errors therein. Clark Steel
Framing Systems did not participate in this project and has not
reviewed the results.

Joist Spans (ft): 33 ksi
(Cold-Formed Steel)

■ 24"oc   □ 16"oc

20 psf live load, **10 psf** dead load: Single Span
L/360 (LL)**, L/240** (LL+DL)

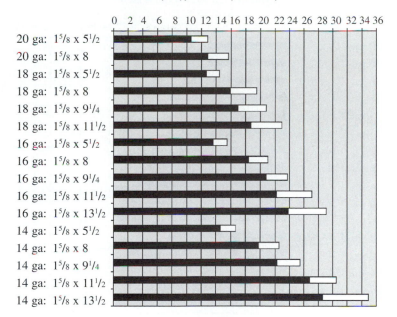

Fig. 2–48.

Joist Spans (ft): 33 ksi
(Cold-Formed Steel)

■ 24"oc   □ 16"oc

20 psf live load, **10 psf** dead load: Two Equal Spans
L/360 (LL), **L/240** (LL+DL)

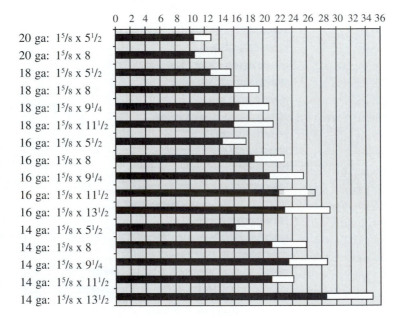

20 ga: $1^5/_8$ x $5^1/_2$
20 ga: $1^5/_8$ x 8
18 ga: $1^5/_8$ x $5^1/_2$
18 ga: $1^5/_8$ x 8
18 ga: $1^5/_8$ x $9^1/_4$
18 ga: $1^5/_8$ x $11^1/_2$
16 ga: $1^5/_8$ x $5^1/_2$
16 ga: $1^5/_8$ x 8
16 ga: $1^5/_8$ x $9^1/_4$
16 ga: $1^5/_8$ x $11^1/_2$
16 ga: $1^5/_8$ x $13^1/_2$
14 ga: $1^5/_8$ x $5^1/_2$
14 ga: $1^5/_8$ x 8
14 ga: $1^5/_8$ x $9^1/_4$
14 ga: $1^5/_8$ x $11^1/_2$
14 ga: $1^5/_8$ x $13^1/_2$

Fig. 2–48 (continued).

Joist Spans (ft): 33 ksi
(Cold-Formed Steel)

■■■ 24"oc   ☐ 16"oc

40 psf live load, **10 psf** dead load: Single Span
L/360 (LL), **L/240** (LL+DL)

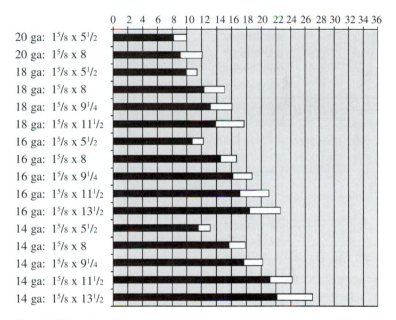

Fig. 2–48 (continued).

Joist Spans (ft): 33 ksi
(Cold-Formed Steel)

■■■ 24"oc   ☐ 16"oc

40 psf live load, **10 psf** dead load: Two Equal Spans
L/360 (LL), **L/240** (LL+DL)

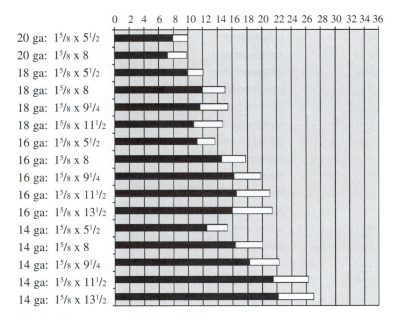

Fig. 2–48 (continued).

Joist Spans (ft): 33 ksi
(Cold-Formed Steel)

■ 24"oc   ☐ 16"oc

50 psf live load, **10 psf** dead load: Single Span
L/360 (LL), **L/240** (LL+DL)

20 ga: $1^5/_8$ x $5^1/_2$
20 ga: $1^5/_8$ x 8
18 ga: $1^5/_8$ x $5^1/_2$
18 ga: $1^5/_8$ x 8
18 ga: $1^5/_8$ x $9^1/_4$
18 ga: $1^5/_8$ x $11^1/_2$
16 ga: $1^5/_8$ x $5^1/_2$
16 ga: $1^5/_8$ x 8
16 ga: $1^5/_8$ x $9^1/_4$
16 ga: $1^5/_8$ x $11^1/_2$
16 ga: $1^5/_8$ x $13^1/_2$
14 ga: $1^5/_8$ x $5^1/_2$
14 ga: $1^5/_8$ x 8
14 ga: $1^5/_8$ x $9^1/_4$
14 ga: $1^5/_8$ x $11^1/_2$
14 ga: $1^5/_8$ x $13^1/_2$

Fig. 2–48 (continued).

Joist Spans (ft): 33 ksi
(Cold-Formed Steel)

■■■ 24"oc   □ 16"oc

50 psf live load, **10 psf** dead load: Two Equal Spans
L/360 (LL), **L/240** (LL+DL)

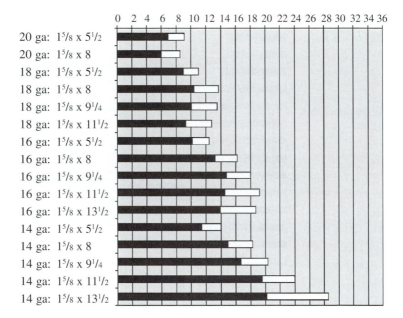

	0 2 4 6 8 10 12 14 16 18 20 22 24 26 28 30 32 34 36
20 ga: 1⁵/₈ x 5¹/₂	
20 ga: 1⁵/₈ x 8	
18 ga: 1⁵/₈ x 5¹/₂	
18 ga: 1⁵/₈ x 8	
18 ga: 1⁵/₈ x 9¹/₄	
18 ga: 1⁵/₈ x 11¹/₂	
16 ga: 1⁵/₈ x 5¹/₂	
16 ga: 1⁵/₈ x 8	
16 ga: 1⁵/₈ x 9¹/₄	
16 ga: 1⁵/₈ x 11¹/₂	
16 ga: 1⁵/₈ x 13¹/₂	
14 ga: 1⁵/₈ x 5¹/₂	
14 ga: 1⁵/₈ x 8	
14 ga: 1⁵/₈ x 9¹/₄	
14 ga: 1⁵/₈ x 11¹/₂	
14 ga: 1⁵/₈ x 13¹/₂	

Fig. 2–48 (continued).

Joist Spans (ft): 50 ksi
(Cold-Formed Steel)

■ 24"oc   ☐ 16"oc

20 psf live load, **10 psf** dead load: Single Span
L/360 (LL), **L/240** (LL+DL)

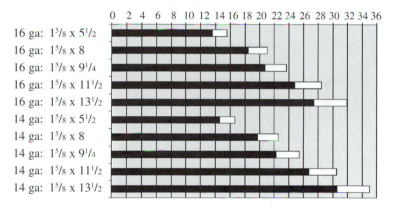

20 psf live load, **10 psf** dead load: Two Equal Spans
L/360 (LL), **L/240** (LL+DL)

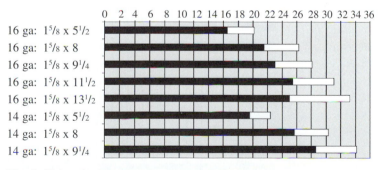

Fig. 2–48 (continued).

Joist Spans (ft): 50 ksi
(Cold-Formed Steel)

■ 24"oc   ☐ 16"oc

40 psf live load, **10 psf** dead load: Single Span
L/360 (LL), **L/240** (LL+DL)

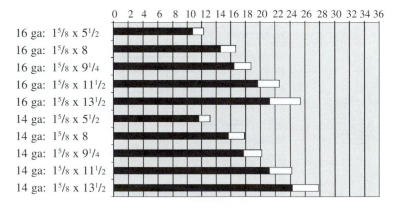

40 psf live load, **10 psf** dead load: Two Equal Spans
L/360 (LL), **L/240** (LL+DL)

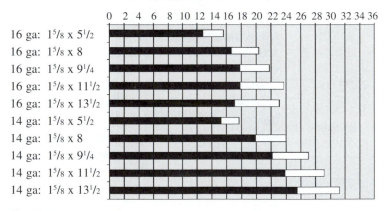

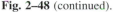

Fig. 2–48 (continued).

Joist Spans (ft): 50 ksi
(Cold-Formed Steel)

■ 24"oc   ☐ 16"oc

50 psf live load, **10 psf** dead load: Single Span
L/360 (LL), **L/240** (LL+DL)

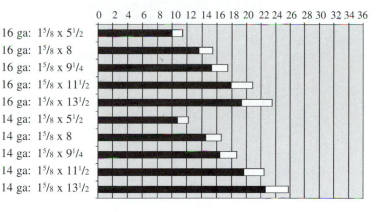

50 psf live load, **10 psf** dead load: Two Equal Spans
L/360 (LL), **L/240** (LL+DL)

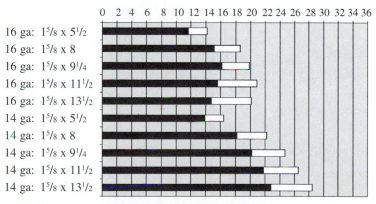

Fig. 2–48 (concluded).

Double Member Beams (Cold-Formed Steel)

Allowable Loads (lbs/ft), L/360

Size: $1^5/_8$" x $5^1/_2$"					
Height (ft)	18 ga 33 ksi	16 ga 33 ksi	14 ga 33 ksi	16 ga 50 ksi	14 ga 50 ksi
3	1982.3	2779.5	3514.1	3643.7	5176.6
4	1232.8	1563.5	1976.7	2049.6	2911.8
5	789.0	1000.6	1265.1	1311.7	1863.6
6	547.9	694.9	878.5	910.9	1157.8
8	308.2	390.9	488.5	396.8	488.5
10	164.6	203.2	250.1	203.2	250.1
12	95.3	117.6	144.7	177.6	144.7
14	60.0	74.0	91.1	74.0	91.1
16	40.2	49.6	61.1	49.6	61.1

Fig. 2–49.

Double Member Beams (Cold-Formed Steel)

Allowable Loads (lbs/ft), L/360

Size: 1⅝" x 8"					
Height (ft)	18 ga 33 ksi	16 ga 33 ksi	14 ga 33 ksi	16 ga 50 ksi	14 ga 50 ksi
3	1344.3	2674.5	5397.7	2674.5	5397.7
4	1008.2	2005.8	3367.2	2005.8	4048.3
5	806.6	1604.7	2155.0	1604.7	3177.1
6	672.1	1178.9	1496.5	1337.2	2206.3
8	476.9	663.1	841.8	871.6	1210.3
10	305.2	424.4	538.7	501.3	619.7
12	211.9	290.1	358.6	290.1	358.6
14	147.6	182.7	225.8	182.7	225.8
16	98.9	122.4	151.3	122.4	151.3
Size: 1⅝" x 9¼"					
Height (ft)	18 ga 33 ksi	16 ga 33 ksi	14 ga 33 ksi	16 ga 50 ksi	14 ga 50 ksi
3	1157.9	2301.6	4639.1	2301.6	4639.1
4	868.4	1726.2	3479.3	1726.2	3479.3
5	694.8	1381.0	2667.9	1381.0	2783.4
6	579.0	1150.8	1852.7	1150.8	2319.5
8	434.2	819.8	1042.1	863.1	1537.1
10	347.4	524.7	667.0	638.0	887.0
12	241.4	364.4	463.2	414.7	513.3
14	177.4	261.2	323.3	261.2	323.3
16	135.8	175.0	216.6	175.0	216.6

Fig. 2–49 (continued).

Double Member Beams (Cold-Formed Steel)

Allowable Loads (lbs/ft), L/360

Size: 1⁵/₈" x 11¹/₂"				
Height (ft)	18 ga 33 ksi	16 ga 33 ksi	14 ga 33 ksi	16 ga 50 ksi	14 ga 50 ksi
3	926.7	1840.0	3702.4	1840.0	3702.4
4	695.0	1380.0	2776.8	1380.0	2776.8
5	556.0	1104.0	2221.4	1104.0	2221.4
6	463.4	920.0	1851.2	920.0	1851.2
8	347.5	690.0	1388.4	690.0	1388.4
10	278.0	552.0	926.2	552.0	1110.7
12	231.7	411.8	643.2	460.0	789.9
14	198.6	302.5	472.6	394.3	558.1
16	165.4	231.6	361.8	301.4	373.9

Size: 1⁵/₈" x 13¹/₂"			
Height (ft)	16 ga 33 ksi	14 ga 33 ksi	16 ga 50 ksi	14 ga 50 ksi
3	1561.5	3139.0	1561.5	3139.0
4	1171.1	2354.3	1171.1	2354.3
5	936.9	1883.4	936.9	1883.4
6	780.8	1569.5	780.8	1569.5
8	585.6	1177.1	585.6	1177.1
10	468.5	941.7	468.5	941.7
12	390.4	683.2	390.4	784.8
14	334.6	501.9	334.6	666.5
16	266.5	384.3	292.8	510.3

Fig. 2–49 (concluded).

Structural Studs (Cold-Formed Steel)

Allowable Heights (ft)

■ 24"oc   □ 16"oc

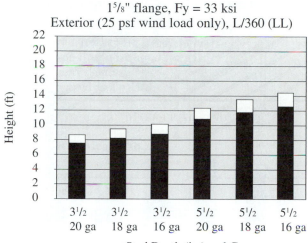

$1^5/_8$" flange, Fy = 33 ksi
Exterior (25 psf wind load only), L/360 (LL)

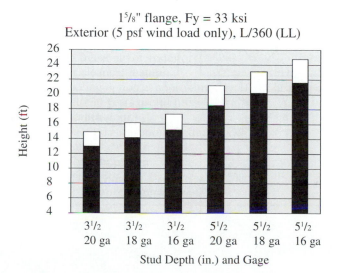

$1^5/_8$" flange, Fy = 33 ksi
Exterior (5 psf wind load only), L/360 (LL)

Fig. 2–50.

Nonstructural Studs (Cold-Formed Steel)

Allowable Heights (ft)

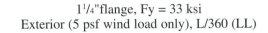

$1\frac{1}{4}$"flange, Fy = 33 ksi
Exterior (5 psf wind load only), L/360 (LL)

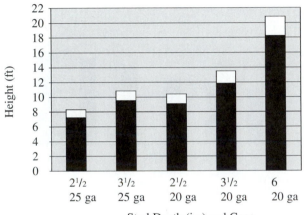

Fig. 2–51.

Structural Studs (Cold-Formed Steel)

Combined Axial Load + Wind Load

1⁵/₈" Flange x 3¹/₂"
5 psf Lateral Load

Allowable Axial Load (kips) @ 16" oc				
Height (ft)	20 ga 33 ksi	18 ga 33 ksi	16 ga 33 ksi	16 ga 50 ksi
8	2.03	2.76	3.55	4.09
9	1.95	2.66	3.4	3.83
10	1.86	2.54	3.22	3.53
12	1.59	2.26	2.83	2.92
14	1.18	1.84	2.4	2.4
16	0.83*	1.35	1.82	1.97
18	0.56*	0.98*	1.36*	1.51*
20	0.37*	0.71*	1.01*	1.16*

Allowable Axial Load (kips) @ 24" oc				
Height (ft)	20 ga 33 ksi	18 ga 33 ksi	16 ga 33 ksi	16 ga 50 ksi
8	2.03	2.76	3.55	4.09
9	1.95	2.66	3.4	3.83
10	1.82	2.54	3.22	3.53
12	1.34	2.13	2.83	2.92
14	0.91*	1.56	2.14	2.35
16	0.56*	1.07*	1.53*	1.73*
18	0.31*	0.72*	1.08*	1.27*
20	0.13*	0.46*	0.75*	0.93*

Fig. 2–52.

* Loads have deflections > L/360.

Structural Studs (Cold-Formed Steel)

Combined Axial Load + Wind Load

1⁵/₈" Flange x 3¹/₂"
25 psf Lateral Load

Allowable Axial Load (kips) @ 16" oc				
Height (ft)	20 ga 33 ksi	18 ga 33 ksi	16 ga 33 ksi	16 ga 50 ksi
8	1.37	2.39	3.37	4.09
9	0.99*	1.95	2.86	3.57
10	0.63*	1.52*	2.34	2.96
12	0.03*	0.75*	1.38*	1.87*
14	0.00*	0.15*	0.63*	1.07*
16	0.00*	0.00*	0.1*	0.51*
18	0.00*	0.00*	0.00*	0.12*
20	0.00*	0.00*	0.00*	0.00*

Allowable Axial Load (kips) @ 24" oc				
Height (ft)	20 ga 33 ksi	18 ga 33 ksi	16 ga 33 ksi	16 ga 50 ksi
8	0.8*	1.82	2.77	3.63
9	0.36*	1.3*	2.16*	2.93*
10	0.00*	0.81*	1.57*	2.27*
12	0.00*	0.00*	0.56*	1.15*
14	0.00*	0.00*	0.00*	0.38*
16	0.00*	0.00*	0.00*	0.00*
18	0.00*	0.00*	0.00*	0.00*
20	0.00*	0.00*	0.00*	0.00*

Fig. 2–52 (continued).

* Loads have deflections > $L/360$.

Structural Studs (Cold-Formed Steel)

Combined Axial Load + Wind Load

1⁵/₈" Flange x 5¹/₂"
5 psf Lateral Load

Allowable Axial Load (kips) @ 16" oc				
Height (ft)	20 ga 33 ksi	18 ga 33 ksi	16 ga 33 ksi	16 ga 50 ksi
8	2.53	3.49	4.65	5.74
9	2.51	3.47	4.61	5.67
10	2.48	3.43	4.56	5.58
12	2.4	3.32	4.42	5.32
14	2.29	3.18	4.22	4.96
16	2.14	2.98	3.96	4.51
18	1.78	2.76	3.66	4.0
20	1.44	2.33	3.3	3.48

Allowable Axial Load (kips) @ 24" oc				
Height (ft)	20 ga 33 ksi	18 ga 33 ksi	16 ga 33 ksi	16 ga 50 ksi
8	2.53	3.49	4.65	5.74
9	2.51	3.47	4.61	5.67
10	2.48	3.43	4.56	5.58
12	2.4	3.32	4.42	5.32
14	2.22	3.18	4.22	4.96
16	1.83	2.92	3.96	4.51
18	1.43	2.42	3.48	4.0
20	1.07*	1.94	2.86	3.28

Fig. 2–52 (continued).

* Loads have deflections > L/360.

Structural Studs (Cold-Formed Steel)

Combined Axial Load + Wind Load

1⁵/₈" Flange x 5¹/₂"
25 psf Lateral Load

Allowable Axial Load (kips) @ 16" oc			
Height (ft)	20 ga 33 ksi	18 ga 33 ksi	16 ga 33 ksi	16 ga 50 ksi
8	2.51	3.49	4.65	5.74
9	2.25	3.47	4.61	5.67
10	1.96	3.26	4.56	5.58
12	1.33	2.57	3.87	5.12
14	0.69*	1.82*	2.98	4.05
16	0.11*	1.1*	2.09*	3.0*
18	0.00*	0.48*	1.29*	2.07*
20	0.00*	0.00*	0.61*	1.31*

Allowable Axial Load (kips) @ 24" oc			
Height (ft)	20 ga 33 ksi	18 ga 33 ksi	16 ga 33 ksi	16 ga 50 ksi
8	2.09	3.43	4.65	5.74
9	1.73	3.06	4.48	5.67
10	1.34	2.65	4.02	5.42
12	0.54*	1.76*	2.99	4.26
14	0.00*	0.87*	1.92*	3.04*
16	0.00*	0.07*	0.93*	1.91*
18	0.00*	0.00*	0.09*	0.98*
20	0.00*	0.00*	0.00*	0.26*

Fig. 2–52 (concluded).

* Loads have deflections > L/360.

Structural Studs (Cold-Formed Steel)

Pure Axial Load, 1⁵/₈" Flange

Allowable Axial Load (lbs): 3¹/₂" depth

Height (ft)	20 ga 33 ksi	18 ga 33 ksi	16 ga 33 ksi	16 ga 50 ksi
1	3108	4406	5711	7935
1.5	3035	4265	5526	7670
2	2936	4077	5281	7315
2.5	2805	3851	4988	6711
3	2644	3595	4660	6058
3.5	2439	3320	4309	5385
4	2224	3034	3934	4723
5	1791	2466	3180	3453
6	1386	1934	2510	2524
7	1068	1478	1963	1963
8	852	1180	1597	1597
9	693	976	1346	1346
10	579	829	1165	1165
12	431	637	829	829
14	341	502	609	609

Allowable Axial Load (lbs): 5¹/₂" depth

Height (ft)	20 ga 33 ksi	18 ga 33 ksi	16 ga 33 ksi	16 ga 50 ksi
1	3196	4596	6074	8321
1.5	3145	4496	5941	8125
2	3075	4359	5759	7873
2.5	2988	4190	5534	7497
3	2872	3993	5271	6959
3.5	2737	3772	4977	6374
4	2568	3533	4659	5763
5	2195	3021	3978	4529
6	1814	2498	3281	3394
7	1449	1994	2610	2610
8	1150	1588	2079	2079
9	939	1300	1700	1700
10	785	1086	1418	1418
12	575	795	1011	1011
14	442	609	742	742

Fig. 2–53.

HVAC

This chapter will assist designers in determining which mechanical components must be accommodated in the schematic design. This permits the architect to plan for such things as louvers in the facade; packaged units inside, outside, and on the roof; baseboard units; ductwork; vents; chases boilers; chillers; air handlers; cooling towers; fuel storage; piping; and other devices associated with the various system choices.

The five tables provided for this purpose are reprinted from *HVAC: Design Criteria, Options, Selection,* and they include advantages and disadvantages of various systems commonly used with selected building types. These entries will help the architect make preliminary system choices early in the design process before the engineer makes specific system information available. Once the probable systems are known, the components required by the systems can then be identified from the tables, and the schematic design can respond to their space requirements.

Accommodating the mechanical equipment and devices early in the schematic process avoids the common pitfall wherein the engineer has to fit the components into a finished design that does not have the space necessary in plan or section for an efficient economical system layout. This chapter, combined with the mechanical and electrical space case studies in Chapter One, provides an early warning to the architect regarding the necessary accommodations for the HVAC systems.

Types of Heating and Cooling Systems for Buildings

The tables below are reprinted from HVAC: Design Criteria, Options, Selection, *by William H. Rowe, III, with permission from the publisher, R.S. Means Company, Inc., Kingston, MA.*

BUILDING TYPE: ASSEMBLY
Churches • Heating (separate): Perimeter radiation. • Cooling (separate): DX. • Heating and cooling (combined): All air central system.
Libraries, museums • Heating and cooling (combined): All air central system. • Remarks: Humidity control.

Movie theaters, cinemas
• Heating and cooling (combined):   All air central system.
• Remarks:
    Large make-up air consideration.
    Check local codes.

Nightclubs, restaurants
• Heating and cooling (combined): All air central system.
• Remarks:
    Smoke and humidity removal requires large make-up air
        consideration.
    Negative pressure in kitchens for odor removal.

Fig. 3–1.

Schools
- Heating (separate):
  Thru-the-wall fan coils.
  Perimeter radiation.
- Remarks: Local codes regulate outdoor air make-up.

Swimming pools
- Heating and cooling (combined): All air central system.
- Remarks: Humidity control.

BUILDING TYPE: **BUSINESS**

Bank
- Heating (separate): Perimeter radiation.
- Heating and cooling (combined): All air central system.

Computer rooms
- Cooling (separate): Tenant supplied unit.
- Remarks: Tie to cooling tower.

Courthouse
- Heating (separate): Perimeter radiation.
- Cooling (separate): Local units.
- Heating and cooling (combined): All air central system.

Lobby
- Remarks: Set 5°–8° buffer.

Lobby, hallways
- Heating and cooling (combined): Separate units.
- Remarks: Separate hours.

Multistory
- Heating (separate): Perimeter-hot water.
- Heating and cooling (combined): All air central system.

Fig. 3–1 (continued).

Offices
- Heating (separate): Perimeter radiation.
- Cooling (separate): Central air.
- Heating and cooling (combined): Package-multizone.

Typical office floor
- Heating (separate): Reheat coils, electric or hot water.
- Cooling (separate): Fan coils, VAV units.
- Heating and cooling (combined): Central air with economizer, heat pumps.
- Remarks: VAV, induction, dual duct, fan coil.

BUILDING TYPE: **COMMERCIAL/RETAIL**

Department store
- Heating (separate): Reheat coils as required.
- Heating and cooling (combined): All air central system.

One-story stores
- Heating (separate): Supplemental radiation at perimeter.
- Heating and cooling (combined): Rooftop HVAC unit.

Supermarkets
- Heating and cooling (combined): Rooftop HVAC unit.
- Remarks: Reclaim heat from refrigeration compressors.

BUILDING TYPE: **FACTORY**

- Heating (separate): Electric, gas-fired space heaters or hydronic.
- Cooling (separate): Special conditions only.
- Heating and cooling (combined): All air central system.

Fig. 3–1 (continued).

BUILDING TYPE: **HAZARDOUS**

- Heating (separate): Hot water.
- Cooling (separate): Chilled water.
- Heating and cooling (combined): Hydronic.
- Remarks: Nonsparking motors and controls.

BUILDING TYPE: **INSTITUTIONAL**

Hospitals
- Heating (separate): Steam-combined with hot water.
- Cooling (separate): Central.
- Heating and cooling (combined): All air-dual duct.
- Remarks: Special ventilation standards.

Penal
- Heating (separate): Hydronic concealed or remote.
- Remarks: Special security standards.

BUILDING TYPE: **RESIDENTIAL**

1 & 2 Family
- Heating (separate): Warm air system or hydronic with radiators.
- Cooling (separate): Split system or window units.
- Heating and cooling (combined): Heat pump (air-to-air) requires booster or with electric reheat.
- Remarks: Operable windows and bathroom exhaust fan.

Mid-rise, multifamily residences and elderly housing
- Heating (separate): Electric or hydronic.
- Cooling (separate): Window units.
- Heating and cooling (combined): Heat pump (water-to-air) fan coil units.
- Remarks: Fresh air to corridors -- bathroom and kitchen exhaust.

Fig. 3–1 (continued).

Hotels
- Heating and cooling (combined): Hydronic or electric fan coil units.
- Remarks: Same as above.

BUILDING TYPE: **STORAGE**

Warehouses
- Heating (separate): Electric, gas, or hydronic unit heaters.
- Cooling (separate):
    Walk-in coolers.
    Built-up direct expansion systems.
- Remarks: Check requirements for material stored.

Existing buildings renovation
Note the type of system presently in the building and compare with the above table. Review the recommendations in the book. See discussion on installing new systems versus renovation. When the renovated use is different from the existing system, check for overall feasibility.

Fig. 3–1 (concluded).

System Selection Chart

The tables below are reprinted from HVAC: Design Criteria, Options, Selection, *by William H. Rowe, III, with permission from the publisher, R.S. Means Company, Inc., Kingston, MA.*

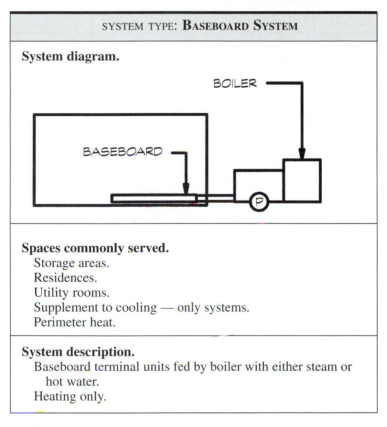

SYSTEM TYPE: **BASEBOARD SYSTEM**

System diagram.

Spaces commonly served.
Storage areas.
Residences.
Utility rooms.
Supplement to cooling — only systems.
Perimeter heat.

System description.
Baseboard terminal units fed by boiler with either steam or
   hot water.
Heating only.

Fig. 3–2.

Advantages.
  Low cost.
  No ducts required.
  Flexible control.
  Minimum space requirements.

Disadvantages.
  Baseboard is exposed.
  May interfere with furniture.
  No ventilation, air conditioning, or humidity control.

System capabilities.
  Heating.

SYSTEM TYPE: **4-Pipe Fan Coil System**

System diagram.

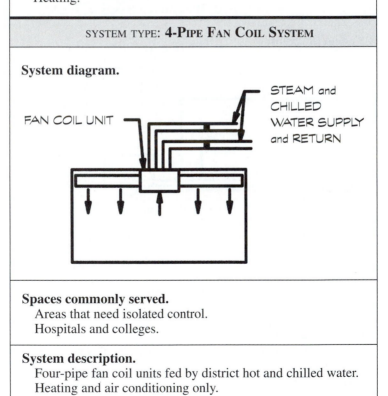

Spaces commonly served.
  Areas that need isolated control.
  Hospitals and colleges.

System description.
  Four-pipe fan coil units fed by district hot and chilled water.
  Heating and air conditioning only.

Fig. 3–2 (continued).

Advantages.
  Low cost.
  Individual room control.
  Minimal space required.

Disadvantages.
  Noisy.
  Limited size range.
  No ventilation.
  Air handler requires space.

System capabilities.
  Heating.
  Ventilation can be achieved by supplying tempered air into
      return air plenum with separate system.
  Air conditioning.
  Humidification possible by adding in-line humidifier.

SYSTEM TYPE: **PACKAGED UNIT SYSTEM**

System diagram.

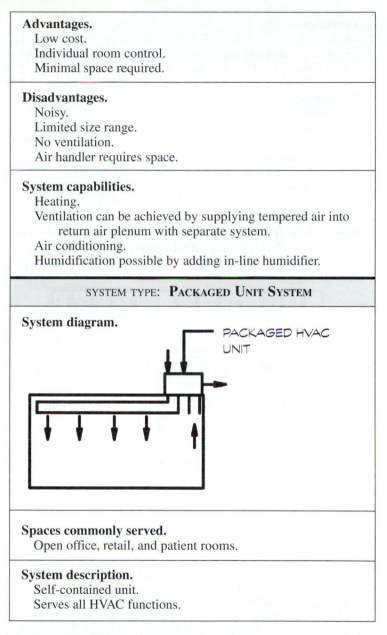

Spaces commonly served.
  Open office, retail, and patient rooms.

System description.
  Self-contained unit.
  Serves all HVAC functions.

Fig. 3–2 (continued).

Advantages.
Quiet.
Easily designed and installed.
Energy costs can be individually billed.

Disadvantages.
Requires maintenance.
Extensive ductwork.

System capabilities.
Heating.
Ventilation.
Air conditioning.
Humidification possible by adding in-line humidifier.

SYSTEM: **SPLIT SYSTEM**

System diagram.

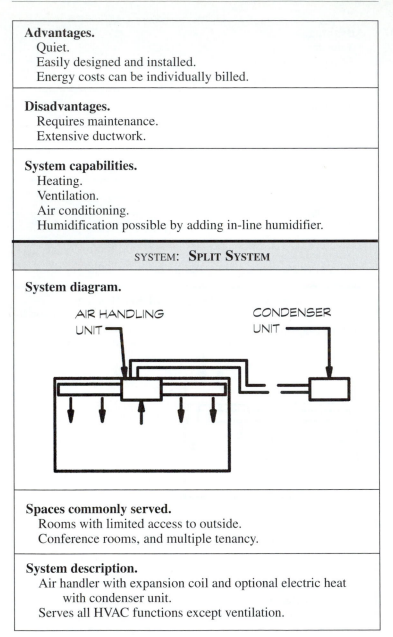

Spaces commonly served.
Rooms with limited access to outside.
Conference rooms, and multiple tenancy.

System description.
Air handler with expansion coil and optional electric heat
    with condenser unit.
Serves all HVAC functions except ventilation.

Fig. 3–2 (continued).

Advantages.
Small indoor component.
Minimal ductwork.
Quiet.
DX—no freezing.

Disadvantages.
Multiple pieces of equipment to maintain.

System capabilities.
Heating.
Ventilation can be achieved by supplying tempered air into
    return air plenum with separate system.
Air conditioning.
Humidification possible by adding in-line humidifier.

SYSTEM: **VARIABLE AIR VOLUME SYSTEM**

System diagram.

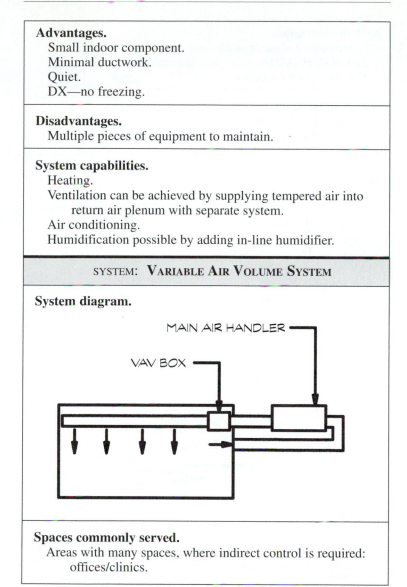

Spaces commonly served.
Areas with many spaces, where indirect control is required:
    offices/clinics.

Fig. 3–2 (continued).

System description.
  Central air handler/air conditioner with VAV boxes.
  Serves all HVAC functions except humidity control.
  Variable speed fan optional.

Advantages.
  Individual room control.
  Good for large applications.
  Can work with economizer system.

Disadvantages.
  Reheat required.

System capabilities.
  Heating.
  Ventilation.
  Air conditioning.

SYSTEM: **INDUCTION SYSTEM**

System diagram.

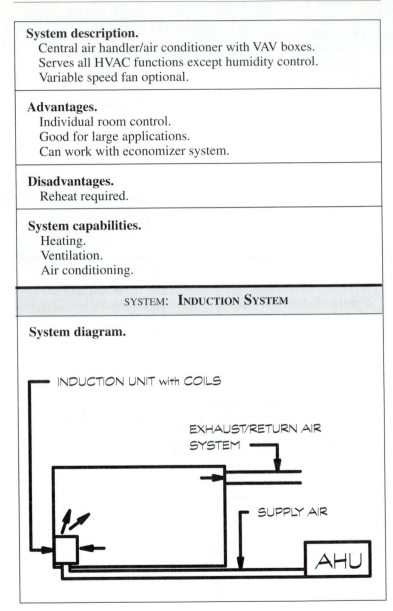

Fig. 3–2 (continued).

Spaces commonly served.
  Spaces with ventilation requirements: offices and patient
      rooms.

System description.
  Central air handler/air conditioner with individual room,
      induction units.
  Serves all HVAC functions.

Advantages.
  No ductwork.
  Minimal amount of equipment to maintain.
  Individual room control.
  Provides ventilation air.

Disadvantages.
  High airflow in rooms.
  Noisy.

System capabilities.
  Heating.
  Ventilation.
  Air conditioning.
  Humidification possible by adding in-line humidifier.

SYSTEM: **HEAT PUMP SYSTEM**

System diagram.

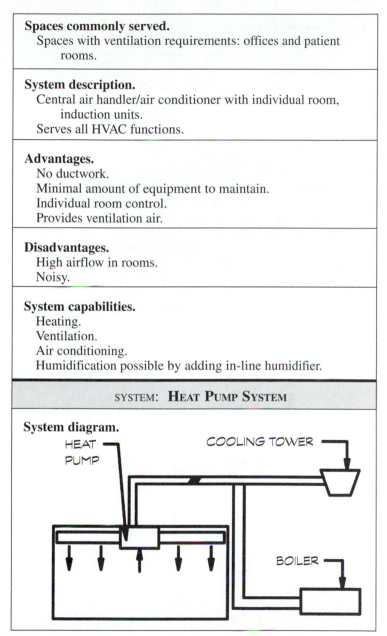

Fig. 3–2 (continued).

Spaces commonly served.
Offices, high-end residences, nursing homes.

System description.
Heat pumps with cooling tower and boiler.
Heating and air conditioning only.

Advantages.
Energy efficient.
Energy moved around building.

Disadvantages.
Will not operate in low air temperatures.
No ventilation or humidity control.
Units require maintenance.

System capabilities.
Heating.
Ventilation can be achieved by supplying tempered air into
    return air plenum with separate system.
Air conditioning.

Fig.3–2 (concluded).

Preliminary Selection of Distribution Systems

The tables below are reprinted from HVAC: Design Criteria, Options, Selection, *by William H. Rowe, III, with permission from the publisher, R.S. Means Company, Inc., Kingston, MA.*

TYPE OF BUILDING SYSTEM: **SEPARATE HEATING**	
Type of Distribution System Conditions	**Select**
Individual room control and/or tenant billing required.	Electric.
Steam heating and other steam uses—industrial.	Steam.
Continuous use buildings.	Hot water.
Intermittent use with freezing potential.	Warm air.

TYPE OF BUILDING SYSTEM: **SEPARATE COOLING**	
Type of Distribution System Conditions	**Select**
One- and two-story buildings.	Air.

TYPE OF BUILDING SYSTEM: **HEATING AND COOLING**	
Type of Distribution System Conditions	**Select**
High-rise office — fan coil units.	Water.
— induction units/central air.	Air and reheat.
— variable air volume.	Air and reheat.

Fig. 3–3.

Generation Equipment—Heating

The tables below are reprinted from HVAC: Design Criteria,
Options, Selection, *by William H. Rowe, III, with permission from
the publisher, R.S. Means Company, Inc., Kingston, MA.*

CAST IRON SECTIONAL BOILERS

Type and R.S. Means No.
Gas fired 155–115
- Capacity:
    80–7000 MBH
    24–2050 kW
- Efficiency: 80%–92%
- Considerations: Gas service required.
- Advantages:
    25 years (plus) useful life.
    Long life.
    Durability.
    Expandable.
    Wide range of sizes.
    Ease of replacement.
    Crack section may be isolated rather than shut down
        entire boiler.
- Disadvantages:
    Heavy.
    Hard to clean.
    High standby losses.
- Related Equipment and Accessories:
    Insulated jacket.
    Type B vent required for gas.
    Push nipples or gaskets required at sections.

Fig. 3–4.

Flue and breeching.
Safety devices.
Two-stage firing available.
May be shipped as a package or broken down for field
assembly.

Oil fired 155–120
- Capacity:
  100–7000 MBH
  30–2050 kW
- Efficiency: 80%–92%
- Considerations: Fuel oil storage and pumping required.
- Advantages:
  25 years (plus) useful life.
  Long life.
  Durability.
  Expandable.
  Wide range of sizes.
  Ease of replacement.
  Crack section may be isolated rather than shut down
    entire boiler.
- Disadvantages:
  Heavy.
  Hard to clean.
  High standby losses.
- Related Equipment and Accessories:
  Insulated jacket.
  Type B vent required for gas.
  Push nipples or gaskets required at sections.
  Flue and breeching.
  Safety devices.
  Two-stage firing available.
  May be shipped as a package or broken down for field
    assembly.

Fig. 3–4 (continued).

<u>Gas/oil combination 155–125</u>
- Capacity:
  720–13,500 MBH
  210–4000 kW
- Efficiency: 80%–92%
- Considerations: Allows for use of least expensive fuel available.
- Advantages:
  25 years (plus) useful life.
  Long life.
  Durability.
  Expandable.
  Wide range of sizes.
  Ease of replacement.
  Crack section may be isolated rather than shut down entire boiler.
- Disadvantages:
  Heavy.
  Hard to clean.
  High standby losses.
- Related Equipment and Accessories:
  Insulated jacket.
  Type B vent required for gas.
  Push nipples or gaskets required at sections.
  Flue and breeching.
  Safety devices.
  Two-stage firing available.
  May be shipped as a package or broken down for field assembly.

<u>Solid fuel 155–130</u>
- Capacity:
  148–4600 MBH
  43–1350 kW
- Efficiency: n/a
- Considerations: Allows for use of inexpensive fuel or burning of waste by-products.

Fig. 3–4 (continued).

- Advantages:
    25 years (plus) useful life.
    Long life.
    Durability.
    Expandable.
    Wide range of sizes.
    Ease of replacement.
    Crack section may be isolated rather than shut down
        entire boiler.
- Disadvantages:
    Heavy.
    Hard to clean.
    High standby losses.
- Related Equipment and Accessories:
    Insulated jacket.
    Type B vent required for gas.
    Push nipples or gaskets required at sections.
    Flue and breeching.
    Safety devices.
    Two-stage firing available.
    May be shipped as a package or broken down for field
        assembly.

STEEL BOILERS

Type and R.S. Means No.
Solid fuel 155–130
- Capacity:
    1500–18,000 MBH
    440–5275 kW
- Efficiency: n/a
- Considerations: Allows for use of inexpensive fuel or
    burning of waste by-products.
- Advantages:
    15 to 25 years useful life.
    Less expensive to purchase.
    Tubes easily accessed for cleaning or replacement.
    Leaking tubes may be plugged for future replacement.

Fig. 3–4 (continued).

- Disadvantages:
  Regular maintenance required to extend boiler life and
      retain efficiency.
  Space allowance to pull or punch tubes.
- Related Equipment and Accessories:
  Insulated jacket.
  Type B vent required for gas.
  Flue and breeching.
  Safety devices.
  Two-stage firing available.
  Must be shipped as one piece (two-piece available on
      special order).

Oil or gas 155–115/135
- Capacity:
  144–23,435 MBH
  42–6868 kW
- Efficiency: 80%–92%
- Considerations: Fuel service and/or storage required.
- Advantages:
  15 to 25 years useful life.
  Less expensive to purchase.
  Tubes easily accessed for cleaning or replacement.
  Leaking tubes may be plugged for future replacement.
- Disadvantages:
  Regular maintenance required to extend boiler life and
      retain efficiency.
  Space allowance to pull or punch tubes.
- Related Equipment and Accessories:
  Insulated jacket.
  Type B vent required for gas.
  Flue and breeching.
  Safety devices.
  Two-stage firing available.
  Must be shipped as one piece (two-piece available on
      special order).

Electric 155–100
- Capacity:
  6–2500 MBH
  2–750 kW

Fig. 3–4 (continued).

- Efficiency: 100%
- Considerations:
    No flue or chimney required.
    No fuel storage required.
    Large electric service required.
- Advantages:
    15 to 25 years useful life.
    Less expensive to purchase.
    Tubes easily accessed for cleaning or replacement.
    Leaking tubes may be plugged for future replacement.
- Disadvantages:
    Regular maintenance required to extend boiler life and
        retain efficiency.
    Space allowance to pull or punch tubes.
- Related Equipment and Accessories:
    Insulated jacket.
    Type B vent required for gas.
    Flue and breeching.
    Safety devices.
    Two-stage firing available.
    Must be shipped as one piece (two-piece available on
        special order).

NOVEL RESIDENTIAL TYPE BOILERS

Type and R.S. Means No.
Pulse/condensing gas fired 155–115
- Capacity:
    44–134 MBH
    13–40 kW
- Efficiency: 90%–95%
- Considerations: Gas service required.
- Advantages:
    No chimney required.
    Less floor space.
    Ease of installation.
- Disadvantages:
    Noisy.
    Acid waste.

Fig. 3–4 (continued).

- Related Equipment and Accessories:
    PVC through-wall flue.
    Plastic drain lines.

Wall hung gas fired 155–115
- Capacity:
    44–64 MBH
    13–19 kW
- Efficiency: 85%
- Considerations:
    Gas service required.
    Available in cast iron or steel.
- Advantages:
    No chimney required.
    Less floor space.
    Ease of installation.
- Disadvantages: Structural support considerations.
- Related Equipment and Accessories: Through-wall flue.

FURNACES—WARM AIR

Type and R.S. Means No.
Electric 155–420
- Capacity:
    30–141 MBH
    9–41 kW
- Efficiency: 100%
- Considerations:
    No flue or chimney required.
    No fuel storage required.
    Large electric service required.
- Advantages:
    Quick response.
    No freeze-up of system.
    Air cleaning feature.
    Cooling option at approximately 1/3 of heating output.
    15 to 30 years useful life.

Fig. 3–4 (continued).

- Disadvantages:
    Space considerations for ductwork.
    Humidification required.
    Large temperature swings.
    Noisy.
    Air filtering required.
- Related Equipment and Accessories:
    Insulated jacket.
    Type B vent required for gas.
    Safety devices.
    Shipped as a package.

Gas 155–420
- Capacity:
    42–400 MBH
    12.5–120 kW
- Efficiency: 80%–92%
- Considerations: Gas service required.
- Advantages:
    Quick response.
    No freeze-up of system.
    Air cleaning feature.
    Cooling option at approximately 1/3 of heating output.
    15 to 30 years useful life.
- Disadvantages:
    Space considerations for ductwork.
    Humidification required.
    Large temperature swings.
    Noisy.
    Air filtering required.
- Related Equipment and Accessories:
    Insulated jacket.
    Type B vent required for gas.
    Safety devices.
    Shipped as a package.

Fig. 3–4 (continued).

Oil 155–420
- Capacity:
  55–400 MBH
  16–120 kW
- Efficiency: 80%–92%
- Considerations: Fuel oil storage and pumping required.
- Advantages:
  Quick response.
  No freeze-up of system.
  Air cleaning feature.
  Cooling option at approximately 1/3 of heating output.
  15 to 30 years useful life.
- Disadvantages:
  Space considerations for ductwork.
  Humidification required.
  Large temperature swings.
  Noisy.
  Air filtering required.
- Related Equipment and Accessories:
  Insulated jacket.
  Type B vent required for gas.
  Safety devices.
  Shipped as a package.

Solid fuel 155–420
- Capacity:
  112–170 MBH
  33–50 kW
- Efficiency: n/a
- Considerations: Allows for use of inexpensive fuel or
  burning of waste by-products, etc.
- Advantages:
  Quick response.
  No freeze-up of system.
  Air cleaning feature.
  Cooling option at approximately 1/3 of heating output.
  15 to 30 years useful life.

Fig. 3–4 (continued).

- Disadvantages:
  Space considerations for ductwork.
  Humidification required.
  Large temperature swings.
  Noisy.
  Air filtering required.
- Related Equipment and Accessories:
  Insulated jacket.
  Type B vent required for gas.
  Safety devices.
  Shipped as a package.

MAKE-UP AIR UNIT

Type and R.S. Means No.
Gas 155–461
- Capacity:
  168–6275 MBH
  50–1840 kW
- Efficiency: 80%–92%
- Considerations:
  Make-up air for kitchens or other large-volume
    considerations.
  May be roof mounted or indoors.
- Advantages:
  Quick response.
  No freeze-up of system.
  Air cleaning feature.
  Cooling option at approximately 1/3 of heating output.
  15 to 30 years useful life.
- Disadvantages:
  Space consideration for ductwork.
  Humidification required.
  Large temperature swings.
  Noisy.
  Air filtering required.

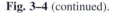

Fig. 3–4 (continued).

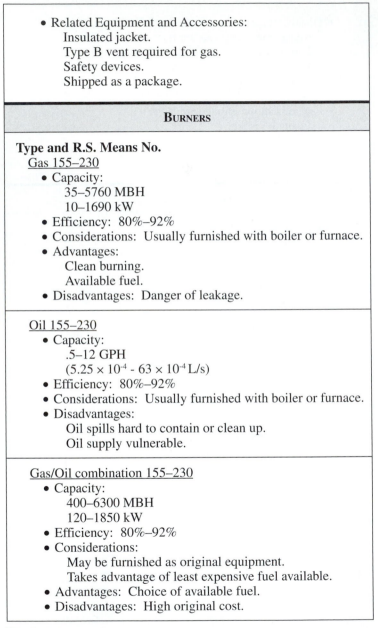

- Related Equipment and Accessories:
  Insulated jacket.
  Type B vent required for gas.
  Safety devices.
  Shipped as a package.

BURNERS

Type and R.S. Means No.
Gas 155–230
- Capacity:
  35–5760 MBH
  10–1690 kW
- Efficiency: 80%–92%
- Considerations: Usually furnished with boiler or furnace.
- Advantages:
  Clean burning.
  Available fuel.
- Disadvantages: Danger of leakage.

Oil 155–230
- Capacity:
  .5–12 GPH
  $(5.25 \times 10^{-4} - 63 \times 10^{-4}\,L/s)$
- Efficiency: 80%–92%
- Considerations: Usually furnished with boiler or furnace.
- Disadvantages:
  Oil spills hard to contain or clean up.
  Oil supply vulnerable.

Gas/Oil combination 155–230
- Capacity:
  400–6300 MBH
  120–1850 kW
- Efficiency: 80%–92%
- Considerations:
  May be furnished as original equipment.
  Takes advantage of least expensive fuel available.
- Advantages: Choice of available fuel.
- Disadvantages: High original cost.

Fig. 3–4 (continued).

Coal Stoker 155–230
- Capacity:
    1000–7300 MBH
    293–2140 kW
- Efficiency: n/a
- Considerations: Uses inexpensive coal or waste by-
    products.
- Advantages: Inexpensive fuel.
- Disadvantages:
    Dirty storage and exhaust.
    Needs coal storage space.
- Related Equipment and Accessories: Conveyor or manual
    feed.

FUEL OIL STORAGE TANKS

Fiberglass underground 155–671
- Capacity:
    550–48,000 gal.
    (2130–186,000 L)
- Efficiency: n/a
- Considerations: Uses inexpensive coal or waste by-
    products.
- Advantages:
    Cannot rust.
    Ease of handling.
    Dielectric material.
- Disadvantages: Leak detection difficult.
- Related Equipment and Accessories:
    Fill vent and sound piping to grade or higher.
    Hold-down pads and anchors.

Steel underground 155–671
- Capacity:
    550–30,000 gal.
    (1950–116,250 L)
- Efficiency: n/a
- Considerations:
    Double wall available.
    Normal caution in backfilling.

Fig. 3–4 (continued).

- Advantages: Inherent strength of steel prevents crushing.
- Disadvantages:
    Leak detection difficult.
    Subject to electrolytic action.
- Related Equipment and Accessories:
    Fill vent and sound piping to grade or higher.
    Hold-down pads and anchors.

Steel above ground
- Capacity:
    275–5000 gal.
    (1065–19,375 L)
- Efficiency: n/a
- Considerations: Visual leakage control.
- Advantages:
    Ease of replacement.
    No excavation or backfill required.
- Disadvantages: Takes up valuable space.

EXPANSION TANKS

Liquid expansion
- Capacity:
    15–400 gal.
    (58–1550 L)
- Efficiency: n/a
- Considerations:
    20–30 years useful life.
    Used on hot and chilled water systems.
- Advantages: Can be atmospherically recharged.
- Disadvantages:
    Subject to flooding.
    Pressures in system can vary.
- Related Equipment and Accessories:
    Diverter fittings.
    Drain valve.

Fig. 3–4 (continued).

Diaphragm (captive air)
- Capacity:
   19–528 gal.
   (7.5–2050 L)
- Efficiency: n/a
- Considerations:
   20 years (plus) useful life.
   Used on hot and chilled water systems.
- Advantages:
   Cannot waterlog.
   Constant pressure possible.
- Disadvantages: Diaphragm can rupture or lose seal.
- Related Equipment and Accessories:
   Diverter fittings.
   Drain valve.

Fig. 3–4 (concluded).

Generation Equipment—Cooling

The tables below are reprinted from HVAC: Design Criteria, Options, Selection, *by William H. Rowe, III, with permission from the publisher, R.S. Means Company, Inc., Kingston, MA.*

Packaged Water Chillers

- R.S. Means No.:
  - 157-110.
  - 157-190.
- Typical uses: Produce chilled water for cooling coils, fan coils.
- Useful life: 15–30 years.
- Capacity range:
  - 2–250 tons.
  - 7–880 kW.
- Advantages:
  - Direct expansion:
    - Chilled water is pipe throughout the building and available on demand.
    - No environmental concern.
  - Absorption:
    - Very competitive where heat source is inexpensive.
    - Few mechanical parts.
    - Use little electrical power for operating.
- Disadvantages:
  - Direct expansion:
    - Reciprocating type can be noisy.

Fig. 3–5.

- ○ Absorption:
  High initial cost.
  Requires frequent maintenance.
  Disposal of lithium bromide is an environmental concern.
- • Remarks:
  - ○ Direct expansion:
    Most chillers operate on electricity.
  - ○ Absorption:
    Energy source is steam or hot water.
    Gas is also used frequently.

CONDENSERS

- • R.S. Means No.: 157-225.
- • Typical uses:
  Cools refrigerant gases leaving compressor; air cooled or
  water cooled.
- • Useful life: 15–30 years.
- • Capacity range:
  20–100 tons.
  70–350 kW (air cooled).
- • Advantages:
  - ○ Air cooled:
    Cools refrigerant gas directly. Fewer overall components
    to maintain.
    Can be grouped for larger capacities.
  - ○ Water cooled:
    Generally integral with hydronic chiller.
- • Disadvantages:
  - ○ Air cooled:
    Limited in size but can be grouped as modules.
    Noisy.
  - ○ Water cooled:
    Cooling tower or evaporative condenser required.
    Freezing of water lines a problem in northern climates if
    winter operation is needed.

Fig. 3–5 (continued).

- Remarks:
    - Air cooled:
        Air cooled preferred when available.
        Heavy loads—check with structural engineer.
    - Water cooled:
        Evaporative condensers are very efficient under certain
            conditions and can be used for the cooling options.
        Local codes regulate their use due to heavy water
            consumption.

ROOFTOP AIR CONDITIONING UNITS

- R.S. Means No.: 157-180.
- Typical uses: Commercial applications.
- Useful life: 10–20 years.
- Capacity range:
    3–100 tons.
    10.5–350 kW.
- Advantages:
    Single package, low initial cost.
    Ease of installation.
    No flue required.
    Valuable floor space not taken up for a mechanical room.
    Very serviceable.
    Minimum field connections.
- Disadvantages:
    Noisy.
    May have to be screened or shielded for aesthetic purposes.
- Remarks:
    Electric for cooling.
    Gas or electric for heating.
    Multizone capability with some units.
    Economizer option recommended.

Fig. 3–5 (continued).

SELF-CONTAINED AIR CONDITIONING UNITS

- R.S. Means No.: 157-185.
- Typical uses: Commercial applications.
- Useful life: 10–20 years.
- Capacity range:
    3–60 tons.
    10.5–17.5 kW.
- Advantages:
    No major remote pieces of generating equipment necessary other than a condenser.
    Can be free-blow without ducts if located in conditioned space.
- Disadvantages:
    Ventilation must be provided separately.
    Takes up valuable floor space.
- Remarks:
    Heating coil may be added to these units.
    Units typically air cooled.
    Fire regulations may require smoke detector in ductwork to shut down unit upon detection.

COOLING TOWERS

- R.S. Means No.: 157-240.
- Typical uses:
    Cools condenser water from refrigerant condenser.
- Useful life: 25–40 years.
- Capacity range:
    60–1000 tons.
    210–3500 kW.
- Advantages:
    o Natural draft:
        Low initial cost.
        Few mechanical parts.
        Quiet operation.

Fig. 3–5 (continued).

- ○ Mechanical draft:
    Energy savings possible by modulating fan speed.
    Acts like natural draft with fans off.
    High capacity is possible.
- Disadvantages:
  - ○ Natural draft:
      All cooling towers require antibacterial water treatment.
  - ○ Mechanical draft:
      High initial cost.
      Noisy.
- Remarks:
  - ○ Natural draft:
      Provide make-up water to replace evaporated water and to
        wash out (blow down) system as water is fouled.
  - ○ Mechanical draft:
      Mechanical draft towers are available as forced draft or as
        induced draft. In northern climates, if winter operation is a
        requirement, closed-circuit cooling towers containing
        antifreeze solution are an alternative.

CENTRAL STATION AIR HANDLING UNITS

- R.S. Means No.: 157-125.
- Typical uses: HVAC of building.
- Useful life: 15–30 years.
- Capacity range:
    1300–60,000 cfm.
    615–28,320 L/s.
- Advantages:
    Combines all HVAC components into one system.
    Energy savings via economizers possible.
    Can be coordinated with VAV systems.
- Disadvantages:
    Ducts and shafts require space.
    Must protect coils from freezing in the event of a power
      failure.

Fig. 3–5 (continued).

- Remarks:
  - Heating:
    steam
    electricity
    gas
    hot water
  - Cooling:
    electric
    chilled water
    direct expansion
  - Check structural loads for floor or roof mounting.

SPLIT SYSTEMS

- R.S. Means No.:
  157-150/187.
  157-230.
- Typical uses:
  Individual space conditioning remote from mechanical
    equipment.
- Useful life: 10–20 years.
- Capacity range:
  1–10 tons.
  3.5–35 kW.
- Advantages:
  Individual cooling coil for each tenant.
  Provides separate cooling for spaces remote from condensing
    unit location.
  No noise in conditioned space.
- Disadvantages:
  Separate ventilation air required.
  Long runs of refrigerant piping.
- Remarks:
  Distance between two sections is limited to approximately
    60'.
  Refrigerant lines between both units must be insulated.
  Optional heating coil.

Fig. 3–5 (continued).

HEAT PUMPS

- R.S. Means No.: 157-160.
- Typical uses: Heating and cooling of spaces.
- Useful life: 10–20 years.
- Capacity range:
    1.5–50 tons.
    5.25–175kW.
- Advantages:
    Individual metering of space possible for electricity.
    Energy efficient, as some heat and others cool.
    Boiler and chiller off for portions of spring and fall.
- Disadvantages:
    Compressor noise in space.
    For winter cooling, a glycol solution in a closed-circuit
        cooling tower or air-cooled condenser is necessary.
- Remarks:
    Boiler must be controlled to limit supply water to 90° F
        maximum.
    Low operating temperatures are conducive to plastic piping.

Fig. 3–5 (concluded).

4

Materials

This chapter provides dimensional limits of a selected group of building components. Although not all variations are illustrated, those shown will inform the designer of the largest standard units available and, in the case of curved elements, the smallest radii that are standard. This information will help the designer produce schematic designs which reduce the need to redesign in the working drawing phase or to use custom products.

The series begins with three less common products, the first two of which are curved. Where curves are desired in a building, structure and glazing often must be curved to produce the desired geometry. The curved glass segment provides size limits to help the designer plan for the required mullions in the composition of the building facade. Also included are radii minimums which help the designer develop realistic geometries in glass. This is followed by information on curved steel. Here approximate maximum sizes of steel members that can be curved with accuracy are shown. Several minimum radii that can be achieved in various sizes are also included. The third section addresses a relatively new product, fire-rated glass. The size limitations and thickness requirements of this series give the designer a realistic preview of the compositional options of glazing in walls required to be fire rated.

The second half of the chapter addresses more traditional products. The next component illustrated is skylights, shown in several configurations. Included in this information are standard sizes among a selected series ranging from the smallest to largest.

This section is followed by a series of large overhead service doors, fire doors, and security grilles. The largest standard sizes of selected weight and construction in steel and aluminum are illustrated. The chapter concludes with information on elevator sizes. This section is useful prior to the final design of the elevators. Small and large standard elevators are shown, thus illustrating the approximate range of areas needed in the floor plan for single or double elevators. In this case, the designer would be prudent to provide space for the largest standard size in multiples of the number of elevators estimated to be needed.

This information is based on products being manufactured at the time of publication, thus the architect is provided with sources from which more specific information can be obtained for detailing purposes or to identify component variations. (Manufacturers bear no responsibility for the interpretation of their data provided here.)

Curved tempered glass

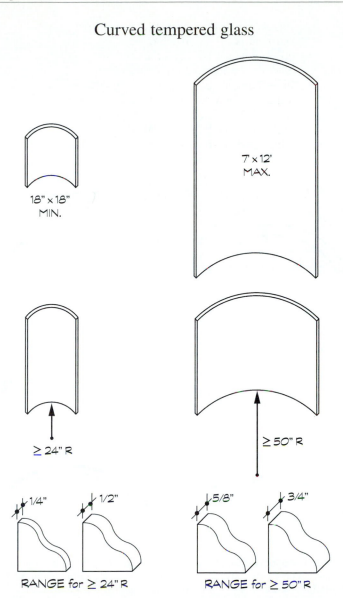

Fig. 4–1. Approximate maximum sizes and minimum radii for curved tempered glass are shown. (The interpretation and reorganization of this data is based on Bentemp® literature from the North American Glass Company, Bensenville, Illinois.)

Curved steel

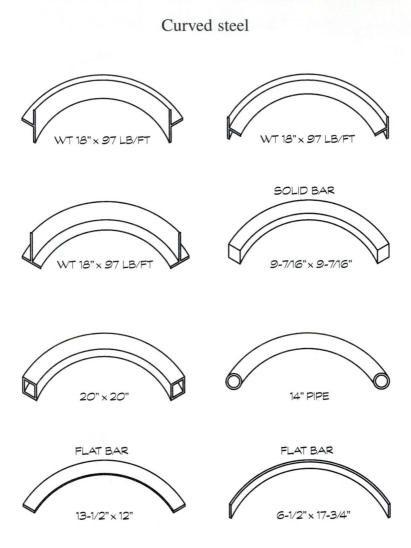

WT 18" x 97 LB/FT

WT 18" x 97 LB/FT

WT 18" x 97 LB/FT

SOLID BAR

9-7/16" x 9-7/16"

20" x 20"

14" PIPE

FLAT BAR

13-1/2" x 12"

FLAT BAR

6-1/2" x 17-3/4"

Fig. 4–2. The approximate largest steel components of various sections that can be curved are illustrated. Minimum radii range from about 30' for a W14x53 to about 45' for a W18x60, rolled against the strong axis. Minimum radii when rolled against the weak axis range from about 10' for a W14x53 to about 20' for a W24x103. (This information is adapted from literature distributed by Falcon Rolling, Inc., Kansas City, Missouri; White Fab, Inc., Birmingham, Alabama; and Chicago Metal Rolled Products Company, Chicago, Illinois.)

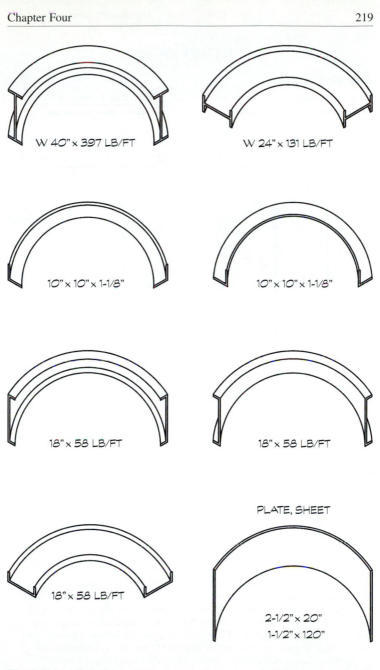

W 40" x 397 LB/FT

W 24" x 131 LB/FT

10" x 10" x 1-1/8"

10" x 10" x 1-1/8"

18" x 58 LB/FT

18" x 58 LB/FT

18" x 58 LB/FT

PLATE, SHEET

2-1/2" x 20"
1-1/2" x 120"

Fig. 4–2 (concluded).

Fire-rated glazing

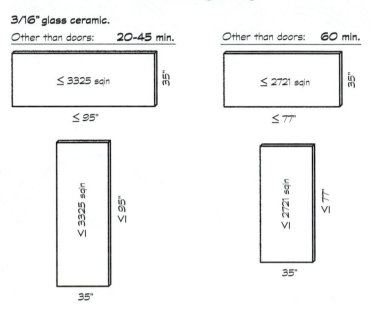

3/16" glass ceramic.

Other than doors: **20-45 min.**

≤ 3325 sqin   35"
≤ 95"

Other than doors: **60 min.**

≤ 2721 sqin   35"
≤ 77"

≤ 3325 sqin   ≤ 95"
35"

≤ 2721 sqin   ≤ 77"
35"

1/4" impact safety-rated toughened glass

Doors: **20 min.**

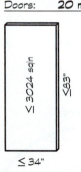

≤ 3024 sqin   ≤83"
≤ 34"

Fig. 4–3. Approximate maximum sizes for fire-rated glazing. Illustrations show the maximum area and maximum dimensions for each panel type. Some doors have maximums for both dimensions of glazing. For other glazing, the shorter dimension shown for each panel is the maximum possible when the longer dimension is set at the maximum allowed. The fire rating is listed with each set of panels. (Data was interpreted and reorganized based on literature from TGP, Technical Glass Products, Kirkland, Washington.)

1/4" impact safety-rated toughened glass for other than doors: 20min.

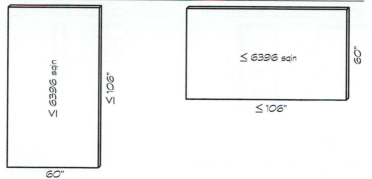

3/16" impact safety-rated glass ceramic with surface film.

Doors: **20 min.**   Other than doors: **20 min.**

Doors: **45 min.**   Other than doors: **45 min.**

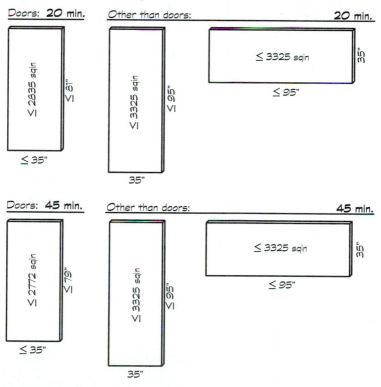

Fig. 4–3 (continued).

3/16" impact safety-rated glass ceramic for surface film.

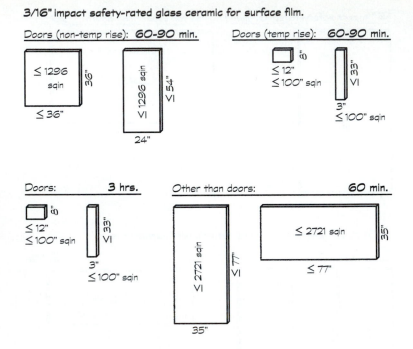

Doors (non-temp rise): **60-90 min.**   Doors (temp rise): **60-90 min.**

≤ 1296 sqin   36"   ≤ 1296 sqin   ≤ 54"   ≤ 12"   ≤ 33"
≤ 36"   24"   ≤ 100" sqin
                                                         3"
                                                        ≤ 100" sqin
                                                        8"

Doors: **3 hrs.**   Other than doors: **60 min.**

8"
≤ 12"   ≤ 33"   ≤ 2721 sqin   ≤ 77"   ≤ 2721 sqin   35"
≤ 100" sqin   35"   ≤ 77"
3"
≤ 100" sqin

5/16" impact safety-rated glass ceramic.

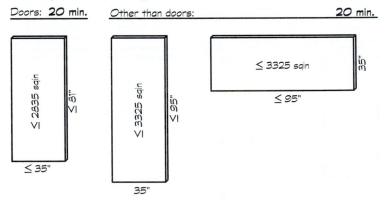

Doors: **20 min.**   Other than doors: **20 min.**

≤ 2835 sqin   ≤ 81"   ≤ 3325 sqin   ≤ 95"   ≤ 3325 sqin   35"
≤ 35"   35"   ≤ 95"

Fig. 4–3 (continued).

5/16" impact safety-rated glass ceramic.

<u>Doors:</u> **45 min.**   <u>Other than doors:</u>   **45 min.**

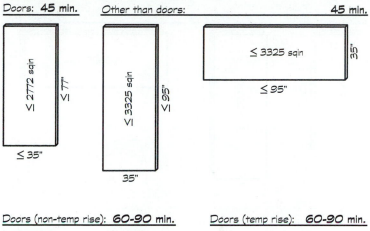

<u>Doors (non-temp rise):</u> **60-90 min.**   <u>Doors (temp rise):</u>   **60-90 min.**

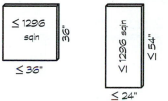   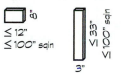

<u>Doors:</u>   **3 hrs.**   <u>Other than doors:</u>   **60 min.**

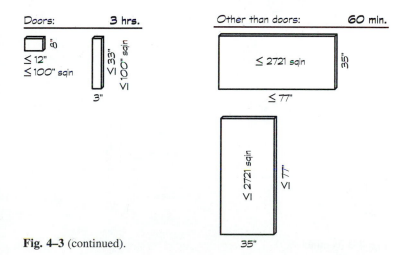

Fig. 4–3 (continued).

1" fire/impact safety-rated insulated glass units.

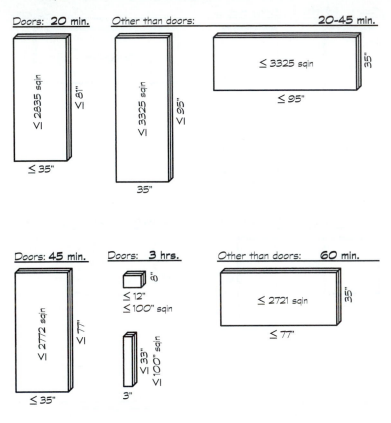

Doors: **20 min.**   Other than doors: **20-45 min.**

≤ 2835 sqin   ≤ 81"

≤ 35"

≤ 3325 sqin   ≤ 95"

35"

≤ 3325 sqin   35"

≤ 95"

Doors: **45 min.**   Doors: **3 hrs.**   Other than doors: **60 min.**

≤ 2772 sqin   ≤ 77"

≤ 35"

≤ 12"
≤ 100" sqin   8"

≤ 33"
≤ 100" sqin

3"

≤ 2721 sqin   35"

≤ 77"

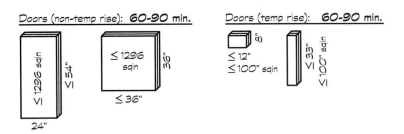

Doors (non-temp rise): **60-90 min.**   Doors (temp rise):   **60-90 min.**

≤ 1296 sqin   ≤ 54"

24"

≤ 1296 sqin   36"

≤ 36"

≤ 12"
≤ 100" sqin   8"

≤ 33"
≤ 100" sqin

Fig. 4–3 (continued).

Impact safety-rated transparent wall panels (thickness as indicated).

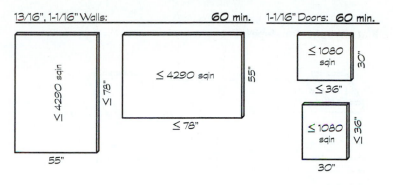

13/16", 1-1/16" Walls: **60 min.**   1-1/16" Doors: **60 min.**

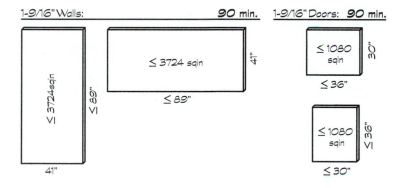

1-9/16" Walls: **90 min.**   1-9/16" Doors: **90 min.**

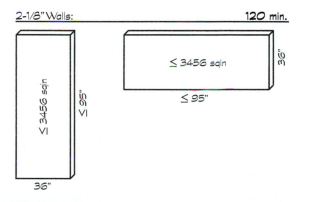

2-1/8" Walls: **120 min.**

Fig. 4–3 (concluded).

Skylights

Flat skylights for slopes.

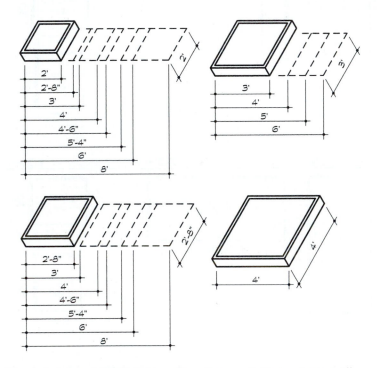

Fig. 4–4. A few of the skylight configurations available are shown with approximate dimensions. These and other units are available in a variety of glass and plastic glazing materials. (This information was interpreted and reorganized based on literature from O'Keefe's, Inc., San Francisco, California.)

Barrel skylights available in l-foot increments.

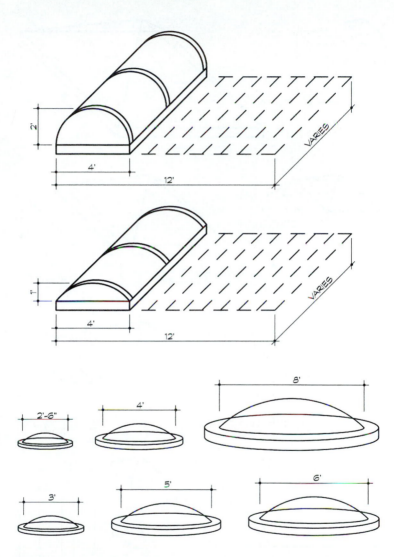

Fig. 4–4 (continued).

Pyramid skylights.

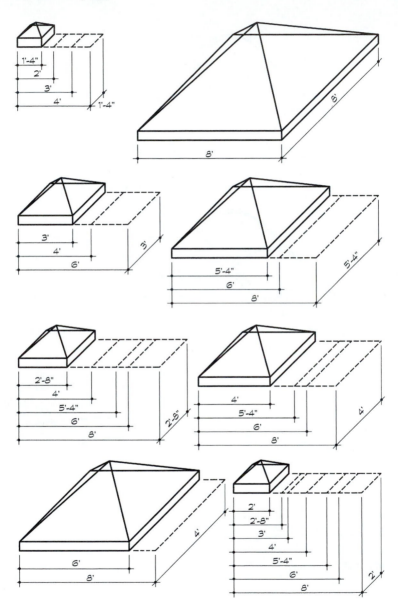

Fig. 4–4 (continued).

Ridge skylights available in 2-foot increments.

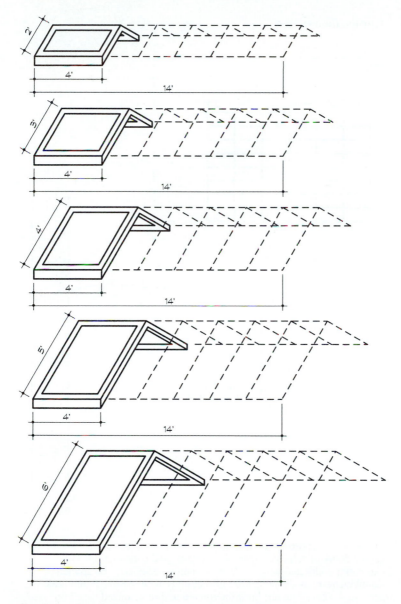

Fig. 4–4 (concluded).

Commercial/industrial doors and grilles

Garage doors.

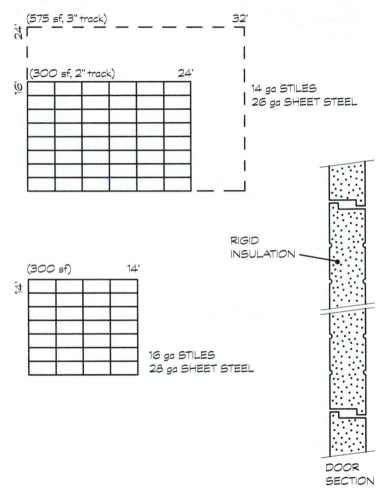

Fig. 4–5. The approximate maximum dimensions and areas are shown for garage doors of selected materials, weights, and construction. The maximum width and height of a door cannot necessarily be applied simultaneously as the door must also comply with the maximum area permitted. (This data has been interpreted and reorganized based on literature published by Raynor Garage Doors, Dixon, Illinois.)

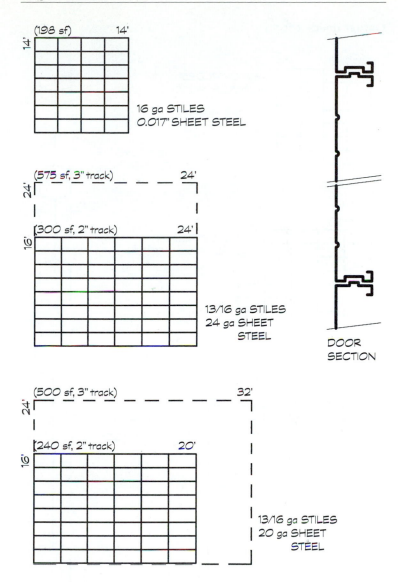

Fig. 4–5 (continued).

Garage doors (concl.)

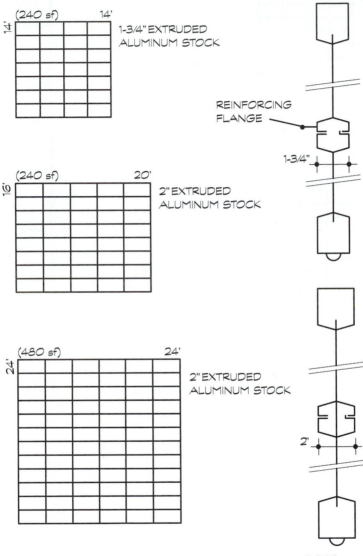

Fig. 4-5 (concluded).

Rolling service doors

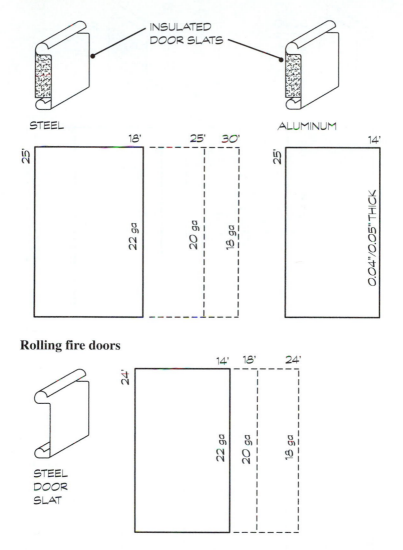

Rolling fire doors

Fig. 4–6. The approximate maximum dimensions are shown for rolling doors of selected materials, weights, and construction. (This data has been interpreted and reorganized based on literature published by Raynor Garage Doors, Dixon, Illinois.)

Rolling service doors (concl.)

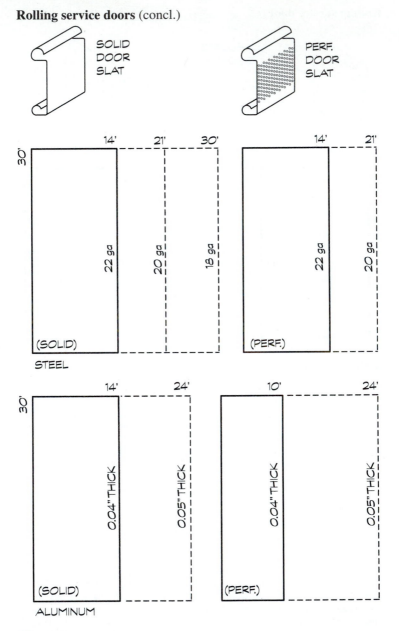

Fig. 4–6 (continued).

Rolling aluminum grilles

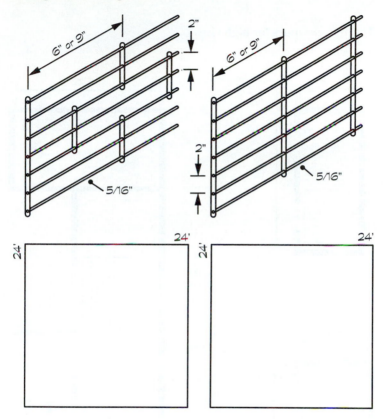

Rolling aluminum doors

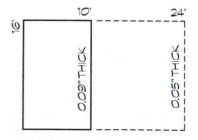

Fig. 4–6 (concluded).

Elevators

Traction elevators for high rises

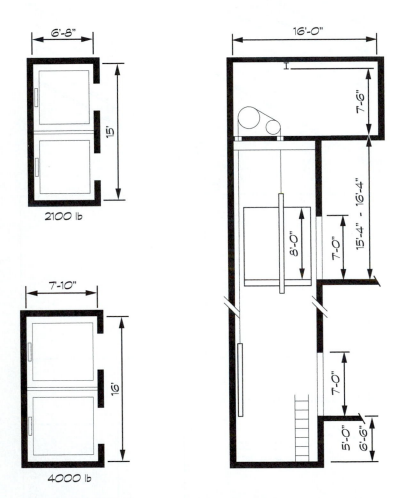

Fig. 4–7. Elevator options are shown in pairs, each being opposite ends of the range of sizes available for the type. Where double dimensions are shown in the section, the smaller applies to the elevator of lower capacity. The types and sizes of elevators shown represent a limited selection of those available. (This data was interpreted and reorganized based on information in the Dover Elevators planning guide.)

Traction elevators for hospitals

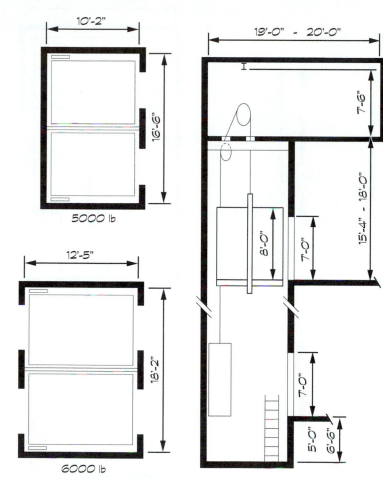

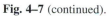

Fig. 4–7 (continued).

DC Gearless traction elevators for high rises

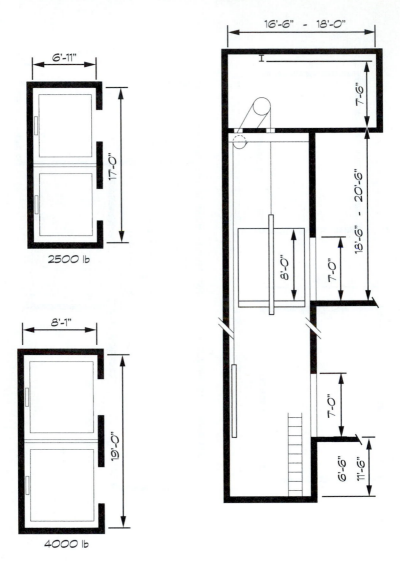

2500 lb

4000 lb

Fig. 4–7 (continued). AC Gearless are within the ranges shown.

Traction elevators for freight

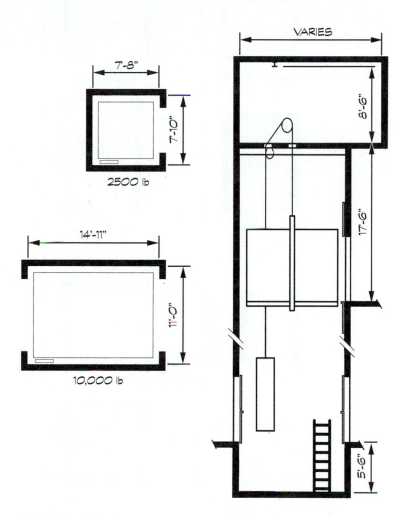

Fig. 4–7 (continued).

Hydraulic elevators

PASSENGER
LOW- AND
MID-RISE

2100 lb — 5'-9" / 7'-4"

3500 lb — 7'-11" / 8'-4"

HOSPITAL
LOW-RISE

4500 lb — 9'-7" / 7'-4"

5000 lb — 7'-11" / 7'-4"

MACHINE
ROOM

S — 1 CAR — 6'-6" / 5'-0"

D   D — 2 CARS — 7'-6" / 15'-0"

MACHINE
ROOM

D — 1 CAR — 5'-6" / 10'-0"

S   S — 2 CARS — 8'-0" / 8'-0"

Fig. 4–7 (concluded). Machine room power units labeled "S" are submersible. Power units labeled "D" are dry units.

Part II

Guidelines
for
Construction Documents

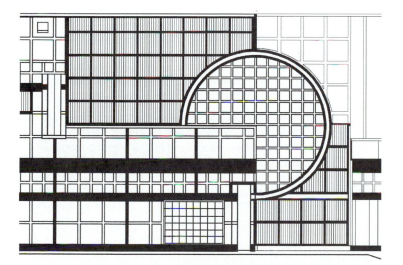

An office and laboratory building, partial elevation.
Gossen Livingston Associates, Inc., Architecture. Wichita, Kansas.

These guidelines are based on contributions from architects, builders, consultants, construction managers, code officials, and computer experts. Examples from actual working drawings are included. Consequently, the information here is based on actual conditions and is a realistic reference for the preparation of working drawings.

The information begins with an overview of computer capabilities in architectural practice and their potential for future applications. This is followed by corporate guidelines for CAD use from RTKL Associates, Inc., which provides a model for both CAD use and for the development of an office manual for computer management. The next chapter addresses both design and production drawing issues as related to the approvals necessary for a building permit. In this regard, building officials and code experts give tips to architects on pitfalls in code compliance based on past experiences. This is followed by input from contractors on problems in construction documents that they have experienced which drive up the cost of construction. Similar comments are made by construction managers representing the owner and working independently. Comments are supplemented by several construction document checklists: One set is based on code compliance, the other is derived from contractor experience. Following these opinions and comments from the building industry, architects have provided their input in the form of working drawing examples from their offices. This chapter provides a library of working drawing styles with examples of similar elements from different offices juxtaposed. The examples do not provide detailing information but show the various symbols, reference notations, and methods for laying out the various subjects in a set of working drawings.

The conclusion of the section broadens in scope to include other practice issues within two specialty realms of practice: design-build and international practice. Thus, a larger context for the subject of architectural working drawings is provided.

5

CAD

In the early days of computer-aided drafting (CAD), an informal survey of errors occurring in architects' offices was conducted to determine if a pattern existed. It was discovered that about half the errors made during a year were CAD related. That is, mismanagement of the computer processes was producing as many errors as were the oversights and misunderstandings typical of the technical aspects of producing buildings. In some cases, office staff were working on the same drawings simultaneously by virtue of being able to access the drawing file from individual computers. The same details were being revised at the same time and then subsequently revised again by others without knowing the original status or goals for the sheet. This sort of confusion was not possible before the introduction of the computer into office practice since only one person could work on a sheet at a time.

Observing the nature of the office errors revealed that although the computer was enhancing production efficiency, it also introduced a new range of problems not common to hand drawing. Although the management of computer systems has become more sophisticated each year, numerous comments from contractors in Chapter Seven verify that certain trends fostered by CAD are frustrating the builder and, in some cases, increasing the cost of construction.

This chapter is intended to provide CAD users with both a realistic overview of the usefulness of the computer as well as its pitfalls. This is unique among computer-oriented publications because working drawings are addressed as opposed to the more popular design and presentation aspects of CAD. A review of two state-of-the-art CAD software packages for producing working drawings is provided which is particularly useful to persons attempting to learn similar software or to their supervisors because the potentials of the programs are examined in a training experience. That is, persons who were not experts with the software attempted to learn to use it. The results revealed the difficulties encountered with the software, and this information can be used to guide production and management staff in their approach to new software in the future. An overview is provided of the potential of CAD in the near future, which is only partially realized at this time.

The chapter concludes with a summary of the "Corporate Standards for CAD" used by the international architectural firm, RTKL. This document is of particular use because it is the actual set of guidelines currently followed by a large and successful architectural practice. In keeping with the spirit of the handbook, actual office documents are provided rather than those based on theoretical goals and standards.

Computer Production of Architectural Working Drawings

Thomas L. Grassi, AIA
Dumont, New Jersey

Drawing clarity

- Computer production can enhance the usefulness of working drawings over hand-drawn versions by improved clarity, precision, and credibility. The mechanical aspects of plotting a computer-generated drawing have eliminated variations in linework and lettering which are typical of hand-drawing and which affect readability. Lines can be thinner without a loss of density thus increasing their exactness. In addition to the improved level of information, the greater uniformity and organization as well as the improved general appearance lend credibility to the working drawings' accuracy, thoroughness, and completeness. This higher level of information and credibility contributes to fewer questions, misunderstandings, and changes.

Changes to drawings

- Multiple changes are possible without physical damage to the document. Multiple erasures in the same area on hand-drawn originals damage the paper or mylar. Added linework might then be difficult to apply and might not match the original, due to the change in paper texture. The result is that readability diminishes.

- Completed sheets are easily reformatted to add or delete drawings and notes. The fixed positions of hand-drawn plans and details, etc., allow only the first layout to look planned and complete. Drawings and/or notes added to or deleted from a completed sheet yield a crowded or disorganized appearance.

Drawing longevity

- The electronic drawing files are not subject to the same kind of physical wear and tear as hand-drawn files.

Drawings for long-term projects, such as hospitals or airports, require repetitive handling by different people over long periods. Hand-drawn originals become dirty, torn, creased, and faded as pencil lead rubs off.

• Lost sheets (paper or computer files) are easily replaced from back-up computer files. Replacement of lost or damaged hand-drawn sheets is labor-intensive and/or results in a reduced quality of appearance when paper copies are converted to reproducible replacements. When drawing with CAD, the "original" drawing is in a computer file so a plot of the file is less valuable than a hand-drawn sheet. It is important to keep electronic copies of one's work on a disk, at a remote location from the original.

Managing drawing files
• Managing the production of computer-drawn working drawings is complex. The single, physical original for each sheet of hand-drawn working drawings simplifies the control of the drawing compared to that of electronic files. While a drawing on a sheet of paper can be changed by only one person at a time, electronic file copies of a sheet can be altered by people simultaneously. Furthermore, each CAD drawing can be composed of numerous layers and externally referenced drawings. A CAD drawing is sometimes compiled just before it is plotted. Some have used the analogy of dressmaking to describe CAD-drawing production because there are pieces of material in many locations until the very end of the process.

The up-to-date status of a sheet and a set of drawings can be less apparent than hand-drawn versions, due to the inconvenience of viewing the document or set of documents as a whole. Unlike the common practice of checking only the "red-lined" changes to hand-drawn originals, the checking of changes to computer drawings must include an examination of the entire drawing every time a change is made. For instance, while changing a drawing, individual layers can be easily turned on and off, and can accidentally be turned off at the time final plots are made.

Potential for errors
• Computer drawing has added the potential for new types of errors due to the nature of the technology. The difficulty of the effort and focus which are required to change hand-drawn working drawings assures that few changes will be made inadvertently. The ease of switching on and off the multiple layers of electronic

files, as well as the ease of deletion, increase the chances of accidental omissions from computer drawings. Whereas parts of the drawings once checked on hand-drawn originals may be assumed to remain unchanged, elements checked on a computer drawing may not. Every sheet should be checked, in its entirety, every time it is plotted onto paper.

Speed of plotting drawings

- The length of time required to plot a computer drawing onto paper makes the checking process more tedious than checking corrected hand-drawn sheets. A large set of computer drawings can take hours to plot. Each set of plotted drawings becomes obsolete when changes are made, thus drawings must be plotted each time a current check-set is needed. This process is more time-consuming and cumbersome than making a set of prints from hand-drawn originals. Computer operators frequently underestimate the time required for production of final plots.

Architect's signature and seal

- Completed, signed, and sealed computer drawings must be protected from accidental changes so as to maintain their legal credibility. A few of the methods that can prevent unauthorized changes from being made to final drawings are as follows:

  ○ On a network, access to the drawing folder can be restricted to certain personnel.
  ○ The final drawings can be distributed on a CD-ROM that can be read but not altered.
  ○ When a Zip drive is used, a password may be required, thus identifying the person viewing the file.

- Changes to completed CAD drawings, which have been signed and sealed, require a prescribed system of handling in order to maintain the legal integrity of the drawings. Changes made by hand to an original CAD drawing do not affect the architect's signature and seal, but negate many of the benefits of CAD. Variations in line weight and lettering will be apparent and the hand work is subject to smudging and deterioration from handling. (Changes made with CAD yield newly plotted drawings, but without the architect's signature or seal.) To avoid the time-consuming process of resigning large numbers of revised drawings, an electronic signature can be "pasted" onto the CAD drawing. There are many third-party programs that use an electronic pen or small tablet to do this. The electronic signature is gaining in popularity but must be managed to insure authorized use.

Another method than can be used to avoid resigning and sealing revised drawings includes using a statement, such as "ORIGINAL DRAWING SIGNED BY: ," with the architect's name and license number printed onto the revised drawings in the area where the signature originally appeared.

Mr. Grassi is an architect and project manager who has been working in New York City for more than fifteen years. He has been responsible for producing both hand-drawn and CAD drawings for numerous large-scale transportation projects. He has been working with CAD since the mid-80s, as both a user and a manager.

Special thanks to Mr. Andrew Thompson, Managing Designer at the Memorial Sloan-Kettering Cancer Center for his assistance.

Architectural CAD: The Future

Joel K. Dietrich, AIA
theEarchitect.com
Norman, Oklahoma

The following essay compares two software programs suitable for the preparation of working drawings as well as other graphic work. The comparison is based on the use of both programs by ten people who were being trained to use the software. The observations, therefore, reflect the nature of the programs as they are revealed in a learning process. The overview of the learning experience is a useful vehicle to shape the expectations of anyone undertaking such an experience or supervising those who are. Some errors and incompleteness of the results are shown in the illustrations as indicators of the challenge to the trainees.

The Promise

The technological transformation of the architect's office has been incredible. Remember when the Lanier word processor was seen as a major advance by revolutionizing the cut-and-paste world of creating specifications? That is correct—architects used to literally cut up old specifications, rearrange them, insert new typed text, and paste them together to create a new specification. The word processor was the advanced technology that allowed them to take old documents and create new documents electronically. Even though the original word processors were expensive, many firms ventured into this area in an effort to make the production of specifications more efficient.

Many architects also spent large amounts of money on big computers to help make the production of working drawings more efficient. Some architects even authored their own software. Those early efforts were whimsically crude, in retrospect. Many of the efforts revolved around the logic of storing commands to tell a pen plotter which way to move the pen on a sheet of paper. Then the architect would watch in amazement as the machine plotted the drawings and they would hope that the plotter pen would not clog or run out of ink.

It is painful to remember trying to produce CAD work on early PCs. Computers with 640K of memory and 10-MB hard drives seemed wonderful, yet "zooming in" and screen regenerations were agonizingly slow. In the early days of networking, often the quickest way to transfer a file was to copy it to a floppy and walk it across the room to the person who would use it next.

Since those early years, computers have doubled in speed approximately every 18 months, and today, with the new processors and gigabyte drives, they are more impressive than ever. Another change has been in the area of networking, which has improved so much that transferring a file across the country or around the world is now done without hesitation. And, software has also continued to advance at a steady pace, marked by the progression of new software releases, each faster than the previous version and loaded with new features.

All of this technology revolutionized the architect's office. In fact, the rate of change has been so great that it has been difficult to keep current. It has also been difficult for the architect to keep up with the computer's increasing efficiency. Although computers have increased in speed over 100 times from what they were 10 years ago, it must be agreed that the architect's increase in productivity in no way approximates that rate of change.

Similarly, most firms are still creating working drawings using two-dimensional CAD software, drafting line by line just as architects did 10 years ago. Most firms are not producing working drawings with the "intelligence" of 3D parametric objects. Granted there are a number of firms that have upgraded to parametric software, but very few are using all of the new features. Instead, they prefer to stick with familiar features with which they are comfortable.

It should be understood that creating designs using 3D parametric objects is the key to increasing productivity. Parametric objects allow the drawing to have intelligence about each component that comprises the building. Instead of lines, arcs, and circles, the drawing is composed of elements such as walls, doors, and windows. Once the software identifies the building by its components, then that data can be used in a wide variety of ways to increase productivity. As a simple example, the production of working drawings can be made more efficient by automatically creating door and window schedules. Another benefit of using 3D parametric objects is that the software can automatically create the sections and elevations. (Fig. 5–1.) But, best of all, as parametric objects are changed, they are updated globally throughout the working drawings. For instance, if the width of a window is changed, it is not only changed in the plan, but its dimensions are also automatically changed, and so are the elevations, the sections, and the window schedules.

Fig. 5–1. Example elevations created in *Architectural Desktop*. (Upchurch)

And this is just the tip of the iceberg. Three-dimensional parametric objects also enable the software to give feedback to the designer. For instance, "on the fly feedback" for energy usage and construction cost can be shown by little meters which appear on the screen as the architect designs. Also, information on code compliance can be given with the addition or movement of each element. Specifically, the distance between two exits or between two corridor walls can be controlled by the software, based on applicable codes. Thus, during the design process the software can inform designers of each potential code violation. Add the power of the Internet to this equation, and the efficiencies become even more exciting. By means of the Internet, manufacturers can automatically make new products available directly to office computers as parametric objects. Furthermore, the Internet makes it possible to automatically check the availability of products as the design progresses. Similarly, codes, standards, and prices can be automatically updated.

The role that working drawings play in communicating the designer's intent could change significantly as contractors use the database. Fabricators could add details to the database where appropriate, and each of the trades could know what the other trades are doing. In this scenario, the database would be able to instruct machines in the creation of components and in the management of the erection of the building.

Another advantage to defining buildings by 3D parametric objects is the efficiency which reaches beyond the architect's office. Because the design becomes a three-dimensional database containing information about all the pieces that comprise the building, the structural and mechanical consultants will be better able to design elements in 3D and benefit from the true conflict avoidance that will result.

One other efficient aspect of this design system is that each consultant will be able to add to the database by way of the Internet, at the appropriate time. For instance, interior designers would add parametric objects for furnishings and finishes that would automatically include information on maintenance, toxicity, and flame spread. This information would allow facility managers to correctly maintain the building throughout its life and use the database as an up-to-date inventory of the building and its contents. As a result, the database would become a source of information to firefighters and assist them in their response to emergency situations. The database would even provide information that would assist in the demolition and recycling of the building and its materials.

However, in spite of the fact that true 3D parametric software has existed for years, many architects have continued designing with 2D CAD software, which offers no intelligence for the individual components. For instance, *ArchiCAD* started in 1984 as true 3D object-oriented software, but, when computers had only 640K of memory and 10-MB hard disks, many designers used simpler options in order to compensate for the lack of speed of the equipment. Keeping track of more information was a luxury when computers were so slow. The vocabulary had to be limited to simple lines, arcs, and circles in order to make the processing delays reasonable.

But now, because of computers' increase in speed and because of the evolution of the software, these 3D parametric capabilities are in great demand. Even Autodesk ®, the authors of *AutoCAD®*, have entered the foray with their *Architectural Desktop* software and, in doing so, have added credibility to the 3D parametric effort. As a result of Autodesk's ability to invest in research and development, all of the related software companies have had to pick up the pace of development as well.

However, not all of the features and promises of 3D parametric software outlined above exist today. In fact, the potential of these features are only now generating excitement. But, regardless of when they are finally implemented, what is important is that the software companies have a vision for the future of this new technology, and that vision can become a reality. This technology holds the promise of increasing the efficiency and productivity of architects, and this is not only something that architects should support, it is something that they should assist in developing. Together, these efforts can result in bringing efficiency to processes that have not changed significantly in years, in reshaping architectural practice, and in giving enhanced value to architectural services.

A Comparison of CAD Software

A course was offered to 10 upper-division students during the 2001 spring semester at the University of Oklahoma entitled *"CAD Shootout."* The seminar compared AutoDesk's *Architectural Desktop (ADT* 3.0) to *ArchiCAD* (6.5) by Graphisoft®. (AutoDesk is indisputably the leader in worldwide CAD software sales; Graphisoft leads in many European countries and is considered the second largest, albeit significantly smaller, architectural CAD software company.)

(The architecture program at the University of Oklahoma is perhaps the most computer-oriented program in the region, with extensive computer facilities that the students use from the freshman class on, therefore, all of the students taking the CAD Shootout course knew *AutoCAD* reasonably well. Two of the students had used *AutoCAD* in offices and could be rated as expert *AutoCAD* users. The remainder of the students had used *AutoCAD* to a significant degree on studio-based design projects. Several students were quite experienced at using *AutoCAD* as a three-dimensional tool, but none of the students had used *ADT* or *ArchiCAD* prior to the course. It should be noted that most school projects do not proceed beyond schematic design. Thus, defining a building in terms of real assemblies and materials, as was the intention of this course, was somewhat abstract to students without office experience.)

The first part of the semester was an introduction to *ArchiCAD* and *ADT,* and the second part of the semester involved designing a house and later a small office building with both software packages. *ArchiCAD* was introduced first, and it's *Step-by-Step Manual* was used to guide the students through the software. This series of exercises uses a simple house to take designers through the process from making a series of standard drawings to the creation of sheets, and teaches the various commands and features throughout. Each step (chapter) includes a file to use as the starting point which is useful in a classroom situation because it keeps everyone at the same place and has the effect of forgiving any errors that might have occurred at any previous step.

The introduction to *ArchiCAD* was followed with the introduction to *ADT*. In a seminar format, the students divided among themselves the primary features of the software, researched its features, and presented those features to the class. This technique actively involved the individual student making the presentation but because it did not require an ongoing exercise or project, it did not require significant involvement by the remaining students. After the presentations, the students felt that, since they were experienced with *AutoCAD*, they understood each feature of *ADT*. But, once the students started their own projects, they realized they did not fully understand each feature and needed considerable time to learn more about them. The students also found that they needed considerable time to relearn each feature of *ArchiCAD*, but that was attributed to the 5-week time span between the instruction and the actual use of the software on their own projects.

Software Observations

The first project was a beach house which was chosen in order to force the students to use a variety of commands and features. The project included a second floor much like an attic, with dormer windows, short walls along the perimeter, and interior walls that sloped with the ceiling. This project caused the students to experience the extremes of emotions, from pure excitement to intense frustration.

They found the automatic functions, like creating stairs and roofs, to be quite incredible. That is, until they tried to modify the parameters, as in the case of designing the stairs they were given in the project. (Fig. 5–2.) But their greatest frustration came from working with walls under dormer roofs. (Fig. 5–3.) A roof on a simple building works great in both programs, but a dormer roof with sloped walls creates a different challenge. *ArchiCAD* has a Trim-to-Roof command that automatically trims the wall to the roof. However, it did not function reliably with the multiple roofs that were involved in the house exercise. Several students uncovered an apparent bug in the command that resulted in the wall not being trimmed completely at the intersection of roofs or at edges. This, in turn, resulted in an unidentified spike protruding through the intersection.

Despite this issue with *ArchiCAD*, the students experienced significantly more frustration with these walls in *ADT*. Remember, the students were exposed to *ArchiCAD* first and were introduced to the Trim-to-Roof command through one of the *Step-by-Step* exercises. (Fig. 5–3.) In contrast, the introduction to *ADT* was student-led even though it was based on the program manual which all of the students received. *ADT*'s function to trim the wall is not named the same as it is in *ArchiCAD*, and, apparently, a number of students did not find the corresponding command in the menu (i.e., Roof Line under the Wall Tools menu). Instead, they tried to manually edit the wall to match the roof through the Wall Properties dialog box. This is a much more difficult route to take since there is no graphical interface for adjusting the wall, so the coordinates must be entered strictly as numeric input, which the students found very frustrating.

It is interesting to note that even though there were multiple ways of accomplishing the same task, the students each believed

Fig. 5–2. Example stairs made with *ArchiCAD*. (Baumeister, Bennett, Ellis, Mashelkar, Nguyen, Zhu.)

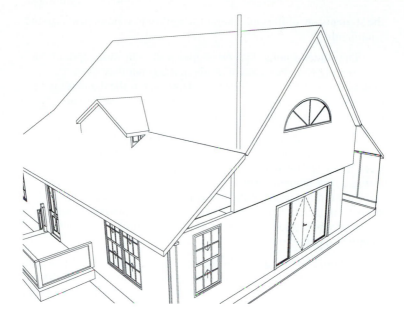

Fig. 5–3. This 3D cut-away illustrates the problem that existed in *ArchiCAD* for some students when trimming walls to an intersection of roofs. (Bennett.)

that the solution he or she found was the one way to complete the task, and did not continue to look for the more appropriate technique. However, the same multiplicity of commands would have solved the apparent bug in *ArchiCAD* by allowing a manual fix to the wall profile.

Since all of the students had some experience with *AutoCAD*, they all found that interface to be the most comfortable. Several students said they missed not having a "command" line in *ArchiCAD*, both for keyboard entry and for feedback on the status of a command. Several noted that they missed not having shortcut commands in *ArchiCAD*, and this was despite the fact that *ArchiCAD* has completely customizable shorthand commands, which were covered in the *Step-by-Step* exercises. Furthermore, many shorthand commands are actually listed beside the commands in the menus. Thus, it appears that not having a command line made the students uncomfortable about the ability to type even shorthand commands.

The students noted that there appeared to be more options for customizing elements such as walls in *ADT*, but they were undecided if that was good or bad. However, if the database is to become truly "intelligent," these elements must have a relatively complete array of appropriate information.

One of the things the students did like about the software was its ability to include standard 3D objects, such as furniture, but they were frustrated by some of the predefined choices. (Fig. 5–4.) For instance, one student documented that several pieces of the *ADT* furniture did not insert at the correct scale. Nonetheless, the students in the class used the objects exactly as provided by the software, and without using any additional sources, such as the Internet, to enhance them.

It should be noted that the management of standard objects has become a major issue in professional practice and, in many offices, is the key to productivity. One approach for resolving this problem is the proposal that the objects should automatically update themselves by way of the Internet, so that their currency is not dependent on a network administrator. Unfortunately, on occasion these "factory" objects are also incorrect. This situation can be remedied easily, however, because when the supplier of the objects discovers the errors, corrected versions of the objects can automatically be sent to all the users of the library.

Several students noted difficulty in creating new objects in both *ADT* and *ArchiCAD*. Several made comments about how easy it was to create new objects in *ADT*, but on inspection, their creations were incorrectly made 3D objects. Since created objects are at the basis of why this software is potentially more powerful than standard 2D CAD, this experience strongly suggests that more initial training should be focused on creating and modifying objects. Although creating objects was included in the *Step-by-Step* approach by *ArchiCAD*, it was obviously not sufficient.

Another feature that the students liked was the concept of multiple stories which *ArchiCAD* embraces for a building with multiple floors. They found the multiple stories aspect easier to use than the referenced drawings method, which is a technique for dealing with multiple floors within *ADT*. (Fig. 5–5, Fig. 5–6 and Fig. 5–7.)

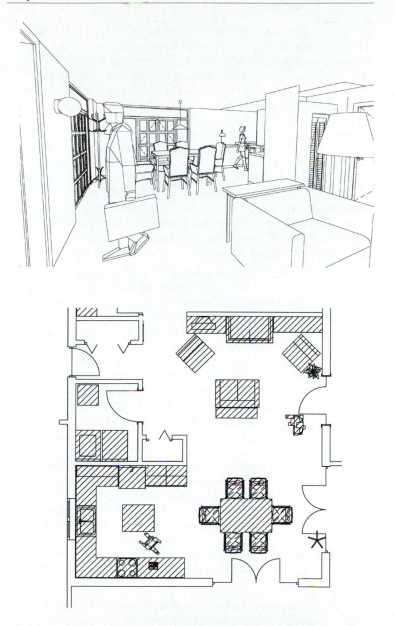

Fig. 5–4. Examples of furniture objects used in *ArchiCAD* for the interior of the building. (Waters.)

The students said that the 3D capabilities of *ArchiCAD* were somewhat superior to those of *ADT*. They noted that creating and rendering a 3D walk-through movie was faster in *ArchiCAD* than in *ADT*, and it produced more appealing results. However, several students noted that the time required to regenerate the 3D window in *ArchiCAD* was excessive. (Fig. 5–8 and Fig. 5–9.)

Outcomes

The course was certainly not a good test of which software is more productive. The students barely became familiar with the software, and thus did not achieve anything close to what could be called productive for either software. A test of real productivity would need to be made by comparing users who are very experienced with the software and know the commands without hesitation. What this experiment did illustrate was the need for more extensive training as software becomes more sophisticated.

Most of the students thought that, since they were familiar with *AutoCAD*, *ADT* would be a snap. Those students actually had more trouble because they felt less compelled to read the manual or try to comprehend all of the new commands. On the other hand, *ArchiCAD,* having such a different interface, caused the students to realize that it was "different" and that they needed to read the manual and try to learn it as "new" software. Although many might see the similarity to *AutoCAD* as *ADT*'s biggest asset, in fact, that similarity might be its biggest hindrance to users actually achieving large gains in productivity, because users might not realize they need to learn this as "new" software.

Conclusions

The need for training coincides with the observation made earlier that a number of firms have purchased 3D parametric software but are not experiencing large gains in productivity. The software purchase needs to be matched with appropriate training to accomplish the gains in productivity. Should or can the software be easy enough to learn right out of the box? That was possible when all that the software did was draw lines, arcs, and circles, but it is unrealistic to believe that training is not necessary for today's software.

It should be noted, however, that the cost of this training is easily outweighed by the gains in productivity. For example, consider an architect who receives an hourly rate of $25 and who, for each week, averages 30 hours of work directly on projects, over

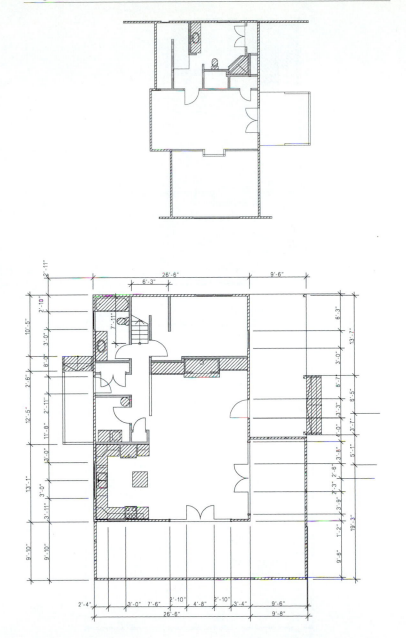

Fig. 5–5. Example floor plans created in *ArchiCAD*. (Bennett.)

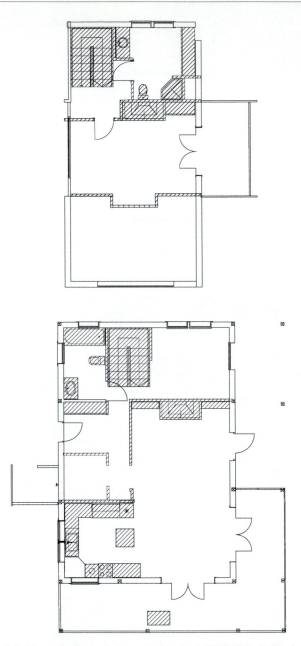

Fig. 5–6. Example floor plans created in *ArchiCAD.* (Mashelkar.)

Fig. 5–7. Example floor plans created in *Architectural Desktop.*
(Upchurch, Zhu.)

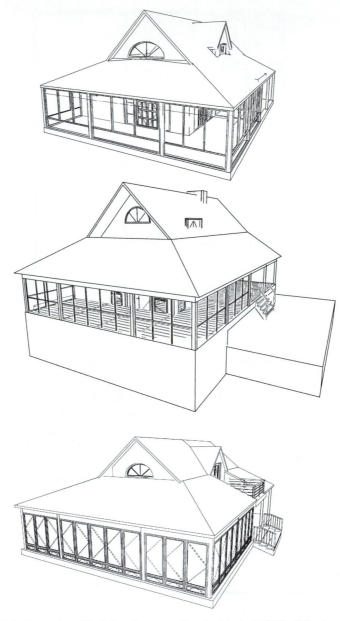

Fig. 5–8. Examples of building forms produced with *ArchiCAD*. (Morris; Nguyen; Zhu.)

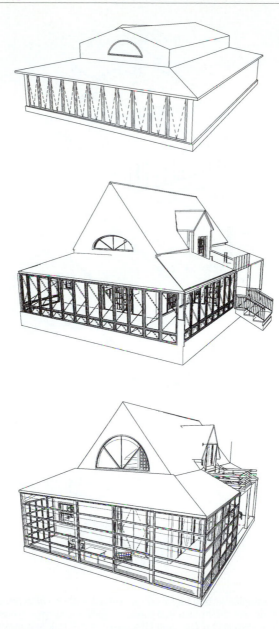

Fig. 5–8 (concluded). (Baumeister; Ellis; Mashelkar.)

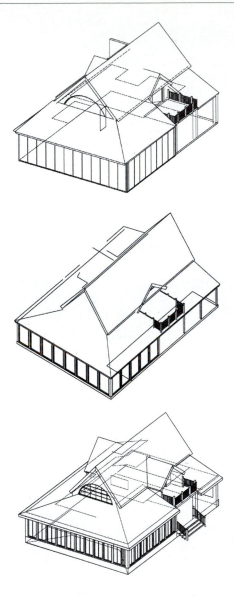

Fig. 5–9. Examples of building forms produced with *Architectural Desktop*. Note that the hidden line function does not always operate properly in *Architectural Desktop*. Obviously, AutoDesk assumes that another of their products will be used for this function. (Mashelkar; Shotts; Ellis.)

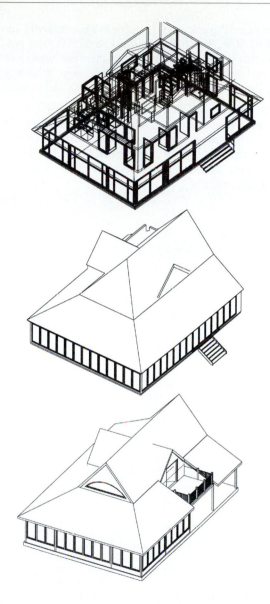

Fig. 5–9 (concluded). (Nguyen; Upchurch; Zhu.)

the course of a 50-week year. If his or her productivity can be increased by 20%, then that amounts to a $7500 gain[1] per 50-week year. And that is based on only a 20% increase in productivity. The potential certainly exists for greater increases in efficiency, as shown by the experiences of other professions and industries.

If architects are to achieve real improvements in productivity, then they need to actively seek additional training with CAD software and they need to sponsor research to advance the field of CAD. Only with that type of attitude can the architecture profession start to make the advances necessary to retain its position as leaders in the building industry.

Note:

[1] ($25 × 30 hr/wk × 50 wk/yr × 0.2) = $7500.

Joel K. Dietrich has been a registered architect since 1978 and is an Associate Professor of Architecture at the University of Oklahoma, with more than 25 years of teaching and consulting experience. He returned to his faculty position in August 2000 after having served as the Director of the Division of Architecture for 6 years, and, prior to that, having held the post of Coordinator of Computer Services for the College of Architecture for 8 years. Mr. Dietrich is also the owner of *theEarchitect.com* , a consulting company that provides computer solutions to the architecture profession.

RTKL
Corporate Standards for CAD

The following document is an edited version of the copyrighted RTKL corporate standards for CAD use. Due to the focus on architectural working drawings and because of space limitatons here, the engineering and demolition drawing references have been omitted from the body of the standards. Also, the AIA CAD layer names have been omitted from section 4 Plot/Sheet File Level/ Layers, which can be found in the second edition of the publication *AIA CAD Layer Guidelines*, by AIA Press. Certain miscellaneous items have been omitted where, for the purposes of this handbook, clarity was enhanced. Virtually all omissions are noted in the RTKL CAD standards table of contents and/or in the body of the text.

This document is useful for two purposes. First, it provides guidelines for the production of architectural working drawings using CAD. Second, it serves as a guide for developing an office manual for CAD standards. To aid in this aspect, the document has not been translated into a generic format. That is, references to RTKL, in the text and file names, have not been omitted because they identify the locations in the document where the firm name is appropriate.

Corporate Standards
for
CAD

Introduction

This document contains the 99B Office Standards for producing
CAD-related project work at RTKL. The 99B Standards have been
set up to be adaptable to a broad range of project types and apply to
projects executed in both MicroStation and AutoCAD.

It is vitally important that new employees become familiar with this
document before starting any CAD-related project work using the
99B Standards.

99B CAD Standards Table of Contents

INTRODUCTION

FUNDAMENTALS

1 – CAD Directory Structure
  1. Introduction
  2. CAD Project Set-up Procedure
  3. CAD Project Directory Structure
      3.1 Two CAD Platforms
      3.2 Project Directory Structure
  4. Project Resource Directories
      4.1 AutoCAD Template Files
      4.2 U99B MicroStation Seed Files
      4.3 RTKL Border Sheets
      4.4 Interface Menus
      4.5 RTKL Standard Color Table
      4.6 Corporate Standard Fonts
      4.7 Corporate Reference Details

2 – CAD File Naming and Creation
  1. Introduction
  2. Definition of File Types
      2.1 Design/Base Files
      2.2 Plot/Sheet Files
  3. File Naming System
      3.1 Base Drawings Files
      3.2 Detail Drawings
      3.3 Plot Drawings/Sheets Files
  4. Discipline/Drawing File Descriptors
  5. Plotting/Sheet File Series Numbers
      5.1 General Series
      5.2 Site Demolition *(omitted)*
      5.3 Site Series
      5.4 Civil Demolition Series *(omitted)*
      5.5 Civil Series *(omitted)*
      5.6 Architectural Demolition Series *(omitted)*
      5.7 Architectural Series
      5.8 Interior Demolition Series *(omitted)*
      5.9 Interior Series
      5.10 Equipment Series *(omitted)*
      5.11 Structural Demolition Series *(omitted)*
      5.12 Structural Series *(omitted)*

8.2 Electrical – Lighting *(omitted)*
8.3 Electrical – Power *(omitted)*
8.4 Plumbing *(omitted)*
8.5 Telecommunication *(omitted)*

4 – CAD Text
1. A99A AutoCAD Fonts
2. U99B MicroStation Fonts
3. Text Size
4. Special Characters

5 – CAD Cell/Block Resources
1. Introduction
2. U99 CAD Standard Cells
   2.1 Libraries
      2.1.1 Component Cell Libraries
      2.1.2 Division Cell Libraries
      2.1.3 Discipline Cell Libraries
   2.2 Locating Cells
   2.3 Scaling Cells
      2.3.1 Component Cells
      2.3.2 Reference Symbol Cells
         2.3.2.1 Determining Imperial Scales
         2.3.2.2 Determining Engineering Scales
         2.3.2.3 Determining Soft Metric Scales
         2.3.2.4 Determining Hard Metric Scales
3. A99 Standard Blocks
   3.1 A99 Standard Block Directory
   3.2 A99 Standard Symbols Directory
   3.3 Accessing Blocks and Symbols
      3.3.1 Pull-down menus

6 – CAD Plotting
1. Introduction
2. Saved Views
3. Level Symbology and Screening
4. MicroStation Plotting
   4.1 Level Symbology
   4.2 Configuring Level Symbology
   4.3 Screening
   4.4 Plot Request Forms
5. AutoCAD Plotting
   5.1 Using CADNET with AutoCAD
   5.2 Additional Information

METHODS AND PROCEDURES

1
CAD Directory Structure

1. Introduction

This section discusses the electronic directory structure setup for all projects. Project directories are organized to place information in a logical location for easy retrieval and automatic access to essential CAD tools. By using information from the project set-up sheet, the appropriate directory structure is put into place.

All of the supporting directory structures are reviewed and modified according to the project needs.

2. CAD Project Set-up Procedure

Information Systems is responsible for creating the directory tree structure for each new project. Information obtained from the Project Set-up sheet will determine what directories will exist within a project, such as project phases, disciplines involved, etc.

It must be decided if the project will use one of the standard options, if it is part of an ongoing project (whereby using the original standard), or the current CAD standards as described in this document. This decision determines which interface menus, configuration files, fonts, symbols, etc., will be used for the project.

3. CAD Project Directory Structure

3.1 Two CAD Platforms – The corporate standard takes into account procedures necessary to create project documents using AutoCAD or MicroStation. This document contains instructions for both AutoCAD and MicroStation. All Filename extensions are .DGN for MicroStation files and .DWG for AutoCAD files. CAD files in this document are shown without the extension to avoid confusion.

3.2 Project Directory Structure – The project directory is set up according to the information on the Project Set-up Sheet.

The standard project tree is located in
V:*Office***\\DIR_TREES\\USTN** or **ACAD**. Each project manager
assigns a project folder name and Information Systems
selects the appropriate folders to create the directory tree. It
is imperative that no folder exceed 8 characters in length.
These directories may contain subdirectories to further
organize the project files.

    PROJECT – Assigned project folder name.

The Project folder contains these folders:
    Cad – Refer to diagram below for additional
        information about this folder. *(omitted)*
    Cca – Construction Administration folders and files.
    Communic – Project correspondence.
    Concepts – Conceptual drawings and information.
    General – General project drawings and information.
    Marketing – Marketing-related information.
    Postcons – Postconstruction information.
    Predgn – Predesign drawings and information.
    Specs – Project Specifications.

The Cad folder contains these additional folders:
(non-architectural omitted)
    Cad – All plot files are stored here.
        3d – Three-dimensional drawings and models.
        Arch – Architectural drawings files and folders.
        Border – Project border file(s).
        Config – Project-specific configuration
            information.
            Keynotes – Project Keynote Database
            Macros – Project Specific
            Prf – Discipline Msprf Config file
            Symb – Project-specific symbology, i.e., fonts.
        Data – Project translation tables, data files, etc.
        Grphx – Graphics drawing files and folders.
        Inter – Interior Architecture drawing files and
            folders.

    (Discipline) – Folders such as Arch, Struc, Mech, etc.
        Base – All floor plans/base drawings.
        Cell or Block – Project-specific cells
            (MicroStation) or blocks (AutoCAD).
        Details – All detail files. May include additional
            folders to organize files.

> **Dwg/dxf or Dgn** – Temporary storage for
> translating CAD files.
> **Prf** – All plot request forms.
> **Schedule** – Project schedules.

4. <u>Project Resource Directories</u>

The directories for the tools and support resources used to design
and produce a project package are as follows:

4.1 AutoCAD template files are saved as read-only files in the
following directories:

> <u>AutoCAD</u>:
> V:\RTKL\A99B\TEMPLATE\
>
> ACAD.DWT
> *(Describe the parameters)*
> <u>Imperial Work Units</u>
> Units –
> Precision –
> Decimal Degrees

4.2 <u>U99B MicroStation</u> seed files are saved as read-only files in
the following directories:
V:\RTKL\A99B\TEMPLATE\
This directory contains the following files:

Purpose	Name	Master Units	Sub Units	mu/su	Su/pu
Architectural English	RTKL2D.DGN	'	"	12	8000
Architectural Soft Metric	RTKL2SMM.DGN	mm	mm	1	315
Architectural Hard Metric (Meters)	RTKL2HM.DGN	m	mm	1000	100
Architectural Hard Metric (Centimeters)	RTKL2HCM.DGN	cm	mm	10	100
Architectural Hard Metric (Millimeters)	RTKL2HMM.DGN	mm	mm	1	100
Planning Hard Metric (Meters)	RTKL2PM.DGN	m	mm	1000	10
Planning Hard Metric (Centimeters)	RTKL2PCM.DGN	cm	mm	10	10
Planning Hard Metric (Millimeters)	RTKL2PMM.DGN	mm	mm	1	10

Purpose	Name	Master Units	Sub Units	mu/su	Su/pu
3D English	RTKL3D.DGN	'	"	12	8000
3D Soft Metric	RTKL3SMM.DGN	mm	mm	1	315
3D Hard Metric (Meters)	RTKL3HM.DGN	m	mm	1000	100
3D Hard Metric (Centimeters)	RTKL3HCM.DGN	cm	mm	10	100
3D Hard Metric (Millimeters)	RTKL3HMM.DGN	mm	mm	1	100

4.3 RTKL Borders are saved as read-only files in the following directories:

V:\RTKL\U99b_RTKL\BORDER\IMPERIAL or
V:\RTKL\A99b_RTKL\BORDER\IMPERIAL

Standard Imperial sheets:

C0811	8^1/$_2$" x 11"
C1117	11" x 17"
C2436	24" x 36"
C3042	30" x 43"
C3442	34" x 42"
C3648	36" x 48"

V:\RTKL\U99b_SUPPORT\BORDER\METRIC or
V:\RTKL\A99b_SUPPORT\BORDER\METRIC

Standard Metric sheets:

CMA0	1189 x 841 mm	46.8" x 33.1"
CMA1	841 x 594 mm	33.1" x 23.4"
CMA2	594 x 420 mm	23.4" x 16.5"
CMA3	420 x 297 mm	16.5" x 11.7"
CMA4	297 x 210 mm	11.7" x 8.3"

V:\RTKL\U99b_RTKL\BORDER or
V:\RTKL\A99b_RTKL\BORDER contains the RTKL
Standard abbreviation, symbol, and drawing index sheets
in both Imperial and Metric:

ABBREV – Abbreviation and symbol sheet.
ABBREV2 – Used for small projects that will also
    include drawing list.
M0ABREV – Metric Abbreviation and symbol sheet.

M0ABREV2 – Used for small projects that will also
include drawing list.
M1ABREV – Metric Abbreviation and symbol sheet
using M1A sheet.
M1ABREV2 – Used for small projects that will also
include a drawing list using sheet CM1A.

Copy border files into the \PROJECT\CAD\BORDER
directory before modifying for project use.

4.4   Interface Menus are useful tools for setting element
parameters. When each project directory is set up the
configuration files and project workspaces set the parameters
to activate interface menus as well as establish project default
settings.

4.5   The RTKL Standard Color Table for MicroStation is
located in the following directory:
V:\RTKL\U99B\DATA\RTKLU99B.TBL

4.6   The Corporate Standard Fonts are located in
V:\RTKL\U99B\WSMOD\DEFAULT\SYMB\
FONTU99B.RSC and V:\RTKL\ACAD_CORE\
WORKSTATION_FILES\ACAD_R14/FONTS or
/ACAD2000/FONTS. For a complete list of fonts see
Chapter 4 – CAD Text.

4.7   Corporate Reference Details are located in
\\BULLWINKLE\TRG\REFDTLS\C_INTER\INTCON\
PARTITN\U97S.

2
CAD File Naming and Creation

1. Introduction

There are several types of CAD files required for the creation of drawings. Files are broadly classified as either Design/Base files or Plot/Sheet files. The file type determines the naming system to be used when creating a CAD file.

2. Definition of File Types

2.1 Design/Base Files

These are files which contain building information. These files contain the bulk of the project information. They differ from plot files in that plot files are specific sheets within a set of drawings. Plan design/base files usually contain the entire building at a given level.

Plan design files are created for each building level using the standard seed or template file. Before drawing any information, the grid file is attached as a reference file to determine the graphic location and boundaries. All graphic elements are drawn at full scale except the text, line terminators, and other information sensitive to the final plotted scale of the file.

2.2 Plot/Sheet Files

Each sheet in a set of drawings has a corresponding plot/sheet file in the computer. The plot/sheet has a project border sheet, structural column grid, floor plan files, and may have other files attached as required. These attached files each contain information necessary to complete the drawing. Each drawing sheet in the drawing set should have a plot/sheet file in the PROJECT\CAD\ directory folder.

Plot/Sheet File Information – Plot/Sheet files contain very little information. The plot file is created using the correct seed or template file determined by the unit type, Imperial or Metric.

3. File Naming System

All file names will have a maximum of 8 characters and a 3-character extension. There are three different systems used in naming CAD files based on the file type. Each of the three systems is described in detail below:

3.1 Base Drawings – These are design files such as floor plans or elevations, typically used as reference files in a number of plot sheets. File names for base drawings are defined as follows:

XX H AP 001
XX = Project name
   H = Building type (hotel in this case)
     AP = Architectural plan (refer to the Appendix for a complete list of descriptors) *(omitted)*
     001 = First floor (building level)

The last three characters designate the building floor level and/or building section. For base floor plans use all three characters to describe the floor level, for elevation drawings these three slots represent the direction and number of the building elevation. When naming the plot files, two characters correspond to the sheet number and the last character is reserved for segment or other descriptor.

Base Floor Plans
   F01 – Foundation Level
   B01 – Basement Level
   M01 – Mezzanine Level
   001 – First Floor Level
   010 – Tenth Floor Level
   R01 – Roof Level or Roof/Penthouse Floor
   R02 – Penthouse Roof
Any level above the roof uses the prefix **R** plus a sequential numbering system.

Elevation Drawings
   E01 – East Elevation #1
   E02 – East Elevation #2
   NE1 – Northeast Elevation #1
   SE01 – Southeast Elevation #1

3.2 Detail Drawings – These are design files of the building for detail drawings are defined as follows:

<u>33 02 7G</u>
33 = Series number as defined in paragraph 5.
  02 = Sheet number in this series.
    7G = Sheet grid coordinates.

3.3 <u>Plot Drawings</u> – These are for drawings that are plotted to produce the documents. File names for plot drawings are defined as follows:

<u>XX H 30 01</u>
XX = Project name
  H = Building type (hotel in this case)
    30 = Series number as defined in paragraph 5.
      01 = Sheet number in this series. This may be extended to 01A for project phases or other special conditions as shown in these examples:
          01 – Sheet number (continued in sequential order 01–999)
          01A – Sheet number and Phase
          02B – Sheet number and Phase (continued in sequential and alphabetical order)

The CADNET plotting software used at RTKL creates a PRF (plot request file) for each sheet in a set of drawings. This software simplifies plotting chores and captures accounting information for reimbursable expenses. The PRF file should have the same name as the plot file with an extension of .prf. Refer to the section on CAD Plotting for additional information.

4. <u>Discipline/Drawing File Descriptors</u>

These codes are the fourth and fifth characters in the base file naming system. Refer to Chapter 3–CAD File Name and Creation for additional information. *(Non-architectural and demolition omitted.)*

  AP – Architectural Plan.
  AD – Architectural Detail.
  AE – Architectural Elevation (or Section).
  AN – Annotation

RC – Reflected Ceiling.
IP – Interior Plan.
ID – Interior Detail.
IE – Interior Elevation (or Section).
IR – Reflected Ceiling.
GP – Graphic Plan.
GD – Graphic Detail.
GE – Graphic Elevation (Sections).

5. Plotting File Series Numbers

The numbers listed below are used to organize sheet numbers in a set of construction documents. Use this list to determine correct file names as described in previous sections.

5.1 General Series Numbers for Plot Files:
Cover Sheet – (No sheet number required)
00 – Contents (Drawing List), Symbol and Abbreviation Sheet
01 – Boring Locations, Logs and Notes
02 – Survey and Legal Description
03 – Code Summary
04 – Fire-rated Construction
05 – Lease Plans
06 – Construction Phasing Plans
07–09 – Unassigned

5.3 Site (Architectural and Landscape) Series Numbers for Plot Files:
10 – Landscape and Architectural Site Plan
11 – Unassigned
12 – Site Elevations
13 – Site Sections
14 – Enlarged Site Plans
15 – Landscape Details
16–18 – Unassigned
19 – Landscape Schedules

5.7 Architectural Series Numbers for Plot Files:
30 – Primary Building Plans
31 – Building Elevations
32 – Building & Wall Sections
33 – Enlarged Plans, Elevations, and Sections

34 – Details
35 – Stairs
36 – Millwork/Casework
37 – Paving Plans
38 – Reflected Ceiling Plans
39 – Schedules

5.9 Interior Series Numbers for Plot Files:
40 – Interior Plans
41 – Power & Data Plans
42 – Interior Reflected Ceiling Plans
43 – Finished Plans
44 – Furniture Plans
45 – Enlarged Plans
46 – Interior Elevations
47 – Sections and Details
48 – Graphics
49 – Schedules

3
CAD Levels/Layers

1. Introduction

1.1 CAD software provides a variety of ways to organize
     information. The most common method of organizing
     information in a CAD file is through the use of levels (in
     MicroStation) and layers (in AutoCAD). Project directories
     and file-naming conventions serve to organize files within a
     project.

1.2 Level/Layer Charts – The charts in this section organize
     drawing information in a logical system of levels/layers. All
     project information should be organized as described in these
     CAD guidelines, unless the client mandates use of a different
     system. These guidelines address the majority of projects
     RTKL does, with some flexibility for unusual or
     project-specific conditions. Deviations from these guidelines

are strongly discouraged. When deviations are necessary, they must be approved by the project architect, communicated to all members of the project team, and documented for future reference.

1.3 Benefits of using Standard Levels/Layers in CAD drawings are as follows:
- Many individuals in several offices can work on a project in a consistent manner.
- New users can be easily introduced to a project.
- All disciplines can coordinate work within a project.
- Information can be easily retrieved and understood at a later date.

2. AIA Level/Layer Names

2.1 The *AIA CAD Layer Guidelines* use nine characters, such as A-WALL-EXTR for level/layer names. The first character, **A** in this example, refers to a Discipline Code. The guideline identifies the following Discipline Codes:

A Architecture and Facilities Management
C Civil Engineering and Site Work
E Electrical
F Fire Protection
G General
H Hazardous Materials
I Interiors
L Landscape
M Mechanical
P Plumbing
Q Equipment
R Resource
S Structural
T Telecommunications
X Other Disciplines
Z Contractor/shop drawings

2.2 The next four characters define a *Major Group*. The Major Group designation identifies the building system. Although major groups are logically grouped with specific discipline codes, it is possible to combine major group codes with any of the discipline codes. Some examples of Discipline Codes and Major Groups are as follows:

A–FLOR   Floors
A–WALL   Walls

2.3 The final four characters represent subdivisions within the
     Minor Groups. This is an optional, four-character field for
     further differentiation of major groups. For example, A-
     WALL-PRHT indicates architecture, new, wall, partial height,
     A-WALL-FULL indicates architecture, new, wall, full height.

2.4 Pull-down menus simplify the use of lengthy layer names.
     Internal mapping relates the MicroStation levels with the
     appropriate AIA layers automatically so the MicroStation-
     numbered level dialogue boxes are still available.

2.5 Numbered/AIA Levels/Layers – All of the numbered levels/
     layers identified in this document have been assigned AIA
     Layer names. In the event that additional layer names are
     required, refer to the second edition of *AIA CAD Layer
     Guidelines* published by the AIA Press for more
     information. Group-, Sector-, or Project-specific level/layer
     requirements should follow the AIA Guidelines. In general,
     the last four characters allow the most flexibility.

     Use of any new levels/layers should be approved by the
     Group or Sector representative or by the Project Manager.
     The information should be properly documented and
     communicated to the project team. Revisions may be
     incorporated into this standard where appropriate and
     approved by the Corporate CAD Committee. (Send all
     requests for revisions to _____ , in the Baltimore
     office.)

3. Pen Table

    One of the attributes assigned to a CAD level/layer is color. It is
    important to maintain consistency in color assignments because
    AutoCAD uses color to determine line weights when plotting.
    Another benefit of consistency is that leveling/layering errors can
    be easily detected and corrected. With 99B Standard a consistent
    color table has been adopted for both platforms for 2D drafting.

    The following chart lists the office standard pen setups and color
    assignments for both AutoCAD and MicroStation. This chart has
    been developed to coincide with the layer by color plotting
    system used for both platforms.

MicroStation & AutoCAD Color Numbers	Acad Pen#	Pen Weight	Pen Width
6,9,12,53,54,62,73,82,84,93,140,154, 186,214,22,250	1	0	0.005
2,4,7,10,11,13,15,21,22,34,35,41,51, 52,61,71,83,85,95,142,151,160 171,201,220,233	2	1	0.010
1,3,5,30,31,40,50,60,200	3	2	0.0175
33,70,144,210	4	3	0.020
150	5	4	0.025
161	6	6	0.030
80	7	8	0.035

AutoCAD has a variety of screens based on color, which are listed in the following table.

A99b AutoCAD Screen Colors	Acad Pen#	Pen Weight	Pen Width
105 (5% screen)	105	1	0.010
115 (15% screen)	115	1	0.010
125 (25% screen)	125	1	0.010
135 (35% screen)	135	1	0.010
145 (45% screen)	145	1	0.010
155 (55% screen)	155	1	0.010
165 (65% screen)	165	1	0.010
175 (75% screen)	175	1	0.010
185 (85% screen)	185	1	0.010
195 (95% screen)	195	1	0.010

The standard CADNET MicroStation pen table has been set up to screen reference files based on the reference file logical name. The screening is based on the first two characters of the reference file logical name as follows:

MicroStation Screens	Beginning of Logical Name
Light Screen (56% screen)	LS
Medium Screen (81%)	MS
Dark Screen (87%)	DS

The MicroStation CADNET pen table has also been configured to plot shapes of colors 100–115 with translucent fill and plot shapes of colors 120–135 with opaque fill.

4. Plot/Sheet and Border Levels/Layers

4.1 Sheet File

Level	Layer Name	Sheet File	Weight	Line Type	Line Code	Color
		Level/Layer Contents				
1–48		*(blank lines)*				
49		Sheet Number and Title	1	cont.	0	140
50		Drawing Issue Date (If not indicated on Sheet Border) Miscellaneous	1	cont.	0	140
51		General Notes (Drawn By, Checked By, Approved By)	1	cont.	0	140
52		Room Names/Numbers and Leaders	1	cont.	0	140, 233
53		Dimensions	1	cont.	0	201, 214
54		Schedule Reference/Revision Numbers & Information	1	cont.	0	140
55		Text, Keynotes	1	cont.	0	140
56		Detail Reference	1	cont.	0	140, 233
57		Revision Block Information	1	cont.	0	142
58		Revision Symbol	2	cont.	0	50
59		Revision Cloud	2	cont.	0	50
60–62		*(blank lines)*				
63		Junk (Non-Plot) (Clip Boundaries)	0	cont.	0	222

4.2 Border File

Level	Layer Name	Sheet Border	Weight	Line Type	Line Code	Color
		Contents				
1		Border Outline, Grid Mapping Numbers	1	cont.	0	142
2		RTKL Logo				

Level	Layer Name	Sheet File	Weight	Line Type	Line Code	Color
		Level/Layer Contents				
3		RTKL IDS LOGO				
4		RTKL Health Care Logo				
5		Consultant Logo/Address	1	cont.	0	140
6		Border Ticks	2	cont.	0	3
7		Border Corner Marks	0	cont.	0	1
8		Line Weight 2	2	cont.	0	9
9		North Arrow	**		**	
10		Baltimore Address and Copyright Information	1	cont.	0	140
11		Chicago Address and Copyright Information	1	cont.	0	140
12		Colorado Address and Copyright Information	1	cont.	0	140
13		Dallas Address and Copyright Information	1	cont.	0	140
14		D.C. Address and Copyright Information	1	cont.	0	140
15		Denver Address and Copyright Information	1	cont.	0	140
16		Houston Address and Copyright Information	1	cont.	0	140
17		Irving Address and Copyright Information	1	cont.	0	140
18		London Address and Copyright Information	1	cont.	0	140
19		Los Angeles Address and Copyright Information	1	cont.	0	140
20		Madrid Address and Copyright Information	1	cont.	0	140
21		Memphis Address and Copyright Information	1	cont.	0	140
22		Tokyo Address and Copyright Information	1	cont.	0	140
23		Address and Copyright Information	1	cont.	0	140
24		Address and Copyright Information	1	cont.	0	140
25		Key Plan Information	**		**	
26		Segment Shading	**		**	

Level	Layer Name	Sheet File / Level/Layer Contents	Weight	Line Type	Line Code	Color
27		Segment Shading	**		**	
28		Segment Shading	**		**	
29		Segment Shading	**		**	
30		Segment Shading	**		**	
31		Segment Shading	**		**	
32		Segment Shading	**		**	
33		Segment Shading	**		**	
34		Segment Shading	**		**	
35		Segment Shading	**		**	
36		Segment Shading	**		**	
37		Segment Shading	**		**	
38		Segment Shading	**		**	
39		Segment Shading	**		**	
40		Line Weight 6	6	cont.	0	161
41		Fill	0	cont.	0	111
42		Line Weight 8	8	cont.	0	80
43–48		*(blank lines)*				
49		Title Block Information (Contract Number, etc.)	1	cont.	0	140
50		Project Issue Date	1	cont.	0	140
51		Project Title/Information	1	cont.	0	140
52		Client Information (Logo Address, etc.)	1	cont.	0	140
53		Phase, Drawing Status Note (Progress Set, Not For Construction, etc.)	1	cont.	0	140
54		Last Revision Date #1	1	cont.	0	140
55		Last Revision Date #2	1	cont.	0	140
56		*(blank line)*				
57		Revision Block Information (Lines, Revision Triangles)	1	cont.	0	142
58		Corner Triangles	2	cont.	0	3
59		Sheet Division Border (Non-plot)	0	cont.	0	3

Level	Layer Name	Sheet File	Weight	Line Type	Line Code	Color
		Level/Layer Contents				
60		Sheet division grid centerlines (Non-plot)	0	center	4	222
61		Sheet division grid lines (Non-plot)	0	dash	3	54
62		Sheet Border Outline (Non-plot)	0	cont.	0	222
63		Junk Non-plot (Point Cells)	0	cont.	0	222

5. Architectural Levels/Layers

5.1 New Architectural & Interior Floor Plans (Building Files)

Level	Layer Name	Floor Plans	Weight	Line Type	Line Code	Color
		Level/Layer Contents				
1		Exterior Walls	3	cont.	0	33
2		Interior Walls through Ceiling	2	cont.	0	1
3		Interior Walls to Ceiling	2	cont.	0	3
4		Partial Height Walls, Window Sills	1	cont.	0	171
5		Demising Walls	1	cont.	0	11
6		Demising Piers, Column Covers	2	cont.	0	30
7		Demountable Partitions	1	cont.	0	95
8		Wall Protection	2	hidden	2	5
9		Lease Lines	1	lease	7	4
10		Patterning/Poché	0	cont.	0	84
11		Miscellaneous Wall Level	2	cont.	0	1
12		Headers – Doors & Windows	2	cont.	0	50
13		Door Jambs	2	cont.	0	31
14		Doors and Swings, Operable Wall	0	cont.	0	6
15		Glass and Frame	1	cont.	0	4
16		Clerestory Glass and Frames	1	cont.	0	61
17		Miscellaneous Plan Elements (Chalkboards, tackboards, etc.)	0	cont.	0	82

Level	Layer Name	Floor Plans	Weight	Line Type	Line Code	Color
		Level/Layer Contents				
18		Expansion Joint	1	cont.	0	71
19		Edge of Slab (EOS) Slab Openings (Structural Reference)	1	cont.	0	2
20		Level Changes, Pits, Slab Depressions, Housekeeping Pads (Elev. Text)	1	cont.	0	4
21		Stairs, Ramps, and Ladders (Circulation) (UP, DN Text)	1	cont.	0	41
22		Handrails and Balustrade	1	cont.	0	143
23		Elevator Cars, Escalators and Equipment	1	cont.	0	21
24		Fire Extinguishers, Cabinets, Hose Valves	1	cont.	0	95
25		Floor Patterns	1	cont.	0	45
26		Raised Flooring	0	cont.	0	12
27		Architectural Specialties and Toilet Accessories	0	cont.	0	54
28		Toilet Partitions / Wall Systems	1	cont.	0	151
29		Architectural Woodwork (Custom Built-in Counters, Desk, etc.)	1	cont.	0	83
30		Casework/Millwork Low	1	cont.	0	51
31		Casework/Millwork High	1	hid.2	5	52
32		Hidden Elements Above	0	hid.x2	3	93
33		Fixed Equipment	1	cont.	0	95
34		Equipment – Service Space for Equipment	1	hidden	2	34
35		Equipment Identifier	1	cont.	0	15
36		Equipment Not In Contract	0	hidden	2	82
37		Electrical Coordination	1	cont.	0	220
38		Mechanical Coordination (Louvers)	1	cont.	0	83
39		Communications Coordination	1	cont.	0	235
40		Plumbing Coordination– (Fixtures in architectural drawings and referenced by	1	cont.	0	201

Level	Layer Name	Floor Plans / Level/Layer Contents	Weight	Line Type	Line Code	Color
		Plumbing; floor and roof drains in Plumbing drawings and referenced into architectural drawings)				
41		Structural Coordination				
42		Floor Finishes (Primary)	0	cont.	0	222
43		Floor Finishes (Secondary)	0	cont.	0	62
44		Floor Finish Identifier	1	cont.	0	21
45		Wall Finish Identifier	1	cont.	0	22
46		Wall/FloorFinishes Misc.	0	cont.	0	62
47–48		*(blank lines)*				
49		Planning Grid/Match lines	0	dash-dot2	4	73
50		Miscellaneous Text (Presentation Text, etc.), Entourage/Presentation Elements	1	cont.	0	21
51		Wall Ties	1	cont.	0	140, 233
52		Room Names/Numbers and Leaders	1	cont.	0	140, 233
53		Dimensions	1	cont.	0	201, 214
54		Door and Window Numbers	1	cont.	0	140, 233
55		Text	1	cont.	0	140
56		Detail References	1	cont.	0	140, 233
57		Roof Outlines	2	cont.	0	60
58		Roof Pavers, Curbs, Level Change	1	cont.	0	10
59		Roof Miscellaneous	1	cont.	0	13
60		Fire Protection	3	cont.	0	210
61		Area Shapes	3	cent.	4	70
62		Non-plot level	0	cont.	0	222
63		Junk (Non-plot)	0	cont.	0	222

5.3 Architectural Reflected Ceiling/Finish Plans (Building Files)

Level	Layer Name	Reflected Ceiling Plans / Level/Layer Contents	Weight	Line Type	Line Code	Color
1		*(blank line)*				
2		Bulkheads – Primary (Stops Grid, Beams, Ref Dashed Line on Plan)	2	cont.	0	40
3		Bulkhead – Secondary (Grid Continuous, Does Not Appear on Plan)	1	cont.	0	73
4–14		*(blank lines)*				
15		Skylights (Primary) Main Truss	1	cont.	0	7
16		Skylights (Secondary) Secondary Truss	0	cont.	0	214
17–22		*(blank lines)*				
23		Smoke Curtains	1	cont.	0	151
24		Fire Shutters	1	cont.	0	41
25		Ceiling Pattern and Poché	0	cont.	0	154
26		Ceiling Grid – Primary	1	cont.	0	160
27		Ceiling Grid – Secondary	0	cont.	0	186
28		*(blank line)*				
29		Diffusers – Architectural	1	cont.	0	83
30		Lights – Architectural	1	cont.	0	220
31		Suspended Ceiling Elements	1	cont.	0	22
32		Fixed Equipment at Ceiling	1	cont.	0	41
33		Public Address Speakers	1	cont.	0	35
34		Fire Alarm Speakers	1	cont.	0	95
35		Miscellaneous Power (Sound Masking)	1	cont.	0	85
36		Exit Signs, Smoke Detectors	1	cont.	0	13
37		Sprinklers	1	cont.	0	201
38		Mechanical Coordination (Grilles, Diffusers)	1	cont.	0	151
39		Electrical Coordination (Lights)	1	cont.	0	10
40		Plumbing Coordination	1	cont.	0	34
41		Demolition – Pattern	0	hidden	2	84
42		Demolition – Ceiling	2	hidden	2	3

Level	Layer Name	Roof Plans	Weight	Line Type	Line Code	Color
		Level/Layer Contents				
43		Demolition Bulkheads	2	hidden	2	40
44		*(blank line)*				
45		Demolition – Skylights	1	hidden	2	142
46		Demolition – MEP	1	hidden	2	85
47		Demolition – Ceiling Grid	1	hidden	2	151
48		Demolition – Text	1	cont.	0	140
49		Planning Grid/Match lines	0	dash-dot2	4	73
50		Miscellaneous Text (Presentation Text, etc.), Entourage/Presentation Elements	1	cont.	0	21
51–52		*(blank lines)*				
53		Dimensions	1	cont.	0	201, 214
54		*(blank line)*				
55		Text, Keynotes	1	cont.	0	140
56		Detail References	1	cont.	0	140, 233
57–59		*(blank lines)*				
60		Fire Protection	3	cont.	0	210
61		Area Shapes	3	cent.	4	70
62		Non-plot level	0	cont.	0	222
63		Junk (Non-plot)	0	cont.	0	222

5.4 Architectural Elevations, Wall Sections

Level	Layer	Roof Plans	Weight	Line Type	Line Code	Color
		Level/Layer Contents				
1		Exterior Walls	3	cont.	0	33
2		Interior Walls	2	cont.	0	1
3		Footing & Foundation Wall System	3	cont.	0	210
4		Wall Ornamentation and Accessories	1	cont.	0	41
5		Demising Walls (Movable & Tenant Layout)	1	cont.	0	11

Level	Layer Name	Roof Plans	Weight	Line Type	Line Code	Color
		Level/Layer Contents				
6		Demising Piers, Column Covers	2	cont.	0	30
7		Control Joints, Reveals	1	cont.	0	71
8		Wall Protection	2	hidden	2	5
9		Metal Panels and Miscellaneous Metals	1	cont.	0	83
10		Patterning/Poché	0	cont.	0	84
11		Miscellaneous Wall Level	2	cont.	0	1
12		Window and Door Sills and Lintels	2	cont.	0	50
13		Door, Window and Wall Trim (Chair rails, Molding, etc.)	2	cont.	0	31
14		Doors & Operable Walls	0	cont.	0	6
15		Windows (Interior/Exterior) Glass and Frame	1	cont.	0	4
16		Skylights	1	cont.	0	34
17		Miscellaneous Floor Elements (Chalkboards, Tackboards, etc.)	0	cont.	0	82
18		Expansion Joints	1	cont.	0	71
19		Floor Slabs, Metal Deck	1	cont.	0	2
20		Floor Lines	2	divide	6	200
21		Stairs, Ramps, and Ladders (Circulation)	1	cont.	0	41
22		Handrails and Balustrade	1	cont.	0	143
23		Elevator Cars, Escalators and Equipment	1	cont.	0	21
24		Fire Extinguishers, Cabinets, Hose Valves, Fire Shutters	1	cont.	0	95
25		Floor System Patterning/Poché	1	cont.	0	145
26		Raised Floors	1	cont.	0	12
27		Grade Lines	3	cont.	0	144
28		Toilet Partitions / Wall Systems	1	cont.	0	151
29		Architectural Woodwork (Custom Built-in Counters, Desk, etc.)	1	cont.	0	83
30		Casework/Millwork Low	1	cont.	0	51

Level	Layer Name	Elevations / Wall Sections	Weight	Line Type	Line Code	Color
		Level/Layer Contents				
31		Casework/Millwork High	1	hid.2	5	52
32		Hidden Elements Above	0	hid.x2	3	93
33		Fixed Equipment	1	cont.	0	95
34		Ceiling System Grid	1	cont.	0	63
35		Ceiling System Bulkheads	2	cont.	0	40
36		Structure	2	cont.	0	30
37		Electrical Coordination	1	cont.	0	220
38		Mechanical Coordination	1	cont.	0	83
39		Communications Coordination	1	cont.	0	235
40		Plumbing Coordination	1	cont.	0	201
41		Demolition – Pattern	0	hidden	2	84
42		Demolition – Walls	3	hidden	2	35
43		Demolition – Structure	3	hidden	2	50
44		Demolition – Doors	0	hidden	2	214
45		Demolition – Glass and Frames	1	hidden	2	142
46		Demolition – MEP	1	hidden	2	85
47		Demolition – Floor Slab	2	hidden	2	40
48		Demolition – Miscellaneous	0	hidden	2	9
49		Grids/Matchlines	0	dash-dot2	4	73
50		Miscellaneous Text (Presentation Text, etc.), Entourage/Presentation Elements	1	cont.	0	21
51		(blank line)				
52		Room Names/Numbers and Leaders	1	cont.	0	140, 233
53		Dimensions	1	cont.	0	201, 214
54		Window Number (On Plan or Elevation, not Both)	1	cont.	0	140, 233
55		Text and Keynotes	1	cont.	0	140
56		Detail References	1	cont.	0	140, 233
57		Roof Outlines	2	cont.	0	60

Level	Layer Name	Elevations / Wall Sections	Weight	Line Type	Line Code	Color
		Level/Layer Contents				
58		Roof Pavers, Curbs, Level Change	1	cont.	0	10
59		Roof Blocking and Accessories	1	cont.	2	13
60		Fire Protection	3	cont.	0	210
61		Area Shapes	3	cent.	4	70
62		Non-plot level	0	cont.	0	222
63		Junk (Non-plot)	0	cont.	0	222

5.5 Architectural Details

Level	Layer Name	Details	Weight	Line Type	Line Code	Color
		Level/Layer Contents				
1		Line Weight 0 (Group Poché)	0	cont.	0	54
2		Line Weight 1	1	cont.	0	22
3		Line Weight 2	2	cont.	0	200
4		Line Weight 3	3	cont.	0	144
5		Line Weight 4	4	cont.	0	150
6		*(blank line)*				
7		Line Weight 6 or Other	6	cont.	0	161
8		*(blank line)*				
9		Profile Line Weight 8	8	cont.	0	80
10–16		*(blank lines)*				
17		Dotted Line Weight 1	1	dot2	1	7
18–24		*(blank lines)*				
25		Medium Dashed Line Weight 0	0	hidden	2	12
26		Medium Dashed Line Weight 2	2	hidden	2	5
27–32		*(blank lines)*				
33		Long Dashed Line Weight 1	1	hid.x2	3	13
34–40		*(blank lines)*				
41		Centerline Weight 1	1	dash-dot2	4	15

Level	Layer Name	Elevations / Wall Sections	Weight	Line Type	Line Code	Color
		Level/Layer Contents				
42–48		*(blank lines)*				
49		Planning Grid/Matchlines	0	dash-dot2	4	73
50		Miscellaneous Text (Presentation Text, etc.), Entourage/Presentation Elements	1	cont.	0	21
51		Wall Ties	1	cont.	0	140, 233
52		Room Names/Numbers and Leaders	1	cont.	0	140, 233
53		Dimensions	1	cont.	0	201, 214
54		Door and Window Numbers	1	cont.	0	140, 233
55		Text, Keynotes	1	cont.	0	140
56		Detail References	1	cont.	0	140, 233
57–59		*(blank lines)*				
60		Reserved for Key and Note	1	cont.	0	140, 233
61		Reserved for Key Only	1	cont.	0	140, 233
62		Reserved for Note Only	1	cont.	0	140, 233
63		Junk (Non-plot)	0	cont.	0	222

6. Architectural Site Level Layers

6.1 Architectural Site Plans

Level	Layer Name	Details	Weight	Line Type	Line Code	Color
		Level/Layer Contents				
1		Contours – Existing	1		2	18
2		Contours – Proposed	2	cont.	0	18
3		Civil Reference points	1	cont.	0	
4		Property Line	4		6	15

Level	Layer Name	Details / Level/Layer Contents	Weight	Line Type	Line Code	Color
5		Project Limit Line	3		4	5
6		Fences/Gates	1	cont.	0	4
7		Retaining Walls	2	cont.	0	8
8		Free-standing Walls	2	cont.	0	8
9–15		(blank lines)				
16		Utilities Right of Way	2		1	3
17		Wetland Limit Line	1		1	220
18–20		(blank lines)				
21		Hardscape Light Line	1	cont.	0	201
22		Hardscape Medium Line	3	cont.	0	210
23		Hardscape Heavy Line	5	cont.	0	161
24		Right of Way	2	dot2	1	5
25		Road Centerline	2	dash-dot2	4	3
26		Road Curb	1	cont.	0	220
27		Sidewalk/Planting Bed/Grates	1	cont.	0	220
28		Path	1	cont.	0	11
29		Ramp	1	cont.	0	195
30		Steps	1	cont.	0	208
31		Paving Outline 1	1	cont.	0	219
32		Paving Outline 2	1	cont.	0	219
33		Paving Option 1	0	cont.	0	209
34		Paving Option 2	0	cont.	0	209
35		Structural Coordination	1	cont.	0	
36		Civil Coordination	1	cont.	0	
37		Electrical Coordination	1	cont.	0	
38		Mechanical Coordination	1	cont.	0	
39		Architectural Coordination	1	cont.	0	
40		Plumbing Coordination	1	cont.	0	
41		Street Lights	2	cont.	0	7
42		Bollard/Bollard Lights	2	cont.	0	7
43		Benches	1	cont.	0	12
44		Tables & Chairs	1	cont.	0	12
45		Building Structure Outline	8	cont.	0	80

Level	Layer Name	Details	Weight	Line Type	Line Code	Color
		Level/Layer Contents				
46		Dumpsters	1	cont.	0	12
47		Misc. Site Furniture	1	cont.	0	12
48		Fountains	2	cont.	0	22
49		Planning Grid/Matchlines	0	dash-dot2	4	73
50		Miscellaneous Text (Presentation Text, etc.), Entourage/Presentation Elements	1	cont.	0	21
51		Site Furniture Text Identifier	1	cont.	0	140
52		Planting Text Identifier	1	cont.	0	140
53		Dimensions	1	cont.	0	201
54		Building, Road, etc. Text Identifier	1	cont.	0	140
55		Text, Keynotes	1	cont.	0	140
56		Detail References	1	cont.	0	140, 233
57		Limit of Construction Lines	0		0,1,2	3
58–59		*(blank lines)*				
60		Fire Protection	3	cont.	0	210
61		Area Shapes	3	cent.	4	70
62		Non-plot level	0	cont.	0	222
63		Junk (Non-plot)	0	cont.	0	222

4
CAD Text

1. A99A AutoCAD Fonts

The fonts listed below are approved fonts for use on CAD documents at RTKL using the A99A Standard. These fonts are located in the folder called V:\RTKL\A99a\FONTS.

Roman and Times New Roman are the basic fonts used on all

CAD drawings. Roman is used for drawing notes. Times New Roman for titles. *(Additional fonts omitted.)*

2. U99B MicroStation Fonts

The fonts listed below are approved fonts for use on CAD documents at RTKL using the 99B Standard. These fonts are located in the V:\RTKL\U99B\WSMOD\DEFAULT\SYMB folder, U99BFONTS.RSC a MicroStation resource file.

Arial – Used for general text.
Times New Roman – Used for plan, detail, schedule, and other titles.

3. Text Size

The RTKL standard minimum text size is 1/8-inch high lettering. The following chart lists text sizes for various scales that will produce 1/8-inch high lettering.

Architectural Scales	MicroStation Text Size	AutoCAD Font Height
Full Size	0:0.125x:.09375	1/8"
6" = 1'-0"	0:0.25x:.1875	1/4"
3" = 1'-0"	0:0.5x:.375	1/2"
1-1/2" = 1'-0"	0:1x:.75	1"
1" = 1'-0"	0:1.5x:1.125	1-1/2"
3/4" = 1'-0"	0:2x:1.5	2"
1/2" = 1'-0"	0:3x:2.25	3"
3/8" = 1'-0"	0:4x:3	4"
1/4" = 1'-0"	0:6x:4.5	6"
1/8" = 1'-0"	1:0x:9	1'-0"
1/16" = 1'-0"	2:0x1:6	2'-0"
1/32" = 1'-0"	4:0x3:0	4'-0"
1/64" = 1'-0"	8:0x6:0	8'-0"

Engineering Scales	MicroStation Text Size	AutoCAD Font Height
1" = 10'-0"	1'-3" x 11.25"	1.25'
1" = 20'-0"	2'-6" x 1'-7.875"	2.5'
1" = 30'-0"	3'-9" x 2'-0"	3.75'
1" = 40'-0"	5'-0" x 3'-9"	5.0'
1" = 50'-0"	6'-3" x 4'-8.25"	6.25'
1" = 60'-0"	7'-6" x 5'-0"	7.5'
1" = 100'-0"	12'-6" x 9'-4.5"	12.5'

Metric Scales	MicroStation Text Size (Millimeters)	AutoCAD Font Height
Full Size	3.715 x 2.38125	3.175 mm
1:2	6.35 x 4.7625	6.35 mm
1:5	15.875 x 11.906	15.875 mm
1:10	31.75 x 23.8125	31.75 mm
1:20	63.50 x 47.6250	63.50 mm
1:50	158.75 x 119.0625	158.75 mm
1:100	317.5000 x 238.125	317.5 mm
1:200	635.00 x 476.2500	635.0 mm
1:250	793.75 x 595.3125	793.75 mm
1:500	1587.5 x 1190.6250	1587.5 mm
1:800	2540.00 x 1905.0000	2540.0 mm
1:1000	3175.00 x 2381.2500	3175.0 mm
1:1500	4762.5 x 3571.875	4762.5 mm
1:2000	6350.0000 x 4762.5000	6350.0 mm

Metric Scales	MicroStation Text Size (Centimeters)	AutoCAD Font Height
Full Size	.3715 x .2381	.343 cm
1:2	.635 x .47625	.635 cm
1:5	1.5875 x 1.19061	1.5875 cm
1:10	3.175 x 2.381	3.175 cm
1:20	6.3500 x 4.7625	6.350 cm
1:50	15.875 x 11.906	15.875 cm
1:100	31.75 x 23.8125	31.75 cm
1:200	63.50 x 47.625	6.350 cm
1:250	79.375 x 59.5312	79.375 mm
1:500	158.75 x 119.0625	158.75 cm
1:800	254.000 x 190.50000	254.00 mm
1:1000	317.50 x 238.125	317.50 cm
1:1500	476.25 x 3571.875	476.25 mm
1:2000	635.00000 x 476.25000	635.00 mm

Metric Scales	MicroStation Text Size (Meters)	AutoCAD Font Height
Full Size	.00317 x .00238	.003175 m
1:2	.00635 x .00476	.00635 m
1:5	.015875 x .011906	.01587 m
1:10	.03175 x .0238	.0343 m
1:20	.0635 x .0476	.0635 m
1:50	.15875 x .11906	.15875 m
1:100	.3175 x .2381	.3175 m
1:200	.6350 x .4762	.6350 m
1:250	.7937 x .5953	.7937 mm
1:500	1.5875 x 1.1906	1.5875 m
1:800	2.5400 x 1.9050	2.5400 mm
1:1000	3.1750 x 2.38125	3.1750 m
1:1500	4.7625 x 3.5718	4.7625 mm
1:2000	6.3500 x 4.7625	6.3500 mm

4. Special Characters for Arial

Arial Character Keys – These special charcters can be used by typing in the associated key combinations.

Characters	Functions
Diameter Symbol	\ 248
Plus Minus Sign	\ 177
Degree Symbol	\ 176
Centerline Symbol	\ 162
Copyright Symbol	\ 169

5
CAD Cell/Block Resources

1. Introduction

1.1 The creation of standard cells and blocks assists the user in delivering a uniform drawing package in a timely manner. This section will give instructions in locating, scaling, placing, and modifying these cells and blocks.

2. U99B CAD Standard Cells

2.1 Libraries

2.1.1 The standard Architectural component libraries are located in V:\RTKL\U99B_RTKL\general\refsymb.cel. This library contains all of the reference symbols to be used by all disciplines.

2.1.2 V:\RTKL\U99B_RTKL\keylibs\. These libraries are named according to the CSI Division in which each element belongs. They contain detail components which will contain intelligent connection to the Keynote Program database in the future.

- Div3.cel
- Div4.cel
- Div5.cel
- Div6.cel
- Div9.cel

2.1.3 The standard discipline libraries are located in the following folders:

- V:\RTKL\U99B_RTKL\ARCH\CELL
- V:\RTKL\U99B_RTKL\ELEC\CELL
- V:\RTKL\U99B_RTKL\MECH\CELL
- V:\RTKL\U99B_RTKL\PLUM\CELL
- V:\RTKL\U99B_RTKL\STRUCT\CELL

2.2 Locating cells – Cells can be located by opening the cell dialog box using the scroll bar.

2.3   Scaling cells

   2.3.1   All component cells are drawn at full scale making
the scaling factor easy to determine, 1 to 1. Therefore
scale factor for placing the cell is **AS=1** (active scale).

   2.3.2   All reference cells which contain text or are related to
text must be placed according to the final plotting scale.
Follow these instructions to assess the active scale for
placing the cell in your file.

      2.3.2.1   Determining Active Scale for Imperial Unit File
Active Scale = The reciprocal of the drawing scale
X 12. **Ex:** The drawing scale is 3/4" = 1'–0" **4/3 X
12 = 16; AS=16**.

As a rule there is no need to set these scales as the pull-down
menus will set them automatically.

      2.3.2.2   Determining Active Scale for Engineering Scales
Active Scale = The reciprocal of the drawing scale
X 12. **Ex:** The drawing scale is 1" = 10'–0" **Active
Scale = 1/10 X 12 = 1.2.**

As a rule there is no need to set these scales as the pull-down
menus will set them automatically.

      2.3.2.3   Determining Active Scale for Soft Metric Scales.
During its transition to requiring metric building
material the United States Government required
metric dimensions to be used on drawings but
allowed the use of non-metric building supplies.
This resulted in most dimensions not being nice
round numbers. During this period RTKL used
"soft" metric working units to conform to this
government requirement so that elements placed in
design files would be the correct, exact size in
inches with no rounding error. These files used 315
PUs per mm which allow the use of the expected
scale factors as follows:

Active Scale = The reciprocal of the drawing scale
Ex: The drawing scale is 1:1000 **Active Scale =
1000/1 = 1000.**

As a rule there is no need to set these scales as the pull-down
menus will set them automatically.

Soft metric files should not normally be used. They are only included in the standard to allow compatability with recently complete GSA projects.

2.3.2.4 Determining Active Scale for Hard Metric Scales. The detail cell libraries used in U99B are created for **Imperial** unit design files. Since the cells in each cell library retain the Positional Unit values of the design file in which the cell was created, special factors must be considered. When placing these cells in a design file that has different working units, where it is different imperial units or metric units, the cell scale value is affected. In the case of placing an imperial unit created cell in a hard metric unit file, the active scale must be multiplied by 0.3175 to correct any difference in working units.

Active Scale = 0.3175 X The reciprocal of the drawing scale. **Ex:** The drawing scale is 1:1000 **Active Scale = 0.3175 X 1/1000 = 317.5.**

In the future hard metric cell libraries will be developed eliminating the need for these special factors. As a rule there is no need to set these scales as the pull-down menus will set them automatically.

The Logic Behind The Correction Factor

Imperial files have 8000 PUs per inch.

Standards bodies have declared that there are 25.4 mm per inch.

Hard Metric files have 100 PUs per mm.

Therefore there are **25.4 X 100 = 2540 PUs** per inch in a hard metric file.

The conversion factor is the ratio of PUs for the same distance in each file.

2540 / 8000 = 0.3175

---

3. A99 CAD Standard Blocks

3.1   The standard Architectural blocks are located in
V:\RTKL\A99a_RTKL\BBLOCKS. These blocks are
components for building plan and detail drawings.

3.2   The standard Architectural symbols are in
V:\RTKL\A99a_RTKL\SYMBOLS. The symbols folder
contains graphic references such as Section Marks, Room
Numbers, etc.

3.3   Accessing the blocks and symbols.

    3.3.1   The A99B interface includes a **BLOCKS** pull-down
menu, listing the available symbols and blocks. See the
A99B Menu Blocks powerpoint presentation for
detailed instructions.

6
CAD Plotting

1. Introduction

It is very important to spend organizational time in the early
planning phases of a computer project to minimize problems
when the time comes to plot the final documents. Early planning
can eliminate coordination problems in later phases. It also
allows the plotter (as a resource) to be used by other teams during
daytime office hours. When running major plotting jobs follow
the rules of etiquette listed below:

- When planning a large job, schedule all plotting deadlines.
  It is a good idea to notify the rest of the office via email
  when you need the plotter for a long period of time.
- Large batches of plots should be sent overnight rather than
  during the day.
- Verify adequate supply of paper (or mylar), toner or ink in
  advance of major plots.
- Verify correct layering in advance of plotting by reviewing
  a printout of a **Plot Request Form**.

- Verify that the plotter and CADNET plot station PC are working properly <u>before</u> sending a large plot job.

2. <u>Saved Views</u>

Saved views may be used in any file to save specific settings associated with a drawing. One very useful application of the saved view is with respect to plot files. One view is set with all the correct parameters and then saved under the name "**plot**." The saved view can be used for plotting instead of picking a window each time a plot is generated.

3. <u>Level Symbology and Screening</u>

Often it is desired to make **reference file information** recede into the background to avoid having it interfere with more important information on the plan. This is used for architectural information on MEP drawings and on architectural and structural drawings to show existing information. The effect of screening can be obtained by the use of level symbology or the screening feature of CADNET Plot Station. Refer to the MicroStation Plotting or AutoCAD Plotting section as appropriate for additional instructions.

4. <u>MicroStation Plotting</u>

4.1   Level symbology should be used if the electronic data is being delivered to a site without CADNET Plot Station or if half-size reductions of the plots will be made. If electronic data is not being delivered to another site, then CADNET screening should be used.

4.2   Configuring Level symbology requires the following steps.

A.   From the Settings pull-down menu, select **LEVEL>SYMBOLOGY,** turn Override buttons off.

Level Symbology						

Level   Color   Style   Weight

				Settings	
				☐ Color	0
2	0	0	0	☐ Style	0
3	0	0	0	☐ Weight	0
4	0	0	0		
5	0	0	0	**Apply**	
6	0	0	0		
7	0	0	0	Overrides	
8	0	0	0	☐ Color	
9	0	0	0	☐ Style	
10	0	0	0	☐ Weight	
11	0	0	0		

Active Design File   **OK**   **Cancel**

B. From the Settings pull-down menu, select **VIEW ATTRIBUTES**, check the Level Symbology box and click All.

View Attributes	

View Number: 1 ▼

☐ ACS Triad	☐ Fill
☐ Background	☐ Grid
☐ Camera	☒ Level Symbology
☐ Constructions	☐ Line Styles
☐ Dimensions	☐ Line Weights
☐ Dynamics	☐ Patterns
☐ Data Fields	☐ Ref Boundaries
☐ Fast Cells	☐ Tags
☐ Fast Curves	☐ Text
☐ Fast Font	☐ Text Nodes
☐ Fast Ref Clipping	

Apply   **All**

C. From the File pull-down menu, select **REFERENCE**. Identify the reference file you would like to screen.

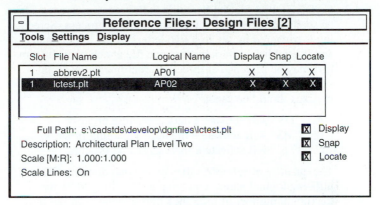

D. From the Reference File Window, pick **SETTINGS>LEVEL SYMBOLOGY**. For each attribute (color, line style, or line weight) to be set turn on the attribute under the Settings category and change to the desired setting. To apply the settings to a level, click the level in the listed box and click Apply, or double click the level. In the Override category select the appropriate buttons according to the changes made in the Settings box. Once all of the levels are set press the OK button.

E. **THEN SAVE SETTINGS!!** from the File menu.

4.3 CADNET Plot Station Screening allows any reference file to
     be screened/half-toned during the plotting process. Screen-
     ing is triggered by the first two letters of the logical name
     and is established during reference file attachment. Informa-
     tion may be screened at three different intensities; light
     screen, medium screen, and dark screen. The following
     prefixes should be used:

   A. "DS" will activate a dark screening process.
   B. "MS" will activate a medium screening process.
   C. "LS" will activate a light screening process.

The quantity of reference files in any one drawing file,
utilizing logical name screening, is only limited by the
maximum number of reference files attached (255). Unlim-
ited quantities and combinations of screening intensities
may reside in one file at any time. The application of
screening is only limited by the user's requirements or
imagination.

4.4 Plot Request Forms (PRF) Files: The PRF File contains the
     information necessary to plot a CAD file. This file is a text
     file that contains the sheet file name, names of any reference
     files associated with the sheet file, drawing scale, view, text
     size, rotation of view, and other information necessary to
     generate the output desired by the user. Plotting is initiated
     when the PRF file is copied to the plotting directory.

Each real paper drawing should have a sheet file and PRF
with the same file name. PRF files are to be stored in a PRF
subdirectory. For an explanation on sheet file naming
conventions refer to Chapter 2 – CAD File Naming and
Creation.

To create the plot request form:

   A. Fence the chosen view area within a design file or plot
       file to be plotted.

```
┌─────────────────────────────────────────────┐
│ ┌───┐                                         │
│ │ ▭ │                                         │
│ └───┘                                         │
│        BYERS PRF GENERATOR for MicroStation   │
│                   Version  6.2.0              │
│  PRF Name: │ S:\CADSTDS\BYERS    │  │ Select ...│
│     Queu: │ msfoq               │  │ Select ...│
│   Plotter: │ DEFAULT            │  │ Select ...│
│  Pen Table: │                   │  │ Select ...│
│  ┌─ Plot Size information ──────────────────┐ │
│  │   Units: │ IN    (inch)              │    │ │
│  │    Size: │ 0.015813.0.010841 │            │ │
│  │   Scale: │ 100 │   Rotation: │ 0.000000 │ │ │
│  │ Rescale: │ 1.000000.1.000 │  Copies: │ 0 │ │ │
│  └──────────────────────────────────────────┘ │
│  ┌─ Customization Palette ──────────────────┐ │
│  │  ☒ View Number:  │ 1 │    │ Options... │  │ │
│  │  ☐ Named Views: │      │   │  Files...  │  │ │
│  └──────────────────────────────────────────┘ │
│  ┌─ Creation Palette ───────────────────────┐ │
│  │  ☒ Create Only │ PRE │  │ Snapshot ... │   │ │
│  │  ☐ Submit Job                             │ │
│  └──────────────────────────────────────────┘ │
└─────────────────────────────────────────────┘
```

B. Then select the CADNET PRF Generator on the Command Menu within MicroStation to open the main CADNET Plot Request Generator dialog box. This dialog box has fields for the following items:

1. The PRF Filename path is used to specify the PRF file name. The PRF file should be named in accordance with the guidelines above. The project disk and directory are supplied by the dialog box. Simply add the PRF subdirectory to the project directory listed.

2. Use the Queue select button to modify the existing selection.

3. The plotter device selection is used to select non-default plotters.

4. For the pen table selection, normally the default is adequate.

5. Units has a drop-down menu with options to choose from. Select the appropriate designation for your project.

6. Size is generally not manually revised, but can be used to force a size if no particular output scale is desired.

7. Enter the proper drawing scale and the system will automatically calculate the drawing size in the box above. Take this time to check your scale input with the sheet size expected.

8. Choose the Fence option from the View Number drop-down menu, unless plotting a particular view.

9. The user also has the opportunity to plot a saved Named View by selecting the File button and clicking the view desired. (See Saved Views for creation.)

10. Check the Create Only box and click the PRF button. Your PRF is now in the appropriate directory.

11. The file can be submitted for plotting by manually copying it to the plotting directory.

12. Modifications can be made to PRF files without recreating them by using the text editor in Windows. Before attempting this, an inexperienced user should seek advice from an experienced user.

5. AutoCAD Plotting

5.1 Using CADNET Plot Station with AutoCAD: CADNET is a plotting utility that works with both AutoCAD and MicroStation. It will benefit all of us by speeding up plotting jobs and providing accurate accounting records of all jobs plotted on our plotters. Following is a step-by-step description of how to use this software with AutoCAD.

   • From within AutoCAD open the drawing that you'd like to plot. If you've made any changes to the drawing, save the drawing before sending it to the plotter.
   • From the CADNET PRF pull-down menu select PRF Generator. An example of this dialog box appears below.

```
CADNET's PRF GENERATOR - VERSION 3.2.05                          [X]

     PRF Name: [Q:\Dal_3000_Acad_Bond_Full\Drawing.prf]        [ Select... ]

        Queue: [Dal_3000_Acad_Bond_Full              ]         [ Select... ]

      Plotter: [DAL_30000_ACAD_BOND_FULL             ]         [ Select... ]

   Paper Size: [0000000.000                          ]         [ Select... ]

    Pen Table: [Amaster.tbl                          ]         [ Select... ]

  ┌─Plot Size Information──────────┐   ┌─Plot Area Information──────────┐
  │                                │   │  ○  Display                    │
  │      Units:  [ in        ▼]    │   │                                │
  │                                │   │  ⦿  Extents                    │
  │   Rotation:  [ 0.000     ]     │   │                                │
  │                                │   │  ○  Limits                     │
  │   Rescale:   [ 1.000, 1.000 ]  │   │                                │
  │                                │   │  ○  View         [        ▼]   │
  │  Plot Size:  [20000000000000000]│   │                                │
  │                                │   │  ○  Window       [ Window... ] │
  │    Copies:   [ 0         ]      │   └────────────────────────────────┘
  │                                │   ┌─PRF Toggles────────────────────┐
  │   Plot Units = Dwg Units       │   │ [X] Create PRF   [ ] Submit PRF│
  │  [ 1.000    ] = [ 1" ]          │   │ [ ] Display Submit Form        │
  │  [ ] Scale to Fit  [Preview...] │   └────────────────────────────────┘
  └────────────────────────────────┘      [ Options... ]  [ Files... ]

              [    OK    ]      [  Cancel  ]

  WARNING:  Plot Size exceeds Paper Size.
```

- The file created by CADNET is copied to a directory to the network where it is processed by the Plot Station computer next to the plotter. Once the PRF has been processed it is deleted from this directory.
- If you'd like to immediately plot the file and are not interested in saving the PRF for future use skip this step. Otherwise, change the entry in the PRF Name: box to a directory location within your project directory structure. Saving PRFs is very beneficial. For future plot jobs, you simply copy the PRFs to the directory where they will be immediately plotted out. The Plot Station computer will read the current CAD files from the server and generate updated plots of all your files even if you've made revisions after the PRF was created. In the event that new reference files were added to the drawing

after the original PRF was created, the PRF file must be recreated or edited.

- Select the appropriate Paper Size. If you need to create a custom paper size refer to the instructions under Additional Information at the end of these instructions.

- The Pen Table is named AMASTER.TBL. This file is located in the \\server\plot\pentbl directory. It sets the pens to match the standard office pen settings. If your project uses a different pen setup a pen table must be created with those settings.

- Units can be set to Imperial or metric measures.

- Set a rotation if required.

- Select a number of copies.

- Select a plotted scale factor.

- Select a Plot Area. Typically you will plot a window or a named view. If you are currently using named views for plotting, the view may need to be adjusted to plot correctly.

- In the PRF Toggles box select create PRF. You will not need to pick the Submit PRF box.

- You can preview an outline of the plot area from within the Byer's PRF Generator dialog box. The full preview option that is available in AutoCAD is not available.

- The log file that is created from your plot will be sent to accounting on a monthly basis. This file tracks the size, employee number, and project number of each plot that is run. One of the limitatons of this log is that the width of the plot is always recorded as the width of the paper roll in the plotter. Since this is the case it is very important to keep the 30" wide roll in the top drawer, and the 36" roll in the bottom drawer.

- **Important:** In order to record accounting information, you **must** select the Options button and fill in your employee number in the User area, and the Project Number in the Project area. An example of this dialog box is shown below.

PRF Options

Optional Information

Accounting: [   ]   [Select...]

User: [   ]   Project: [10-94501.10]

Text1 : [   ]

Text2 : [   ]

Text3 : [   ]

Qualifiers : [   ]

[OK]   [Cancel]

- Typically you do not need to change any of the settings in the Files dialog box. Xrefs are plotted by default so this setting does not need to be changed.
- Click on OK to create the PRF. If you've saved the file in one of the directories on the Q:\ drive such as Q:\Dal_3000_Acad_Bond_Full, the drawing will plot immediately. If you've saved the file to a project directory, you will need to copy it to the appropriate directory on the Q:\ drive before the file will plot.

5.2   Additional Information

- CADNET Plot Station plots postscript fonts as outlines only. If you have any postscript fonts in your drawings please take the time to run a test plot and check the plotted appearance of the fonts. Typical AutoCAD fonts like Architxt are not postscript fonts and will plot just fine.
- There is no way to hide lines when plotting through Byer's. If you've got 3D drawings that need to plot after hiding the lines use the standard AutoCAD plotting utility.
- If you're having problems with Byer's don't panic, the standard AutoCAD plotting utility will still work. Just remember that you're not recording any accounting information and you can't replot the drawings without going through the complete plotting process again.

- If you need to add a nonstandard paper size to the list of sheet sizes, consult the instructions below.
- The dialog box depicted below is accessed from the CADNET PRF menu. Select Configure PRF, then Edit the Active configuration. Select the Plotting button and the Plot Information dialog box will apear. Click on the Select button beside the Plotter and the Plotter Information box will open. Select a plotter and click on the Edit button. The dialog box below will open.

Plotter Parameters

┌─ Plotter Specific Overrides ──────────────────────────────────┐

PRF Ext: [   ]   Path: [   ]   Select...

Rotation: [   ]   Units: [▼]

Rescale: [   ]   Plot Units = Dwg Units

Copies: [   ]   [   ] = [   ]

Active Paper Size : E   Max Size: [   ]

┌─ PRF Paper Size List ─────┐   ┌─ Paper Sizes Available ──────┐

A	10.5	8.00	in
B	16.00	10.00	in
C	21.00	16.00	in
D	33.00	21.00	in
E	43.00	33.00	in

[Remove>]   [<Add]   [<<Addall]   [Delete]

┌─ Additional Paper Sizes ──────────────────────────────────────┐

Size: Width: Height: Units:
[   ]   [   ]   [   ]   [in ▼]   [Create]

[OK]   [Cancel]

- Modifications can be made to PRF files without recreating them by using the text editor in Windows. Before attempting this, an inexperienced user should seek advice from an experienced user.

7
MicroStation Methods and Procedures

1. <u>MicroStation Project Workspace</u>

   The Project Workspace file is modified according to the assigned project folder name. The project manager and the Project Set-Up sheet determine the directory path of the project.

   Before opening MicroStation the user must choose the old or new standard option:

   > Click Windows **START** command
   > Click **PROGRAMS**
   > Click **MICROSTATION** or **MICROSTATION SE**
   > Click **OLD STANDARDS** or **NEW STANDARDS**

   This process overwrites the Msconfig.cfg and Mslocal.sfg files with the correct files for the desired standard. The user must exit MicroStation each time they need to select a different standard for their project. The correct configuration file is read each time MicroStation is opened. When the user opens MicroStation and the MicroStation Manager tutorial appears, search the project pull-down menu for the appropriate project workspace and the appropriate discipline interface.

2. <u>CAD Leveling Menus</u>

   CAD Leveling is covered in detail in Chapter 3 – CAD Levels/ Layers. This section covers the use of several different menus for working with levels in MicroStation. RTKL has developed interface menus to customize MicroStation to the way RTKL uses the program. Three types of sidebar menus have been developed.

   2.1   Interface Menus: These menus are modified by the MicroStation configuration files. They contain the same information as the sidebar menus but are more conveniently placed on the screen. To activate these menus run the USENEW.BAT batch file located in C:\WIN32APP\USTATION\CONFIG\. Open MicroStation and at the MicroStation Manager tutorial, choose the correct discipline "Interface" from the pull-down menu. Search the

"Project" menu for the appropriate project workspace.

2.2   Text Menus: This sidebar menu sets text and dimension attributes to the RTKL standard levels, font type and sizes for differing plot scales for both Imperial and metric files. The menu may also be used to set the scaling factor for Imperial and metric cells as well as the active angle. The sidebar menu, which provides these functions is named CTEXTDIM, Text and Dimensions.

2.3   Cell Menus: This menu activates cell libraries listed in the user preference or project preference files. The intent of the menu is to encourage the use of standard cells. The sidebar menu which provides this function is named CSYMB, Reference Symbols.

2.4   Menu Attachment: The sidebar menus need to be attached while working in MicroStation. To attach the menus, the user needs to enter the following key strokes:

AM=<NAME>,SB<N>
Name: path and name of the menu to be attached
N: designates the numerical position on the
             screen for the menu to appear
             (1, 2, 3 or 4)

Menus can be attached by using different function key combinations. To use the function menu, log into MicroStation. In the **Workspace** menu, open the **Function Keys** tutorial. In the tutorial under the **File** menu choose **Open** and select the function key menu path and file name: V:\OFFICE\USTN\WSMOD\DEFAULT\DATA\CORPFKEY.MNU

<SHIFT><F1>   CTEXTDIM
<SHIFT><F2>   CSYMB
<SHIFT><F3>   CPLAN
<SHIFT><F4>   CELEVSEC
<SHIFT><F5>   CRCP
<SHIFT><F6>   CDETAIL
<SHIFT><F7>   Check E-Mail

3. CAD Color Tables

The standard table should be used on all projects. If an individual has difficulty in "seeing" a specific color (because of color blindness or screen resolution), then the standard color table can be modified to display a different color. Only the computer of the individual affected should be modified. The original color/level association remains the same for the entire team.

4. <u>Creating Enlarged Plan Details</u>

   4.1 Enlarged Plan Details: The procedure for creating and naming any enlarged plan detail is similar to the detail format. Determine the plot file and grid locaton of the plan detail and name the file accordingly. Attach the building floor plan as a reference file, fence clip, and scale the area of enlargement. Add the detail and text information needed and attach this file to the corresponding plot file in the correct grid location. The building floor plan is saved in the V:\PROJECT\ARCH\CAD\BASE\ folder, the enlarged detail drawing is saved in the V:\PROJECT\ARCHCAD\DETAIL\ folder, and the plot file is saved in the V:\PROJECT\ARCH\CAD directory.

   4.2 Example: AAWAP04.DGN is the architectural fourth level building plan base file located in \BASE\. 330210A.DGN is the file where the enlarged plan detail is completed and saved in \DETAIL\. If completing the enlarged plan detail consists of only dimensioning and notation, there is no need to create the detail file (330210A.DGN). In this case attach the scaled plan section to the plotting file (AAW3302.DGN) and add the dimensions and notes in this file. AAW3302.DGN is the Enlarged Plan, Elevation and Section plot file with the above two drawings attached as reference files and stored in the \CAD\ folder.

5. <u>Reference File Logical Names</u>

   Logical Names are used when attaching plans as reference files. This standard naming convention allows files to be manipulated (modify levels) through batch procedures. Following is a list of standard logical names, which are to be used throughout the project. The format is "**Discipline + Drawing Type + Building Level + _Number of times referenced**."

APB	Architectural Basement Floor Plan
AP1	Architectural First Floor Plan
AP1_2	Architectural First Floor Plan attached the first time.

AP2_2	Architectural Second Floor Plan attached a second time.
APR	Architectural Roof Plan.
GRD	Grid sheet.
GRD_1	Grid sheet attached the first time.
GRD_2	Grid sheet attached a second time.
SHT	Sheet Border.
AX1	Architectural Existing First Floor Plan.
AP	Architectural Plan.
AD	Architectural Detail.
AE	Architectural Elevation.
AX	Architectural Existing.

6. Border Files

   6.1   The border file contains the border information. The border
         size and type are determined during the planning stages by
         the project architect. After the desired standard border file
         has been copied into the project directory, information
         common to all sheets such as project number, title block,
         and issue date are added. Sheet titles and numbers are
         placed in each individual plotting file. The following steps
         are required.

   6.2   Copy the appropriate border from V:\LIBS\BORDER into the
         project directory. Rename the border file to BORDER.DGN.
         If the project calls for more than one type of border, modify
         the file name as required.

   6.3   If the owner supplies the border file, check and/or add the
         following items as required.
         • Define a scale reference point at the bottom right-hand
           corner of the sheet.
         • Add a leveling chart. See 3–CAD Levels/Layers. Level
           any sheet information according to this leveling scheme.
         • Add title block text information such as contract
           number, issue date, scales, and addendum information.
         • Add a north arrow.
         • Add prototype drawing number data field(s).
           Government projects often require multiple drawing
           numbers on each sheet.
         • Modify title block information to be project-specific if
           required.

- Add border reference grid. If not permitted by owner place the grid on a non-plot level.

6.4 The border is drawn at full size allowing the same border file to be used for multiple drawing scales within the project. Refer to the chart in the Appendix *(omitted)* for correct scale factors. Scale the border file about the scale reference point, located at the bottom right-hand corner of the border.

Place information on the appropriate levels according to the border level/layer chart. Plan-specific information such as north arrows and key plans should be turned off on detail sheets by level manipulation.

- Title block graphics.
- Project number.
- Issue date. (If disciplines have different issue dates then assign each discipline a level for their issue date.)
- Fill in project-specific level information in the leveling chart.
- North arrow.
- Key plans.
- Package label. (Not for Construction, For Bid Only etc.)

All project-specific information should be placed on a designated level and documented in the project border level chart. It is the responsibility of all users to keep this leveling scheme up to date. Anyone adding information to the border must place it on a project-assigned level and update the level chart.

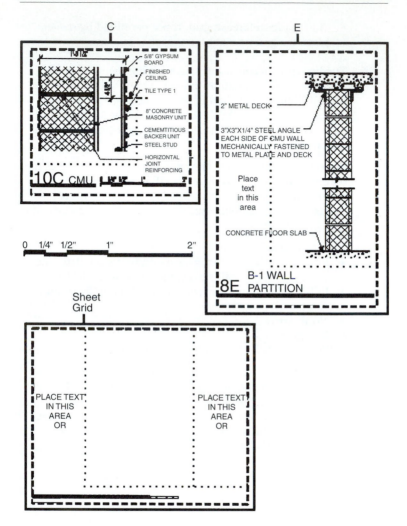

C

10C CMU

- 5/8" GYPSUM BOARD
- FINISHED CEILING
- TILE TYPE 1
- 8" CONCRETE MASONRY UNIT
- CEMEMTITIOUS BACKER UNIT
- STEEL STUD
- HORIZONTAL JOINT REINFORCING

0   1/4" 1/2"   1"   2"

E

2" METAL DECK

3"X3"X1/4" STEEL ANGLE EACH SIDE OF CMU WALL MECHANICALLY FASTENED TO METAL PLATE AND DECK

Place text in this area

CONCRETE FLOOR SLAB

B-1 WALL
8E   PARTITION

Sheet Grid

PLACE TEXT IN THIS AREA OR

PLACE TEXT IN THIS AREA OR

7. Sheet File Structure

7.1   Sheet File Structure: There are several ways the sheet file may be structured depending on whether there is one building level plan per drawing, several building level plans on one drawing, or several drawings per building level. The drawing layout must be determined in the early planning stages of the project. Sheet files are named according to the file naming standards defined elsewhere in this document. The following procedures should be used when creating sheet files:

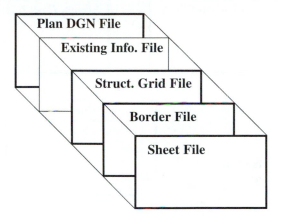

7.2   Single Plan Per Drawing: These are the steps to follow when creating a plot file with a single plan file per drawing. The diagram above depicts this type of file.

- Create the sheet file using normal design file creation methods.
- Attach the project border using the proper logical name. (See Section 5 above.)
- Reference scale the border using the reference point.
- If the grid is not displayed within the border, reference move the border to align with the grid. Do not reference move the grid file.
- If necessary, attach and display the existing information file using reference screening or level symbology. Refer to the plotting section for information on these procedures.
- Attach the new building plan file using the proper logical name.
- Attach any other reference files that may be required for the drawing (e.g., architectural reflected ceiling plans for mechanical/electrical drawings).

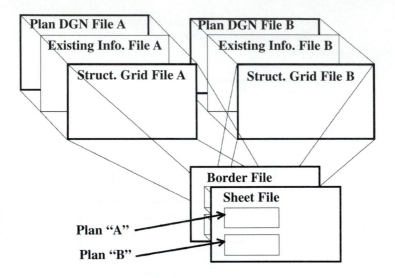

7.3   Multiple Plans Per Drawing: These are the steps to follow
      when creating a sheet file with multiple plan files per
      drawing. The diagram above depicts this type of file.

- Create the sheet file using normal design file creation
  methods.
- Attach the project border using the proper logical name.
- Reference scale the border using the work point.
- Attach the grid as reference file using the proper logical
  name.
- Reference move the border so the first plan is oriented
  correctly and allows space for the other plans.
- If necessary, attach and display the existing information
  file using reference screening or level symbology. Refer
  to 6–CAD Plotting for information on these procedures.
- Attach the new building plan file using the proper
  logical name.
- Attach any other reference files that may be required for
  the drawings (e.g., architectural reflected ceiling plans
  for mechanical/electrical drawings).
- Fence and clip bound all files for this plan
  simultaneously.

- Repeat the previous three steps for the second plan and assign standard logical names with descriptions. It may be necessary to attach the same files multiple times for different part plans on the same building level.
- Reference move all files attached for the second plan as required to properly locate them within the border.
- Calculate a distance from the plan's original location to the new area on the design plane. When using the move reference file command input a cumulative distance for all files. Document these distances with the description for future use and additions.
- Repeat as required for any additional plans placed on this drawing.

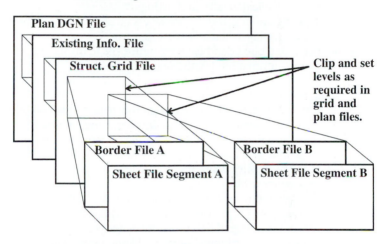

7.4 Segmented Plan Drawings: These are the steps to follow when creating sheet files for segmented plan drawings. The diagram above depicts these types of files. Repeat the following steps for each sheet file to be created. One sheet file is created for each segment.

- Create the sheet file for this segment using normal design file creation methods.
- Attach the project border using the proper logical name.
- Reference scale the border using the work point.
- Attach the grid as a reference file using the proper logical name.
- If the grid for this segment is not displayed within the border, reference move the border to align with the grid.

All but one of the sheet files will require the border be
reference moved to align with the correct area of the
plan. The distance the borders are moved should be
documented with the logical name description for the
project team.

- If necessary, attach and display the existing information
  file using reference screening or level symbology. Refer
  to the plotting section for information on these
  procedures.
- Attach the new building plan file using the proper
  logical name.
- Attach any other reference files that may be required for
  the segment (e.g., architectural reflected ceiling plans
  for mechanical/electrical drawings).
- Turn the grid and design file levels on and off according
  to the leveling scheme for this segment.
- Fence and clip bound each reference file to display the
  correct information for the segment.

7.5   Enlarged Detail Drawings
- Create the sheet file using design file creation methods.
- Attach the border sheet using the proper logical name.
- Reference scale the border using the reference point.
- Attach the grid and all necessary floor plan design files
  as reference files using the proper logical names and
  appropriate scale.
- Turn off and/or on the correct levels in the reference file
  to ensure the proper information is displayed.
- Attach the enlarged detail file created as a reference file
  using the proper logical name and appropriate scale.
- Fence and clip bound each reference file to display all
  the information intended for this particular enlarged
  detail.
- Reference move each file the same distance to the
  correct sheet grid location. Document the distance
  moved in the logical name description for team and
  future use.

7.6   Normal Detail Drawings
- Create the sheet file using normal design file creation
  methods.
- Attach the project border using the proper logical name.
- Reference scale the border using the reference point.

- Attach the detail file as a reference file using the proper logical name and appropriate scale.
- Fence and clip bound each reference file to display all the information intended for this detail.
- Reference move the detail file to the correct sheet grid location. Include the distance moved with the logical name description for team and future use.

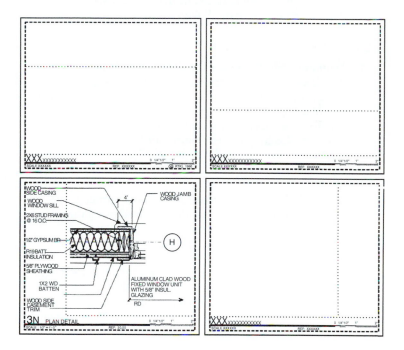

8
AutoCAD Methods and Procedures

1. Drawing (DWG) Files

1.1   Drawing files are files that contain building information. These files contain the bulk of the database information.

They differ from sheet files in that sheet files represent a
specific drawing. Plan drawing files usually contain the
whole building at a given level.

1.2   Plan drawing files for each building level are created using
the standard prototype drawing. Before drawing any
information, the grid file is attached as a reference file to
determine the graphic location and boundaries. All graphic
elements are drawn at full scale and the text size is
determined by the desired plotted text height.

2. Sheet Files

2.1   Definition: Sheet files are the files to which all other
drawing-related files are attached. Sheet files assemble a
group of reference files in a particular configuration (such
as a building segment for plotting as a drawing or sheet).
There is one sheet file for each sheet in the set of project
drawings. Each sheet file requires a PRF that contains its
plotting parameters. Refer to 6–CAD Plotting for more
information on PRF files.

2.2   Sheet File Information: Sheet files usually contain very
little information. The sheet file is created using the
appropriate template file determined by the unit type,
Imperial or metric.

2.3   Each drawing sheet should have a sheet file and PRF with
the same file name prefix. Sheet files are to be kept in the
project \CAD\ directory as drawing files. Sheet and PRF
files should have the same name with extensions of .dwg or
.prf for any single project.

2.4   Sheet File Structure: There are several ways the sheet file
may be structured depending on whether there is one
building level plan per sheet, several building level plans on
one sheet, or several sheets per building level. The sheet
layout must be determined in the early planning stages of
the project. Sheet files are named according to the file
naming standards defined elsewhere in this document. The
following procedures should be used when creating sheet
files.

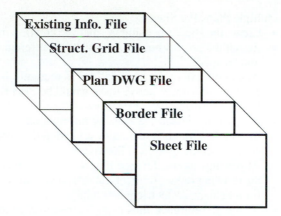

2.5 Single Plan Per Sheet
  • Create the sheet file using normal file creation methods.
  • Attach the project border as an external reference file in
    model space.
  • Attach the new building plan file at the appropriate scale
    factor as an external reference file. The structural grid
    drawing should be referenced into the plan file prior to
    attaching the drawing to the plot file.
  • Attach any other reference files that may be required for
    the drawing (e.g., mechanical/electrical drawings, etc.).

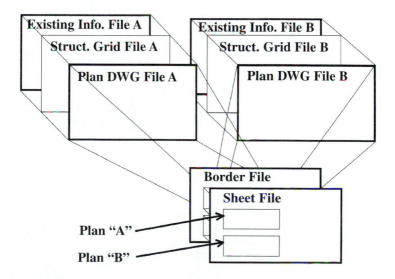

2.6   Multiple Plans Per Sheet
- Create the sheet file using normal file creation methods.
- Attach the project border as an external reference file in model space.
- Attach the external reference files as required. In the example illustrated above these would be Plan DWG File A and Plan DWG File B.
- If necessary, attach the existing information file. This file can be plotted/screened by assigning the appropriate color to all the reference file layers.
- Attach any other reference files that may be required for the drawing (e.g., architectural reflected ceiling plans for mechanical/electrical drawings).
- Attach all reference files using an insertion point of 0,0 and then move the reference file to the correct location on the sheet. All reference files should be attached with the current layer set to 0 (zero).

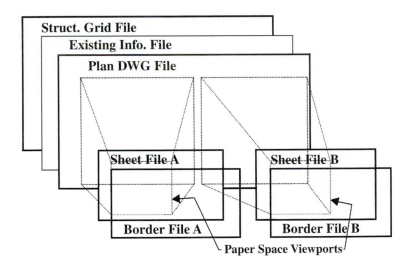

2.7   Segmented Plans & Elevations
- Repeat the following steps for each sheet file to be created. One sheet file is created for each segment.
- Create the sheet file for each segment using drawing file creation methods.
- Attach the project border in paper space.

- Create floating viewports as required. The viewport should be drawn on a layer that can be frozen for plotting.
- With Tilemode set to 1 attach the reference file drawings.
- Return to Paper space by setting Tilemode to 0. Type MS at the command prompt and click in one of the viewports to set it current. Zoom and Pan as required to set the correct drawing view and scale. Repeat for each viewport.

2.8   Detail Sheet File

- Create the sheet file using normal drawing creation methods.
- Attach the project border in Model Space at 0,0 with a scale factor of 1.
- Attach the detail files as reference files using the appropriate scale factor.
- Move each detail file to the correct sheet grid location.

CAD Glossary

AutoCAD - The most widely used CAD software in the A/E profession first released on the original IBM PC in the early 1980s. This software is produced by Autodesk.

Autodesk - The company that writes and markets the AutoCAD program. They are located in northern California.

Base File - The design or drawing file that contains information related to the project design and its construction.

Bentley Systems - The company that writes and markets the MicroStation program. They are located in eastern Pennsylvania.

Border File - The design or Drawing file that contains the drawing border, title block, and other information that is common to all drawings in a particular project.

Byers Engineering - Former name of CADNET.

CADNET - The company that writes PRF generator and plot station software. They are located in Atlanta, Georgia.

CALS - A vendor-independent plotter input language.

Cell File - A file used by MicroStation to store **cells**.

Design File - A file used by **MicroStation** to store graphic information.

Directory - The part of the file specification after the disk drive and before the file name.

Dot - The period between a **file name** and a **file extension.**

Drawing File - A file used by **AutoCad** to store graphic information.

English Units - The system of measurement that uses units of feet and inches. This name is commonly used in the United States but is not generally understood in the United Kingdom.

File - A set of information stored on a computer disk that can be loaded into an application program.

File Extension - The part of the file specification after the **dot.**

File Name - The part of a file specification after the folders/folders and before the dot.

Folder - A modern term for **directory** originally used on Apple MacIntosh computers. Folders are shown on the desktop and in Windows Explorer as file folder icons.

HPGL2 - A plotter input language developed by Hewlett-Packard for their line of Pen and Ink Jet plotters.

IGDS - An abbreviation for Intergraph Graphics Design System. This was the name for the predecessor of MicroStation that was originally created by **Intergraph.**

Imperial Units - The system of measurement that uses units of feet and inches. This name is the correct term for this system in the United Kingdom.

Intergraph - The company that originally created IGDS, the predecessor of MicroStation. MicroStation files use a superset of the information stored in IGDS files. MicroStation still is able to read IDGS files from the early 1980s. Intergraph is located in Huntsville, Alabama.

Metric Units - The system of measurement that uses meters, centimeters, and millimeters. Many Americans assume this system to be uniform throughout the world. However, there are many variations on this system depending on what country you are in. Local inquiries should be made before starting to work in an unfamiliar location to determine what local variations are required.

MicroStation - A widely used CAD software package that had its beginnings as **Intergraph IGDS** on Digital PDP- I Is in the mid-1970s. The software is written and marketed by **Bentley Systems.**

Plot File - The file that contains the commands necessary to make a plotter create output. Examples are HPGL2 and Postscript. AutoCAD typically uses a PLT extension for this file. MicroStation often uses a .000 extension for this file. In the past RTKL referred to Sheet Files as Plot Files.

Postscript - A vendor-independent printer input language often understood by plotters as well.

PRF - An abbreviation for Plot Request File. A small text file that contains specifications regarding reference files, level, fonts, and other information required by CADNET to plot a drawing. This term was created long ago by **Intergraph** when MicroStation's predecessors ran on PDP- I Is and VAXs.

Reference File - One or more design files that are attached and viewed with a **MicroStation design file or an AutoCAD drawingfile** in a manner similar to the individual sheets used in pinbar drafting.

Sheet File - The design or drawing file that contains information related to a specific drawing. This includes the title, issue date, revision information and dates, and special notes such as "not for construction." In the past RTKL referred to this type of file as the **Plot File.** This practice was changed to avoid confusion with the typical AutoCAD usage of the term **Plot File.**

UNC - A way of specifying a network drive without using a drive letter. This term is short for Uniform Naming Convention.

XREF - Another name for an external reference file. One or more drawing files that are attached and viewed with an **AutoCAD drawing file** in a manner similar to the individual sheets used in pinbar drafting.

RTKL Associates Inc. (RTKL) <www.rtk1.com> is one of the world's largest multidisciplinary design firms, featuring projects in over 60 countries. Headquartered in Baltimore, the firm employs more than 900 professionals in 12 offices worldwide.

Beginning in the 1950s with the redevelopment of Baltimore's urban core and Inner Harbor, RTKL carved out a niche in master planning for government and private clients. Over the succeeding decades, RTKL evolved into a full-service firm adding the disciplines of engineering, interior architecture, landscape architecture, and environmental graphic design, and new project specialties including offices, retail centers, hotels, and health sciences projects. The 1980s and 1990s brought further expansion with mixed-use, federal government, and entertainment assignments.

RTKL has a successful track record of crossing cultural and physical frontiers to serve a wide variety of clients in the public and private sectors. From Baltimore to Shanghai, comprehensive service, design expertise, and global experience allow RTKL to successfully usher any project from start to finish. RTKL prides itself on combining the service of a small practice with the professional and technical resources of a large firm.

Multidisciplinary Design Services
Planning and Urban Design
Architecture
Interior Architecture
Structural Engineering
Mechanical, Electrical, and Plumbing Engineering
Landscape Architecture
Environmental Graphic Design

Project Specialties
Hospitality
Residential
Corporate Facilities Planning and Design
Retail/Commercial
Healthcare
Mixed-Use
Public

Working Drawings and Building Code Compliance

A common issue faced by architects is that building codes often contain language that obscures their meaning. This problem of code interpretation frequently leads to the rejection of a set of construction documents submitted for a building permit. Such rejections are frustrating, delay the building process, and can be expensive for the architect (and, ultimately, the client). This is particularly true if the revisions required extend beyond detailing and material selection and into the design itself, because the redesign time can be extensive. In that case, the revisions are done at no cost to anyone except the architect, and result in the design office doing the same work twice but for no extra fee.

In order to help the architect reduce the number of revisions required to secure a building permit, this chapter provides advice from building officials in all model code jurisdictions. Building departments across the nation were queried as to the most problematic aspects of the codes for architects, and their responses range from general comments to citations of specific paragraph numbers in specific codes. Regardless of the model code used by each building official, their comments apply, in principle, to all jurisdictions, including the new *International Building Code*.

Troublesome Code Sections

A survey of building officials was conducted in order to identify code requirements commonly violated in plans which have been submitted for building permits. The following comments indicate where architects should focus extra attention and/or seek help to verify compliance, prior to the submission of a project for review by the building department. A brief summary of the key requirements of each section is also provided. Although the codes are not universal, the troublesome subjects are likely to apply to all jurisdictions because of the similarities of the model codes.

1997 Uniform Building Code

Chapter 1 Administration

- Sec. 106.3.2 Submittal documents.
  Lists the documents required for submittal to the building official for a building permit.

  Problem: Omitting one or more required documents in the submittal.

- Sec. 106.3.3 Information on plans and specifications.
  Requires that documents submitted for a building permit include all information to verify compliance with the building code.

  Problem: Documents are submitted with information omitted such as structural connections, fire penetration protection, and typical partition construction.

Chapter 5 General Building Limitations

- Sec. 504.3 Allowable floor area of mixed occupancies.
  Defines the method for determining the allowable area on a floor with mixed occupancies.

  Problem: Confusion in the computation using actual areas of individual occupancies in order to determine the total allowable area for a floor.

- Sec. 506 Maximum height of buildings.
  Limits height of buildings based on occupancy and
  construction type.

  Problem: Using the correct construction type and understanding
  when the use of sprinklers permits a height increase.

Chapter 7 Fire-resistant Materials and Construction

- Sec. 709.1 Walls and partitions; and Sec. 710.1 Floor ceilings or
  roof ceilings.
  Specifies the materials and the configuration of their
  assemblies that qualify for various fire-resistance ratings.

  Problem: Substitutions of untested materials into listed
  assemblies without supporting documentation.

  Problem: Claims of fire ratings for surface coatings such as
  intumescent paint.

  Problem: Alteration of detailing or nailing requirements in listed
  assemblies without supporting documentation.

  Problem: Exceeding the number or size of penetrations permitted
  in fire-rated ceilings.

Chapter 10 Means of Egress

- Sec. 1003.2.8 Means of egress identification.
  Describes the location, graphics, illumination, and power
  required for exit signs.

  Problem: Failure to place exit signs that meet code specifications
  in the required locations.

- Sec. 1003.3.1.8 Type of lock or latch.
  Requires that exit doors be operable from the inside without a
  key or special effort.

  Problem: Specifying locking systems for exit doors not permitted
  by the rule or its exceptions.

- Sec. 1004.2.2. Travel through intervening rooms.
  Prohibits the interruption by an intervening room of direct
  access to an exit from any point in a building.

  Problem: Distinguishing between a corridor and a hallway (terms
  which are not interchangeable and both of which are used in
  this section).

  Problem: Exercising exceptions without qualifying for them.

- Sec. 1004.2.4 Separation of exits or exit-access doorways.
  Requires that where two or more exits are required, they be
  separated by a travel distance at least as long as half the longest
  diagonal of the area served.

  Problem: The methods of measuring the lengths of the diagonal
  and travel distances.

- Sec. 1004.3.4.3.1 Fire-resistive materials.
  Specifies where fire-resistive materials are required in exit-
  access areas.

  Problem: Failure to use noncombustible panels or tile in a ceiling
  suspended below a fire-resistive rated structural ceiling.

- Sec. 1005.3.3 Exit enclosures.
  Requires that stairs be enclosed for fire protection in specified
  construction.

  Problem: Failure to enclose stairs or otherwise circumvent the
  nature of the construction required for their enclosure.

  Note: Typically aesthetic goals are the motivation for these
  problems and redesign after completion of the working
  drawings is typically difficult.

- Sec. 1005.3.3.6 Use of space under stairway or ramp.
  Prohibits enclosure of space under exit stairs or ramps and
  requires that the space under them remain unused.

  Problem: Enclosing space under exit stairs.

Chapter 11 Accessibility
- Sec. 1103.2.2 Accessible route; and Sec. 1103.2.3 Accessible
  entrances.
  Indicates where accessible routes are required in buildings and
  on sites.

  Problem: Incomplete drawings addressing the requirements of
  these sections.

  Problem: Ramps provided do not meet accessibility
  requirements. (Architects should specify that the formwork for
  a concrete ramp be inspected prior to placing the concrete, in
  order to verify that the ramp will comply with accessibility
  requirements.)

- Sec. 1105.2.2 Toilet facilities.
  Requires the provision of accessible toilets and specifies the necessary quantity.

  Problem: The required number of accessible toilet facilities are not provided in a design.

  Problem: Toilet rooms are designed too small to provide the 5-foot turning radius required for wheelchair accessibility.

Chapter 23 Wood

- Sec. 2320 Conventional light-frame construction design procedures.
  Defines the types of buildings to which the section applies and specifies the detailing of the construction that is acceptable.

  Problem: Applying the details prescribed in the section to projects outside its applicability.

  Note: This section tends to apply to houses at the low end of the market which are not usually designed by architects using this code. More expensive houses with multistory windows, first floor exterior walls that are highly open, an open plan, and many re-entrant corners, might be structurally unstable if built by the guidelines of this section. Such houses should be designed based on engineering principles prior to the submission of plans since it is usually less expensive to do so than after the plans are rejected for a building permit.

Chapter 24 Glass and Glazing

- Sec. 2406.4 Hazardous locations.
  Lists locations requiring safety glazing.

  Problem: Failing to specify safety glazing where the glazing is within 24 inches from the vertical edge of the door and the bottom edge of the glazing is within 5 feet of the floor.

  Problem: Failing to specify safety glazing where the glazing is within 5 feet of the bottom or top of a stairway, and the bottom edge of the glazing is within 5 feet of the floor.

1996 BOCA® National Building Code

Chapter 10 Means of Egress

- Sec. 1010.4 Emergency escape and rescue.
  Requires an escape window of specified characteristics for sleeping rooms in certain occupancies and locations.

  Problem: Failure to meet the size or detailing requirements for the required escape window.

- Sec. 1014.0 Stairways.
  Requirements for size, detailing, materials, doors, and locks for stairways.

  Problem: Failure to meet all restrictions specified.

- Sec. 1017.4.1.2 Special locking arrangements.
  Restrictions on door locks in a means of egress for selected occupancies with sprinklers or fire detection systems.

  Problem: Failure to comply with all seven requirements related to the unlocking of such doors.

- Sec. 1021.0 Guards.
  Size and detailing requirements for guard rails to be provided along elevated walking surfaces.

  Problem: Failure to meet detailing requirements, especially the limitations on openings in the guards.

- Sec. 1022.0 Handrails.
  Size and detailing requirements for handrails.

  Problem: Failure to meet detailing requirements, especially graspability characteristics and termination configuration.

1997 SBCCI Standard Building Code

Chapter 7 Fire-resistant Materials and Construction

- Sec. 704.2 Interior wall and partition fire-separation requirements.
  Fire-separation requirements of interior walls.

  Problem: Failure to seal openings in fire-rated walls that meet the requirements necessary to maintain the fire-resistance rating of the wall.

Problem: Failure to provide the fire dampers necessary in ducts penetrating fire-resistance-rated walls.

Chapter 18 Foundations and Retaining Walls

- Sec. 1804.1.1 Footings and foundations.
  Requirements for the soil under foundations.

  Problem: Failure to place foundations on undisturbed soil or properly compacted fill.

- Sec. 1804.1.3 Footings and foundations.
  Specifies the required depth for foundations.

  Problem: Failure to place the bottom of foundations below the frost line, or at least 12 inches below finish grade.

Common Problems
In Working Drawings

Richard R. Faubion
Hospital Construction Inspector
Redlands, California

---

*The following guidelines respond to common errors and omissions
that hinder the approval of drawings by the building department
and/or affect constructability. Some are simple, some are complex,
but all can be pitfalls.*

ARCHITECTURAL ISSUES

Administrative

• Make sure all drawings are stamped and signed by the architect
and consultants.

• Indicate on drawings the codes being enforced by the local
jurisdiction. Identify the correct editions. Refer to the correct
governing agencies. Don't forget the local fire marshal's
requirements. Fire marshal requirements can usually be secured
from the local fire chief. Any fire department knows where to
locate these requirements. Many times when a set of plans is
submitted to the building department, a set of plans must also be
submitted to the fire department for review, or else the building
department will forward them. The fire marshal (or the fire chief)
will be interested in fire life-safety, and also in such things as fire
hydrants, size of fire lines, fire department access to the building,
and identification of the buildings. Most fire chiefs want big
numbers on buildings so they can find them when they are called
to the scene. When they respond to emergencies, such as heart
attacks, there is no fire or smoke to help identify the building.

• Indicate on the drawings items that are to be deferred for
approval, such as fire alarms. Often the fire alarm drawings are
not ready when the architectural working drawings are submitted
to the building department for approval. Some states require that

note be put on the cover stating that approval for these drawings is to be deferred.

- Indicate the type of building construction (Type I, II, III, IV, V, and subcategories where applicable).

- Identify all rooms.

Site
- Show property lines, assumed or actual. Provide civil drawings. For purposes of protecting against the spread of fire between buildings on the same lot, codes require the identification of imaginary property lines between the buildings. Certain code restrictions are based on distances measured to these lines.

Detailing
- Verify that the referenced details are applicable to the project and to the element generating the reference. Sometimes a referenced detail has nothing to do with the original item. Make sure that, when referring to details in a drawing note, the correct detail is indicated and that the detail can be found in the drawings at the location identified.

- Do not include details that do not apply to the project. Details that do not apply cause confusion. The ease with which details can be copied from a CAD detail library exacerbates this problem.

- Be consistent in the layout of details. In some projects, details are numbered beginning at the bottom of the sheet and proceeding right to left. Some details might be numbered starting at the top of the sheet and proceeding in any of the various directions. In the United States, reading is done left to right and top to bottom, therefore, it makes sense to follow this pattern in the numbering of details. But, regardless of the ordering system employed, use the same sequence on each sheet for layout of details.

- Make sure all legends and symbols are clear and readable.

- Do not show fire-rated doors in non-rated walls. This is unnecessary and a waste of money.

- Indicate the roof type and all components of the roof drainage system. The class of roof with regard to fire resistance (Class A,

B, or C) must be indicated and must comply with code and
ordinance requirements.

Dimensioning

- Provide dimensions that are clear, consistent in their format, and
  accurate. Dimensions must always refer to similar points in walls,
  i.e., either the finished face or the face of stud. The sums of
  parallel dimensions between the same points must be the same.

Schedules

- Verify the accuracy of door schedules. Indicate correct fire-
  resistance ratings. For instance, do not indicate a 90-degree door
  closure for a 180-degree door swing. Do not list doors with fire-
  protection ratings other than 20-minutes for 1-hour walls. Do not
  list other than 90-minute doors for 2-hour walls. Fire-protection
  ratings required for doors are clearly indicated in the model
  codes.

- Verify the accuracy of hardware schedules. Indicate the hardware
  types appropriate for the use of the door, i.e., office, classroom,
  corridor, etc. It is expensive when the contractor buys hardware
  that is discovered to be incorrect upon installation.

Code Requirements

- Verify that corridor widths and heights meet code minimums.
  For instance, hospital corridors must be at least 8 feet wide and 8
  feet high. The protrusion of soffits, sconces, and other objects
  into the space defined by these dimensions is limited by code.

- Do not permit dead-end corridors to be excessive in length.
  Dead-end corridors are a common problem. The length that a
  corridor can extend past an exit or an exit access is limited by
  code, if the corridor does not terminate at an exit.

- Provide door openings which meet required clear-width
  requirements. Panic hardware can no longer protrude into
  required clear width.

- Provide storage rooms over 100 sf with 1-hour fire-resistance-
  rated walls.

Elevations

- Indicate actual elevations of the finished floor and footings in
  relation to standard benchmarks, such as a plate in the street or

pin in a utility pole. Elevations related to finished grade are not accurate, given the lack of precision and consistency in the height of the adjacent landscape and paving.

- Provide complete interior elevation dimensions. Drawings of the walls showing casework, electrical outlets, fixtures, clocks, handrails, and so forth should indicate vertical dimensions above the finish floor and, where applicable, horizontal dimensions to a reference point such as a wall. Sometimes these dimensions conflict with another drawing, such as where electrical outlets are shown at one height on the architectural drawings and at another height on the electrical drawings.

Specifications
- Do not use specifications that are generic or obsolete. It causes confusion and wastes time to include specification entries that do not apply to the job or that refer to materials and components that are no longer available. Verify that every line item applies to the project, and incorporates current references.

ADA Requirements
- Reconcile detailing with ADA (Americans with Disabilities Act) requirements. Common violations include the incorrect clearance at the door latch side; incorrect or omitted heights of toilets and other fixtures; the required 5-foot diameter wheelchair turning clearance not provided; handicap showers incorrectly designed; incorrect or omitted dimensions of fixtures, seats, and drain location; incorrect height of handrails in corridors and stairs; requirements for handrail extensions at stair landings not met; incorrect or omitted curb cuts and ramps; incorrect parking provisions.

- Show accessible routes as defined by the ADA, if indicating them on the drawings is required by the local building department.

Fire Life Safety

Administrative
- Clearly indicate the fire-resistance ratings for walls with legible symbols. Symbols used to indicate the fire-resistance ratings of walls are especially difficult to understand as they tend to look similar. The various dashes and dots used to indicate 1-hour walls, 2-hour walls, etc., must have distinct identities and be easily distinguished from each other. It's difficult for a plan

checker to check corridor wall ratings, if they can't tell what the wall type is.

- Tabulate square footage of smoke compartments to verify code compliance.

- Verify that exit hardware is tested and approved by the appropriate agency, such as UL (Underwriters Laboratories) for the application specified.

- Show testing requirements in the specifications. This includes testing fire dampers, fire alarm systems, kitchen hood fire-suppression systems, and the pressure testing of piping.

Design and Detailing
- Provide approved design number and detail for rated walls, ceilings, roofs, and floor penetrations as developed by UL and other testing agencies.

- Indicate occupancy, area and smoke separation walls in correct locations and with correct fire-resistance ratings. Separations sometimes do not extend to the exterior walls and to the structure above as required by code. Doors and other penetrations in the separation must have the correct fire-protection ratings.

- Indicate locations of exit signs and verify that both normal and emergency power is provided to them. Some jurisdictions allow self-contained battery systems; check current codes.

Fire-Protection Systems
- Verify that mechanical drawings show fire/smoke damper locations. Dimension the location of the components used to activate the dampers to verify code compliance.

- Provide fire alarm drawings. This is an area of many errors including location, height, distances, and type of devices. Components requiring attention include smoke detectors, pull stations, strobes, chimes, power supplies, wiring, and audio-visual signals.

- Provide fire sprinkler drawings if required. This must be a system designed by a licensed fire-sprinkler design engineer. Many states require separate licenses for designers and installers. Do not leave the design to be done by a person who is not licensed to do so.

• Indicate locations of fire extinguisher cabinets and hose cabinets.

Kitchens
• Address the special requirements of kitchen areas. In kitchens, duct work may be required by fire code to be enclosed in 2-hour shaft, fire sprinklers might be required throughout, and under-hood dry chemical systems might be necessary. Local authorities may have special ordinances governing kitchen areas. The fire marshal or fire chief will typically inspect and witness tests of these systems. Deep fat fryers usually have special requirements. Fire-protection systems usually must deactivate power and gas to cooking devices. Equipment needs to be securely anchored. Check seismic requirements in this regard. The architect must be familiar with the local code requirements for these and other fire-protection issues.

Richard R. Faubion is a California Certified Hospital Construction Inspector. His background includes construction management, plan review, eight years with the Kaiser Permanente Facilities Design and Construction Department, Director of Plant Operations and Maintenance for major hospitals, and 22 years in U.S. Navy Engineering.

Avoiding Code Compliance Problems

Aaron J. Goodman
Mount Vernon, WA

Mr. Goodman is a former Plans Examiner for the city of Mount Vernon, Washington.

THE NEED FOR A PRESUBMITTAL REVIEW

A widely accepted strategy for identifying code compliance problems, prior to the finalization of a project's design and detailing, is to participate in a presubmittal review of the work at the permit office. This process is efficient for both the architect and the building department because it cuts the paperwork generated by deficiencies in the drawings by half, or more in some cases. Performing this review without charge by the city has proved to be cost effective and encourages architects to participate in it.

KEY ISSUES TO DISCUSS IN A PRESUBMITTAL REVIEW

The egress scheme.
Architects should prepare floor plans for the purpose of showing the intended exit paths in the building. This clear format of illustrating intention provides an opportunity for the building official to provide feedback, and for the architect to propose code-based justification for certain design decisions. This approach is particularly useful in business and mercantile occupancies and in assembly areas without stages (other than for business or education), and serving 300 or more people. Examples of buildings in particular need of egress drawings include large discount stores, grocery stores, churches, and large office buildings.

Location of smoke and fire dampers.
The mechanical engineer should attend the presubmittal meeting with the architect to discuss the duct penetration of fire-

resistance-rated ceilings and walls, and the locations of smoke and fire dampers. The building official should be able to preapprove the locations of the dampers, if a plan showing them is left with the office.

Past problems.
The architect should bring to the presubmittal meeting a list of field corrections from the previous project that were required by the building inspectors. The building official should provide a list of commonly required field corrections. The reoccurrence of problems, similar to those of the past, tends to diminish because discussion of the reasoning behind the field corrections clarifies the interpretation of the code which can be anticipated in current and future work.

CITATION OF SPECIFIC STANDARDS IN DOCUMENTS

Field corrections.
Indicate by agency and number the approved assembly used to comply with fire-protection (or other) requirements. Underwriters Laboratories, the Gypsum Association, the various model code groups, and other testing and quality control agencies have specific requirements for assemblies that meet various standards required in the code. These requirements, as provided in literature from the agencies, often include details. By being specific in the drawings and specifications regarding the exact assembly which is required from a specific agency, confusion in the field and field corrections can be avoided.

Aaron J. Goodman resides in Mount Vernon, WA. He is a Certified Building Official, Building Plans Examiner, and Building Inspector. Mr. Goodman has worked in county and city jurisdictions for more than 11 years, with a total of 22 years in the field of construction. He holds a Bachelors Degree in Business Administration and is currently working as a Cost Estimator for a northwest Washington general contractor.

Code Compliance Problems In Architectural Working Drawings

Harwood W. Loomis, AIA
Consulting Architect
Woodbridge, Connecticut

The following are common major problems found in architectural working drawings submitted for building permits.

The system of egress is insufficient in number, capacity, or distribution.

- An insufficient number of exits occurs most often in assembly occupancies, since most other use groups do not have large enough occupant loads to require more than two (possibly three) exits based solely on occupant load.

- An insufficient capacity of exits can occur in any occupancy classification, since many architects forget that stairs must be 50% wider than doors, corridors, or ramps to accommodate an equal capacity. It is common to find a designer basing his or her exit capacity on the door sizes, only to find that the limiting factor is not the doors but the aggregate stair widths.

- Inadequate distribution of exits is most often a problem in irregular plan low-rise buildings such as schools. In a typical medium- to high-rise office building, the floor plan is fairly uniform from floor to floor, and egress travel distances are usually easily controlled. In low-rise buildings that tend to spread out, it is easy to lose track of the egress travel distance from one or more portions of the building. This results in isolated pockets where egress is deficient because of excessive exit-access travel distance.

- Designers often measure travel distance to an exit along a diagonal path, forgetting that codes require exit-access distance to be measured along the actual path of egress travel. It is usually impossible to walk through a furnished room or space on a straight diagonal. Therefore, code officials are taught to measure travel along a rectilinear path with square corners where the path of travel changes direction.

The building is too large for the type of construction.

- Chapter 5 of the various building codes limits building height and floor area based on the type of construction as defined in Chapter 6.

The design fails to meet accessibility requirements.

- The worst accessibility problems are maneuvering clearances at doors and landings, and toilet accommodations. Also, in renovation work particularly, the fact that accessibility standards define "accessible route" as including the toilet facilities, which serve the accessible space, is a concept that many designers overlook.

- Another common problem is failure to provide for areas of refuge, or "areas of rescue assistance," in ADAAG (Americans with Disabilities Act Accessibility Guidelines) terminology. For example, the 1996 and 1999 editions of the BOCA® *National Building Code* differ subtly from ADAAG requirements. Both the ADAAG and all of the national model building codes agree that, when a space is required to be accessible, accessible means of egress must be provided from the accessible portion or portions of the building. With respect to stairs, designation as an accessible means of egress might require special provisions.

    According to the ADAAG and the 1996 and 1999 editions of the BOCA® *National Building Code*, in order to be considered an accessible means of egress, a stair must be either provided with an adjacent area of refuge (a safe area where a person in a wheelchair can await rescue by emergency personnel), or incorporate such an area of refuge within the exit stair enclosure itself. However, the ADAAG specifically requires that stairs are not part of an accessible route, except when they connect floors not served by an elevator. The ADAAG also states that areas of rescue assistance are not required in fully sprinklered buildings.

    Using the 1996 and 1999 BOCA® *National Building Codes* as examples for building code requirements, the criteria are different from the ADAAG requirements. A stair is considered part of an accessible means of egress. Where a stair comprises part of an accessible means of egress, the stair must be provided with, or incorporate an area of, refuge, and the stair must have a minimum clear width between handrails of 48 inches. This is to facilitate emergency personnel carrying a wheelchair down the stairway. An exception states that the area of refuge and the 48-inch clear width are not required in a fully sprinklered building. Although the functional requirements are essentially the same, it must be recognized that a stair is not part of an accessible means of egress under the ADAAG, although it is part of an accessible means of egress under the building codes.

The ADAAG does not address any stair which is not part of an accessible route. According to the national model building codes and the NFPA *101 Life Safety Code*, however, all stairways are regulated by the same dimensional criteria, irrespective of whether or not they are exit stairs. In the model codes, stairways are part of an accessible route even in buildings and between levels which are served by an elevator. This makes sense. A person who is mobility-impaired, but not confined to an elevator, should be able to use the stairs to exit a building without having to wait for an elevator or negotiating an uncomfortably steep stair.

The following are also problems found in architectural working drawings which might cause a delay in issuing the building permit.

The of numbers of toilet fixtures is insufficient.
- This is not confined to accessible fixtures. In most occupancies, the actual (projected) occupant load is usually lower than the occupant load calculated in accordance with the floor area ratios called for under the codes. The codes are clear that the building must be designed for the calculated occupant load or the actual occupant load, whichever is greater. Many designers remember this in designing for exits but forget that the occupant load used to design exits also applies to establishing the required number of plumbing fixtures.

Basic code-related information provided on the drawings is insufficient.
- Information must be provided to define for the plan reviewer the parameters to use in the review. Such information might

include: type of construction; use group; locations of rated walls; occupant count and method used to determine occupant count; name and edition of code with which the plans comply; presence or absence of sprinklers; area of building; and height of building, in feet and stories.

Drawings with this information tend to fare better in the review process than those without it or those with the information scattered throughout the documents. The data should be in a concise table near the front of the set.

The working drawings lack clarity.

- Lack of clarity in the documents is a big issue. Often, the information is in the documents somewhere, but it isn't where one might expect to find it, and the documents are not internally cross-referenced in a way that makes it easy to find code-required information.

  To avoid this problem, someone in the architectural firm or an outsider such as a consultant, who is not involved in the project, should do a trial code review midway through the project. The reviewer must not be given any background information other than that which is in the documents. If the reviewer has to ask a lot of questions to establish the basic parameters for review, the code official will have the same problems. This indicates that the drawings are either incomplete or badly organized and/or coordinated.

The following observations address general issues in code compliance and plan reviews.

Code violations generated by aesthetic demands.

- Fire stairs are a common example of a conflict between aesthetic goals and code limitations. The designer might want a stair to be a glazed enclosure, either for aesthetics or even for security. An exit stair must be enclosed in either 1-hour or 2-hour construction. Plain glass won't provide the required rating. Wired glass won't provide it because it is acceptable only as an opening protective in limited size openings. Even certain proprietary products, such as Fire-Lite ™, don't provide the required fire-resistance rating, because these products have been tested only as an opening protective (i.e., as a clear substitute for wired glass) and not as a fire-resistance-rated wall assembly. But a designer might balk at spending the extra money for one of the newer, hi-tech ceramic glass products that has been tested as a rated fire-separation assembly. The result might be a failure to achieve the issue of a building permit on the first submission due to a glazing detail at the fire stair that is in violation of code requirements.

- An attempt to use an open stair as a required means of egress is sometimes a problem.

- The omission of fireproofing, where it is required on exposed structural members, is a problem on occasion.

Where a culture of mutual antagonism exists between the architect and the building department, problems are exacerbated.

- Architects should avoid treating code officials with mistrust. They are licensed by the state in the interest of protecting the public safety, health, and welfare, the same basis on which architects are licensed. They are part of the system of checks and balances that is intended to ensure safety in buildings. While the code officials should not be expected to design corrections for the errors in design or detailing made by architects, it is much easier to agree on corrections if the building officials are not blamed for the problem. The plan review process will proceed more smoothly and with more acceptable results if the architect integrates code requirements into the building design before it is finalized.

Harwood W. Loomis, AIA, is an architect and licensed building official in Connecticut. He is also licensed as an architect in California and Maine, and has been practicing architecture for more than 25 years. Mr. Loomis was a founding member of the Building Performance and Regulations Commission of the Connecticut chapter of the AIA, and has served as Chair of the commission. He is a member of BOCA® and ICBO, and he served three terms as President of BOCA® Professional Chapter Number 1 (Connecticut). Mr. Loomis is a member of the New England Building Code Association, of which he is a past President, and he is also a member of the Connecticut Building Officials' Association.

Problems in Code Compliance

Daniel F. Kaiser
Senior Building Inspector
City of Corona, California

Accessibility

- Building design and detailing commonly fail to meet disabled access requirements, including those for the wheelchair-bound as well as for sight and hearing impaired persons.

- Decorative items (pictures, ornate lighting fixtures, artwork) often project into paths of travel beyond that permitted for disabled access.

Means of egress

- Exit paths often fail to meet code requirements with regard to location and size.

- Door swings into the exit path of travel often violate code restrictions.

Guardrails

- Decorative guardrail designs often do not meet code requirements.

Building services

- Access to plumbing, HVAC, and electrical systems for maintenance is often inadequate.

- Adequate combustion air for fuel-burning appliances is rarely provided.

Fire and smoke protection

- Decorative wall and ceiling finish materials often exceed the minimum developed smoke and flame spread ratings allowed by code.

*The following problems in drawings submitted to the building
department hinder or prevent verification of code compliance and
can slow the process or require resubmission.*

Drawing problems

- Penetrations of membrane surfaces and penetrations entirely
  through fire-rated assemblies are rarely detailed adequately.

- Where seismic requirements apply, the proper attachment of the
  plumbing, electrical, and mechanical systems is often lacking in
  the required details.

- Shaft construction is often not adequately detailed.

- Detailing for fire-rated protection where required for structural
  members is sometimes omitted.

- Cross-referencing of details and the drawings to which they relate
  is often inadequate.

- General notes, which are taken from previous projects,
  sometimes do not apply to the current work and are, therefore,
  confusing.

- Most drawing sets contain outdated details from previous
  projects, which obstruct the review process.

Daniel F. Kaiser is a senior building inspector for the City of Carona,
California. He has also served as building inspector for the cities of
Calabasas and Rialto in California. He has multiple certifications
including Certified Building Official and Certified Plans Examiner.
His inspector certifications include the categories of building,
mechanical, plumbing, accessibility/usability, reinforced concrete,
spray-applied fireproofing, fire code, and others. He maintains
numerous professional memberships including that of the
International Conference of Building Officials (ICBO), National Fire
Protection Association (NFPA), International Association of
Plumbing and Mechanical Officials (IAPMO), International
Association of Electrical Inspectors (IAEI) and others.

Minimizing Code Compliance Problems

The following recommendations are based on comments from code officials in Uniform Building Code jurisdictions but which apply to any region of the United States.

- Contact the code authority having jurisdiction over the project (usually the city building department) early in the design concept stage. Ask this code official to help identify potential areas of code conflict in the current project and discuss possible solutions. Take notes during the meeting and provide a copy to the code official. If there is a disagreement about the meaning of a section, find out who has the authority to make official interpretations.

- Find out if there is an appeals process and how it works. Often these areas of conflict are not identified until late in the design process, making changes and adjustments more difficult.

- Code interpretations and local amendments can vary from city to city. Don't assume that all jurisdictions are the same even if they have adopted the same codes.

Error-prone chapters

- Review the issues related to handicapped accessibility (Chapter 11) because this is an area which commonly has errors. Although most agencies normally do not enforce the ADAAG, the building code incorporates similar requirements and might be more restrictive than the federal law in some cases.

- Review the issues related to the use of the space, and occupancy identification (Chapter 3). This is another common problem area. Errors in this realm have broad ramifications because many code requirements are based on the occupancy designation.

Contractors
and
Working Drawings

The desire for a trouble-free process for constructing a building is universal among architects, contractors, and owners. Given this common goal, it is logical to assume that architects and contractors would collaborate during the production of working drawings in order to make them more realistic and less vague. Where this occurs the building process can be expected to be smoother with fewer misunderstandings and unexpected expenses for all parties involved. It is these advantages of early and continuous communication between architect and builder, therefore, which have spawned the design-build industry (see Chapter 12) which continues to grow in popularity.

As an introduction to what can be learned about working drawings by talking to contractors, this chapter provides comments from builders throughout the United States. Dozens of general and subcontracting firms were asked to identify the major problems with architects' working drawings, as well as the aspects that work best. (The subcontractors queried included those from two key trades, roofing and fire protection.) Due to the relationship between specifications and working drawings, many of their comments on specifications are also included.

The surveys indicated that the architects' working drawings are thought to be generally too vague. The question as to whether or not it is possible to have too many details was also answered. Apparently, there are never enough details in working drawings for nonresidential work. In residential work, there is a trend toward underdetailing so as to give the builder freedom to construct standard details in an economical way. However, the following study of working drawings is focused on nonresidential construction, and the consensus was that, as a rule, more details are needed.

Another common complaint about working drawings is CAD related. Due to the ease with which it is possible to insert a detail into a drawing from a CAD library of details, many details are included which do not pertain to the project. This disrupts the estimating process and drives up the cost of the building. For instance, bids might include coverage for installing details which do not exist, or they might include increases in the builder's overhead due to the unnecessary time spent on each verification of a detail's relevancy. The same problems exist in the use of irrelevant specifications for the same computer-based reason. Consequently, contractors generally agree that uncertainty in the drawings increases the amount of the contractor's bid.

Survey Results from "Architectural Working Drawings: Problems and Suggestions"

A survey soliciting responses from contractors to 5 questions about working drawings was conducted. The questions and responses are listed below.

1. Of project bids coming in over budget, approximately what percent of these are due to inadequacies of architectural working drawing information (as opposed to expensive materials and assemblies)?

<u>Average response</u>
   10–20% of project bids coming in over budget are due to inadequacies of architectural working drawing information.

<u>Contractors' comments</u>
- Typically there is confusion regarding the division between plumbing and mechanical work. This confusion tends to increase bids by both subcontractors.

- Except for design-build work, nearly every project has gone over budget as a result of working drawing errors and deficiencies.

- Poor working drawings can force bids to be unnecessarily high, although a lack of sufficient details in the drawings, regarding project requirements, can result in a bid that is too low. In particular, unintended vagueness in the drawings can result in interpretations by the contractor which lead to a bid that is different from the costs projected by the architect. In these cases, it is especially important that the architectural and engineering cost projections be accurate so that comparisons can be made between them and the bid in order to discover the discrepancies prior to committing to a contract.

- Working drawings that are not clear or have missing details cause bids to be more conservative and result in driving up the cost of the construction.

- Vague and incomplete architectural working drawings result in a project bid which is based on the contractor's understanding of the requirements. But, after construction begins and the architect clarifies the intention of the drawings, a more expensive version of the project is required to be built by the contractor. These added costs are not recoupable and encourage subsequent bids to be higher than might otherwise be necessary.

- Project documents contain excessive specifications and details which are not specific to the project. These drive up the bid because they require that a cost be assigned to them in order to be sure that no required element is omitted from the estimate.

2. Approximately what percent of change orders are due to inadequate architectural working drawing information?

Average response

40–50% of change orders are due to inadequate architectural working drawing information.

Contractor comments

- Often the plans do not show mechanical rooms that are large enough for the equipment, and/or they show stairways that are not large enough to meet code requirements.

- Change orders tend to be generated by the owner's changes or are the result of conditions that are unforeseen.

- Because it is difficult to secure money from the owner to cover errors and omissions in the drawings, the architect will often approve fewer change orders than the contractor believes are necessary.

- Approximately half of the change orders generated on a project are due to the owner's changes, the other half result from inadequate working drawings.

- The quality of working drawings has declined during the last 10 to 15 years and continues to deteriorate.

- The inadequacies in a set of working drawings are revealed by change orders.

3. Of the change orders which increase cost unnecessarily, what percent are due to a lack of detail or lack of working drawing information?

Average response

40–50% of the change orders which increase cost unnecessarily are due to a lack of detail or lack of working drawing information.

Contractor comments

- "Unnecessarily" is a relative term. In most cases, adequate working drawing information would have caused the cost of a potential change order to have been included in the original bid. The misrepresentation of the actual cost of a project, which results from inadequate working drawings, is a mis-service to the owner.

- Change orders are usually denied by the architect, who claims that the contractor should have understood the drawings or clarified the requirements before bidding.

- Change orders are usually due to a lack of details in the working drawings, inaccurate field dimensions, or errors in drawings for existing construction and which are incorporated into drawings for additions and renovations.

- The cost of construction, which is unnecessarily increased by change orders, would be higher than it is except for the fact that contractors help identify potential problems and contribute solutions to hold down the cost of solutions.

4. Prioritize the list of inadequacies of architectural working drawing information with "1" being the greatest problem, "9" being the smallest problem, and "0" being an insignificant problem.

(The inadequacies are listed in order of greatest to smallest problem, according to the average response given by the survey participants.)

1. Information missing
2. Information not clear
3. Vagueness
4. Information confusing
5. Duplicated information did not match
6. Information difficult to use
7. Dimensions incorrect
8. Format difficult to use
9. Inefficient dimensions

Contractor comments

- The biggest problems in architectural working drawings are that they lack necessary information and they lack correct information. Without enough information, the contractor must make assumptions regarding the nature of a requirement and, in order to remain competitive, bids the cheapest accommodation. This does not assure that the available budget will be adequate to provide the necessary quality, should the architect have a different and more expensive solution in mind.

- Vagueness and incorrect dimensions are the two biggest problems in working drawings because these are difficult to correct during the bid phase. The other items on the survey list should be identified during the bid process.

- Architects and draftspersons are not learning the fundamentals of preparing working drawings.

- The most serious problems result when duplicated information in the drawings do not match.

- A trend toward the use of keynotes increases the likelihood that the contractor will miss information during bidding.

- A major problem is that, too often, the architectural drawings do not agree with related information on the mechanical, electrical, structural, site, and food service, etc., drawings.

- On remodeling projects, problems result from the lack of field verification of conditions shown on the drawings. Also, about half of the time, required details are missing.

- The CSI (Construction Specifications Institute) format is very helpful for organizing and clarifying information. It is recommended that architects continue to use it.

5. What impact has the increased use of CAD for architectural working drawings had on the cost of construction?

Response

    69% believe that the impact on construction costs is insignificant.

    23% believe that construction costs are increased.

    8% believe that construction costs are decreased.

Contractor comments

- As when they were done by hand, working drawings created with CAD are only as good as the architect who draws them.

- The failure of CAD operators to put enough information on the drawings has increased costs because of the number of change orders required to remedy the deficiency. However, because shop drawing submittals can be generated from the original drawing files, CAD has reduced costs in this area.

- CAD working drawings are much clearer and easier to read in the field.

- The biggest obstacle to the production of better working drawings is that the architectural fees are too low to support the extra time required to produce more complete and better reviewed drawings. This fact must be conveyed to owners.

- Changes to hand-drawn working drawings required an extensive thought process, consequently, the related information was coordinated. Changes made in CAD are easier and faster to make, and, therefore, often result in the failure to consider the implications for related information elsewhere in the drawings.

- Today, CAD-produced construction documents lack the necessary final review for consistency, errors, and omissions.

- CAD has caused architects to use more typical details in a set of working drawings but there are still not enough details describing conditions that are not typical.

- The biggest problems result from working drawing preparation that is done too quickly and, thus, lacks the necessary coordination between drawings.

Contractors' Views of Architects' Construction Documents

Comments on architects' working drawings and specifications were solicited from contractors in order to determine where the problem areas are. This section lists contractors' responses including problems and recommendations. Similar comments from additional contractors are listed as an indication of the sentiment in the industry.

Training for architects

- Before being licensed, architectural interns should be required to spend two years in the construction industry, either in office or field work. This would help them learn how to prepare working drawings that are both buildable and within budget, two things which are much needed today.

- Architectural programs need to teach the basics of construction, not just the theory, so that students know how each material works with the other. For instance, they should know how steel works with masonry and how concrete masonry works with clay masonry in a range of environments, such as, from Michigan to Oklahoma. This will help architects prepare working drawings that are more realistic than some that are produced now.

- Architectural educators must have field experience, either in a construction or architectural capacity so as to be able to prepare graduates who can produce working drawings that are complete and realistic. The inadequacies of working drawings distributed for bids suggest that many educators have never had practical experience. This would explain why these drawings show detailing that is unnecessarily costly and difficult to build.

- In the "old days," a fledgling architect would be assigned to the jobsite to monitor field progress as a member of the contract administration. There, he or she would acquire a first-hand knowledge of how to convert product descriptions and drawings into a physical structure. Sadly, contract administration by the architect and by that apprenticeship program has evolved away from the "design" group because of a subrogation of supervisory responsibilities to authorities conducting special inspections and municipal inspections. Today's architect sorely lacks the perspective of the construction side of the industry.

- Working drawings would be improved if architects had more experience with construction. The architect is not only responsible for the design in general, but also for the workability and code compliance of the design. To this end, designers implicitly warrant that they have exercised diligence, competence, skill, and good judgment throughout the design process and contract preparation.[1] They further warrant this through their professional stamp, insurance, and the contract with the owner. If the diligence, competence, skill, and good judgment of the architect are inadequate for the delivery of sufficient working drawings, then perhaps greater involvement in the construction of the project through the older version of jobsite contract administration should be revived.

- An opportunity for the architect to achieve more construction-related experience is provided by recent changes in the *1997 Uniform Building Code*, 1701 Special Inspections. This section withdraws responsibility for special inspections from the contractor, and specifically assigns it to the owner (and, thus, to the designer). It is hoped that the designers will step in and completely take over this process, because if a new Special Inspection industry emerges to assume jobsite quality control, the designers will lose this perfect apprenticeship opportunity, and the inspectors will become the experts. In that case, the owners will never know who to believe, and the courts will have to settle disagreements.

Document review
- A major problem in the process of producing a building occurs when the owner imposes a rigorous schedule requiring the architect to issue working drawings that are not finished, and are not reviewed, either for missing information or inconsistencies. This causes problems during the bidding process and results in increased costs for the contractor, the architect, and the owner.

- Never issue a revised drawing without identifying the revision date. Use "clouds" or notes to describe the revision, and distinguish it from detailing which has not been revised.

- Always have a person not familiar with the project review the drawings before the final printing for bidding.

Thoroughness
- Detail all conditions that vary from the norm, as well as all miscellaneous conditions, in order to minimize both the number of contractor requests for information (RFIs; see Appendix C.) and the requests for clarifications (RFCs). The items below are summaries of a few problems requiring additional information from architects because the drawings and specifications did not contain enough information, or were not compatible with each other:

  o The materials specified for the air conditioning ductwork and insulation do not match that which are called for in the drawings.

  o The specified concrete mix designs and water/cement ratios do not match those noted on the drawings.

  o The concrete fibermesh and/or colored concrete indicated on the drawings are not included in the specifications.

  o The concrete fibermesh and colored concrete included in the specification are not shown on the drawings.

  o The waterproofing of hard tile floors indicated under Section 7 of the specifications is not always compatible with the hard tile application required in the drawings.

  o Details and clarification of installation requirements are required for owner-furnished equipment and materials.

  o In Section 8710–Finish Hardware of the specifications, some cabinet harware is not included.

- Do not assume that expectations will be met without providing detailed graphic and written information as to requirements and goals.

- Provide sections for all walls.

- Show details of all elements to be constructed.

- Verify that all of the technical and engineering designs required for a project are provided in the drawings. Unfortunately, the trend is to leave much engineering design to be accomplished by the contractor. This causes bids to be based on planned work which is dissimilar in scope and quality. It also stresses relationships between parties to the contract when expectations are not fulfilled during construction.

- Indicate reference elevations of all structural components.

Project strategy
- Provide at least 15 sets of working drawings to the contractor for any project of any size.

- Design based on sound construction practices. Don't sacrifice quality for aesthetic goals.

- Architects who make mistakes in the design or construction should not expect the general contractor to cover or pay for those mistakes. Admit the mistake and contribute to it's resolution.

- A better building will be produced if the architect views the general contractor as an ally rather than as an adversary.

Specification strategy
- FOIC ("furnished by owner and installed by contractor") items are common in building construction. Where these items are required, the architect should supply the vendors' installation instructions within the specifications. This is necessary because there are many items, such as wall coverings, that require special wall priming or installation procedures on which a subcontractor can not bid without the instructions.

Specification relevancy
- Construction documents are commonly found to be incomplete, with "canned" specifications that include many sections which are irrelevant to the project. Architects need to understand that cost is added to a project where the documents are improperly prepared.

- Verify that construction documents include only products and components that are currently available. It is common to see, in drawings and specifications, requirements for items that have not been in use for more than 20 years.

- Verify that all specified products are available and are not outdated or discontinued.

- Verify that all portions of the specifications are applicable to the current project, and not generic or directed to work from a previous project.

Working drawing strategy
- Working drawings must be clear, complete, concise, and comprehensible. Keep in mind that the architectural documents have to be understood without excessive research by dozens of people from all segments of the industry, including the owner. When working drawings aren't understood, they will surely be argued in the courtroom.

- Provide a separate working drawing sheet for each type of work. Do not provide multiple "overlays" on one sheet, such as overlaying a furniture plan onto a dimensioned floor plan.

- Provide details in the working drawings for all configurations of the materials and components required. Do not rely on descriptions in the specifications in lieu of details.

- Use full-size working drawing sheets.

- On the same plan sheet, show the demolition requirements and the new construction in the demolition area.

Detailing strategy
- Owners' loss of faith in architects' abilities is the catalyst for the design-build movement. The resulting trend is for a construction manager to hire an architect simply as a draftsperson to prepare working drawings under close supervision so that the constructability of the project within budget can be assured.

- If it is desired to have fire sprinkler heads centered in ceiling panels, require it in the specifications. Otherwise, do not assume that the subcontractor will center them. Centering the heads increases the cost of the system, so this requirement must be known to the contractor prior to bidding.

- Design and draft buildings comprehensively. For instance, prepare a cabinet detail with the understanding that it relates to the wall finish, which relates to the mechanical and electrical rough-in and trim out, which relates to the framing, which relates to the steel, which relates to the masonry, which relates to the concrete, and so on. Accommodate, in the detailing, the technical and installation-sequence demands of all the elements.

• Always use materials that are available locally.

Contractor input

• When designing or detailing building elements about which little is known, architects should consult people who can determine whether or not it can be built. It should not be assumed that because it can be drawn, it can be constructed. (Fig. 7–1.)

• Be open to recommendations from tradespeople (laborers, masons, operators, etc.) because many have extensive practical knowledge of detailing configurations and installation procedures that is buildable and cost effective.

• Do not require a contractor to be the first person ever to build an element in a particular way.

• Ask contractors how they have built a particular element before. They are willing to share ideas if asked.

• Use product information and drawings from manufacturers and suppliers when developing details and specifications. Seek the advice of people experienced in the installation of such products.

Coordination

• From the contractor's viewpoint, the majority of document problems arise from a lack of coordination among design teams. Quality control begins with the design, and when the parts and pieces do not fit, it causes a lot of turmoil. By the time the problem is solved, many egos have been bruised and the loser is the owner, who has to pay for duplicated work and delays.

• The architectural working drawings might show a water fountain, hose bibb, or an item requiring either plumbing and/or electrical service. But the mechanical, plumbing, or electrical drawings might not have water service or an electrical circuit shown for these items. In this case, even though the architectural drawings cearly identify such an item, a subcontractor will submit a change order because the engineering drawings did not specifically call out the item. To prevent such change orders, the

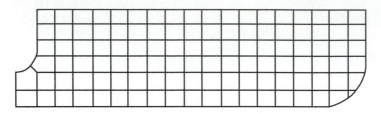

Paving "A"

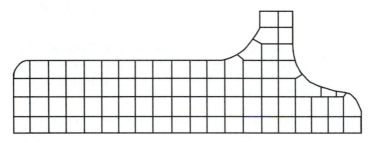

Paving "B"

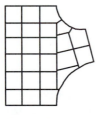

Paving "C"

Paving "D"

Paving "E"

Fig. 7–1. Paving plans. This is an example of a project documents not being compatible with the practical demands of construction. In this case, the specifications called for a slipform paver to produce the paving on the project. The paving as shown in the drawings is not all compatible with this process. Paving "A" and "B" can be done with the slipform paver. The other configurations would not be cost effective by this process. Paving "E" is particularly inappropriate for this machine due to its very small size. This problem could have been avoided if the architect had requested input from the contractor on the best method of installing the paving prior to finalizing the construction documents.

architect should cross check his or her drawings with those of the consultants. Also, the subcontractor should be held responsible for bidding the work regardless of where it is shown in a set of working drawings, rather than limit their responsibility to the sheets normally within the scope of their trade.

- Never put consultants' work (structural, mechanical, electrical, interior design, audio/visual, etc.) into the construction documents without reviewing it. If the architect is not clear as to the intent of the consultants' drawings, then the implementation of the drawings cannot be coordinated and the drawings are vulnerable to conflicts with the other consultants' designs.

- Indicate whether the mechanical contractor or the electrical contractor is responsible for running the low-voltage wire to the thermostats. Confusion over who is to do this occurs whenever it is not assigned in the specifications.

- On the mechanical and electrical working drawing sheets, refer the contractor to any notes pertaining to them which occur on other sheets, such as the structural sheets. Often the mechanical and electrical contractors will see only their respective sheets when bidding, and they will miss miscellaneous notes in other parts of the working drawings.

Site information
- For sitework, indicate both existing and new grades on the same plan. Show the scale of the drawing and the north arrow on *every* plan sheet.

- Using dimensions, define the limits of surfacing and landscape areas.

- Provide details of all structures, surfaces, and engineered designs.

- Include geotechnical information in the working drawings.

Dimensioning
- Do not use architectural dimensioning (feet and inches) or architectural elevation notation (such as 100.0) on civil plan sheets. Do not use architectural scales (such as 1/8" = 1'- 0") on civil plan sheets.

- Provide ample dimensions and verify that they are accurate.

- Do *not* mix metric and imperial units on the same drawing.

- Rough-in dimensions, such as for an overhead door on a wood strucrure, must have 3 inches added for liners and true plumb framing. For instance, it is common for a garage door opening to be dimensioned on the footer and foundation plans as 16 feet between blocks, although this should be 16'-3". Errors of this type are normally caught during the preconstruction review but might be missed by a new builder.

- Dimension to the centerline of interior partitions and to the top of the outside face of the foundation for exterior walls. In some areas this is called the "building line," and the outside face of a brick veneer is the "brick line." Confusion occurs where dimensions run to both the "building line" and the "brick line" in the same set of drawings.

Bidding strategy

- Where the bids for a project are over the budget, negotiate with the lowest bidder to find changes which can be made that will lower total cost, rather than revise and re-bid the work.

- Notify all participants of the bid results promptly after bidding is concluded. Always reveal the amounts of all bids.

- When issuing addenda to construction documents that have been distributed for bidding, provide adequate time for proper consideration of the changes prior to the bid date. Do not issue addenda on the same day as bids are due.

- Do not require that the manufacturers or suppliers, which are to be used by the contractor, be reported as part of the bid package. Instead, require that they be identified by the successful bidder within 24 hours after being selected.

Note
[1]Andrew M. Civitell, Jr., *Contractor's Guide to Change Orders* (Upper Saddle River, NJ: Prentice-Hall, Inc.,1987), p. 34.

Recommendations for Architectural Working Drawings

Wintford Taylor III, President
William Taylor & Co., Inc. General Contractors

Format

- Use as small of a drawing sheet size as possible, but keep floor plan scales at least 1/8" = 1'-0" or larger. Sheet sizes in excess of 24" x 36" are difficult and cumbersome to manage in field conditions.

- Limit floor plan scales to 1/8", 1/4", or 3/8". Scales of 1/16" are too small to read and scales of 3/16" and 5/16" are not usually found on standard architectural scales used for manual quantity take-off in the estimating phase.

- Use detail books in lieu of placing the architectural details on the full-size sheets. Detail books should be on 8-1/2" x 11" pages in order to allow details to be easily faxed. Detail books should be bound with plastic ring binders and covers.

- With the advent of CAD drafting, it is very handy to have a half-size set of drawings for use in the field. Although the details are not as readable, the intent of the drawings remains intact.

- Room finish schedules <u>including ceiling heights </u>should be located on the floor plan drawing, as close to the details as possible, or in a separate detail book in order to avoid searching for the finish schedule.

- Alternates to the base bid should be limited to one single major alternate (involving change in scope with multiple crafts) and a small number of minor alternates (comparison of different type or quality of materials or equipment). The drawings and specifications must exactly describe the scope and details of such alternative bids and their ramifications should be separately placed in each section of the relevant specifications.

Keynotes

- Do not use <u>keynotes</u>. Drawings without the keynote system are easier to read and understand than the keynote-style drawings.

- If keynotes are used on elevations and sections within a drawing, provide a keynote legend on <u>each</u> and <u>every</u> page the keynotes are used.

- If keynotes are used, keep the numbers on the keynotes consistent from sheet to sheet in the drawings, i.e., #10 = brick no matter on which sheet it appears.

- If keynotes are used, use a simple single or duplicate numbering system (1, 2, 3 . . . 50, 51 . . .) in lieu of tying the keynote numbers to the specification section. The multidigit system is fine in specifications but encourages errors in reading the keynote number accurately.

Specifications

- Always specify the desired trade to install the control wiring for HVAC equipment. Much confusion can occur between the electrical contractor and mechanical contractor as to who is responsible for furnishing and installing control wiring and other miscellaneous wiring.

- When using MASTERSPEC® carefully edit specifications to avoid including a section of the specs that does not exist or which was not desired in a particular job.

Content

- Doors should be numbered individually versus numbering them as groups of door types. This allows all parties to be able to describe a door unit using a number instead of "the type 3 door on the south end of hall 100." This also reduces punch list confusion.

- If the design professional is using a number of interior wooden trims or moldings, an elevation and typical section of the wall showing details would be helpful.

Completeness

- Architects and design professionals should resist the owner rushing them to have the plans issued for bidding before the drawings are complete. A large number of addenda only serves to drive up the cost of construction by causing uneasiness in the contractor's submission of bids for the work.

William Taylor & Co., Inc. General Contractors was founded in 1954 by William W. Taylor, Jr. and operated as a sole proprietorship from 1954 to 1981. William Taylor was joined by Ford Taylor in 1982, and the company operated as a partnership until 1991, when it was incorporated. The company has extensive experience in commercial and light industrial construction, including rigid-frame metal buildings and tilt wall concrete construction. General construction projects have included apartment and motel construction, nursing homes, warehouses, office buildings, and commercial centers. The company concentrates on projects of up to three stories in height with budgets of up to ten million dollars. Company management has developed a strong team of highly skilled and loyal employees and because of this, it has worked closely with owners, architects, and engineers, developing a reputation for attention to detail and for dedication to quality construction.

Roofing Contractors' Views of Construction Documents

Comments on architects' working drawings and specifications were solicited from roofing contractors in order to determine where the problem areas are. This section lists contractors' responses including problems and recommendations.

Working drawing strategy
- Where possible, provide all of the roof details on one or two adjacent sheets.

- A birds-eye perspective is useful in describing a roof which has numerous changes and elements, such as hips, dormers, and bays.

- Verify that all skylights and vents are included because they are sometimes omitted from the drawings.

- Always include a roof plan in the working drawings.

- Provide wall sections at exterior walls and reference their locations on the roof plan.

- Provide sections at changes in roof elevation and reference them on the roof plan. This is necessary because it affects the amount of flashing to be used and the contractor must know the configuration of the flashing.

- Show details of every condition that affects the roof, and reference the details on the roof plan. Such details should include air conditioning units, vents, exhaust fans, curbs, etc.

Detailing strategy
- On the roof plan, indicate the slope of the roof surface in inches per foot, and report how the slope is achieved. If the slope is structural, the tendency is to omit this information from the roof plan, but it takes time for the person preparing a bid to examine

the structural drawings to verify that it is sloped. If the roof slope is achieved by tapered insulation, its location must be indicated on the roof plan since the roofing contractor is responsible for installing it. Identifying the location of tapered insulation is particularly important where the overall slope of the roof is achieved by a slope of the structure and where crickets are formed by tapered insulation. If the tapered insulation is indicated only in a detail and not on the roof plan, it might be missed during bidding.

- In drawings, provide the following quantities applicable to roofs:
  ○ The square footage of the roof at each pitch.
  ○ The length of valleys in feet.
  ○ The size and length of facia and trim board on rakes and eaves.
  ○ Using dimensions, indicate the location of roof vents (hat type) or the length of the ridge vent, in feet.

- Drawings must include flashing details for every different condition and they must indicate the type of metal required, as well as profiles for counter flashings. This information will simplify bidding by clarifying exactly what the roofing contractor must provide.

- Where a "dead valley" occurs, provide ample details to describe exactly how the valley is to be constructed. (Fig. 7–2.)

Completeness
- The roof plan must show every item that is necessary to prepare a bid for the roofing contract. The common practice of showing little more than the outline of the roof is not adequate.

Coordination
- Reconcile specifications with drawings. Sometimes they are in conflict with each other, or sometimes an item referenced in one is not included in the other.

- Verify that the details in the drawings coincide with the materials specified, and vice-versa.

Specification relevancy
- A common problem with working drawings for EPDM (Ethylene Propylene Diene Monomer) roofing projects is that generic details are used which do not match the specific job or which are modified inaccurately. To avoid this, architects must obtain

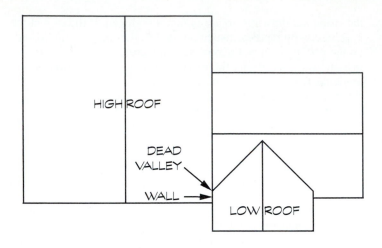

Fig. 7–2. Roof plan with a dead valley. A dead valley occurs where the flow of water down the valley to grade is interrupted. In the case above, a valley abuts a wall, thus becoming a dead valley.

current detail drawings from manufacturers to use in working drawings. The architects must then verify that the detail drawings accurately portray the conditions to be constructed on the current project.

- Show all crickets and saddles on the roof plan. Also indicate how they are constructed, i.e., with plywood, tapered insulation, or other materials. If the deck is warped so as to send water toward the drains, state it on the roof plan.

- Do not include more than one specification for an element (such as a valley) where only one is applicable. This occurs where, instead of selecting the appropriate entry from a palate of generic specifications, the architect lists all of the choices. In this case, the contractor is forced to search the drawings in order to verify that only one is applicable and that there actually is a choice between the entries. Then the cost for each of the specifications must be estimated in order to determine the lowest cost. This process is inefficient and wastes time. Instead, with the help of the contractor prior to bidding, the architect should determine which detail is the most cost effective and should omit the specifications for all other configurations which do not apply.

Documenting Painting and Wall Coverings

Amy B. Williams, Estimator
Brewer Paint and Wallpaper Company, Inc.
Rocky Mount, North Carolina

- When using wall coverings, always select one on which to base the proposal, or provide a price allowance per linear yard.

  Wall coverings are sold by the linear yard. Without this information, contractors will base their bids on patterns having different costs. Listing only "manufacturer's standard type II, 24 oz," for example, is too vague, even if the manufacturer is identified. Many patterns of various prices fit such a description.

- Show wall-accent configurations and dimensions with interior elevations. (Fig. 7–3.)

- Always indicate where epoxy paint is to be used.

  This affects paint pricing since the price of epoxy paint differs from that of other paints.

- Indicate where split-face block and/or synthetic stucco are to be painted.

  Since these can be prefinished, it is necessary to clarify whether or not they are prefinished or require painting. Locating this information in the working drawings, rather than specifications, is preferred for easier access.

- List ceiling heights for every room.

  This is necessary to calculate the square footage of wall space to be painted or papered. The heights can be on the floor plan, the finish schedule, a reflected ceiling plan, or in building sections. This is often overlooked by the architect.

- When using two wall finishes in one area, such as for accents, show a detail or describe where each finish begins and ends.

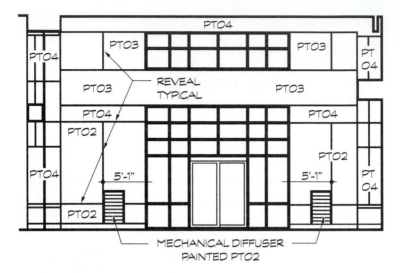

Fig. 7–3. Lobby elevation. The paint pattern is noted on the elevation by designations "PT02," "PT03," etc. Each designation refers to the following type of information, as given for PT02: Manufacturer (Devoe, Number 2H8P); Sheen (Eggshell); Texture (Orange Peel); Color (Clover Sweet); Type (Latex). A healthcare center. HKS, Inc., Architects, Engineers, Planners, Dallas, Texas.

This affects prices due to the differing costs of various finishes as further affected by greater or smaller surface areas.

• Indicate the specific surfaces and components in mechanical and electrical rooms to be painted.

List items, such as exposed bare and insulated pipes and ducts, hangers, exposed steel and iron work, primed metal surfaces of mechanical and electrical equipment, etc., if these are to be painted. Indicate whether or not the ceilings (typically exposed structures) and walls are to be painted. A statement requiring paint for "all exposed items and surfaces" is too vague. If "occupied rooms" are cited for painting, indicate whether or not mechanical and electrical rooms are occupied rooms. These spaces are often overlooked in painting instructions and will unnecessarily increase the bid if included when they should not be part of the work.

• On drawings of existing buildings, indicate the surface material of all walls, such as gypsum board, CMU, etc.

This might save the contractor a visit to the building to identify these finishes, thus reducing overhead costs.

• Do not position wall covering joints on "outside corners," such as for a change of pattern. (Fig. 7–4.)

The coverings will eventually peel back at the joint unless a corner guard is used.

• Use the smallest sheet size possible for working drawings.

If the work will fit on a 24" x 36" sheet, do not use a 30" x 42" size. Subcontractors often duplicate sheets from working drawing sets for bidding purposes. Unnecessarily large sheets are expensive to duplicate and increase overhead costs.

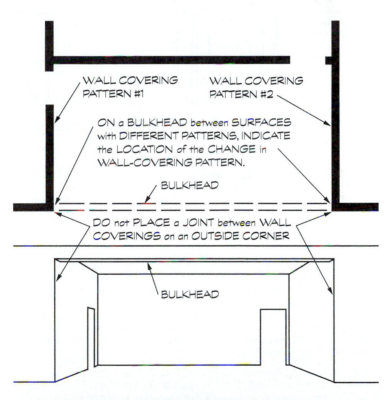

Fig. 7–4. Plan and perspective. Examples of outside corners and a bulkhead between walls with coverings of different patterns.

- Do not skip numbers in the sequence of room numbers.

  If changes require the omission of a number, renumber the rooms to provide a continuous sequence. Omitted numbers and numbers listed as "not used" in the finish schedule can be confusing during bidding and construction.

- Place finish schedules and door schedules as close to the floor plans as possible in working drawings. (Fig. 7–5.)

  Place on the same page if possible. Schedules remotely located from plans require extensive handling of drawing sheets. This increases overhead costs.

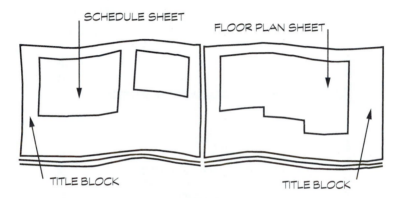

Fig. 7–5. Working drawing set layout. Schedule sheets are bound facing related floor plan sheets. Used by PBK Architects, Inc., Houston, Dallas/Fort Worth, San Antonio, Austin, and League City, Texas, for such projects as a high school and an elementary school.

Brewer Paint and Wallpaper Company was founded in 1927 by J.B. Brewer, Sr. Still operated by family members, Brewer now serves most of North Carolina and the surrounding areas, from two offices. The main office is located in Rocky Mount, N.C., and the second office is in Greensboro, N.C. Brewer also offers interior design services, as well as equipment rentals and sales. Brewer Paint and Wallpaper Company, Inc., is a member of Carolina's Associated General Contractors as well as Carolina's Council PDCA.

Brewer Paint and Wallpaper Company, Inc., P.O. Box 7906, Rocky Mount, North Carolina 27804. J.B. Brewer, Jr., President; J.K. Brewer, Jr., Vice President; J.B. Brewer, III, Secretary/Treasurer; Amy B. Williams and Jim Gray, Estimators.

Construction Documents for Pier Foundations

Don McGee, P.E., Drilling estimator
Austin Traffic Signal Construction Co.
Round Rock, Texas

Specification relevancy
- Omit all specifications and details that do not apply to the project. Specification entries that are included but do not apply to the work waste the time of the bidders in their attempts to verify the location of associated details and they also increase the cost of the construction due to the uncertainty they cause.

Specification information
- Always include boring logs from the geotechnical engineer. These are sometimes omitted by the architect.

- Always list unit prices for pier construction that runs deeper or shallower than shown in the drawings. This list is often omitted from the construction documents.

- If casings are not required by the drawings, the specifications must provide for additional payment to the subcontractor for mobilization and demobilization of crews as well as for the equipment for installing casings, should they be needed. Some geotechnical companies do not report the presence of water when encountered in their test drilling, so that no cost is included in the bid for these projects. Where the drilling contractor encounters water, casing equipment and crews must be assembled, and casings must be installed. States require a permit and fee each time this equipment is moved to a job, so this cost must be added to that of the installation of casings.

- Unit prices for pier depths that run longer or shorter than that shown in the drawings should be provided regardless of the pier length specified in the drawings. Such prices are necessary in spite of the availability of test boring information because substrate suitable for pier bearing is sometimes found at depths that vary from those which are expected.

Location of foundation drawings

- All foundations, regardless of type, should appear only in the structural drawings. Some projects have included foundation information in several drawing categories. For instance, landscape drawings have included foundation details for fountains and retaining walls; architectural drawings have included foundations for out-buildings (mechanical rooms, shops, etc.); and no information on these foundations was provided in the structural drawings. The estimator has to search the entire set of drawings to identify foundation work and can easily miss miscellaneous items if they are not located in the structural set.

Working drawing information

- The architect should require the engineer to show the same "bid depth" for all piers. (Fig. 7–6.) If all piers are shown to be the same depth in the drawings, all contractors will bid on the same length. The specifications then must list a price per lineal foot to be paid to the contractor where it is discovered during construction that the piers must run deeper. A price per lineal foot must also be provided in case piers run to less depth than shown in the drawings. The latter unit price is typically about 2/3 of the former. This approach places the risk of unknown site conditions appropriately on the owner, with costs controlled to the extent possible.

- Providing a single bid depth in the working drawings also reduces the bid errors that can result in financial hardship for the design team, owner, and contractor, if the errors are not discovered until after construction begins. The alternative of showing multiple pier lengths encourages mistakes. (Fig. 7–7.) In one project, numerous top and bottom elevations were required for piers. The low bidder was $80,000 under the next higher bid, due to mistakes in computing the volume of the pier holes. In this case, the error was caught prior to letting the contract and it was awarded to the next higher bidder, thus avoiding serious financial difficulties at a later date.

- The information necessary to determine pier size should be provided on the same sheet of drawings and they should be in close proximity to each other. In some instances, drawings have

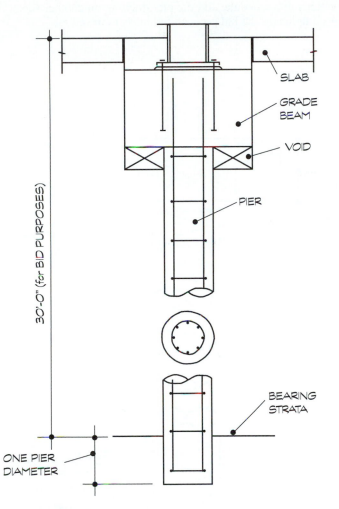

SLAB

GRADE
BEAM

VOID

PIER

30'-0" (for BID PURPOSES)

BEARING
STRATA

ONE PIER
DIAMETER

Fig. 7–6. A pier detail that simplifies bidding. This detail shows a 30'-0" "bid length" for the pier. All contractors bid on this same length for every pier, thus providing consistency in the basis of the bids and reducing errors. The bid length extends to the top of the slab, and, therefore prevents different slab elevations and grade beam thickness from affecting the estimated cost of each pier. Differences between the bid and the cost of actually constructing piers which vary from this length are covered by a unit price which is added to or subtracted from the base bid according to pier diameter. (Other information in the detail has been omitted for simplicity.)

placed the top elevations of piers on a floor plan, the bottom
elevations in a schedule, and the pier drawing on another sheet.
This complicates the bid process and leads to mistakes.

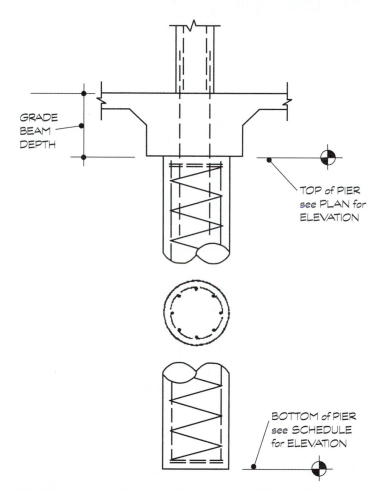

GRADE
BEAM
DEPTH

TOP of PIER
see PLAN for
ELEVATION

BOTTOM of PIER
see SCHEDULE
for ELEVATION

Fig. 7–7. A pier detail that complicates bidding. This detail requires the
estimator to examine the floor plan for the top elevation and the pier schedule
for the bottom elevation of each pier, in order to determine its volume. In this
project, the schedule requires five different bearing elevations for various
piers, thus requiring a different calculation for each one. Variations in the
grade beam depth further complicate the calculation of total steel and concrete
required. (Other information in the detail has been omitted for simplicity.)

Recommendations for Fire Protection

The following recommendations apply to the design and specification of fire-protection systems. They are based on comments made by contractors and other professionals in the fire-protection industry in response to a survey conducted to identify problems and issues related to the preparation of construction documents.

Applicable standards

• The names and editions of the codes that govern the work must be identified. Rules for fire-protection systems vary from edition to edition of the codes, and the subcontractor must know which requirements apply.

• The owner's insurance company must be identified. Insurance companies, such as Industrial Risk Insurers (I.R.I.) and Factory Mutual (F.M.), have requirements for fire-protection systems which affect cost and configuration. These requirements might vary from the applicable codes, and must be considered in the bid and installation. The name and phone number of the insurance underwriter should be listed in the specification.

Code references

• If the building qualifies as "high rise" according to the definition in the applicable building code, then identify the building as such. Buildings meeting code definitions for a high-rise building have special requirements, such as the addition of a standpipe system according to NFPA 14.

• The commodity classification of any combustible substances to be housed in the building must be identified. These classifications are defined in NFPA 231 and 231C (Chapter 2). They affect the requirements of the fire-protection system. Knowing these classifications is helpful where working drawings do not show the design of the sprinkler system in an area where a system is required. These unknowns can cause a bid for the system to be "qualified," which could result in misunderstandings of project cost and cause subsequent change orders, which increase costs.

Code requirements

- Quick-response sprinklers cannot be provided for extra hazard occupancies.

- The design route for sprinkler supply lines should not be blocked by an electrical room. The National Electrical Code does not permit sprinkler pipes to pass over equipment in an electrical room. The positioning of an electrical room which requires an inefficient routing of sprinkler pipes around it drives up the cost of the system.

- Any draftstops and closely spaced sprinklers required for openings in floors by codes and NFPA 13, 4-13.3.4 (1996), must be provided.

Sprinkler trade-offs

- The architect should take advantage of alternative solutions for meeting code requirements for fire protection, where they are cost effective. For instance, unnecessary cost is added to a project when buildings are designed as if there were to be no sprinkler system, even though a sprinkler system will be included. But, if a sprinkler system is employed, certain fire separation walls could be omitted or reduced in scope, thus making the construction less expensive. So, from the outset, architects should design a building that takes advantage of the cost-effective code-compliance options offered by a sprinkler system. This approach should be used whenever sprinklers are to be installed, whether or not they are required by code. (Single- and multiple-family housing should be included in such consideration.)

Information needed by the contractor

- The function of the building must be identified.The fire-protection designer needs to know if the space will be an office, manufacturing facility, warehouse storage, etc., because code requirements for fire protection vary with use.

- The fire-protection contractor must be provided with reflected ceiling plans in CAD files. Failure to provide CAD files to the contractor increases the cost of the sprinkler system because the

reflected ceiling plans must be redrawn. Some architects provide
the CAD files to the contractor in exchange for a signed
disclaimer waiving the architect's liability for problems resulting
from their use. This has convinced some insurance companies
that the architect's liability is minimized.

Water pressure
- The water pressure and flow volume available to the site must be
  verified as adequate for the required sprinkler system. The results
  of the water flow test should be listed in the specification so that
  all sprinkler contractors are bidding on the same conditions.

- The minimum pressure required of a standpipe system's outlet,
  which is most remote from the water supply main, should be
  specified. Typical requirements are 65 psi or 100 psi.

Applicability of specifications
- Specifications must be prepared specifically for the project.
  Using generic specifications or those prepared for a previous
  project leads to confusion and leaves questions about the current
  project unanswered due to the failure to include all necessary
  information. In addition, irrelevant information is included, thus
  requiring time to reconcile discrepancies between specification
  entries and drawings. Due to the unknowns in these cases,
  fire-protection contractors are forced to take risks in preparing
  their bids. This tends to increase bid prices and cause change
  orders.

- Specifications must match current editions of standards, and
  products listed therein must be currently available.
  Fire-protection components change from year to year so the use
  of specifications from previous work might include references to
  products which are no longer available. For example, alarm
  check valves and water motors, once frequently used, are now
  obsolete.

- The design criteria specified must apply to the actual use of the
  building. A pitfall of reusing specifications or portions of which
  were written for another project, is that differences between the
  use of the new building and the previous one might render some
  sections irrelevant to the current project.

Specification of components
- The ramifications of using concealed sprinkler heads must be

considered prior to specifying them. Since these are virtually
hidden from view, they do not readily provide the psychological
benefit of knowing that one is in a building protected from fire
by sprinklers. Also, they have moving parts which might require
maintenance in order to be in working condition at all times.

- Surface-mounted light fixtures should not be specified without
  coordination with the sprinkler designer. Surface-mounted light
  fixtures tend to interfere with the distribution of water from the
  sprinkler heads. Lights are usually mounted after the sprinkler
  heads which sometimes means that the heads have to be moved
  to prevent the light fixture from affecting their spray pattern. In
  this case, the heads must be mounted lower than the ceiling
  using a special sleeve, which is large and unsightly.

- Polished brass fire department connections should not be
  specified without verification from the owner that the necessary
  maintenance will be available to maintain their appearance.
  Owners usually don't have the maintenance budget to polish
  these. Without maintenance these connections will turn black
  within a year.

Location of components
- The supply riser for a sprinkler system should be located at the
  low side of a roof slope. This permits the piping to drain by
  gravity when it is necessary to empty the system.

- The water line acting as the fire main feed coming to the
  building should run into the building but stop no more than 2
  feet from the outside wall. Stopping the feed line 5 feet outside
  the building is a dated practice and should no longer be done
  because it creates a warranty issue and brings up the question of
  who is responsible for testing the last underground joint in the
  line. If the company installing the main runs it into the building,
  responsibility for its proper function is clarified. If the main runs
  farther than 2 feet into the building, a leak can eventually cause
  structural failure because there is no alarm or other warning of
  the leak.

- The compatibility of both ESFR (early suppression, fast
  response) sprinklers and extended coverage sprinklers with the
  ceiling slope and configuration for which they are proposed must
  be verified by the manufacturer. Special sprinkler heads such as
  the aforementioned, which are relatively new to the industry,

function most efficiently where smooth and unobstructed ceilings slope less than 2 inches per foot. In certain cases, the use of ESFR sprinklers could reduce the need for supplemental in-rack sprinklers. Extended coverage sprinklers can reduce the total number of sprinkler heads required. In both cases, however, cost savings can be realized, if the ceiling conditions permit proper function of the sprinkler heads.

Reflected ceiling plans

- Ceiling plans should be coordinated with the mechanical and electrical engineers in order to show the actual location of the equipment as they have designed it.

- The sprinkler designer must be informed of any changes in the building design that affect the sprinkler system as soon as they are known. Changes in the structure, room layout, and building occupancy, etc., might require changes in the sprinkler system design.

- For storage facilities, the sprinkler designer must be provided with information necessary for compliance with NFPA 231C. The sprinkler designer must know aisle widths, storage rack configurations, storage heights, and the commodity classifications of stored items.

- The reflected ceiling plans must show all ceiling fixtures, such as soffits, valences, etc.

Centered sprinkler heads

- The requirement to center sprinkler heads in ceiling panels or to position them exactly in any location should be avoided because it drives up the cost of the system.

  - Not only does it increase labor costs, but centering sprinkler heads in ceiling panels adds material costs because of the need for extra nipples and 90-degree ells. By one estimate, 15 minutes of labor is added to each sprinkler head that must be centered (depending on the ceiling height). And, according to another estimate, each centered head costs the owner about $50.

  - Architects specify centered sprinkler heads in order to enhance their visual compatibility with the ceiling pattern, but the expense of this system is not justified when the sprinklers are the "hidden" type. The reduced visibility of these sprinklers logically negates the consideration of their visual impact.

- When centered sprinkler heads are specified, providing a 3-inch tolerance for each head would ease installation and save money.

Ceiling grids
- Making grids for suspended ceilings which are continuous across partitions is recommended because the sprinkler piping will be more economical. There will be fewer pipe length changes, and more repetitive dimensions, thus, labor will be saved and material waste will be reduced.

- A starting point for the grid of a suspended ceiling should be fixed in order to prevent the installer from shifting the grid to gain economy in its installation. By fixing the grid, it remains in the position on which the sprinkler contractor based the bid. A grid that is moved might save in the cost of the ceiling but might increase the cost of the sprinkler system.

Vertical space requirements
- Where sprinkler pipes are to run above a suspended ceiling, an extra 12 inches of space dedicated to them must be provided. This 12-inch space must sit above the light fixtures, which protrude into the concealed space. The subcontractor's anticipation of having space above a ceiling which is inadequate for the sprinkler system drives up the bid for the work. In this case subcontractors must raise the bid price to protect themselves against the possibility of having to install complex piping configurations due to a congestion of utility lines, or having to re-route lines from the original plan. The provision of adequate space, therefore, is cost effective for new installations and can save maintenance costs and the expense of future renovations.

  In hospitals and other healthcare facilities, where more room is needed above the ceiling for utilities, architects should increase the floor-to-floor heights of the buildings rather than further limit the space available for sprinkler piping.

- Adequate space for the slope of pipes in dry sprinkler systems must be provided. Dry systems require greater slope than do wet systems, so architects who are used to providing space for wet systems should refer to NFPA 13, section 4-14.3.3 for the proper dry-system slope.

Plan requirements

- Pump rooms must be provided with adequate space and access in order to house and maintain all sprinkler equipment and required piping, including backflow prevention equipment. Refer to NFPA 20, A-2-14.1.2, note 2, for information relative to this requirement. For example, top or bottom connections of a suction pipe require a clearance of not less than five pipe diameters. For side connections of a suction pipe, a clearance of not less than ten pipe diameters is required. Verify that space is available for packaged fire pump units if they are to be used.

  For instance, a 12-foot by 12-foot room is the minimum allowable space where 6-inch pipes are used. A 20-foot by 20-foot room is the minimum allowable space where 10-inch pipe is used (probably a High-Hazard building). A minimum of 3 feet is required around all equipment for service; adequate space is necessary because, once a year, the fire pump is tested, and this is a dangerous procedure if there is not ample space around the equipment.

- Fire-protection equipment and water service should not be located in a closet of an office. This space is usually very limited and if the building is expanded, the closet will not likely be able to accommodate additional equipment. Additional concerns include the disruption of office activities when the equipment is serviced, and the possibility that the backflow prevention device might dump water into the space.

- A fire sprinkler valve room should not be located adjacent to an office or an apartment.

Standpipes

- Standpipes should be located so that the fire hoses connected to them can reach all areas of the building.

- Standpipe hose connections should be located between floors at intermediate landings of exit stairs. (Although NFPA 14 recommends that these connections be located on intermediate landings, it is not common practice to do so.) Do not place hose connections on floor-level landings unless the authority having jurisdiction over the project approves. The reason for this is that a standpipe is 6 inches in diameter and is typically positioned at a small distance from the wall. Consequently, where space is limited, it can encroach on the minimum egress clearance required in the stairwell.

Intermediate landings are a better location for hose connections. This is because egress clearance at these landings of U-shaped stairs is defined by a semi-circle which does not include the outer corners of a rectangular landing, thus providing more room for the installation of the standpipe without affecting egress minimums.

In any case, landings must be large enough to accommodate egress dimensions plus any standpipe hose connection located on them. It has been known that entire stairwells have had to be enlarged after their construction in order to accommodate the standpipe hose connections located on landings therein.

Elevator requirements
• For hydraulic elevators and elevator machine rooms, sprinkler heads with easily accessed shut-off capability must be provided where required by local codes. These sprinkler heads might not be required in all locales, however, and the subcontractor should be made aware of any such requirement prior to bidding.

Structural support
• Where sprinkler piping is to be supported under a large skylight or atrium, the adequacy of the skylight structure to carry the extra weight and afford attachment of the piping must be verified.

• Sprinkler piping should be run perpendicular to joists or beams. This orientation permits support of the piping from the joists or beams, at periodic points along the piping.

Piping hangers
• The design for attachments of sprinkler piping to composite wood I-joists must conform to manufacturers' recommendations, and the budget must accommodate the process necessary to hang the system from this structure. For support of piping, some manufacturers of wood I-joists require a screw rod to be located at the exact center of the bottom chord. Other manufacturers require that the attachment be made off center so as to avoid the composite panel web insert into the chord. Additional considerations regarding the attachment of sprinkler piping to wood I-joists include the following:
   ○ Holes must be drilled for these attachments which requires time.

- ○ Where the piping will be exposed below a gypsum board ceiling attached to the I-joists, two trips to the site are usually required by the subcontractor, one to install the hangers and a second to install the pipe after the gypsum board is attached.

- ○ The fire marshal will generally want to see the hanger attachment prior to the installation of anything that would cover it in subsequent construction.

- ○ Hanging a 4-inch pipe from a single wood I-joist is not permitted.Usually two joists are used to hang a 2-½-inch pipe.

- Hangers for the sprinkler piping that are stronger than required by NFPA 13 should not be required. Mechanical engineers might specify hangers that are stronger than necessary for sprinkler piping due to their experience with supporting mechanical system piping. (Mechanical equipment piping tends to move because the systems are turned on and off throughout the day. Thus, they require stronger supports than do sprinkler piping which does not move on a daily basis.) But, requiring hangers for sprinkler piping that are stronger than those required by NFPA 13 drives up cost unnecessarily.

Cost considerations

- Irregular geometries and level changes in the ceiling should be minimized because they increase the cost of sprinkler systems due to the extra labor required to configure the piping. Where a constant ceiling height cannot be maintained, changes in level should be kept to less than 12 inches in order to minimize cost premiums.

- Quick-response sprinklers should be provided in all light hazard occupancies and should be considered for use in ordinary hazard occupancies. Quick-response sprinklers are permitted in ordinary hazard occupancies and are recommended, in spite of the fact that they cost more than standard sprinkler heads.

- Architects should review area limitations for sprinkler systems as defined by NFPA 13, 4-2. This will help architects understand the number of sprinkler systems required for a building, and whether or not draft curtains and other special elements are required.

Coordination of consultants' designs

• Verify that the mechanical and electrical consultants have coordinated their designs so that all of the wiring required for the fire-protection system is included in the contract documents.
  In order to make this verification, the architect can require the consultants to provide a checklist of all the system devices that require electrical wiring. Then the consultants should be asked to acknowledge that all the necessary provisions for the devices are included in the drawings and specifications. (This process can also provide a check of the consultants' extent of knowledge and experience with fire-protection systems.)

     It has been found that solenoid valves, supervisory switches for control valves, flow switches, or control panels have been shown on the mechanical drawings without any indication of the electrical wiring necessary to support them. There have been cases where no supervisory switches for fire sprinkler control valves were shown on the mechanical drawings or electrical drawings, in spite of the fact that they were required by code in the project jurisdiction. (The function of these switches is important because the malfunction of a control valve can reduce the effectiveness of the fire-protection system.)

• Adequate heat must be provided in a building with wet sprinkler systems in order to keep the water from freezing.

Quality control

• The services of a fire-protection engineer should be secured to reduce omissions and errors, to oversee the design of the fire-protection system, and to verify that all the components necessary to the system are covered in the contract documents.

• The fire-protection contractor should be involved in the development of the project during the conceptual phase. Request help to find creative solutions to fire-protection requirements where the design is unique. Modify the design where possible based on input from the contractor, in order to accommodate a more economical and efficient fire-protection system.

• Unless architects have extensive experience in the design of fire-protection systems, they should not prepare the system layouts. A lack of experience in fire-protection design can result in the failure of a system to accommodate code requirements, principles of economy, and current technology. This causes discrepancies in bidding.

Guidelines for Cost-effective Sprinkler Systems

Jon R. Ackley
Vice President of Operations
Dalmatian Fire, Inc.
Indianapolis, Indiana; Cincinnati, Ohio; Columbus, Ohio

Scope of work

- Assign the entire responsibility for the water line which feeds the sprinkler system to the fire sprinkler contractor. If this is impractical, the site utility contractor is often chosen, especially if the distance between the building and the city main is short. Regardless of who is chosen, do not divide responsibility for the line at the once traditional point of 5 feet outside of the building. Instead, terminate the responsibility for the line installed by the contractor at a point inside the building and 12 inches above the floor.

    It is not cost effective for a contractor to mobilize labor and equipment only to install a short run of buried pipe. (The timing of the work is also inefficient.) The original installing contractor could finish the "stub-up" for less than $1000, whereas a subsequent contractor could cost as much as $5000.

- Be clear on the scope of work assigned to the sprinkler contractor especially in contrast to work assigned to the plumber. Assign all electrical wiring relating to the sprinkler system to the electrician. Assign all painting relating to the sprinkler system to the painting contractor.

    It is not cost effective to assign the painting of exposed sprinkler piping in the mechanical room to the sprinkler contractor. It is difficult for the sprinkler contractor to get bids on such a small amount of work. Consequently, such painting is typically more expensive than it needs to be when it is not done by the painting contractor.

Building layout

- Where rooms are just over 20, 40, or 60 feet, etc., in length or width, consider adjusting the room size to an exact multiple of 20 feet. Extended coverage sprinkler heads cover 20 feet. A 21-foot dimension requires an additional head, thus significantly increasing the cost per square foot of the system.

- Space open-web joists in multiples of 5 feet for all ESFR (early suppression fast response) systems. The most efficient sprinkler head layout is on a 10-foot by 10-foot grid. Sprinkler heads must be 1 foot from joists to avoid disruption to the spray pattern. Thus, an odd spacing, such as 5-feet 3-inches, eventually forces an interruption to the repetitive installation of the sprinkler heads. This changes component dimensions and increases labor costs.

- Dedicate the zone 8 inches above a ceiling to the sprinkler system. While this zone will be shared with the electrical and lighting systems, ductwork should not be permitted closer than 8 inches to the ceiling to allow room for the sprinkler system.

Standards

- Inform the sprinkler contractor of any variances to standard building-code options that have been agreed to by the authorities upon the request of the architect or engineer. The sprinkler contractor knows the requirements of the building code and NFPA standards. He or she will exploit the various options in the standards to yield the most cost-effective system even when only one option is shown in the drawings. The sprinkler contractor must be informed, if the building official and architect have come to an agreement limiting certain options which change the significance of the drawings from that of being an illustration of one choice to being the only choice. To take the approach that the sprinkler drawings are always the only choice in all cases is not cost effective.

- Let the sprinkler contractor design the system according to NFPA 13. (If there are additional insurance company requirements, inform the sprinkler contractor in advance of preparing the design.) Do not restrict the innovative sprinkler contractor with a large number of additional requirements in anticipation of, perhaps, producing a better system. This is not cost effective and might not yield an improved system.

An example of this is the common reluctance to use Schedule 10 lightwall pipe as allowed by NFPA 13. Schedule 40 pipe, often the preferred choice, can be weaker at the joints and more vulnerable to corrosion. This is because the cutting of threads in Schedule 40 pipe reduces the thickness of the pipe to a thinner dimension than that of Schedule 10, which is deformed, rather than cut, to make its grooves. On the other hand, it is understandable that architects might wish to avoid threadable lightwall pipe (due to the thinness produced by cutting threads). Schedule 5 pipe requires special methods of connection due to its thinness and should only be allowed with approved fittings (i.e., Victaulic's "pressfit system").

CAD files

- At no cost, provide the sprinkler contractor CAD files for the building shell. In some cases, insurance companies might not permit the architect to provide these drawings. Redrawing the building shell sheets can increase the cost of the sprinkler system by $3500, depending on the size of the building. If it is necessary, secure a waiver from liability relating to errors and omissions in the CAD files in order to release the files to the sprinkler contractor.

Sprinkler technology

- Use sprinkler hangers permitted by NFPA 13 rather than requiring typical plumbing hangers. Typical plumbing hangers are 1/2-inch in diameter and, therefore, over-sized compared to the 3/8-inch sprinkler hangers which are adequate and meet the NFPA standard. Over-sizing the hangers costs more and does not produce a better system.

- Allow the use of extended coverage sprinklers. Routine practices need to be updated if extended coverage sprinklers are not yet permitted. This technology is cost effective.

- Use quick response sprinklers, except in certain extra hazard conditions. Routine practices need to be updated if quick-response sprinklers are not yet permitted. This technology is cost effective.

Dalmatian Fire, Inc. was founded in 1989 by Richard Ackley, its current president and chairman, and, in 2000, it generated revenues of 24.6 million dollars. The company is headquartered in Indianapolis, Indiana, and has branch offices in Cincinnati and Columbus, Ohio. Dalmatian Fire serves the industrial, institutional, commercial, and residential markets in Indiana, Ohio, Kentucky, and Illinois, at the local, state, and federal government levels. Jon Ackley has been in the fire sprinkler industry since 1974 and is a NICET Level IV Senior Engineering Technician.

Construction Managers
and
Working Drawings

Members of the construction management profession are in a unique position to judge the effectiveness of architects' working drawings because, unlike architects and contractors, they generally do not have a financial interest in the project. Since both the architect and the contractor have financial liability at risk for additions or corrections to the work, this might affect their views of the solution, should there be a disagreement regarding the intent of the drawings. Construction managers who are financially independent from the design or building team, however, can be considered truly disinterested parties, and free to judge the meaning of a drawing without financial consequences to themselves for the remedies deemed necessary.

Considering this objectivity, several construction managers were asked to comment on the state of architects' working drawings, and a variety of responses are provided, from general guidelines to specific problems and solutions. In one example, a significant savings in construction cost is demonstrated based on the construction manager's recommendation to change the architect's detailing *prior* to bidding. Another manager focuses on the detailing of flashing as a recurring deficiency in working drawings.

Recommendations for Working Drawings

Jerry Bronstein, AIA
Director of Design
International Management Consultants, Inc.
Malvern, Pennsylvania

The competitive fee structure for architects, which is demanded by owners, requires that architects expedite projects quickly, which sometimes results in construction document deficiencies such as the following.

Working drawing details
• Plans, sections, and other drawings are not coordinated with details. In some instances, especially on projects that have many documents, incorrect references to details appear which might cause confusion during the bidding process as well as during the actual construction.

• Many drawings include standard details that have been utilized on other projects and which sometimes do not apply to the present project. Detailing sheets sometimes show a cursory review of the details with the nonapplicable details crossed out. Nonapplicable details and specifications that are crossed out create added drawings which are unnecessary. Documents are often cumbersome without added piecemeal documentation. The overall impression of the construction documents also suffers based on a "messy" appearance.

• In some instances, the details are unnecessarily expensive, not practical in the field, or are more time consuming because they are dependent on the completion of work by multiple trades in a fixed sequence. (Fig. 8–1 and Fig. 8–2.)

    As an example, wood blocking details have been drawn with configurations that waste lumber and were eventually changed in the field to a more cost-effective use of materials. Some details suggest a lack of thought as to how the parts will actually be

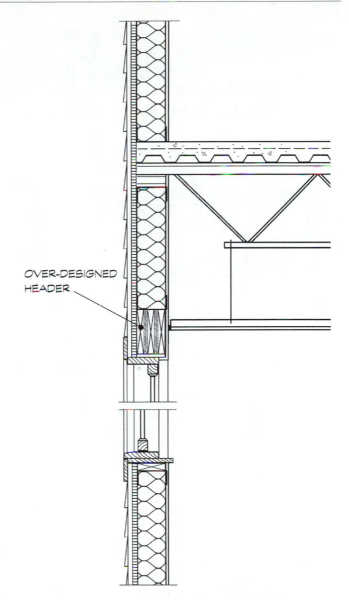

OVER-DESIGNED
HEADER

Fig. 8–1. The header over the window as drawn in the wall section is over-designed with three 2x10s and two ½-inch plywood flitch plates. A metal channel and a single flat 2x4 would be sufficient for the 3-foot to 4-foot wide windows.

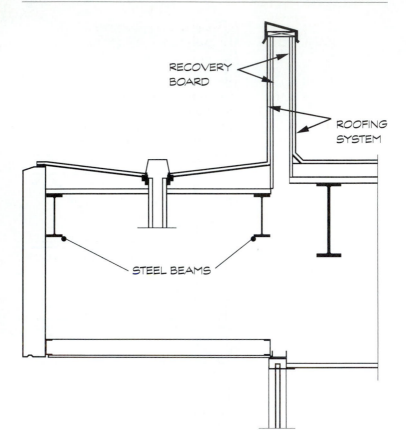

Fig. 8–2. Steel beams, as shown above, were originally proposed to support the overhang. It was suggested and approved to change the detail by running the beams perpendicular to the building façade and span between them with steel angles. The new detail was simpler and reduced the tonnage of steel required, thus reducing the cost of the support. The recovery board shown on the parapet wall in the illustration above was originally in the detail. This board does not comply with the manufacturer's warranty for the roofing system. During preconstruction meetings it was determined that the warranty required treated exterior plywood which was subsequently substituted for the recovery board in the detail, thus saving a considerable amount of cost that would have been incurred if the wrong material had been installed.

assembled on the job. They sometimes appear to be a haphazard placement of wood, in order to accommodate gaps and fastener requirements.

- On occasion, details do not comply with the warranty requirements which affect the warranty validation. (Fig. 8–2.) This is common for roofing systems with such items as substrate materials, flashing details, allowable structural supports, and important dimensional characteristics which do not match the manufacturer criterion for warranty compliance. Typically, the necessary literature and detailing can be found in manufacturers' system description catalogues. Specific requirements for adherence to warranty requirements are sometimes listed with their details.

- Compliance with certain UL-rated fire-resistant systems has been required where other systems would be more cost effective. In one example, spray fire proofing within a steel joist ceiling system was required by the construction documents, but it was more cost effective to use fire-resistance-rated ceilings and control the number of ceiling penetrations in order to maintain the fire rating. (Fig. 8–3 and Fig. 8–4.)

Coordination of specifications and drawings
- Specified concrete mix designs have not matched the engineering requirements on the drawings.

- Drawings sometimes contain details which do not adhere to very specific and specialized references within the specifications. As an example, performance specifications sometimes use obscure references from trade organizations which are not illustrated in the details. For instance, on one project a standard configuration of ceramic tile on drywall with metal studs detail was shown in a wall section and plan for a locker room/shower room application. The detail included cementitious board and a thinset ceramic tile. The specifications required adherence to the Ceramic Tile Institute Guideline Specifications. The specifications were not readily available, thus requiring research time to secure them. Upon reference to these specifications, it was discovered that a waterproof membrane, rigid insulation, and a vapor barrier were also required, none of which where shown in the wall section of the working drawing. Therefore, unless tradespeople are sophisticated and up to date on the referenced

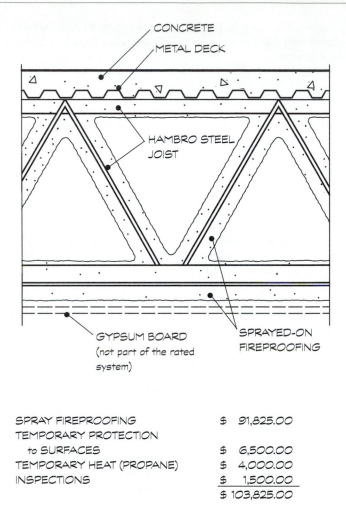

SPRAY FIREPROOFING $ 91,825.00
TEMPORARY PROTECTION
   to SURFACES $ 6,500.00
TEMPORARY HEAT (PROPANE) $ 4,000.00
INSPECTIONS $ 1,500.00
                                      $ 103,825.00

Fig. 8–3. This steel joist ceiling system with sprayed-on fireproofing was originally specified and drawn but proved to be more expensive than an alternative system with the same fire-resistance rating and which costs $15,000. It was also observed that the UL listing for the fire rating of this system specified Hambro joists, which were not planned for the project.

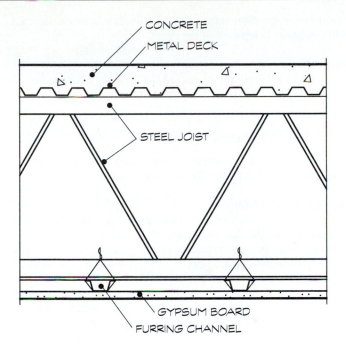

<table>
<tr><td>SPRAY FIREPROOFING</td><td>$</td><td>0.00</td></tr>
<tr><td>FIRE DAMPERS (100 maximum
   DAMPERS @ $50.00 ea.)</td><td>$</td><td>5,000.00</td></tr>
<tr><td>SHEATHING and/or TENTING
   INSULATION at LIGHT FIXTURES
   (BUDGET)</td><td>$</td><td>10,000.00</td></tr>
<tr><td></td><td>$</td><td>15,000.00</td></tr>
</table>

Fig. 8–4. This steel joist ceiling system was recommended as a substitution for the system originally specified which would have cost $103,825.00. This alternative was logical because the system was less expensive and had the same fire-resistance rating as the originally proposed system.

organization requirements, an installation might be constructed without critical elements of the detail.

Specifications
- Many times sections are contained within the specifications that do not apply to the specific project.

- Restrictive carpeting specifications which apply to a hospital requirement have appeared in a specification for an office project.

- The galvanizing of all steel components has been specified where such is not required by the project conditions.

General recommendations
Include a qualified construction manager as a part of the building team early during the design process. The owner, the architect, and the construction manager typically meet according to a prearranged schedule and address issues similar to those listed above, as the process and design develops toward the final construction documents. This process has worked very well in the past and has produced cost and time savings on a consistent basis. The key to this success is that the team is developed early, it understands the mission, and it keeps the owner's goals as a primary priority.

IMC Construction is a nationwide, general contracting/construction management firm located in Malvern, Pennsylvania. Founded more than 25 years ago, IMC has completed projects totaling well over one-half billion dollars in such industries as elderly housing, assisted living, retail malls/strip centers, warehouse distribution, schools, athletic facilities, office/commercial, pharmaceutical, laboratory, medical office, and industrial markets. IMC is consistently ranked as one of the top ten retail construction firms in the United States.

IMC's staff of project managers, architects, superintendents, schedulers, estimators, and support staff perform all facets of preconstruction and construction services. The team approach to value engineering, cost control, fast-track, and established-project management procedures affords the owner control of important

construction issues, as if IMC were a member of their own
organization without the owner taking the risk and liability.

Winner of numerous awards, IMC has most recently been the
recipient of the Building Excellence Award for the Woodbridge
Assisted Living Facility, Kimberton, Pennsylvania, and the Jewish
Community Center, Cherry Hill, New Jersey, as well as the 1999
Historic Architectural Preservation Award for the Devereux Arthur 0.
Edward Center at Villanova, Pennsylvania.

Key staff include Tom Williams, President; Robert Cottone, Executive
Vice President, and Jerry Bronstein, AIA, Corporate Secretary and
Director of Design.

Improving Working Drawings

Hank Falstad, AIA
Principal
Pentacore ADA Consulting, Inc.
Las Vegas, Nevada

- Each sheet must be well organized regarding the placement and emphasis of information, and it should also be easy to read. For a drawing to be easy to read there must be open space between the information.

- Written information needs to be conveyed in a consistent manner. The construction personnel will miss information if there is no consistency in the presentation. The same information or similar information should always be located in the same position on the individual sheets.

- Architects need to understand what information is important to the construction personnel. It is pertinent that the most important information be easily understood. The working drawings then become a written presentation of this information with emphasis on the most important information. Construction personnel need to be able to look at a sheet and determine which is the most important information, and which is the least important.

- First impressions of working drawings are very important. If the drawings are well organized, neat, and easy to follow, they suggest that the architect is competent.

- Where a drawing refers to information found elsewhere in the set, it must be easy to find. Such information must be thoroughly cross-referenced.

- All details should have a scale listed. Construction personnel scale the drawings, so it is important to reduce the chance of error from this process by being consistent in the scale of the details.

Hank Falstad, AIA, is a principal in Pentacore ADA Consulting, Inc. The firm provides consulting services to evaluate building compliance with Americans with Disabilities Act (ADA) and/or Department of Housing and Urban Development (HUD) accessibility requirements. The company does repeat business with large architectural firms, hotel/casino properties, and major development corporations. Their personnel staff of 10 has analyzed working drawings for over 8 billion dollars worth of construction. Offices are located in California, Nevada, Arizona, and Utah.

Common Problems in Working Drawings

Glenn Strong
Sea Hawk Enterprises
Aptos, California

Flashing and waterproofing

- Flashing for openings in exterior walls is omitted from drawings or is not detailed adequately. It is often left to the contractor to assemble the flashing without guidance. Incorporate details from SMACNA (*Architectural Sheet Metal Manual* from the Sheet Metal and Air Conditioning Contractors' National Association) <www.smacna.org>.

- The flashing and waterproofing of decks above habitable space are inadequate or incorrect, especially at the meeting of the horizontal surface with a wall.

- Windows above a shed roof do not have adequate space between the sill and the roof below for adequate flashing.

- Expansion joints are not provided every 20 to 30 feet of flashing. There can be 1/16" movement in 100' of typical flashing due to temperature fluctuations.

- Specifications for waterproofing and flashing are general in nature and not written specifically to apply to the project at hand.

- Penetration of parapets is not detailed with regard to waterproofing and flashing.

- Flashing of joints between materials with different coefficients of expansion is not detailed properly.

- Dampproofing and waterproofing of foundation walls at basements are not detailed or are detailed incorrectly.

Roofs

- Roof construction details are lacking. Incorporate details from the *NRCA Roofing and Waterproofing Manual* available from the National Roofing Contractors Association, <www.roofonline.org>.

- Penetrations of the roof for mechanical equipment are not detailed.

- Primary and overflow roof drains are not detailed or not detailed correctly.

- Railings for roof decks are not detailed.

Structure

- Vertical and lateral load-resisting elements are not detailed adequately. The architect must understand the path of load distribution to the foundation in order to check the engineer's design. Hold-downs are required at the ends of shear walls and need to be detailed. Various anchor systems and details can be found in the "High Wind-Resistant Construction Connectors" catalog of the Simpson Strong-Tie Company, Inc. as well as other publications from this company, <www.strongtie.com>.

EIFS

- Inadequate detailing and direction are provided for EIFS (exterior insulation and finish system) projects. Details for EIFS installations may be obtained from Senergy, Inc., <www.senergy.cc>, or from Dryvit, Inc., <www.dryvit.com>.

Coordination

- Ducts are drawn in the same locations as beams. Working drawings must be overlaid to find conflicts between the various building systems. The architect must understand all the components of a building's technology in order to comprehend the consultants' drawings and anticipate interface problems.

Accessibility

- The design and detailing do not meet accessibility requirements. Doors don't have the necessary clearance. A 5-foot turning radius is not provided in toilets. Obstructions exist in the toilet area. Required clearances can be found in various references including the ADAAG (Americans with Disabilities Act Accessibility

Guidelines for Buildings and Facilities) publication,
<www.access-board.gov>.

Omissions

Drawings which fail to include all the details necessary for the
construction of a building tend to increase the cost of construction
and the overhead of both the contractor and architect. When
omissions are encountered in the bidding or construction phases, a
request for information (RFI; see Appendix C) is typically
submitted to the architect by the contractor, which takes the
contractor time to prepare and which requires that the bid or
construction process work around the unknowns. The architect is
then obliged to respond, thus, more time is lost in research and
preparation of a written reply.

Glenn W. Strong, CSI, CDT is president and CEO of Sea Hawk
Enterprises, Inc. He is a general contractor, independent building
inspector, and planning consultant, with over 30 years experience in
the building industry. Mr. Strong is licensed in California, Arizona,
and Nevada as a Contractor. He is also a Construction Superintendent
and Project Manager with expertise in all aspects of the construction
trade.

Sea Hawk Enterprises, Inc., offers complete project management for
new construction, as well as for reconstruction of single-family,
multiresidential, condominium, and commercial projects. Services
include the preparation of Construction Specification Institute (CSI)
Project Manuals and Specifications. Consulting on Planning and
Development permits and red tag negotiations is available.
Specializations also include the Construction Management of
historical restoration and other renovation projects. Mr. Strong
provides inspections and testimony as an expert witness in arbitration
hearings and in construction dispute mediation services.

Clients and
Working Drawings

This chapter provides ideas from a cross-section of government agencies for improving working drawings. The special view of working drawings common to government clients makes their comments particularly useful for upgrading the quality of the drawings done for both the public and private sectors. City- and state-level clients also provided input, and the military and several universities are represented as well.

Government clients have repetitive building programs and usually act as construction managers for the work. This gives their managers a different view of the working drawings compared to that of independent construction managers. In this case, the clients' managers have a vested interest in the quality of the work as described by the architect in the drawings. For instance, in a prebid review of the drawings, the client may find them to be insufficient in graphic and written descriptions necessary to achieve the quality of building required. The architect may have a high quality of work in mind while preparing the drawings, but the client, in this case, knows whether or not the drawings are enforceable in this regard because the client has been through the construction process before and has had to enforce the requirements of architect's working drawings many times. This experience gives the client the ability to identify weak points in the drawings.

One set of observations is in the form of actual comments made by a client on architects' working drawings submitted for prebid reviews over a period of time. In this case, the advice comes not in the form of reflection but by way of the same words delivered to the architects doing the government work. Some design issues are addressed as are specification concerns. Although the focus is on working drawings, the other comments provide a context for the working drawing discussion thus completing the larger picture of the challenge.

The comments come from specific entities but are universal in nature. It is not anticipated that many architects will do work for the same agencies represented here. The comments in this chapter, however, provide an overview of the quality of drawings required for government work in general.

General Guidelines for the Production of City Facilities

Bradley G. Black, Architect
Project Manager, City of Eugene
Eugene, Oregon

The City of Eugene owns and maintains over 150 buildings serving a myriad of service-delivery-related functions including park structures, multiple fire stations of varying sizes, police facilities, the 911 center, city hall, office structures, a large performing arts center, and public works facilities. Because of the wide range of facility types, it is not practical for the city to have written guidelines for building development. Therefore, the city doesn't maintain a specific or special set of guidelines for the design of its facilities.

The one unwritten, but well-understood policy, that the city does maintain for its new capital projects is related to the quality of the projects undertaken. That is, the city council has an informal policy stating that the city should be an "exemplary developer." This policy often results in the inclusion of amenities in a project which are not required by the building or land use codes. The amenities are included to provide an example of how "good" development should be undertaken, to be a model for private developers.

CIRCULATION/CORE

Elevators, escalators, stairs, corridors, foyers, toilets, janitors' closets, drinking fountains, etc.
The City of Eugene's lack of specific guidelines for the development of its facilities should not imply that there is not consistency among the facilities. Consistency does exist on a number of levels. For instance, throughout the design process serious and on-going consideration is given to how the building

components, such as elevators, escalators, stairs, corridors, foyers, toilets, janitors' closets, and drinking fountains, are incorporated into the project. Whenever possible, the city attempts to design facilities where such components are centralized in single-story buildings or stacked in multiple-story facilities, the goal being to create a building that is "readable" by the public. For instance, components such as elevators, stairs, toilets, and drinking fountains should be placed so that they are easily located by the public as part of their routine use of the facility. Relying upon signage or staff assistance to find these components results in a building which the public finds less than "user friendly." Locating these elements in areas of high traffic and visibility also results in an increased perception that the area is safe.

In addition to designing facilities to be functionally and aesthetically pleasing, the City of Eugene attempts to design and construct all of its facilities with public safety in mind. Therefore, since the safety of the city's staff and the public is a major design consideration for public buildings, the components listed above are routinely examined for locations which "design out" opportunities for vandalism or threats. The city is fortunate to have an officer in the police department who has the expertise and experience to contribute to the development of building designs that foster public safety. For instance, from consultation with the police department it has been learned that elevator lobbies can be a location where heightened security awareness is required, and, so, such lobbies are always located in high-traffic areas, they are well lit, and they are open to public view. It also has been learned that pay telephones provide an opportunity for an individual with bad intentions to appear to have a legitimate reason for being in an area for an extended period. Such individuals might act as though they are using the phone while they are really waiting to victimize someone by snatching a purse, or waiting to perform some other form of theft. Deliberately locating pay telephones in high-traffic, well-supervised areas is a design response that tends to improve safety for the building users.

Accessibility is also important when looking at the specifics of many building components. We often find that the requirements of the Americans with Disabilities Act (ADA) are a driving force behind many design responses. A good example of making decisions around ADA and life-safety issues is the design of elevators. Within the city's facilities, all newly installed elevators either meet or exceed ADA requirements. Usually located in the core of the building, elevator cars are sized to allow emergency evacuation of a person in a stretcher. This criterion, combined with ADA requirements, establishes the minimum size of the elevator cab. In meeting these requirements, the functional requirements of the elevator are also met or exceeded. In this example, the city standard for elevators is set by code and emergency response requirements, not by functional need.

Another aspect for which the city lacks a set of fixed guidelines is the location and size of restrooms. These elements are not mandated by city policy because the diversity of facility types creates range of functional considerations for restrooms which cannot be addressed in a set of hard and fast rules. One such consideration is the need to provide adequate restrooms; another consideration is the issue of security. For example, in the city's existing library, the restrooms are located on the second floor, away from regular staff presence and oversight. This remote location of the restrooms makes them difficult to access by disabled patrons, and the lack of surveillance by staff leaves them vulnerable to possible illegal activity. In designing the new main library, now under construction, the potential use pattern by a minority of individuals was taken into account. Thus, the location of the restrooms was a significant functional and design issue, which was successfully addressed by the architects who located all public restrooms in areas where there is high traffic and easy staff supervision.

Another issue for the city regarding the design of restrooms is that the division between the number of fixtures in men's and women's restrooms is problematic. The building code leads to a distribution of fixtures between men's and women's restrooms that is not really workable, particularly in high-use facilities. For high-volume facilities, such as the city's Hult Performing Arts Center, having an equal number of fixtures in each restroom is not a useful distribution as evidenced by the fact that there is never a line of patrons for the men's restrooms, while there are often long lines for the women's. This is a sensitive issue, and in new facilities, the issue of distribution of fixtures is examined carefully and adjustments are made where possible. However, no city-level solution has been established. (European-style restrooms have been considered but were not found to be acceptable because of their reduced privacy.)

Parking

The City of Eugene has extensive parking guidelines/requirements, many of which are land-use code driven. In addition to meeting code requirements, the city is attempting to create as many full-size parking spaces as possible, while resorting to the creation of compact spaces only when absolutely necessary. For example, one recent project has 735 parking spaces on three underground levels. To maximize the stall count, the number of the total compact-size spaces was increased to nearly 50%. This will result in operational problems when a truck or other large vehicle parks in a compact space because that is all that is available. This will lead to crowding the adjacent cars, as well as to reducing the drive aisle width. For some projects involving a significant number of parking spaces, parking consultants have been used but with mixed results. The city has its own well-qualified staff assigned to the management of the car parking program and they are directly involved in the design of the parking from the outset of projects containing a large number of spaces.

An important factor in reducing user confusion is the signage used in public parking garages. The city maintains a standard set of entrance and traffic control signage for all public parking areas. Through experience, it has been determined that consistency of signage is a significant factor in the public's ability to efficiently use the parking facilities.

Besides car parking, the city emphasizes the use of alternative modes of transportation throughout its land-use code. This includes the use of public transportation and bikes. For instance, the new public library project was not required to provide parking for bikes, but under the exemplary developer concept, the project included a significant amount of on-site bike parking. This provision was in response to community input as well as being a direct result of the city council's desire for the city to be a model developer. Although this bike parking facility presented a financial impact on the project, the encouragement of alternative transportation modes was deemed to be a higher priority within the community.

Structure

Normally, structural decisions are left to the architect. However, the city's project managers often require the architect to consider several different systems, depending upon the type of structure. For example, the new 911 center is classified by the building code as an "essential facility," and as such it must survive earthquakes and other natural disasters, and be 100% operational. Given the size of the facility (about 12,000 sf) and the initial decision to limit construction to a one-story building to fit within the existing "campus" setting, the architect was asked to look at a number of different options for the structure, in particular, wood vs. steel. It was found that designing wood shear walls in accordance with current code (the city is in the Uniform Building Code seismic zone 3) results in a nailing pattern for plywood diaphragm walls which nearly cuts the plywood into strips. As a result, the architects were asked to consider a steel framing system, which proved to have greater seismic resistance, as well as being more fire and rot resistant than wood. In addition, a public building with an intended life span in excess of 50 years, which is built in Oregon and constructed of wood, requires more money for long-term maintenance than does steel.

Structurally, the new library project presented a challenge because the structural module for the parking areas below the library were not the same as the structural module required for the efficient layout of book stacks. This functional difference drives the design of the library's structural system, including the design of the floor plates, the major transfer girders, and the lateral load-resisting systems. Based on past performance and flexibility problems, the architect was not permitted to use any type of post-tensioned concrete structural system. Although the city has a number of concrete post-tensioned structures, it has found that this structural system limits the future ability to modify the facility, including the ability to penetrate the floor plate. For instance, the city's existing city hall is a post-tensioned structure, and, without an x-ray (each x-ray examination costs about $2000), one can't drill a hole through the slab. Even with the x-ray examination, the result is often the inability to penetrate the desired location due to the presence of a tendon. Therefore, a post-tensioned concrete slab system creates a set of restrictions that are unacceptable on a programmatic level for the library facility design and for the library's need for future flexibility.

Since a steel system was ruled out early in the design process because its floors would be too lively (due to its heavy loading), the city asked the architect to design a cast-in-place structural system. The decision to use a cast-in-place structure might have cost more than other alternatives, but it allowed for future flexibility. In the case of the new library facility, the city was willing to pay more to get a more flexible structural system.

Materials

The City of Eugene controls the use of some exterior materials as a standard policy. For instance, single-ply roofing systems are used wherever possible for flat roofs because experience has shown that built-up systems do not last the intended life span, and result in earlier than anticipated replacement costs. Similarly, built-up roof membranes also require more yearly maintenance to lengthen life span. As a result, the city has found that a higher initial price is paid for the single ply, in exchange for lower long-term maintenance costs and increased membrane longevity. Experience has also shown that single-ply assemblies result in fewer leaks and roofer call-backs.

The city's policy also addresses sloped roofs, and, despite being in the heart of "wood" country, it does not use wood shakes or shingles on its projects. Wood roofs present an increased risk of fire and the quality of wood roofing materials has declined over the past two decades, resulting in wood roofs that do not have extended life spans. In place of wood, asphalt shingles or metal roofing is being used. For higher slope roofs, either architectural-grade asphalt shingles or metal roofing is preferred, due to the greater life span and the lower maintenance. In areas of high vandalism, metal roofs are used due to their higher resistance to damage.

Other than the roof membrane standard, the city does not have requirements for exterior materials. Instead, it is up to the city's project managers to find a balance between the budget, aesthetics, and long-term maintenance. For instance, the city currently uses masonry whenever possible because of its low maintenance and attractive appearance. The city's land-use code does not provide direction on the selection of exterior materials, so the building code often drives the interior and exterior material choices, based upon fire-resistance requirements.

The City of Eugene also maintains a policy on sustainability issues, and, whenever possible, its projects use "green" materials and incorporate sustainability concepts. Moreover, for new projects and major remodels, the city participates in the U.S. Green Building Council's Leadership in Energy and Environmental Design (LEED) Program. This is a voluntary program designed to use principles of sustainability and green building concepts to produce buildings that are more environmentally sound and which require less energy to operate. In order to meet some of the LEED certification criteria, the city uses a variety of "green" materials and sustainable products, including carpet, wood products, and roofing.

One example of a green directive to the design team by the city, is the use of Milliken's "Earth Square" carpet, which, for most new and remodel projects, is the carpet specified for use. Created by a process developed by Milliken which renews and reuses existing modular carpet (carpet tiles), Earth Square carpet has a completely new installation life and a performance guarantee equal to that of a new product. The city's participation in this process of recycling old carpet helps reduce landfill disposal of old carpet, reduces the added energy and raw materials required to recycle old carpet into another product, reduces off-gassing of chemical compounds into new structures, and, most importantly, reduces up-front costs of the carpet by approximately 50%.

In addition to requiring sound initial choices regarding materials to be incorporated into its facilities, the city also requires the recycling of construction waste for all major projects. Contracts require that the general contractor develop, maintain, and manage an on-going construction waste recycling program. Typically, the city expects the general contractor to recycle wood waste, metals, drywall (gypsum products), soil, concrete, and asphalt. For example, the new public library project has recycled nearly 20,000 cubic yards of topsoil and bar run fill, in addition to the on-going recycling of its construction waste. Recycling construction waste for small projects, however, has not proven to be cost effective.

BUILDING SERVICES AND COMMUNICATIONS

Controls of systems for HVAC, plumbing, fire suppression, fire alarm, electrical, lighting, security, telephone, computing, etc.
The City of Eugene dictates the type of Direct Digital Control (DDC), fire alarm, security, telephone, and computer cabling systems that are used in all of its facilities. Due to the large number of facilities within the city, the use of the "single source" system is required because it would not be cost effective to maintain different, noncompatible building control and security systems. For these systems, the city mandates the use of particular manufacturers and suppliers. The architect is not given a range of choices.

The city has a set of well-established requirements for telephone and computer cabling. These are minimum requirements and are often exceeded in the project design. For example, the new 911 center needed cable trays which allowed for flexibility and future cable modifications without interruption of service. The guidelines didn't address cable trays, but once they were installed in the 911 center and were found to be workable, then this same cable tray system became the standard for cable trays to be used in the new public library project.

The city also mandates the creation of dedicated rooms for telephone and data use. Each city facility is required to have a room that is a minimum of 8 feet x 8 feet to house telephone and computer equipment. Each room must have at least two walls covered with 3/4-inch MDO-faced plywood, designed to accept the installation phone connection blocks and terminals. The room must also have dedicated circuits for the equipment and ventilation, and which are tailored to the amount of equipment installed. Security for these rooms is also addressed by the city, which understands that these areas are potentially vulnerable areas of its computer network.

The locations for mechanical rooms, electrical closets, telephone closets, etc., are dependent on the type of facility being built, its site, and its design. The goal is to locate these spaces so that maintenance access is easy. (Proximity to maintenance parking is also a concern.) In the performing arts facility, one major mechanical room is on the third floor and it is only accessible by an internal service stair. There is no elevator access to the area, and everything needed in the space has to be hand-carried up multiple flights of stairs. This makes repairs difficult, costly, and may reduce the frequency of preventive maintenance, thus decreasing the expected life span of the equipment.

Acoustics
There are no formal requirements by the city for sound transmission class (STC) or impact insulation class (IIC) ratings. Acoustical requirements for each facility or space are individually considered and the appropriate response implemented. For instance, the new 911 center has many acoustical controls because of the nature of the facility's function, but the new fire stations have no equipment which is out of the ordinary. The new library project includes a mix of sound attenuation solutions which are dependent on the different locations. However, one routine practice in acoustical installations is that whenever sound insulation is installed in a wall, an attempt is made to eliminate sound paths around the insulation and between the spaces. But, regardless of the desired response to the acoustical requirements of a space, acoustical

considerations are always evaluated in relationship to the project budget.

Energy

Energy conservation is mandated by the City of Eugene to its design professionals. With over 100 facilities in its system, each small energy savings makes a difference by contributing to the larger, organization-wide savings. Responsible for energy management is a full-time staff person, who works within the Facility Management Office, and who interfaces with the operations and maintenance branch of the organization, as well as with the design and construction branch.

According to the building code, all city projects must meet the State of Oregon's energy code. The city, however, maintains a strong commitment to exceed code requirements whenever possible, and it voluntarily participates in an interactive, cooperative energy-saving program with the local utility company. In addition, the city participates in the U.S. Green Building Council's Leadership in Energy and Environmental Design (LEED) Program which establishes guidelines for building orientation; limitations on glazing area; use of low E glazing; insulation in excess of code minimums; use of day-lighting practices; and, in some cases (for swimming pools), the use of solar energy for water heating. Heat recovery is utilized in buildings whenever possible. The LEED program, combined with the expertise of the local service utility company, provides direction and opportunities to the city for energy-saving strategies to be included in projects.

Of course, each situation and each project is different. In general, architects/engineers are required to incorporate as many energy-saving strategies as possible just as a routine approach to design. Routinely, the city strives to produce facilities that use between 20 and 30% less energy than that allowed under the current energy code. A good example of how this interactive approach can produce a more energy-efficient facility is illustrated by the new public library project. When the design process began, the target energy savings established by the city was 20% less than that allowed under the current energy code. Through work with the local utility company and with innovative solutions from the design team, the projected savings are 30%, well below that allowed by code. The additional 10% in savings was achieved through a cooperative effort by the serving utility, the design team, and the city, as the owner. And, despite the significant savings projected for this facility, there is not expected to be a significant increase in the maintenance costs for the facility.

In order to achieve the desired energy savings and to produce acceptable user comfort, the new public library project required the use of Direct Digital Control (DDC) systems. Because the city has found that building systems are too complex to manage as they have been in the past, requiring more real-time information, data logging, and interactive control, it has been determined that the only effective way to manage all of the building systems to achieve and maintain energy savings is through the use of a DDC system. Such systems are mandated by the city for all major new and remodel projects.

Maintenance
To reduce the maintenance required by its facilities, the city dictates many materials and products to the architect, including flush valves, carpet, roofing, electrical panels, DDC systems, fire alarm systems, and, whenever possible, the manufacturer of the HVAC equipment. When about 30% of the working drawings are complete, the project manager meets with the maintenance staff, reviews the project and products with them, and considers their input. For example, it was learned from the staff that using a standardized type of flush valve requires that the plumber have only one type of rebuild kit. Otherwise, the plumber must stock several different types or make repeated trips to the wholesale house for parts, thus wasting time. Project managers are always looking at the long-term costs of any solution, and this includes maintenance.

GUIDELINES FOR COMPUTER-GENERATED
WORKING DRAWINGS

The computer is a valuable tool for producing production drawings. It allows the city almost constant access to the architect/ engineer's work as it progresses, and it allows the city to maintain an electronic record of the information, which makes updates easier and affords greater accuracy.

Cover sheet
Renderings of the project are not required on the cover sheet by the City of Eugene because they are expensive to produce and the contractor does not need them.

Differences between architects' material symbols are minor and usually don't create problems for the city. Problems occur, however, when a new symbol is used in the drawings without identification. This might happen when a new draftsperson joins the team and draws a symbol he or she is familiar with but which is not included in the working drawing legend.

Site

The City of Eugene requires that the site plan show the legal boundaries of the site, the known utilities, and the other items on the site. Of course, there might be unknown site elements which will be omitted from the plan, such as unknown underground utilities, which pose a routing problem and source of significant added expense. Either contingencies for contractors to address such occurrences is allowed, or else the city does all of the site work and addresses the unknowns itself, thus establishing exactly how much of the budget remains for the project. (In one case, three unknown underground storage tanks were discovered, and the clean-up cost was in excess of $250,000.)

Also required for major new buildings is a series of soil borings, done both for geotechnical and environmental information. A site-specific seismic analysis is also done. These procedures avoid significant problems but other problems occur when the architect uses the surveyor's data file without examining the information closely. In some of these cases, the survey includes information that was of no use, and, in other cases omitted information that was needed. These problems happen when the wrong layers from the computer file are selected.

The city has a very extensive Storm Water Management plan including a length list of "dos" and "don'ts." Therefore, city projects are monitored more closely than a private project might be.

Floor plans

A common problem in floor plans is that matching dimension strings do not add to the same total length. As an aid to finding dimensioning errors during reviews, dimension strings are required to have common reference points, but, in some cases, there seems to be less care checking dimensions when the drawings are done on CAD, than when the plan is drawn by hand. It might be believed that the computer will prevent these errors.

Regarding the use of arrowheads in dimensions, the city prefers that slashes be used because they tend to work for all scales of drawings.

Architectural drawings for the city are in feet and inches; civil drawings are in decimals. At this time, there is no trend by the city toward metric dimensioning.

Roof plans
Roof plans are required for all projects, and they sometimes have problems. For instance, often it is discovered that fall-protection tie-offs have been omitted from the drawing or that walk pads to roof-mounted equipment are missing, thus causing change orders and extra expense if not caught prior to bidding.

Reflected ceiling plans
Ceiling plans are required by the city. Often, light fixtures are in conflict with other ceiling, and above-ceiling, items. It is desirable, therefore, that during the construction drawing phase the consultants superimpose drawing-file layers of lights, fire sprinkler, piping, electrical, and structural drawings, and search for such conflicts.

Elevations
The sea-level reference is used for floor elevations rather than the alternative of 100.00', which, otherwise, might be assigned as the first-floor elevation. All elevations are tied to an elevation benchmark within the city, which is an elevation above sea level. It is preferred to stay with these benchmark notations for locating important items on elevations and/or sections. Otherwise, using other reference points results in a mixture of elevation dimensions on the drawings in both decimals, and feet and inches, and grade problems have resulted from misunderstandings regarding this mixture.

Building sections
There are often not enough building sections drawn. In the cases where a minimum number are provided on the working drawings, a condition not anticipated in a section which has been omitted can become a problem. (Stair sections are common examples of this.) Sections are considered very important by the city because they bring the project into the third dimension and show that the architect visualized how the building would be assembled vertically.

Wall sections

The extent to which wall sections are drawn varies from architect to architect, but they must always be clear and of adequate scale to be informative. Wall sections are useful when they respond to building specifics because they can eliminate problems.

Window and door details

There is often not enough detailing for windows and doors. An example of this comes from a previous city project with fire-rated glazing in it, but for which no hollow metal frame sections were drawn; the openings were just shown in elevation and specified. The shop drawings were approved, and the frames were fabricated and installed, but the 1-1/2 inch thick glass would not fit into the frame because there was only a 2-inch recess to receive glazing tape on both sides, as well as a 5/8-inch stop. A simple, accurate section would have shown this problem in advance. One solution, after the fact, would be to take the frames out of the masonry walls and install new ones using epoxy anchors, thus resulting in a reduction of quality.

Details

Projects are never over-detailed. Generally there are too few details. There is the assumption that the contractor will work the details out in the field, but this leads to results that are less than acceptable in many cases. Where extensive detailing occurs, fewer problems and added costs are encountered during construction.

Schedules

Problems with schedules often include instances where rooms are without numbers, or where rooms are left off altogether. Errors in the finish matrix are also a common problem, and they result from inadequate double-checking of the data. An example of such an error would be the case where epoxy paint was scheduled for a lay-in ceiling system that was actually required to be left unpainted for acoustical purposes.

General information

Preferred for larger jobs is the standard 36-inch x 42-inch sheet size, which can be reduced to sheets of 18 inches x 21 inches, also a standard size. The relationship between these sizes is especially useful because for larger projects, half-size reproductions are always prepared.

Providing contract drawings on CD ROM to contractors is being considered by the city. This is currently being done on federal projects for bidding purposes. From some agencies, a CD is issued rather than a set of drawings. One then has to use a CAD system to do the quantity take-off, etc.

General problems
Some problems encountered by the city include one or more sheets are missing from working drawings, and the use of uncommon scales, such as 3/16"=1'-0", on drawings which are not recommended. Another problem is that often data which should be on the drawings is listed in the specifications, and vice versa. (When similar information occurs in both places, conflicts are common.)

Contractors complain about a lack of enough clear information, and they are often required to sort through a whole series of sheets to get the answer to a question. For instance, a plan might read, "see the section," and the section might read, "see the structural," and the structural might instruct the reader to look elsewhere, until, finally, there is a reference to an architectural detail, some place. Put all together, one can arrive at an answer, but it is a time-consuming and confusing process. Therefore, clarity of information and its presentation is important. And it is also important to minimize the areas where the contractor has to assume something. There is an economical limit to the time which the owner can invest in answering contractors' questions arising from problems in drawings.

There can be a gap or lack of coordination regarding where the architectural/engineering drawings end and where the civil drawings begin. An assumed boundary for the architectural/engineering work is 5 feet outside of the building line, and beyond that is the area of work which belongs to the civil engineers. The coordination at this boundary is often found to be lacking.

Construction administration
It has been observed that the construction administration phase of a project is the most problematic. Difficulties arise when the architects administering construction contracts do not entirely understand the terms of the contracts, nor the rights and responsibilities of each party. This has resulted in unanticipated costs, project delays, and additional work for the city project managers.

In the past, it has been found that among the various consultants, architects are generally the best equipped to prepare and administer construction contracts, due to their traditional assignment as the prime consultant in private work. Their coordination of other consultants in this role has given them a global view of project needs, a posture necessary in construction administration for the city.

Brad Black is a licensed architect living in Eugene, Oregon, and he works for the City of Eugene as the owner's representative/project manager. In this role, he manages the City of Eugene's new $34.2 million public library project. Other city projects successfully managed by him include the $11 million Broadway Place project, a multi-use, public-private housing/parking garage facility which received the Governor's Award for Livability. In addition to his 10 years of experience as a project manager/owner's representative, Mr. Black holds the Certified Construction Specifier (CCS) status with the Construction Specification Institute. He has been a licensed architect since 1980, and has practiced architecture in Oregon and Oklahoma. In addition to his practice, Mr. Black has also held the position of Assistant Professor of Architecture at both the University of Arkansas and the University of Oklahoma, and he has been Adjunct Faculty at the University of Oregon.

Frequently Repeated Comments for the Construction Documents Phase

William S. Morrison
Assistant Director
Facility Planning and Control
Division of Administration
Baton Rouge, Louisiana

The following are typical comments made by authorities in the office of Facility Planning and Control, State of Louisiana, in response to construction documents prepared for state work and submitted to the office for review. The comments are general in nature and, therefore, apply not only to documents prepared for state projects in any state but are also applicable to documents prepared for any construction project. It should be noted that the entries marked with an asterisk (*) relate either to office policy or to Louisiana statutory requirements and might not be applicable to other states.

SPECIFICATIONS

Administration

- "Use original or properly authorized copies of AIA Document A201 in the documents issued for bidding."

- "There are some items that need to be added or clarified in the specifications. Please see the notes on the attached copy."

- "Do not use unit prices except for pile length and well depth. In any case they must be stated as single price which may be added or deducted. In general the best approach to providing for conditions that can not be accurately defined prior to bidding, such as roof decking if reroofing is included, is to include a stated quantity in the documents and set it up so that the amount will appear as a line item in the Schedule of values."*

- "The Designer alone is responsible to the Owner for this project and is the administrator of the construction contract. We do not want this issue confused by the use of other professional titles in the documents such as Architect/Engineer, Engineer if the Designer is an Architect, Architect if he is an Engineer, etc. Please revise any such references."*

- "If a project sign is used, specify a sign specifically for this project and limit wording to the project name, project number, State of Louisiana, name of Governor, Architect, Contractor. Do not include subcontractors, Board members, or any other information."*

Applicability
- "Your specifications contain a large amount of verbiage that does not apply to this project. Carefully review your documents and eliminate everything that does not apply to this project."

- "Be sure that the performance requirements you have stated are appropriate for this project."

Coordination
- "Coordination of the specifications. Be sure that the Table of Contents is accurate, pages are in order, etc."

- "Be sure that general requirements in the separate sections are coordinated with the General Conditions and Supplementary Conditions. This comment is typical for any requirements that are defined in more than one place."

Contractor
- "Our contract will be with the general contractor. We will have no contractual relationship with any subcontractors. All specifications shall be directed to the general contractor and it will be his responsibility to allocate work and other aspects of the project to the various subcontractors."

- "Do not burden the Contractor with unnecessary administrative procedures. Please review the following sections and be sure that they require only submittals and other information necessary to the proper administration of the project."
    - Application for Payment
    - Construction Schedules
    - Cutting and Patching
    - Project Closeout
    - Project Record Documents
    - Quality Control

    o Shop Drawings, Product Data, and Samples
    o Temporary Facilities

- "Coordinate temporary facilities and utilities with the User
  Agency and designate specific areas and utilities for the
  contractor's use. Require that any facilities used by the contractor
  be returned to the condition in which they were found at the start
  of the project and see that condition is noted and recorded before
  work starts."

Technology

- "Reasons for allowing substitution should include only those that
  provide a substantial advantage to the Owner or are related to
  conditions beyond the control of the Architect or Contractor that
  have changed since the project was bid. For example: a warranty
  can not be provided because the manufacturer that offered it at
  the time of bidding no longer does so."

- "The specifications appear to include copies of standard
  documents. Be sure that these apply to this project and edit them
  if necessary. If copyrights apply to any of these documents, be
  sure the documents have been properly obtained. The Designer
  will be responsible for any problems caused by reliance on
  standard documents."

- "Be sure that all such things as doors, windows, hardware, etc.,
  are completely scheduled."

- "I am enclosing a list of low-slope (flat) roofing systems that are
  approved for use on State projects. Please specify two or more of
  these for the low-slope roofs on this project. If you have a
  compelling reason for using another system please submit
  complete manufacturer's data for this system to this office for
  review. If it is approved it will be added to the list. Also attached
  is a list of criteria that must be met if the system is to be
  approved. Metal roofing is not affected by this."*

- "Structural systems seem to be over-designed in some cases.
  Please review your calculations."

- "Southern Yellow Pine is specified exclusively. Name other
  acceptable species unless there is a compelling reason for using
  this species."

Standards

- "In some sections the contractor is instructed to comply with ADA Guidelines, ANSI Guidelines, NFPA requirements, "local codes," "governing authorities," ACI, CRSI, DOTD, SDI, AISC, etc. Such statements are acceptable but they are not to be used as a substitute for design. The Designer is responsible for these decisions."

- "In many sections under "Available Products" the following phrase is used: 'Subject to compliance with requirements . . .' It is acceptable to include such a phrase but it is not a substitute for the Designer's review and approval of products."

- "The specifications appear to rely heavily on standard documents such as the Louisiana Standard Specifications for Roads and Bridges and/or others. Be sure that these apply to this project and be sure that you have in your possession, or ready access to, copies of all such standards referred to in your documents. The Designer is responsible for the decisions covered by these standards and any problems caused by reliance on them."*

- "Please be sure that you have in your possession copies of all reference standards referred to in your documents and that you are familiar with their contents and their application to this project. This includes 'manufacturer's written instructions.' "

- "The contractor should be reminded that all requirements of OSHA must be met including the Hazard Communication Standard."

DRAWINGS

General

- "The drawings include incomplete items and inconsistencies and do not appear to be ready for bid. They also lack coordination in some areas, need more referencing and, in some places, are difficult to read. Examples are marked on the drawings."

- "Be specific. Be sure that bidders know exactly what to bid on."

- "The [name omitted]'s documentation is disorganized and inconsistent in presentation. This makes the project difficult to bid and increases the possibility of misunderstandings on the job."

- "Be sure that the appropriate Architect's and Engineer's stamps are on the drawings."*

- "For the [name omitted] much design is left to the Contractor. Be very sure that design and/or design criteria is provided by you. We do not want change orders or to have to compromise the integrity of the building because the work is not adequately defined. This includes but is not limited to profiles, sizes, joints, support bracing, connections, and coordination with other building systems."

Technology
- "We have had reports of termites tunneling through silicone sealant. Please be careful in using this type of sealant."

- "Be sure that there are enough fire extinguishers and that they are in the right places."

- "In the office areas the partitions should be constructed on the carpet and stop at the ceiling."*

- "The roof has many penetrations and many of them appear to be unnecessary. Please review the design of the roofing, the roof structure, mechanical systems, etc., to determine how this roof can be simplified."

- "Show all sprinkler piping, pipe sizes and locations of sprinkler heads on plans."

GENERAL COMMENTS

Administration
- "Extent of the specifications. The specifications have gone from a condition of not having enough information to having, in some cases, too much. Some items of work are covered more extensively than necessary. Be sure that all documents are edited for this project."

- "Do not include details or specifications that do not apply to this project. Be sure that all references to other projects are deleted or revised."

- "Be sure that drawings and specifications are clear and unambiguous. As Mark Twain said, and I am paraphrasing here,

'Do not write so that you can be understood. Write so that you can *not* be *mis*understood.' "

Format

- "The Federal Government requires that many federally funded projects use the metric system of weights and measures. Does this affect this project? Please verify this with the federal agency that administers the funds for this project if you have not already done so."

- "Do not use exculpatory clauses that attempt to cover situations which may not have been covered, or poorly covered, in the documents. Examples of such statements include 'to the satisfaction of the Architect,' 'as directed by the Architect,' 'unless otherwise directed,' or 'at the discretion of the Owner.' Such statements are open ended, do not give the contractor a basis on which to bid, and leave him exposed to demands to do work which is not called for in the documents. The scope of work must be completely defined within the documents."

- "Consistent terminology. Be sure that consistent terminology is used throughout the documents and particularly between the drawings and specifications."

Performance

- "Your budget estimate indicates that the construction cost of the complete facility will exceed the amount available for construction (AFC). If the low base bid exceeds the AFC the project will have to be redesigned to the extent necessary to bring the cost within the AFC *and* to include all program requirements. We applaud and encourage efforts to provide good design but our definition of 'good design' includes meeting all the program requirements."

- "The documents appear to contain incomplete items. Though most of these are small, there are many of them and they indicate that the documents were not complete as required by your contract for submittal at this phase. This means that your contract time was not complete with this submittal. Your contract time will resume when you receive this letter."

Coordination

- "Coordination of the drawings. Be sure that all drawings agree and that all systems are appropriate for this project and work together. Be sure that all such things as doors, windows, finishes, etc., are completely scheduled."

- "Coordination of drawings with the specifications. Some items shown on the drawings are not covered in the specifications and some items covered in the specifications are not called for on the drawings. Do not include specifications that do not apply to this project and be sure all items called for on the drawings are specified."

Technology
- "Please keep in mind the availability of materials for maintenance when specifying or calling out materials or equipment."

- "No 'equipment' is to be included in construction contracts. Equipment means items that do not require a mechanic to install them, such as refrigerators, microwave ovens, etc."*

- "Conditions for the metal building have not been detailed. It appears that you are relying on a 'manufacturer's standard' system and you have listed manufacturers but no specific systems. Does each of these manufacturers provide only one system and if so is each of them acceptable? If not, name the systems that are acceptable. In any case you must address the "model number" concept. If the manufacturer has more than one system, name the one that is to be used. If not, make it clear that this is the case. For instance:

   "American Steel Building Co., Inc., Superduper System A-1 Armco Steelox Building Systems, Manufacturer's Standard System"

   "Even if a manufacturer has only one system he usually has a name for it and if so it should be used. Any options within a system also must be addressed."

   "The metal building must be treated *either* as a system which is designed and detailed by the designer *or* as a product that the Designer has evaluated and specified by manufacturer and "model number." In either case the object is to provide specific and detailed criteria by which the end product and shop drawings can be evaluated. If this is addressed by manufacturer and model you must have in your possession, or ready access to, printed product information that clearly describes and details the system. My recommendation is to obtain specific product information from at least two manufacturers, review and verify the adequacy of the system from this information and list the manufacturers and models in the specifications. Prior approvals and shop drawing review can be based on this information. You must be sure that the system available at the time of construction does not vary from the printed information."*

Energy
• "Please be sure that all appropriate elements are addressed in the Energy Conservation Analysis. For example: building orientation, glazing, thermal characteristics of the building envelope, illumination, energy-consuming and heat-producing equipment and alternate HVAC systems. See the Designer's Package for more information on this."*

Life-safety
• "It is understood that a sprinkler system is not required by code. However, the exclusion of this item should be carefully considered by the Designer and the User."

• "The Code Analysis references the _____ NFPA Life Safety Code. This building is required to meet the requirements of the _____ Edition of this code."

Standards
• "Use the Americans with Disabilities Act Accessibility Guidelines (ADAAG) to address the Americans with Disabilities Act."

• "Be sure that you can comply with all requirements of the Americans with Disabilities Act."

Facility Planning & Control administers the capital outlay budget for all building construction for the State of Louisiana. Typically there are approximately 650 projects totaling 1 billion dollars in various stages of design and construction. The office also handles all real estate leasing for the State of Louisiana with a total of 4,700,000 square feet of leased space. The office is headed by the Director, Roger Magendie.

Architectural Work for the U.S. Navy

Stephen L. Reece, Architect
Bainbridge Island, Washington

General

You don't have to be a naval architect to work for the Navy.

Providing architectural services for the U.S. Navy is rewarding because the building types are diverse, the fees are just, payment is prompt, and the government counterparts to civilian architects are design professionals.

The U.S. Navy Civil Engineers Corps Officers, through the Naval Facilities Engineering Command (NAVFACENGCOM), are responsible for planning, programming, designing, and constructing buildings for the U.S. Navy. NAVFACENGCOM uses acquisition teams comprised of architects, engineers, program managers, contract specialists, and contract administrators to produce buildings.

Architects desiring work with the Navy must be skilled in assembling consultants who best meet the requirements and solicitations for A-E services. Architectural services are procured through Commerce Business Daily[1] solicitations. The Architect must assemble a team of individuals who best meet the selection factors listed in the CBD Announcement for the specific project.

Submissions

When responding to a solicitation, make certain that the SF-254 (Architect-Engineer and Related Services Questionnaire) and SF-255 (Architect-Engineer and Related Services Questionnaire for Specific Project) forms[2] list only skill and experience that directly relates to the specific project or selection criteria requirements. Be accurate and complete in filling out the forms, and explain, specifically, how the proposed team of consultants best meets the selection criteria. The response to a CBD solicitation will receive attention from a Slate Panel, whose mission is to prepare a list of five to eight of the most highly qualified A-E firms for interview by a Selection Board. The intention of the Slate Panel is to review all submissions, but they will eliminate all incomplete or inconsistent proposals at the outset. The Slate Panel will probably review 50 to 80 submissions within a 3-day period. Don't give the Slate Panel any excuse for early dismissal of your submittal.

Interviews

The slated short list of A-E firms will be invited for an interview by the Selection and Negotiation Board. Each firm will be allowed about 30 minutes to present their unique qualifications followed by 30 minutes of questions and answers. Focus the presentation and response to the CBD Solicitation factors in priority order. All firms interviewed are qualified to do the job, so the chemistry and interaction with the Selection Board is very important. Be natural, but be memorable. Bring no more people to the interview than is necessary to present the proposal. Explain the contribution of each member.

Bring name place cards to identify each member of the team and his or her role. No matter how many times the architect has been across the table from the same Selection Board, he or she must always present his or her unique and specific qualifications for that specific project. Remember it's not the names of the team members that are important, but their specific skills, knowledge, and experience that count.

Fee Proposal

The selected firm will be invited to submit a fee proposal for purposes of determining a fair and reasonable price for the required A-E services. The services are described in a detailed Scope of Work. Prepare the fee proposal in direct man-hours by discipline and by phase. Obtain a copy of the *Federal Register*[3] to understand what the "6-percent rule" applies to. Negotiations will be based on the level of effort required, so bring supporting calculations. List all drawings by discipline for each submittal phase. Calculate all printing and correspondence costs. Be prepared to discuss allowable elements of overhead and profit. Travel and per diem rates are established by Government Travel Regulations. Use the negotiation to clarify the program, refine the scope of work, define special services, and to quantify submission requirements. Tie down the delivery schedule according to phases, and, if possible, set the review time.

Design and Production
Never exceed the authorized square foot area nor the construction
cost budget amount without written approval of
NAVFACENGCOM. Learn the Department of Defense method of
gross area calculation. It is different than for any other code. Don't
exceed authorized project scope without written approval.

NAVFACENGCOM highly values clear and concise
construction documents prepared on schedule. Your first successful
project delivery is the most reliable way of being considered for
repeat work. Watch the CBD announcements for future
solicitations.

Notes
[1] The CBD can be accessed at <http://cbdnet.gpo.gov/read-gd.html>.

[2] Forms SF-254 and SF-255 can be accessed at
<http://hydra.gsa.gov/forms/zero.htm>.

[3] *Federal Register*, vol. 41m, no.15, January 22, 1976, page 3293.

Stephen L. Reece has 25 years experience with the United States
Navy as an engineering officer, an Officer in Charge of a SEABEE
team, a Resident Officer in Charge of Construction, Architect, a
Planning Engineer, a Community Planner, and a Supervisory
Architect. His responsibilities have included housing, institutional
and urban design, interior design, project management, and team
supervision. He was a Supervisory Construction Analyst for the U.S.
Department of Housing and Urban Development for 4 years. Mr.
Reece is a licensed architect in the state of Washington.

Comments on Working Drawings

Charles G. Jeffcoat
Director/University Architect
Office of Facilities Management
University of South Carolina
Columbia, South Carolina

Predesign requirements

- For renovation projects it is imperative that the architect/engineer visit the site and survey it to document existing conditions prior to preparing renovation bid documents. These visits will eliminate the need for change orders due to architectural, mechanical, plumbing, and electrical conflicts in the field resulting from insufficient space, clearances, etc.

- For new projects, sufficient geotechnical (quality control) testing should be done on a new building site to eliminate change orders resulting from unknown conditions.

Coordination of utilities

- Architectural and engineering drawings should show clear details of mechanical/plumbing shafts and all of the utilities that are to be housed in them. Often the utilities are crowded in these shafts. It must be verified that space will be adequate for the utilities and that they are accessible, where appropriate.

- It is imperative that architectural, mechanical, plumbing, and electrical working drawings be coordinated during the design and construction document phase in order to eliminate conflicts and change orders during construction.

- Coordinate heights of beams, ducts, pipes, and conduits. When the positions of utilities above the ceiling are left up to the contractor, a less than desirable ceiling height might result. Also, if it is not verified that there is enough space for all of the utilities above the ceiling, it might be discovered, on the job, that they do not fit. In one case, the lack of coordination of beam height and utilities resulted in lowering a ceiling from the 9-foot height that was planned to 8 feet. The sprinkler piping still would not fit, however, and it had to be relocated above the ceiling of an adjacent space.

Student safety
- Some measures needed for student safety include security screens at lower-level windows to keep students from using them as a means of ingress and egress. Also, safety stops must be provided at upper-level windows to prevent student access to ledges and/or roofs.

Components
- When components requiring custom manufacturing are required, they should be identified to contractors bidding on the work. In a previous case, bidders were not aware of the requirement for a custom component in an emergency generator system. After the bids, a $36,000 change order was required for the item.

Completeness of drawings
- Working drawings and construction bid documents for university construction have to be more detailed and complete than drawings for the private sector, due to public advertisement and bidding to meet state procurement code requirements. Documents that are complete eliminate misinterpretation or guesswork during the bidding process. In a previous case, steel bracing above a storefront entrance wall was not clearly shown in the construction documents, and resulted in a change order request by the contractor.

- Clear details of window installation, including how they are fastened to the structure, are required. Details of interior and exterior sills, trim, etc., must be included.

- All of the larger project drawings are reviewed by the Office of the State Engineer. During this review, many code issues are identified that would have been costly change orders, if not found prior to bidding. The same issues could be identified through a plan checking service, prior to submission to the university. Architects should employ such a service or other means in order to verify that drawings are complete and that all code requirements are met.

Facilities Planning and Construction and Facility Services are responsible for the renovation and construction, and operations and maintenance of all academic and administrative facilities on the University of South Carolina Columbia campus. Facility Services operates and maintains 150 buildings and approximately 5 million square feet of building space on the Columbia campus. Facilities Planning and Construction manages approximately $200 to $250 million in renovation and new construction projects on an ongoing basis for all South Carolina university campuses. In addition to the Columbia campus, Facilities Planning and Construction is responsible for managing the work and costs associated with renovation and new construction projects conducted on seven campuses across the state of South Carolina.

Recommendations
for Working Drawings

Ted Curtis, AIA, NCARB
Vice President for Capital Planning
and Facilities Management
University of Akron
Akron, Ohio

Detailing strategy

- Details should be provided to show the configuration of all items
  that are required to be installed on the project. On occasion a
  brief note such as "caulk" is used in lieu of a detail. Instead, a
  detail should indicate exactly where the caulk should be placed.

- Details should be drawn at a scale larger than is typical. The
  detail must be large enough so that no questions remain for the
  bidder as to how the architect would like to see the various
  materials installed.

Flashing

- Flashing should be installed at joints vulnerable to water
  penetration. At times, caulking has been used in lieu of flashing,
  but it is not a satisfactory solution for an extended period.
  Caulking should be used only as a secondary line of defense to
  back up protection by flashing.

Contractor input

- Input from tradespeople should be incorporated into the
  preparation of details, showing how the materials and
  components of the respective trades are to be installed. The
  people who actually install the materials and components know
  the practical considerations which should affect the architect's
  design of the assembly. Sound advice from the various trades is
  available for the asking.

Mr. Curtis has been a registered architect for 43 years and is registered in 11 states. In addition to having his own architectural firm for more than 20 years, he was also the Chief Corporate Architect for the Hilton Hotels Corporation for 6 years. He has been a consultant for several years and joined the University of Akron administration in 1999.

The University of Akron is a publicly assisted metropolitan institution. It offers comprehensive programs of instruction from associate through doctoral levels, pursues a vigorous agenda of research in the arts, sciences, and professions, and provides service to the community. The University of Akron pursues excellence in undergraduate and graduate education, and distinction in selected areas of graduate instruction, inquiry, and creative activity.

Working Drawing Checklists

This chapter provides checklists for working drawings, the use of which will help avoid omissions and errors of a special nature. Nine lists are provided by two key sources in the building industry, a code consulting firm and a contractors' association. As could be anticipated, the three lists from the code consultant have a code compliance focus, unique among checklists commonly available.

The six checklists provided by the contractors' group cover the architect's and consultant's working drawings. They are based on the members' collective experience regarding shortcomings of working drawings as well as opinions and ideas of others in the building industry who were consulted during the development of the document. The "field-experience" basis for the lists makes them unique and particularly useful.

Plan Review Checklists

Kelly P. Reynolds & Associates, Inc.
Building Code Consultants
Chicago, Illinois

The following lists are an outline of basic information compiled to expedite plan review time and approvals. Prior to submitting Plans and Specifications, review the appropriate list to be sure all necessary information is included in your submittals. To avoid unnecessary delays, be sure to include TWO complete sets of plans and specifications. (Check with local building department for number of complete sets they require.)

BUILDING PLAN REVIEW CHECKLIST

1. Title block which includes:
   - Total square footage
   - Type of construction
   - Use group
   - Occupant load calculations
   - List of all installed fire protection
   - List of all design options
2. Site plan.
3. Complete building plans showing use of all areas.
4. All appropriate wall, floor, and foundation sections.
5. Complete door schedule with catalog cuts for all doors and hardware, including locksets.
6. Complete window and glazing schedule.
7. Complete interior finish schedule with flame spread ratings.
8. Complete specifications.
9. List of all rated assemblies, including a diagram of assembly and design numbers.
10. Details showing all handicap requirements.

11. Occupant load for all areas.

12. Statement indicating that shop drawings will be submitted for all fire-protection systems.

13. Electrical plans, showing the location of all exit and means of egress lighting.

14. List of all design loads for the building.

15. Complete information on special occupancy requirements (floor opening, high rise and covered mall).

16. Complete information for all special structures (sky lights, roof, panels, awnings, etc.).

17. Soil test.

18. Signed and sealed plans, and structural calculations.

19. Sequence of operations for all special systems (smoke control, elevator recall, etc.).

SPRINKLER PLAN REVIEW CHECKLIST

1. Water flow test, including pressures, location, time, date, witness, and seasonal adjustment.

2. Type of pipes, joints, fittings, dimensions, and lengths of pipes.

3. Indicate sprinkler protection for all areas and square footage per sprinkler.

4. Number, type, and temperature ratings for all sprinklers.

5. Catalog cuts for special sprinklers.

6. Building occupancy, describing process or storage commodity.

7. Section and plan views of racks or shelving.

8. Storage heights.

9. Description of special systems, showing valves and all trim.

10. Indicate locations of gauges, main drains, auxiliary drains, and test valves.

11. Plan showing arrangement, piping drainage, threads and height of the Fire Department Connection.

12. Statements indicating that all tests and flushing will be completed.

13. Hose rack layout.

14. Storage areas complying with NFPA 231 series.

15. Detail and location of all hangers.

16. Supervision of valves and flow switches where applicable.

17. Hydraulically calculated systems.

18. Complete calculations.

19. Completed sprinkler system summary sheet.

20. Flow diagram showing nodes or reference points.

PLUMBING/MECHANICAL REVIEW CHECKLIST

1. Upon selection of mechanical equipment and appliances, submit manufacturer's installation instructions to the Building Department.

2. Submit cleaning schedule for commercial kitchen exhaust hood and duct system.

3. Submit details showing construction of commercial kitchen hood and duct system.

4. Submit specifications for commercial kitchen exhaust hood suppression system. Indicate pipe size, minimum and maximum length, number of elbows, and installation procedures and tests.

5. Submit ventilation schedule indicating amount of supply air, exhaust air, and outside air.

6. Submit specifications for fixtures, pipe materials, joints, and connections for all plumbing systems.

7. Submit gas piping plans showing location, pipe sizes, and material.

8. Submit plans showing complete water piping system, including all sizes.

9. Indicate the location of drinking fountains or indicate that bottled water will be provided.

10. If copper tubing is to be installed, indicate solder for copper tubing for potable water distribution to be lead-free solder.

11. Submit working drawings for the required fire protection, suppression, and detection systems when a contractor is chosen.

12. Submit riser diagram for drainage, waste, and vent system.

13. Provide smoke duct detection, if HVAC system has more than 2000 cfm.

14. Provide 110V outlet for servicing rooftop appliances.

Kelly P. Reynolds & Associates, Inc., offers a comprehensive third-party plan and specification review service, specializing in examinations based on the model codes. The scope of services includes BOCA®, Uniform, and Standard, Building, Mechanical, Plumbing, Electrical, and Fire Codes; NFPA National Fire Codes; National Electrical Code; disability standards; and International Codes (ICC). State and local amendments to these codes are included. The company also provides fire and life safety consulting, as well as code seminars.

Kelly P. Reynolds is a former Chief Fire Protection Engineer with BOCA® International. He has extensive experience in plan review, product research, and code evaluation. His expertise includes code interpretations, technical publishing, and seminars for professionals in the field. Reynolds leads a team of review technicians and former code officials, all of whom are certified by BOCA®, ICBO, or SBCCI in their particular fields of code expertise.

Working Drawing Checklists

Nevada Chapter of the AGC
Reno, Nevada

---

*The following checklists are provided by the Nevada Chapter of the
Associate General Contractors of American, Inc., Reno, Nevada,
Jack N. Tedford III, President, John D. Madole, Jr., Executive Director.
They were developed for designers, owners, and contractors by the
chapter, its Board of Directors, and its AIA/Design Committee,
Mario Bullentini, Chairman. The checklists were designed with the input
from various public agencies and other interested groups, and have been
distributed in the area served by the Nevada Chapter.*

DESIGN CHECKLIST -- MASTER

Yes	No	n/a	Item	Comments/Notes
			Site Checklist:	
			Coordinate architectural, structural, civil, landscape, plumbing, electrical, mechanical and fire sprinkler.	
			Square feet of landscaping per code.	
			Number of required parking spaces.	
			Zoning setbacks per code.	
			Utility locations.	
			Handicap parking and access routes.	

Fig. 10–1.

DESIGN CHECKLIST -- MASTER

Yes	No	n/a	Item	Comments/Notes
			Accessibility:	
			Structural details for railings, heights, access widths, and opening sizes between rails.	
			Structural details of ramps for maximum slope, cross slope, etc.	
			Coordinate locations of mechanical, plumbing, electrical and fire sprinkler-meter, piping, ducts and riser locations to not conflict with handicap access widths, wheelchair turning, toilet stall sizes and quantity.	
			Eliminate references to the Americans with Disabilities Act. For code compliance, references should be made to the UBC and ANSI standards and the applicable governing authority. ADA compliance may differ from code requirements in some cases and needs to be met, but the building department reviews plans for code compliance only.	
			Coordination between disciplines:	
			Overlay correlation drawings completed.	
			Coordinate structural floor and roof framing plans with mechanical duct openings, mechanical unit sizes and weights, lighting fixture sizes and weights, weights of piping and fire sprinkler system.	

Fig. 10–1 (continued).

DESIGN CHECKLIST -- MASTER

Yes	No	n/a	Item	Comments/Notes
			Architectural ceiling plans, electrical fixtures, mechanical ducts and supply/return grills, fire sprinkler system.	
			Eliminate or minimize contractor-determined or "field verified" requirements on the project.	
			Reviewed special use permit for compliance with drawings.	

REVIEWED BY

_____	_____
Firm	By
_____	_____
Signature	Date

Revised 04/98   J:WP\Design\Design Checklists

Fig. 10–1 (concluded).

DESIGN CHECKLIST -- SITE/CIVIL

Yes	No	n/a	Item	Comments/Notes
			Owner has met with all project team members prior to design to confirm scope of work and establish realistic schedules for completion of plans and specifications. Milestone meetings are set to review conceptual and preliminary site layout. Owner has decided on whether utilities will be owner/ applicant or utility company installed.	
			Geotechnical investigation has been provided to address foundations, site grading, pavement structural sections, and potential construction problems.	
			Geotechnical consultant has reviewed plans and specifications to ensure compliance with geotechnical investigation recommendations.	
			Design level topographic map with 1- or 2-foot contours (subject to site conditions), boundary information, existing utilities, with limits corresponding to local agencies' requirements has been provided to civil engineer.	
			Civil site plan(s) addressing on-site improvements, horizontal geometric layout of site including building location(s), curb & gutter, on-site circulation and striping have been provided.	

Fig. 10–2.

DESIGN CHECKLIST -- SITE/CIVIL

Yes	No	n/a	Item	Comments/Notes
			Civil grading plan(s) addressing building(s') finished floor elevations, general site drainage, on-site storm drainage system. Top of curb elevations have been prepared and provided in accordance with local agency requirements.	
			ALTA survey has been completed on the property proir to beginning of design. ALTA survey meets ACSM/ ALTA standards. Copy of ALTA survey included in bid documents.	
			Detail sheet(s) to support civil, site & grading plan(s) have been provided.	
			Utility design, sanitary sewer/storm drainage/water (for some local providers) have been incorporated into civil drawings or provided on separate civil utility drawings.	
			Specifications, in either note or book form, depending on project requirements, have been provided.	
			Hydrology study, as required by local agency, has been provided. Project team members advised of City/County setback standards prior to design.	
			Project team has coordinated utility connections and potential conflicts. Project team has coordinated with utility company on utility connections and availability.	

Fig. 10–2 (continued).

DESIGN CHECKLIST -- SITE/CIVIL

Yes	No	n/a	Item	Comments/Notes
			At the 60-70% construction document phase in the project, a full set of construction drawings was sent to utility company for review. Proposed to owner that complete plan sets, including utility company design, be reviewed prior to stamping by any design team members. Civil engineer checked utility company plans prior to final submittal and wet stamp.	
			Advised owner of potential cost increases due to nonstandard specifications for items used during construction (i.e., asphalt, concrete, fencing, etc.). Emphasized use of standard materials/design specifications.	
			Provided geotechnical report as a portion of project specifications.	
			Specified site area that can or cannot be used by contractor for staging or storage.	
			Defined usage of roads and/or access to site.	

REVIEWED BY

_____   _____
Firm   By

_____   _____
Signature   Date

Revised 04/98

Fig. 10–2 (concluded).

DESIGN CHECKLIST -- ARCHITECTURAL

Yes	No	n/a	Item	Comments/Notes
			GENERAL Provide sufficient time for each of the consultants to review completed plans of other disciplines. Incorporate comments of review prior to distribution.	
			Minimize or eliminate notes relating to future construction unless necessary to define the scope of the project.	
			Clearly define phasing if applicable.	
			Verify that consultants have used the most current plans for their drawings.	
			Ensure that all materials are defined in the specifications.	
			Use keyed notes where necessary. Notes should be listed on same sheet where keyed.	
			COVER SHEET Provide a thorough description of code compliance through the use of notes and diagrams. Indicate occupancies, construction types, fire ratings, and other elements pertinent to building department review.	
			SITE PLAN Provide thorough and sufficient dimensions for the site layout if not provided elsewhere.	
			Indicate setback requirements.	

Fig. 10–3.

DESIGN CHECKLIST -- ARCHITECTURAL

Yes	No	n/a	Item	Comments/Notes
			Indicate scope of work for the project. Clearly label all elements included in the project. Label existing elements and items to be removed.	
			Verify dimensions of property with site survey.	
			Verify compliance with applicable planning ordinance in regard to planting areas, trash enclosures, and equipment screening.	
			FLOOR PLAN Verify column grids with structural plans.	
			Check wall thicknesses with structural requirements.	
			Eliminate duplicate dimensions and dimension only what is necessary.	
			Indicate rated walls. Check mechanical plans for dampers at wall penetrations, corridors, and rated walls.	
			ROOF PLAN Indicate all mechanical equipment accurately and coordinate the location of equipment with architectural elements.	
			BUILDING SECTIONS Provide sufficient and accurate sections and label all materials.	
			Dimension wall heights.	

Revised 04/98

Fig. 10–3 (continued).

DESIGN CHECKLIST -- ARCHITECTURAL

Yes	No	n/a	Item	Comments/Notes
			Key all details and detailed wall sections.	
			Check wall sections against elevations.	
			Verify wall heights and materials against structural drawings.	
			EXTERIOR ELEVATIONS Indicate all materials and key details.	
			Check wall elevations against building sections.	
			Verify that finish grade is shown accurately. Check against grading plan.	
			EXTERIOR DETAILS Eliminate details which are provided to other disciplines or check for consistency.	
			INTERIOR ELEVATIONS Provide interior elections where necessary to define specialty finish elements.	
			REFLECTED CEILING PLAN Check light fixture layout against electrical plans.	
			Check diffuser layout against mechanical plans.	
			Verify ceiling materials against finish schedule.	

Revised 04/98

Fig. 10–3 (continued).

DESIGN CHECKLIST -- ARCHITECTURAL

Yes	No	n/a	Item	Comments/Notes
			RESTROOM PLANS & DETAILS Locate all accessories and indicate mounting heights.	
			Provide sufficient dimensioning to verify compliance with applicable accessibility requirements.	
			Check enlarged plans against overall floor plans.	
			PARTITION SCHEDULE & DETAILS Check against floor plan and verify fire-rating requirements.	
			ROOM FINISH SCHEDULES, DOOR SCHEDULES & DETAILS Check all elements against plans, sections, and interior elevations.	
			Check that all finish materials are defined in the specifications.	
			Key all details to their appropriate locations.	

REVIEWED BY

_____

Firm   By

_____

Signature   Date

Revised 04/98

Fig. 10–3 (concluded).

DESIGN CHECKLIST -- STRUCTURAL

Yes	No	n/a	Item	Comments/Notes
			Dimensions are complete and match architectural.	
			Column location, type, and orientation on structural match architectural.	
			Structural perimeter slab edges match architectural plan. (Dimensions should be given.)	
			Location and extent of depressed or raised slabs match architectural. (Slopes required.)	
			Foundations are identified, located and sized on a schedule or plan.	
			Walls are identified and sized on a schedule or plan.	
			Braced frame diagonal bracing is coordinated with locations of doors, windows, openings, etc.	
			Structural jambs and hold downs are coordinated with mechanical, plumbing and electrical components and are shown on foundation and structural plans.	
			Beam, column, wall and slab joints are detailed and coordinated with other disciplines.	
			Roof framing plan column grid and column locations match foundation plan.	

Revised 12/97

Fig. 10–4.

DESIGN CHECKLIST -- STRUCTURAL

Yes	No	n/a	Item	Comments/Notes
			Roof elevations, slopes and locations of ridges and valleys are shown and match architectural roof plan. Roof can freely drain.	
			Openings and support framing for mechanical roof and wall penetrations (ducts, fans, etc.) and locations of heavy equipment (with maximum weight) are indicated on structural, mechanical, and architectural plans.	
			Structural supports required for mechanical and electrical equipment are indicated and coordinated wiith mechanical and electrical drawings.	
			Separation/expansion joint locations and widths match other disciplines.	
			Stair plans and details area coordinated with architectural.	
			Locations of electrical conduit runs, floor trenches, and openings are coordinated with architectural and electrical plans. Location of electrical conduits should be shown, if allowed on slab on grade and slab on metal deck details.	
			Necessary sections and details are provided, complete, keyed, and coordinated with other disciplines.	
			Drawing notes do not conflict with specifications and are customized to project.	

Revised 12/97

Fig. 10–4 (continued).

DESIGN CHECKLIST -- STRUCTURAL

Yes	No	n/a	Item	Comments/Notes
			Column schedules indicate column on floor plans with appropriate footings, base plates, and anchor bolts.	
			Length of column shown matches length shown in section and elevation.	
			Eliminate nonapplicable details on detail sheets.	
			Elevator framing addressed and coordinated.	

REVIEWED BY

_____   _____
Firm   By

_____   _____
Signature   Date

Fig. 10–4 (concluded).

DESIGN CHECKLIST -- MECHANICAL

Yes	No	n/a	Item	Comments/Notes
			Coordinate trades for services installation: ☐ Ductwork ☐ Piping ☐ Fire Sprinkler ☐ HVAC ☐ Plumbing ☐ Electrical ☐ Structural	
			Designed spaces are sufficiently sized for installations and maintenance or replacement.	
			Complete overlay of all systems including structural to verify clearance and accessibility.	
			Structural design is complete and coordinated.	
			Systems should be complete and not require redesign through shop drawings.	
			Life/Safety items defined by design team (NOT contractor team).	
			Design responsibilities: ☐ Design incorporates most efficient components. ☐ Maintenance and serviceability provided for. ☐ Equipment platforms designed considering structural design.	
			Power requirements for the mechanical system are specified in design.	

Fig. 10–5.

DESIGN CHECKLIST -- MECHANICAL

Yes	No	n/a	Item	Comments/Notes
			Sprinkler design is part of the bidding documents.	
			Specifications define responsibility for various systems and components.	
			Objectives: ☐ Specifications provide for "or equals" on equipment. ☐ Specifications and system design allow for maximum competitive bidding. ☐ Systems are designed for energy efficiency.	
			Design meets current specifications and building codes.	
			Utility locations indicated: sewer, gas, water, storm drain.	
			Recommendation to include fire sprinkler design consultant on design team.	
			Gas and electric meter sets located and coordinated among disciplines.	

REVIEWED BY

_____   _____
Firm   By

_____   _____
Signature   Date

Fig. 10–5 (concluded).

DESIGN CHECKLIST -- ELECTRICAL

Yes	No	n/a	Item	Comments/Notes
			Site:	
			Plans reflect serving utility. Firm designs for power, telephone, TV.	
			Vaults properly sized for conductors with service loops and future capacity.	
			Vaults specify required cover loading.	
			Light pole bases designed correctly for soil conditions and poles specified.	
			Building Switchgear:	
			Switchgear interrupting ratings meet available fault currents. Fault calculations and coordination study completed for entire project.	
			Equipment specified has been sized and will fit into electric rooms with proper clearances.	
			Building Special Systems *(Fire/ Life Safety)*:	
			Fire alarm system design matches local fire department codes. UBC and NFPA not always adequate. Design responsibility of design team; *not* contractor.	
			Supplier/installer of duct detection identified. Duct detection compatible with detection system specified and coordinated among mechanical and electrical contractors.	

Fig. 10–6.

DESIGN CHECKLIST -- ELECTRICAL

Yes	No	n/a	Item	Comments/Notes
			Supplier/installer of fire bells, flow and tamper switches identifed and coordinated among mechanical and electrical contractors.	
			Supplier/installer of smoke evacuation system identified and coordinated among mechanical and electrical contractors.	
			Smoke dampers/life safety system operations defined and coordinated among mechanical and electrical contractors.	
			Building Special Systems *(System Wire):*	
			Plans specify type of system wire and raceways to be used. CL2 rated or plenum wire required.	
			Building Special Systems *(Data Systems):*	
			Phone data area designed with at least 100 square feet of room with necessary power and ventilation.	
			Phone data requirements verified with owner or end user.	
			Rough In	
			Underground raceways do not conflict with building slab.	
			Design allows for raceways in metal decks and roof decks. Limitations listed.	

Fig. 10–6 (continued).

DESIGN CHECKLIST -- ELECTRICAL

Yes	No	n/a	Item	Comments/Notes
			Design coordinated with structural engineers for roof support requirements and requirements are detailed.	
			Roof penetration types specified and requirements for roof conduits identified.	
			Ceiling spaces adequate for raceways, light fixture clearances, cable trays, etc., and are coordinated with other trades.	
			Fireproofing requirements defined and specified in this division.	
			Generator:	
			Supplier/installer of fuel tanks/day tanks identified and coordinated among mechanical and electrical contractors.	
			Supplier/installer of exhaust system identified and coordinated among mechanical and electrical contractors.	
			Proper ventilation supplied with auto or manual louvers. Coordinated among disciplines.	
			Generator exhaust discharges properly away from intake air both for generator ventilation and building make-up air. Coordinated among disciplines.	
			Light Fixtures:	
			Light fixtures overlaid/coordinated with reflected ceilings and ceiling types.	

Fig. 10–6 (continued).

DESIGN CHECKLIST -- ELECTRICAL

Yes	No	n/a	Item	Comments/Notes
			Mechanical/Kitchen:	
			Feeds coordinated with equipment specified.	
			If disconnects and starters required, supplier identified.	
			Connections defined.	
			If control wires required, installer identified.	
			Syrup lines defined by specification section.	
			Specifications and Notes:	
			Specifications meet current design.	
			Notes clarify work detailed.	
			Items specified allow for competitive bidding by several manufacturers.	
			Gas and electric meter sets located and coordinated among disciplines.	

REVIEWED BY

_____   _____
Firm   By

_____   _____
Signature   Date

Fig. 10–6 (concluded).

The Nevada Chapter of the Associated General Contractors, Reno, Nevada, has been serving its members, community, and the building industry since 1939. It has 350 members. <www.nevadaagc.org>

11

Working Drawing Case Studies

This chapter provides examples of formats and information from working drawings prepared by 19 architectural firms from a broad geographical distribution of locations. Drawing types are duplicated with variations of drawing techniques demonstrated. Although reference books typically suggest that there is one correct way to format drawings and details, in reality there are many ways succeeding in the production of buildings. It is the intent of this chapter to illustrate several options which are currently in use.

The documentation begins with tables of contents for working drawing sets which indicate that the general order of sheets is fairly standard. These tables of contents can be used to verify that all desired subjects are covered in a set of drawings from the beginning and throughout the architectural sheets. (Engineering and other sheets that follow the A-sheet section are omitted from the series.) This is followed by a comprehensive collection of abbreviations assembled from several offices into a single list. In this case, variations of abbreviations representing the same word were omitted leaving a single entry for each word. Rather than a menu of choices, therefore, the list provides a document which can be incorporated directly from the handbook into a set of drawings without editing.

Nearly every set of working drawings includes general notes. A comprehensive set of notes from a single office is provided here. Although some entries are typical of the firm's location (i.e., California), most apply to any project in any location. For projects involving existing facilities, a set of demolition notes is provided from another office. The notes are followed by two types of symbols. The first group contains a series of drawing conventions for which alternatives for each type are shown. Size variations found in the working drawing sources affect the presentation of the symbols so that the series lacks a rigid uniformity. Therefore, variations of styles between offices are reflected. The second group of symbols indicate materials. To aid in the readability of this section, the length of the symbols is held constant, although their vertical dimensions fluctuate with variations between working drawing sets.

Examples of drawings constitute the remainder of the chapter. In selecting the illustrations, comments from contributors in Part II of the handbook were considered. Consequently, many of the concerns of contractors, construction managers, and code officials are addressed in the samples. For instance, the drawings begin with several examples of code information which is needed by building officials to approve a set of drawings for a building permit. Subsequent pages include partial plans, elevations, sections, schedules, and details, most of which have been simplified to facilitate readability. Most dimensions have been removed, leaving a focus on the methods of depicting references to other drawings. The graphic reference system is a concern of many builders who have to reconcile all related drawings in order to bid and build a project.

Working Drawings Tables of Contents Case Studies

The contents of architectural and preceding sheets are listed. Only the first sheet is listed where a series contains the same type of drawings.

A MULTISTORY RESIDENTIAL BUILDING
Ankrom Moisan Associated Architects. Portland, Oregon

CS Cover Sheet	A-3.4 Elevations, enlarged windows
A-1.0 Site survey	A-3.5 Building sections
A-1.1 Site plan	A-3.7 Wall sections
A-1.2 Courtyard, paving	A-4.1 Exterior details
A-1.3 Courtyard details	A-5.0 Reflected ceiling plan
A-2.0 Floor plans	A-5.4 Interior elevations
A-2.7 Roof plan	A-5.8 Interior details
A-2.8 Wall types, wall intersections	A-5.10 Floor finish plan
A-2.9 Egress diagrams	A-6.1 Stair plans/sections
A-3.1 Elevations	A-6.2 Enlarged lobby plans
	A-6.3 Enlarged plan

CITY HALL AND RENOVATION ADDITION
David Woodhouse Architects. Chicago, Illinois

Title Sheet	A6.1 Exterior wall sections, details
A1.1 Materials, symbols, abbreviations, index	A6.3 Exterior details
A2.1 Demolition drawings	A7.1 Reflected ceiling plans
A3.1 Basement plan, roof plans	A8.1 Interior elevations
A3.2 Floor plans	A9.1 Interior details
A4.1 Exterior elevations	A10.1 Door details, window details, types
A5.1 Building sections	A11.1 Schedules, partition types

Fig. 11–1.

A POLICE DEPARTMENT
Cromwell Architects Engineers. Little Rock, Arkansas

T1.1 Title sheet	A1.8 Toilet plans
T1.2 Symbols, abbreviations, index of drawings	A2.1 Door schedule
	A2.2 Finish schedule
C1.1 Site survey	A3.1 Exterior elevations
C2.1 Site layout plan	A3.2 Building sections
C2.2 Site grading, drainage	A4.1 Wall sections
C2.3 Site utilities plan	A5.1 Exterior details
C3.1 Site details	A5.4 Miscellaneous details
L1.1 Landscape plan	A5.5 Exterior details
A1.1 Floor plans	A6.1 Stair details
A1.3 Dimension floor plans	A6.4 Interior details
A1.5 Reflected ceiling plan	A6.6 Door & window details
A1.7 Roof plan	A6.7 Interior details

AN OFFICE, STORAGE, AND MAINTENANCE FACILITY
Wilson Darnell Mann P.A., Architects. Wichita, Kansas

C Cover Sheet	A1.1 Reference plan
C.1 Key map	A1.2 Floor plans
C.2 Site demolition	A1.5 Enlarged floor plan
C.3 Site utility	A2.1 Building elevations
C.4 Site grading & storm sewer	A3.1 Building sections
	A4.1 Wall sections & details
C.5 Paving joint layout	A5.1 Roof plans & details
C.6 Sanitary sewer manhole	A6.1 Room finish schedule
C.7 Miscellaneous details	A6.2 Door and window schedules
C.8 Backfill details	
C.9 Curb inlet details	A6.3 Door details
C.10 Storm water sewer manhole details	A6.4 Window details
	A7.1 Ceiling plans
C.11 Manhole frame & cover details	A8.1 Interior elevations
	A8.2 Administration desk – plans, elevations, details
C.12 Pavement details	
C.13 Erosion control details	
SA1.1 Site layout	A8.3 Reception desk – plans, elevations
SA1.2 Site details	
PL1.1 Planting plan	A8.4 Reception desk – details
PL1.2 Planting details	A9.1 Canopy details
IR1.1 Irrigation plan	A9.2 Van canopy details
IR1.2 Irrigation details	A9.3 Miscellaneous details

Fig. 11–1 (continued).

A University Sports and Fine Arts Complex
Gossen Livingston Associates, Inc., Architecture. Wichita, Kansas

T1.1 Title Sheet	A5.4 Exterior door details
G-1 Survey	A5.5 Window schedule and details
CS Code Sheet	A5.6 Details
A1.1A Floor plans	A6.1 Enlarged floor plans
A1.4 Partition types	A7.1 Interior elevations
A2.1 Building elevations	A7.6 Interior details
A2.2 Enlarged elevations	A8.1 Stairs and Elevators
A2.4 Building sections	A9.1A Floor finish plans
A3.1 Wall sections	A9.3A Ceiling Plans
A4.1 Roof plan	A9.5 Ceiling Details
A4.2 Roof details	A9.6 Court Striping Plan
A4.7 Waterproofing	A10.1 Miscellaneous Details
A5.1 Door schedule	A11.1 Millwork
A5.2 Door details	

An Elementary School
HKT Architects, Inc. Somerville, Massachusetts

A-0.1 Notes, symbols, abbreviations	A-3.8 Classroom plan, millwork details
A-0.2 Code compliance	A-3.9 Science center – plans, elevations, details
C-1.1 Plan, construction area limits	A-3.10 Stair rail modifications
D-1.1 Demolition plans	A-3.11 Administration entry – plan and details
D-1.2 Demolition plans and details	A-3.12 Door schedule, and frame types, plaque schedule
L-1.1 Landscaping plan, site features	A-3.13 Window types
A-1.1 Floor plans	A-3.15 Finish schedule, partition types
A-1.4 Reflected ceiling plan	A-3.16 Classroom interior elevations
A-2.1 Exterior elevations	A-3.17 Window details
A-3.1 Auditorium/performing arts – plans, details	A-3.19 Alternate 1 – plans, elevations
A-3.2 Entry ramp – plans and elevations	
A-3.3 Entry ramp – sections and details	

Fig. 11–1 (continued).

A VOCATIONAL-TECHNICAL HIGH SCHOOL
HKT Architects, Inc. Somerville, Massachusetts

	Cover Sheet		
T-1	Abbreviations,	A-1.02A	Roof plan and
	Symbols, Notes		details—Alternate 1
A-0.01	Code Analysis—	A-1.03	Floor plans
	New Campus Plan	A-1.11	Enlarged plans
A-0.02	Code Analysis—	A-1.16	Stair Plans, Sections
	Floor plans		and Details
A-PH.00	Staging Plan	A-1.17	Enlarged Plans
A-PH.01	Phase 1	A-2.01	Reflected ceiling
A-PH.02	Phase 2		plans
A-PH.03	Phase 3	A-3.00	New Campus
A-PH.04	Phase 4		Building Elevations
G-1	Geotechnical Survey	A-3.01	Building Elevations
	Data	A-4.01	Building Sections
X-1.1	Existing Conditions	A-5.01	Wall Sections
	Survey	A-6.01	Plan Details
C-1.1	Site Preparation	A-6.10	Section Details
	Plan	A-7.01	Interior Elevations
C-2.1	Site Layout Plan	A-7.03	Stairs and Ramps
C-3.1	Site Grading Plan	A-7.04	Interior Elevations
C-4.1	Site Utility Plan	A-8.01	Door Schedule
C-5.1	Site Details	A-8.02	Door Types, Frame
EX-1.01	Existing campus		Types, and Interior
	plans		Windows
D-1.01	Demolition plans	A-8.03	Window Schedule
D-1.04A	Alternate #1		and Details
A-1.01	New Campus Plans	A-8.04	Storefront Plans and
A-1.02	New Campus Roof		Elevations
	Plan & Details	A-9.01	Finish Schedule
		A-9.03	Partition Types

Fig. 11–1 (continued).

AN ELELMENTARY SCHOOL
PBK Architects, Inc.
Houston, Dallas/Fort Worth, San Antonio, Austin, League City, Texas

A0.00	Cover	A3.01	Roof plan, roof details
A0.01	Index of drawings	A4.01	Enlarged toilet plans
	Drawing conventions	A4.02	Plan details
	Materials symbols	A4.04	Partition types and
	Code information		miscellaneous details
	Site location map	A5.01	Building elevations
	Project summary	A6.01	Building sections
C0.00	Pre-rated assemblies	A6.03	Wall sections
C0.00	Survey	A6.05	Vertical details
A1.00	Site plan, site details	A6.07	Miscellaneous vertical
A1.02	Site details, service		and plan details
	yard	A7.01	Door and window
A1.03	Site amenities		elevations
A1.04	Enlarged site plan	A7.02	Door details
A2.00	Composite floor plan	A7.03	Window details
A2.01	Schedules and floor	A8.01	Casework elevations
	plans on facing sheets	A9.01	Reflected ceiling plans
A2.07	Mezzanine floor plans,		
	details		

A SCHOOL DISTRICT CENTRAL KITCHEN
Phillips Metsch Sweeney Moore Architects.
Santa Barbara, California

A0.0	Sheet index, code plan,	A2.2	Roof plan
	building data, vicinity	A2.3	Alternate No. one
	map, symbols	A2.4	Schedules
A0.1	Code plan	A3.1	Building sections
A0.2	Title 24 energy	A3.2	Exterior elevations
	compliance	A5.1	Interior elevations
A1.0	Topographic survey	A6.1	Reflected ceiling plan
A1.1	Site plans	A8.1	Exterior details
A1.3	Grading plan	A9.1	Interior details
A1.4	Site details	A9.2	Suspend ceiling details
A2.1	Floor plan, code plan,		
	floor finish legend		

Fig. 11–1 (continued).

AN OFFICE AND FACTORY BUILDING
Spencer Godfrey Architects. Round Rock, Texas

0.0 Cover	A–1.2 Enlarged site plans and details
0.1 Abbreviations	
0.2 Building code evaluation site plan	A–2.1 Dimensioned floor plan and details
0.3 Building code evaluation floor plan	A–2.2 Reflected ceiling and roof plan, and details
C–1 Grading and drainage plan	A–3.1 Building elevations
	A–3.2 Enlarged panel elevations
C–2 Water and wastewater plan	A–4.1 Wall sections and details
C–3 Construction details	A–5.1 Door and window schedules and details
C–5 Water and wastewater details	A–6.1 Interior elevations
A–1.1 Dimensioned site plan	A–6.2 Millwork details

A WAREHOUSE ADDITION
Stephen Wen + Associates Architects, Inc.
Pasadena, California

T-0.0 Cover sheet	A-5.2 Sections, elevator and stairs
T-0.1 General notes, sheet Index, abbreviations, vicinity map	A-6.1 Finish schedule
	A-6.2 Door and window schedules
T-0.2 General notes	A-6.3 Door details
T-0.3 Disabled access notes	A-6.4 Window details
C-1 Topographic survey	A-7.1 Interior elevations
C-2 Grading plan	A-8.1 Reflected ceiling plans
C-3 Notes and details	A-9.1 Site details
C-4 Grading notes	A-9.2 Roof details
A-2.1 Site plan	A-9.3 Miscellaneous details
A-2.2 Floor plans	A-10.2 Elevator and miscellaneous details
A-2.4 Roof plan	
A-3.1 Building elevations	A-10.3 Miscellaneous details
A-4.1 Wall sections	
A-5.1 Enlarged floor plans	

Fig. 11–1 (continued).

AN OFFICE AND LABORATORY BUILDING

Gossen Livingston Associates, Inc., Architecture. Wichita, Kansas

I1   Cover Sheet
R1   Reference floor plan
R2   Site survey
R3   Soil borings
SD1 Site demolition plan
SG1 Site grading, utility plan
SA1 Site layout plan
SA1.2 Site details
SA2.2 Exterior stair details
SL1 Site landscape plans
A1.1 Demolition floor, and ceiling plans
A1.2 Partition schedule
A1.3 Floor plans
A1.6 Enlarged toilet plans/ elevations
A1.7 Plan details
A2.1 Building elevations
A2.2 Building sections
A3.1 Wall sections
A4.1 Stair sections
A4.3 Stair details
A5.1 Roof plan
A5.2 Roof details

A6.1 Door schedule and elevations
A6.2 Curtain wall and storefront elevations
A6.3 Door and window details
A6.4 Storefront details
A6.5 Miscellaneous door and window details
A7.1 Translucent panel and window elevations
A7.2 Translucent panel and window details
A7.3 Translucent panel details
A8.1 Room finish schedule
A9.1 Floor finish plans
A10.1 Reflected ceiling plans
A10.4 Ceiling details
A11.4 Enlarged lab plans
A12.1 Interior elevations
A12.3 Miscellaneous details
A12.4 Cabinet elevations

Fig. 11–1 (concluded).

Working Drawing Abbreviations

*The following abbreviations were compiled from several lists
currently used by architectural firms. Where different abbreviations
were used for the same word, the more common one was selected,
or the shorter one was used where terms were equally common.*

℄	and	A.P.	access panel
&	and	A/C	air conditioning
"L"	angle	ABV	above
∠	angle	AC	acoustical
∡	angle	ACC	access
@	at	ACC	accessory
/	by	ACI	American Concrete
℄	centerline		Institute
[	channel	ACOUS	acoustical
°	degree	ACOUS BD	acoustical board
⌀	diameter	ACOUS T	acoustical tile
=	equal	AD	access door
(E)	existing	ADD	addendum
'	feet	ADD'L	additional
FL	flow line	ADH	adhesive
'	foot	ADJ	adjacent
"	inch(es)	ADJ	adjustable
#	number	AFF	above finished floor
/	per	AGGR	aggregate
%	percent	AL	aluminum
PL	plate	ALT	alternate
±	plus/minus	ANCH	anchor
#	pound	ANOD	anodized
⌀	round	APPD	approved
⊕	square	APPROX	approximate
A.B.	anchor bolt	APPROX	approximately
A.D.	area drain	ARCH	architect
A.E.	architect-engineer	ARCH	architectural
A.M.H.S.	automatic material	ASB	asbestos
	handling system	ASPH	asphalt

ASSOC	association	C. CONC.	cast concrete
ASSY	assembly	C. TO C.	center to center
ATTEN	attenuation	C.B.	catch basin
AUTO	automatic	C.B.	chalk board
AVER	average	C.C.G.	concrete curb and
AWG	American wire		gutter
	gage	C.F.C.I	contractor furnish,
B.B.D.	bulletin board		contractor install
B.F.	both faces	C.G.	corner guard
B.M.	bench mark	C.I.	cast iron
B.O.	bottom of	C.I.P.	cast iron pipe
B.O.	by others	C.J.	construction joint
B.P.	base plate	C.J.	control joint
B.U.	built-up	C.L.	centerline
B.U.R.	built-up roofing	C.L.F.	chain link fence
B.U.R.	built-up roof	C.M.P.	corrugate metal pipe
B.W.	both ways	C.O.	clean out
BATT	battery	C.R.	cold rolled
BB	baseboard	C.R.S.	cold rolled steel
BD	board	C.T.	ceramic tile
BDRM	bedroom	C.W.	cold water
BEL	below	C.W.	concrete walk
BET	between	C/O	cased opening
BEV	beveled	CAB	cabinet
BEY	beyond	CALK	caulk
BITUM	bituminous	CCM	cubic centimeter
BLDG	building	CEM	cement
BLK	block	CEM	cementitious
BLKG	blocking	CEM. PLAS.	cement plaster
BLVD	boulevard	CER	ceramic
BM	beam	CFM	cubic feet per minute
BOT	bottom	CIR	circle
BRG	bearing	CIR	circular
BRK	brick	CIR	circumference
BRKT	bracket	CL. GL.	clear glass
BRZ	bronze	CL. W. GL.	clear wire glass
BSMT	basement	CLG	ceiling
BTH	bathroom	CLKG	caulking
BTN	batten	CLO	closet
BVL	bevel	CLR	clear
C	Celsius	CLR	clearance
C	channel	CLRM	classroom
C	course	CM	cubic meter

CMM	cubic millimeter	D.C.	drainage conductor
CMU	concrete masonry unit	D.F.	drinking fountain
		D.H.	double hung
CNTR	counter	D.L.	dead load
CO	company	D.O.	door opening
CO2	carbon dioxide	D.R.	dressing room
COL	column	D.S.P.	dry standpipe
COMB	combination	D.W.	dry wall
COMP	computer	DBL	double
COMPR	compressed	DEG	degree
COMPR	compressor	DEMO	demolition
COMPT	compartment	DEPT	department
CON	conference	DET	detail
CONC	concrete	DIA	diameter
CONC. FL.	concrete floor	DIAG	diagonal
COND	condenser	DIAG	diagram
COND	condition	DIAG	diagrammatic
CONN	connect	DIFF	diffuser
CONN	connection	DIM	dimension(s)
CONST	construction	DISP	dispenser
CONT	continue	DIST	distance
CONT	continuous	DISTR	distribute
CONTR	contract	DISTR	distribution
CONTR	contractor	DISTR	distributed
CONV	convector	DIV	divider
COR	corridor	DIV	division
CORR	corrugated	DMBW	dumbwaiter
CPG	coping	DN	down
CPR	copper	DO	ditto
CPT	carpet	DOC	documents
CPT	carpeted	DP	dampproofing
CR	crushed	DP	deep
CSG	casing	DR	door
CSK	countersink	DS	downspout
CSK	countersunk	DW	dishwasher
CSK/S	countersunk screw	DWG	drawing
		DWR	drawer
CSMT	casement	E	east
CTG	coating	E. TO E.	end to end
CTR	center	E.B.	expansion bolt
CU	cubic	E.C.	electrical conduit
CU. FT.	cubic feet	E.C.	electrical contractor
CY	cubic yard(s)		

E.F.	each face	F.A.I.	fresh air intake
E.J.	expansion joint	F.B.	face brick
E.P.	electric panel	F.B.	flat bar
E.P.B.	electrical panel	F.D.	floor drain
	board	F.D.C.	fire department
E.W.	each way		connection
E.W.C.	electric water	F.DR.	folding door
	cooler	F.E.	fire extinguisher
EA	each	F.E.C.	fire extinguisher
EIFS	exterior insulation		cabinet
	and finish system	F.F.	finish floor
EL	elevation datum	F.F.&E.	furniture,
EL	elevation view		furnishings &
ELAST	elastic		equipment
ELAST	elastomeric	F.H.	fire hose
ELB	elbow	F.H.	flat head
ELEC	electric	F.H.C.	fire hose cabinet
ELEC	electrical	F.H.R.	fire hose rack
ELEC. CLO.	electrical closet	F.H.S.	flat head screw
ELEV	elevator	F.JT.	flush joint
EMER	emergency	F.L.	flow line
ENC	enclose	F.O.	face of
ENCL	enclosure	F.O.C.	face of concrete
ENGR	engineer	F.O.F.	face of finish
ENT	entrance	F.O.M.	face of masonry
EQ	equal	F.O.S.	face of studs
EQUIP	equipment	F.S.	far side
EST	estimate	F.S.	full size
EXC	excavate	F.V.	façade view
EXC	excavation	F.V.	face view
EXH	exhaust	FAB	fabricate
EXIST	existing	FAB	fabricated
EXP	expansion	FAB	fabrication
EXPD	exposed	FBD	fiberboard
EXT	extension	FD	fire damper
EXT	exterior	FDN	foundation
F	face	FED	federal
F	Fahrenheit	FH	fire hydrant
F. HYD.	fire hydrant	FIG	figure
F. TO F.	face to face	FIN	finish
F.A.	fire alarm	FIXT	fixture
F.A.A.	fire alarm	FL.CO.	floor cleanout
	annunciator	FLASH	flashing

FLEX	flexible	GL	glass
FLG	flooring	GL	glazed
FLR	floor	GL	glazing
FLR. MTD.	floor mounted	GL. OPG.	glass opening
FLUOR	fluorescent	GLZ. TILE	glazed tile
FP	flat point	GND	ground
FPM	feet per minute	GOVT	government
FPRF	fireproof	GPM	gallons per minute
FPRF	fireproofing	GR	grade
FPS	feet per second	GYP	gypsum
FR	frame	GYP	gypsum drywall
FR	framed	GYP. BD.	gypsum board
FR	framing	H	high
FT	feet	H. PT.	high point
FT	foot	H.B.	hose bibb
FTG	footing	H.C.	hollow core
FUR	furred	H.D.	hair dryer
FUR	furring	H.D.F.	handicap drinking
FURN	furnace		fountain
FURN	furnish	H.E.W.C.	handicap electric
FUT	future		water cooler
G	gas	H.H.D.	handicap hair dryer
G.B.	grab bar	H.L.AV.	handicap lavatory
G.C.	general	H.M.	hollow metal
	contractor	H.MI.	handicap mirror
G.F.	granular fill	H.P.	horse power
G.I.	galvanized iron	H.R.	handrail
G.R.	guardrail	H.S.D.	handicap soap
G.S.	galvanized steel		dispenser
G.W.B.	gypsum wall	H.S.H.	handicap shower
	board		head
G/B/O	gypsum board	H.U.	handicap urinal
	opening	H.W.	hot water
GA	gage	H.W.C.	handicap wall-mounted
GA	gauge		wall closet
GAL	gallon	HC	handicap
GALV	galvanized	HC	handicapped
GD	guard	HD	head
GEN	general	HDBD	hardboard
GEN	generator	HDNR	hardener
GFRC	glass fiber	HDR	header
	reinforced	HDW	hardware
	concrete	HDWD	hardwood

HEX	hexagonal	JCT	junction
HK	hooks	JNT	joint
HOR	horizontal	JR	junior
HOSP	hospital	JST	joist
HP	high point	JT	joint
HR	hour	JTS	joints
HT	height	K	kip (1000 lbs)
HTG	heating	K. PL.	kick plate
HTR	heater	K.D.	knock down
HVAC	heating,	K.O.	knock out
	ventilation, and	KIT	kitchen
	air conditioning	KW	kilowatt
HVY	heavy	L	length
HWY	highway	L	long
HYD	hydrant	L.B.	lag bolt
I.D.	inside diameter	L.CMU	lightweight core
I.D.	interior diameter		masonry unit(s)
I.P.S.	inside pipe size	L.F.	linear foot
IC	intercom	L.G.	lead glass
IMPR	impregnate	L.H.	left hand
IN	inch(es)	L.L.	live load
INC	incorporated	L.L.H.	long leg horizontal
INCAND	incandescent	L.L.V.	long leg vertical
INCIN	incinerate	L.P.	low point
INCL	include	L.RM.	living room
INCL	included	L.W.C.	light weight concrete
INCL	including	LAB	laboratory
IND	industrial	LAD	ladder
INDIV	individual	LAM	laminate
INFO	information	LAV	lavatory
INSL	insulate	LB	pound
INSL	insulating	LIN	linen
INSL	insulation	LKR	locker
INST	install	LOC	location
INT	interior	LT	light
INT	internal	LTL	lintel
INTERM	intermediate	LVR	louver
INV	invert	M	thousand
ISOL	isolate	M. PART'N	movable partition
ISOL	isolation	M.C.	mechanical
IV	intravenous		contractor
J.B.	junction box	M.C.	medicine cabinet
JAN	janitors closet	M.C.	miscellaneous

	channel	MULT	multpile
M.C.	structural shape	MUT	muntin
	misc channel	N	north
M.E.	match existing	N.C.	noncorrosive
M.H.	manhole	N.I.C.	not in contract
M.L.	metal lath	N.S.	near side
M.O.	masonry opening	N.S.	nonslip
M.S.	masonry shelf	N.T.S.	not to scale
MACH	machine	N2O	nitrous oxide
MACH. RM.	machine room	NARC	narcotics
MAS	masonry	NFPA	National Fire
MAS. BLK.	masonry block		Protection Assn
MAT	material	NIP	nipple
MAX	maximum	NO	number
MB	markerboard	NOM	nominal
MBR	member	NORM	normal
MECH	mechanical	NRC	noise reduction
MED	medical		coefficient
MED	medium	O. TO O.	out to out
MED. STO.	medications storage	O.C.	on center(s)
MEMB	membrane	O.D.	outside diameter
MEMO	memorandum	O.F.C.I.	owner furnish,
MEZZ	mezzanine		contractor install
MFD	manufactured	O.F.O.I.	owner furnish,
MFG	manfacture		owner install
MFR	manufacturer	O.F.S.	outside face of
MGR	manager		stud
MIN	minimum	O/	over
MIR	mirror	O2	oxygen
MISC	miscellaneous	OA	overall
MK	mark	OB	obscure
MLDG	moulding	OBS	obsolete
MOD	model	OFF	office
MOD	modular	OH	overhead
MOD	module	OPNG	opening
MON	monitor	OPP	opposite
MON	monument	OPPH	opposite hand
MOV	movable	ORIG	original
MTD	mounted	ORN	ornament
MTG	mounting	OV. H.S.	oval head screw
MTG. HT.	mounting height	OVHG	overhang
MTL	metal	OWN. FURN.	owner furnished
MUL	mullion	OZ	ounce

P	page	PKWY	parkway
P.A.	public address	PL	plate
P.B.	panic bar	PLAS	plaster
P.C.P.	portland cement plaster	PLAT	platform
		PLF	pounds per linear foot
P.C.T.	precast terrazo		
P.G.	plate glass	PLMB	plumbing
P.L.	property line	PLYWD	plywood
P.LAM.	plastic laminate	PNEU	pneumatic
P.P.GL.	polished plate glass	PNL	panel
		PNLG	paneling
P.R.V.	pressure reducing valve	PNT	paint
		POL	polish
P.S.	plan section	PORT	portable
P.T.	pressure treated	POS	position
P.T.D.	paper towel dispenser	PR	pair
		PRCST	precast concrete
P.T.D./R,	combination paper towel dispenser & receptacle	PRD. GYP.	poured gypsum
		PREFAB	prefabricate
		PREFAB	prefabricated
P.T.D./R.	paper towel disp/recp	PREFIN	prefinished
		PREP	preparation
P.T.STA.	pneumatic tube station	PROD	product
		PROJ	project
P.W.GL.	polished wire glass	PROP	property
		PSF	pounds per square foot
PAR	paragraph		
PAR	parallel	PSI	pounds per square inch
PARA	parapet		
PART. BD.	particle board	PT	part
PASS	passage	PT	point
PAT	patent	PT. CRV.	point of curve
PC	piece	PT. TAN.	point of tangency
PC.C.	precast concrete	PTD	painted
PCF	pounds per cubic foot	PTN	partition
		PVC	polyvinyl chloride
PED	pedestal	PVC.P.	PVC pipe
PERF	perforate	PVMT	pavement
PERF	perforated	PWR	power
PERM	permanent	Q.T.	quarry tile
PERP	perpendicular	Q.T.B.	quarry tile base
PH	phase	Q.T.FLR.	quarry tile floor
PHOTO	photograph	QRY	quarry

QTR.	quarter	S	south
QTY	quantity	S.B.	splash back
R	radius	S.C.	self closing
R	riser	S.C.	sill cock
R.A.	return air	S.C.	solid core
R.B.	rubber base	S.C.D.	seat cover
R.C.P.	reinforced concrete		dispenser
	pipe	S.C.T.	structural clay tile
R.D.	roof drain	S.D.	soap dispenser
R.H.	right hand	S.D.	storm drain
R.H.R.	right hand reverse	S.F.	square foot
R.O.	rough opening	S.F.	storefront
R.W.L.	rain water leader	S.G.	semigloss
RAD	radiator	S.G.D.	sliding glass door
RAD	radius	S.H.	shower head
RD	road	S.N.D.	sanitary napkin
RE	refer		dispenser
RECIRC	recirculation	S.N.R.	sanitary napkin
RECOMM	recommendation		receptor
RECP	receptacle	S.P.	starting point
RECT	rectangle	S.S.	sanitary shower
RED	reducer	S.SNK.	service sink
REF	reference	S.V.	sheet vinyl
REFG	refrigerator	S.Y.	square yard
REG	regulator	SAD	saddle
REINF	reinforced	SAN	sanitary
REINF	reinforcement	SC	scale
REINF	reinforcing	SCH	schedule
REPR	repair	SCM	square centimeter
REPRO	reproduce	SCN	screen
REQ	require	SDG	siding
REQD	required	SEAL	sealant
RESIL	resilient	SEC	second
RESIST	resistant	SECT	section
RET	return	SEP	separation
REV	reversed	SERV	service
REV	revise	SF.GL.	saftey glass
REV	revision	SFTY	safety
RFG	roofing	SH	shelf
RGTR	register	SHLVG	shelving
RM	room	SHT	sheet
RR	railroad	SHTHG	sheathing
S	sink	SHWR	shower

SIM	similar	SWBD	switchboard
SKL	skylight	SYM	symmetrical
SL	slab	SYN	synthetic
SL	sliding	SYS	system
SMLS	seamless	T	tread
SOF	soffit	T&B	top & bottom
SP. CTG.	special coating	T&G	tongue & groove
SPC	space	T. P. HLDR.	toilet paper holder
SPC	spacer	T.B.	tack board
SPCG	spacing	T.B.	towel bar
SPEC	specification	T.D.	towel dispenser
SPECS	specifications	T.G.	tempered glass
SPKR	speaker	T.O.	top of
SQ	square	T.O.C.	top of curb
SQ. IN.	square inch	T.O.M.	top of masonry
ST	street	T.O.W.	top of wall
ST. PART.	steel partition	T.P.	top of pavement
ST. STL.	stainless steel	T.P.D.	toilet paper
ST.S.	storm sewer		dispenser
STA	station	T.S.	towel strip
STAG	staggered	T.S.	tube steel
STC	sound transmission	T.V.	television
	class	TANG	tangent
STD	standard	TECH	technical
STER	sterilizer	TECHS	technicians
STIFF	stiffener	TEL	telephone
STIR	stirrup	TEMP	temperature
STL	steel	TEMP	tempered
STOR	storage	TEMP	template
STOR. CL.	storage closet	TEMP	temporary
STR	structural	TERM	terminate
STR	structure	TERR	terrace
STRIPG	stripping	TERR	terrazzo
SUB	substitute	THD	thread
SUP	supply	THK	thick
SUP	support	THK	thickness
SUPP	supplement	THR	threshold
SUPT	superintendent	THRU	through
SUR	surface	TLT	toilet
SUSP	suspend	TRANS	transformer
SUSP	suspended	TRTMN'T	treatment
SUSP. CLG.	suspended ceiling	T'STAT	thermostat
SW	switch	TYP	typical

U.H.	unit heater	VIN	vinyl
U.N.O.	unless noted otherwise	VIT	vitreous
		VOL	volume
U.O.N.	unless otherwise noted	W	water
		W	west
U.S.	utility shelf	W	wide
UC	undercut	W. CAB.	wall cabinet
UG	underground	W. GL.	wire glass
UL	Underwriters Laboratories, Inc.®	W.C.	water closet
		W.F.	wide flange
ULT	ultimate	W.H.	wall hydrant
UNEX	unexcavated	W.H.	water heater
UNF	unfinished	W.L.	water line
UR	urinal	W.R.	water-resistant
V	valve	W.S.	weather stripping
V	volt	W.T.W.	wall to wall
V.A.T.	vinyl asbestos tile	W.W.F.	welded wire fabric
V.B.	valve box	W.W.M.	welded wire mesh
V.B.	vapor barrier	W/	with
V.B.	vinyl base	W/O	without
V.C.P.	vitrified clay pipe	WD	wood
V.C.T	vinyl composition tile	WH. C.	wheel chair
		WHSE	warehouse
V.I.F.	verify in field	WNDW	window
V.T.R.	vent through roof	WP	waterproof
V.W.C.	vinyl wall covering	WP	waterproofing
VAC	vacuum	WP	weatherproof
VAR	variable	WP	weatherproofing
VAR	varies	WSCT	wainscot
VAR	varnish	WT	weight
VENT	ventilate	X	by (as 6'x8')
VENT	ventilation	Y.P.	yield point
VENT	ventilator	Y.S.	yield strength
VERT	vertical	YD	yard
VEST	vestibule		

The abbreviations were taken from working drawings produced by the following architectural firms: Gossen Livingston Associates, Inc., Architecture. Wichita, Kansas; The Hollis and Miller Group, Inc. Lee's Summit, Missouri; Perkins Eastman Architects, P.C. New York, New York; Spencer Godfrey Architects, Inc. Round Rock, Texas; Stephen Wen + Associates Architects, Inc. Pasadena, California.

Working Drawing Notes

The following is an example of a thorough set of general and construction notes for working drawings. These notes were written for a specific project[1] in a specific state but many of the notes would apply to any project in any location.

GENERAL NOTES

1. CONTRACTOR SHALL VERIFY AND COORDINATE ALL NEW AND EXISTING CONDITIONS AND DIMENSIONS AT JOB SITE FOR COMPARISON WITH DRAWINGS AND SPECIFICATIONS PRIOR TO BIDDING AND START OF AND DURING CONSTRUCTION. IF ANY DISCREPANCIES, INCONSISTENCIES OR OMISSIONS ARE FOUND, THE ARCHITECT SHALL BE NOTIFIED, IN WRITING FOR CLARIFICATION PRIOR TO PROCEEDING WITH WORK.

2. DO NOT SCALE DRAWINGS. CONTRACTOR SHALL RELY ON WRITTEN DIMENSIONS AS GIVEN. THE CONTRACTOR SHALL NOTIFY THE ARCHITECT FOR CLARIFICATIONS. ALL DIMENSIONS SHALL BE FIELD VERIFIED BY CONTRACTOR AND COORDINATED WITH ALL OF THE WORK OF ALL TRADES. IF DISCREPANCIES ARE FOUND, THE CONTRACTOR SHALL NOTIFY THE ARCHITECT IN WRITING FOR CLARIFICATION BEFORE THE COMMENCEMENT OR RESUMPTION OF WORK.

3. ABBREVIATIONS THROUGHOUT THE PLANS ARE THOSE IN COMMON USE. NOTIFY THE ARCHITECT OF ANY ABBREVIATIONS IN QUESTION.

4. CONTRACTOR SHALL COORDINATE THE INSTALLATION OF THE VARIOUS TRADE ITEMS WITHIN THE SPACE ABOVE ALL CEILINGS (INCLUDING, BUT NOT LIMITED TO: STRUCTURAL MEMBERS, MECHANICAL DUCTS AND INSULATION, CONDUITS, RACEWAYS, SPRINKLER SYSTEM, LIGHT FIXTURES, CEILING SYSTEMS, AND ANY SPECIAL STRUCTURAL SUPPORTS REQUIRED) AND SHALL BE RESPONSIBLE FOR MAINTAINING THE FINISH CEILING HEIGHT ABOVE THE FINISH FLOOR INDICATED IN THE DRAWINGS AND THE FINISH SCHEDULE. (CEILING HEIGHT DIMENSIONS ARE TO THE FINISH SURFACE OF CEILING.

5. ACCESS PANELS SHALL BE PROVIDED AND INSTALLED
    WHEREVER REQUIRED BY BUILDING CODE OR FOR THE
    PROPER OPERATION OR MAINTENANCE OF MECHANICAL OR
    ELECTRICAL EQUIPMENT, WHETHER OR NOT INDICATED ON
    THE DRAWINGS. CONTRACTOR SHALL COORDINATE SIZE,
    LOCATION, AND TYPE OF ACCESS PANEL WITH OTHER
    CONTRACTORS' WORK AND RECEIVE APPROVAL OF THE
    ARCHITECT. ACCESS PANEL SHALL BE AS SPECIFIED. NO
    ACCESS PANEL SHALL BE LOCATED, FRAMED OR INSTALLED
    WITHOUT THE EXPRESSED APPROVAL OF THE ARCHITECT.

6. DIMENSIONS SHOWN ON FLOOR PLANS, SECTIONS,
    ELEVATIONS, AND DETAILS ARE TO FINISH FACE OF STUD,
    MASONRY, OR CONCRETE. GRIDLINES, UNLESS OTHERWISE
    NOTED.

7. IN THE CASE OF A CONFLICT BETWEEN THE DRAWINGS AND
    THE SPECIFICATIONS, SPECIFICATIONS SHALL TAKE
    PRECEDENCE. CONTRACTOR SHALL NOTIFY THE
    CONSTRUCTION MANAGER OF ANY CONFLICT BEFORE
    PROCEEDING WITH THE WORK.

8. ALL DUCT PENETRATIONS THROUGH PARTITIONS AND CEILING
    SHALL BE PROVIDED WITH NECESSARY FRAMES AND
    BRACING AROUND THE OPENING AND SHALL BE PROVIDED
    WITH AUTOMATIC FIRE DAMPERS AS REQUIRED BY THE
    BUILDING DEPARTMENT FOR FIRE-RATED PENETRATIONS.

9. THE SPECIFICATIONS AND ALL CONSULTANT DRAWINGS ARE
    SUPPLEMENTAL TO THE ARCHITECTURAL DRAWINGS. IT SHALL
    BE THE CONTRACTOR'S RESPONSIBILITY TO COORDINATE
    WITH THE ARCHITECTURAL DRAWINGS BEFORE THE
    INSTALLATION OF ANY OF THE CONSULTANTS' WORK AND TO
    BRING ANY DISCREPANCIES OR CONFLICTS TO THE
    ARCHITECT'S ATTENTION IN WRITING, FOR CLARIFICATION.
    IMPROPERLY INSTALLED WORK SHALL BE CORRECTED
    BY THE GENERAL CONTRACTOR AT HIS EXPENSE AND AT NO
    EXPENSE TO THE ARCHITECT, HIS CONSULTANTS, OR THE
    OWNER.

10. CONTRACTOR SHALL PROVIDE AND INSTALL ACCESS
    PANELS WHERE SHOWN ON THE REFLECTED CEILING PLANS
    AND AS REQUIRED BY THE BUILDING DEPARTMENT OR
    NORMAL GOOD PRACTICE TO PROVIDE ACCESS TO ALL
    TERMINAL BOXES, VOLUME DAMPERS, AND VALVES, ETC.
    (ALSO SEE NOTE 5.)

11. THE ARCHITECT SHALL BE CONSULTED IN ALL CASES WHERE
    CUTTING INTO AN EXISTING STRUCTURAL PORTION OF ANY
    BUILDING IS EITHER EXPEDIENT OR NECESSARY. PRIOR TO

PROCEEDING WITH WORK, REINFORCEMENT AND/OR
SUPPORT SATISFACTORY TO ARCHITECT AND STRUCTURAL
ENGINEER SHALL BE PROVIDED BY CONTRACTOR PRIOR TO
CUTTING INTO STRUCTURAL PORTIONS OF ANY BUILDING.

12. ALL EXIT DOORS SHALL BE OPENABLE FROM THE INSIDE
     WITHOUT THE USE OF A KEY OR ANY SPECIAL
     KNOWLEDGEOR EFFORT AND SHALL BE ACCESSIBLE BY THE
     HANDICAPPED.

13. MAXIMUM EFFORT TO OPERATE DOORS SHALL NOT EXCEED
     THE FOLLOWING:
     A. INTERIOR DOORS: 5 POUNDS
     B. EXTERIOR DOORS: 8.5 POUNDS
     C. FIRE DOORS: 15 POUNDS

14. LEGAL EXITS SHALL NOT BE BLOCKED AT ANYTIME.

15. ALL EXIT LIGHTING AND SIGNS TO HAVE MINIMUM 6-INCH-
     HIGH LETTERS IN ACCORDANCE WITH TITLE 19, CHAPTER 33.

16. EMERGENCY LIGHTING SHALL BE PROVIDED GIVING A VALUE
     ONE FOOTCANDLE AT FLOOR LEVEL. EXIT SIGNS SHALL BE
     ILLUMINATED BY TWO SEPARATE SOURCES OF POWER PER
     LOCAL FIRE DEPARTMENT. (ONE SOURCE ON EMERGENCY
     POWER, SEE ELEC. DRAWINGS.)

17. TEMPORARY PEDESTRIAN PROTECTION SHALL BE PROVIDED
     AS REQUIRED BY LOS ANGELES CITY CODE.

18. FINAL CLEAN UP AND DISPOSAL:
     REMOVE DEBRIS, RUBBISH AND WASTE MATERIAL FROM THE
     OWNER'S PROPERTY TO A LAWFUL DISPOSAL AREA AND PAY
     ALL HAULING AND DUMPING COSTS. CONFORM TO
     PERTAINING FEDERAL STATE AND LOCAL LAWS,
     REGULATIONS AND ORDERS UPON COMPLETION OF WORK,
     ALL CONSTRUCTION AREAS SHALL BE LEFT VACUUM-CLEAN
     AND FREE FROM DEBRIS. CLEAN ALL DUST, DIRT, STAINS,
     HAND MARKS, PAINT SPOTS, DROPPINGS, AND OTHER
     BLEMISHES.

19. PRIOR TO INSPECTION OF THE EXISTING FACILITY, THE
     CONTRACTOR MUST RECEIVE PERMISSION FOR SITE ACCESS
     FROM THE OWNER OR THE DESIGNATED REPRESENTATIVE.

20. WHEN IT IS NECESSARY TO INTERRUPT ANY EXISTING UTILITY
     SERVICE TO MAKE CORRECTIONS AND/OR CONNECTION, A
     MINIMUM OF 48 HOURS ADVANCE NOTICE SHALL BE GIVEN
     THE OWNER. INTERRUPTIONS IN UTILITY SERVICES SHALL BE
     OF THE SHORTEST POSSIBLE DURATION FOR THE WORK AT
     HAND AND SHALL BE APPROVED IN ADVANCE BY THE
     OWNER.

21. IN THE EVENT THE UTILITY SERVICE IS INTERRUPTED WITHOUT THE REQUIRED 48 HOURS NOTICE, THEN THE CONTRACTOR SHALL BE FINANCIALLY LIABLE FOR ALL DAMAGES SUFFERED BY THE OWNER DUE TO THE UNAUTHORIZED INTERRUPTION. RECONNECTION SHALL BE MADE IMMEDIATELY.

22. IF THE CONTRACTOR ASCERTAINS AT ANY TIME THAT REQUIREMENTS OF THIS CONTRACT CONFLICT WITH, OR ARE IN VIOLATION OF, APPLICABLE LAWS, CODES, REGULATIONS AND ORDINANCES, HE SHALL NOT PROCEED WITH WORK IN QUESTION, EXCEPT AT HIS OWN RISK, UNTIL ARCHITECT HAS BEEN NOTIFIED IN WRITING AND WRITTEN DETERMINATION IS MADE BY THE ARCHITECT. WHERE COMPLETED OR PARTIALLY COMPLETED WORK IS DISCOVERED TO BE IN VIOLATION WITH APPLICABLE LAWS, CODES, REGULATIONS AND ORDINANCES, CONTRACTOR SHALL BE REQUIRED TO REMOVE THAT WORK FROM THE PROJECT AND REPLACE SUCH WORK WITH ALL NEW COMPLYING WORK AT NO ADDITIONAL COST TO THE OWNER OR ARCHITECT.

23. ANY WORK INSTALLED IN CONFLICT WITH THE CONTRACT DOCUMENTS SHALL BE CORRECTED BY THE CONTRACTOR AT HIS EXPENSE AND AT NO ADDITIONAL EXPENSE TO THE OWNER, ARCHITECT, OR CONSULTANTS.

24. FINISH FLOOR ELEVATIONS ARE AS ESTABLISHED DATUM LINE, UNLESS OTHERWISE NOTED.

25. THE CONTRACTOR WILL BE RESPONSIBLE FOR VERIFYING FLOOR-TO-FLOOR ELEVATIONS. THE NEW BUILDING EXPANSION'S GROUND FLOOR SHALL ALIGN IN ELEVATION WITH RESPECTIVE FLOORS IN EXISTING BUILDING.

26. THE CONTRACTOR SHALL FURNISH ALL MATERIALS, LABOR, EQUIPMENT, TRANSPORTATION AND SERVICES NECESSARY FOR THE SATISFACTORY COMPLETION OF WORK UNLESS DESIGNATED (N.I.C.) OR (O.F.O.I.). ALL EQUIPMENT, WORK AND MATERIALS SHALL COMPLY WITH ALL CURRENT AND LOCAL APPLICABLE CODES AND GOVERNING REGULATIONS, AND THE CONTRACT DOCUMENTS.

27. THE CONTRACTOR SHALL PROTECT ALL FINISH WORK AND SURFACES FROM DAMAGE DURING THE COURSE OF CONSTRUCTION AND SHALL REPLACE AND/OR REPAIR ALL DAMAGED SURFACES CAUSED BY CONTRACTOR OR SUBCONTRACTOR PERSONNEL TO THE SATISFACTION OF THE OWNER AND ARCHITECT.

28. THE CONTRACTOR SHALL PROVIDE ALL NECESSARY PERMITS AND INSPECTIONS.

29. SIZE OF MECHANICAL AND ELECTRICAL EQUIPMENT PADS AND BASES ARE APPROXIMATE ONLY. THE CONTRACTOR SHALL VERIFY DIMENSIONS WITH RESPECTIVE EQUIPMENT MANUFACTURER.

30. SPECIAL NOTICE TO CONTRACTORS: ALL CONTRACTORS PERFORMING WORK ON THE PREMISES SHALL BE RESPONSIBLE FOR INITIATING, MAINTAINING AND SUPERVISING A REASONABLE AND PRUDENT SAFETY PROGRAM INCLUDING BUT NOT LIMITED TO THE ISOLATION OF WORK AREAS AND THE PROMPT REMOVAL OF ANY DEBRIS OR TOOLS WHICH MIGHT ENDANGER VISITORS AND STAFF OF THE OWNER OR ARCHITECT.

31. CONTRACTOR SHALL PROVIDE AND INSTALL ALL STIFFENERS, BRACINGS, BACK-UP PLATES AND SUPPORTING BRACKETS REQUIRED FOR THE INSTALLATION OF ALL CASEWORK, TOILET ACCESSORIES AND OF ALL FLOOR-MOUNTED OR SUSPENDED MECHANICAL AND ELECTRICAL EQUIPMENT.

32. THE CONTRACTOR SHALL VERIFY THE LOCATION OF ALL EXISTING UTILITIES BELOW GRADE AND RELATED SERVICE CONNECTIONS WITH THE RESPECTIVE UTILITY COMPANIES.

33. THE CONTRACTOR SHALL COORDINATE THE REMOVAL, ABANDONMENT, AND/OR RELOCATION OF EXISTING UTILITIES ABOVE OR BELOW GRADE WITH THE RESPECTIVE UTILITY COMPANIES.

34. THE CONTRACTOR SHALL PERFORM ALL WORK WITHIN PUBLIC RIGHTS-OF-WAY ACCORDING TO THE CITY OF LOS ANGELES STANDARD PLANS AND SPECIFICATIONS. CONTRACTOR SHALL OBTAIN PERMITS FROM APPROPRIATE AGENCIES.

35. THE CONTRACTOR SHALL PROVIDE TEMPORARY BRACES, SHORES AND GUYS REQUIRED TO SUPPORT ALL LOADS TO WHICH THE BUILDING STRUCTURES, UTILITIES AND RIGHT-OF-WAY MAY BE SUBJECTED DURING CONSTRUCTION.

36. THE CONTRACTOR SHALL PROVIDE SANITARY FACILITIES FOR WORKERS' USE. EXISTING FACILITIES SHALL NOT BE USED.

37. THE CONTRACTOR SHALL OBTAIN OSHA PERMITS FOR ANY VERTICAL EXCAVATIONS OVER 5'-0" DEEP INTO WHICH PERSONS MUST DESCEND.

38. THE CONTRACTOR SHALL COORDINATE WITH REPRESENTATIVES OF WATER, ELECTRICAL, GAS, TELEPHONE AND TELEVISION COMPANIES TO VERIFY AVAILABLE FACILITIES AND, IF APPLICABLE, TO ESTABLISH TEMPORARY FACILITIES.

39. CONTRACTOR SHALL VERIFY ALL COLUMN COORDINATES
    AND CHECK THEM AGAINST DIMENSIONS SHOWN ON PLANS
    AND DETAILS. CONSTRUCTION MANAGER SHOULD BE
    NOTIFIED OF ANY DISCREPANCIES DURING STAKING.

40. CONTRACTOR AND SUBCONTRACTORS SHALL BE
    RESPONSIBLE FOR OBTAINING AND PAYING FOR ALL PERMITS
    AND FEES REQUIRED, NOT NORMALLY COVERED BY THE
    BUILDING PERMITS.

41. SUBSTITUTIONS:

    A. REFERENCE TO MAKERS, BRAND, MODELS, ETC., IS TO
       ESTABLISH THE TYPE AND QUALITY DESIRED;
       SUBSTITUTION OF ACCEPTABLE EQUIVALENTS WILL BE
       PERMITTED IF APPROVED BY THE ARCHITECT AND OWNER
       PRIOR TO BID (UNLESS NOTED OTHERWISE).

    B. THE ARCHITECT, ACTING AS THE OWNER'S DESIGNATED
       AGENT FOR THE DESIGN FOR THIS PROJECT, WILL
       EXERCISE SOLE AUTHORITY FOR DETERMINING
       CONFORMANCE OF MATERIALS, EQUIPMENT AND
       SYSTEMS WITH THE INTENT OF THE DESIGN.

42. ONLY NEW MATERIALS AND EQUIPMENT OF RECENT
    MANUFACTURE, OF QUALITY SPECIFIED, FREE FROM DEFECTS,
    WILL BE PERMITTED ON THE WORK.

43. SHOP DRAWINGS:

    A. SHOP DRAWINGS SHALL BE SUBMITTED FOR ALL
       EQUIPMENT AND MATERIALS WHICH MUST INTERFACE
       AND COORDINATE WITH OTHERS, WHETHER DETAILED OR
       NOT.

    B. SHOP DRAWINGS SHALL BE SUBMITTED IN A MINIMUM OF
       3 COPIES AND ONE OZALID TRANSPARENCY; BROCHURES
       IN NOT LESS THAN 8 COPIES.

44. TEMPORARY FACILITIES:

    A. THE CONTRACTOR SHALL PROVIDE A STAGING AND
       MATERIAL STORAGE AREA ADJACENT TO THE AREA OF
       CONSTRUCTION. LOCATION SHALL BE COORDINATED
       WITH THE OWNER.

    B. THE CONTRACTOR SHALL MAKE NECESSARY
       CONNECTIONS TO EXISTING UTILITIES FOR TEMPORARY
       POWER AND WATER SUPPLIES, AND SHALL COORDINATE
       SUCH USE WITH THE OWNER PRIOR TO CONNECTION.

    C. THE CONTRACTOR SHALL PROVIDE TEMPORARY
       BARRICADES TO SEPARATE CONSTRUCTION AREAS FOR

PUBLIC SAFETY AROUND ENTIRE PERIMETER OF CONSTRUCTION AREA.

45. THE CONTRACTOR SHALL PROVIDE A BLANKET ONE (1) YEAR GUARANTEE FOR THE CONTRACT PROJECT WITH SEPARATE GUARANTEES AS SPECIFIED FOR TRADES/EQUIPMENT ITEMS WITH NAMES OF LOCAL REPRESENTATIVES TO BE CONTACTED FOR SERVICE. PROVIDE OPERATING MAINTENANCE BROCHURES, AND GUARANTEES AS REQUIRED.

46. THE CONTRACTOR SHALL PROVIDE ONE COMPLETE SET OF AS-BUILT XEROX VELLUM REPRODUCIBLE DRAWINGS INDICATING ALL DISCREPANCIES, CHANGES, ETC., AND ACTUAL LOCATIONS OF CONCEALED WORK TO THE ARCHITECT AT THE COMPLETION OF WORK PRIOR TO FINAL PAYMENT. CHANGES MUST BE DRAFTED. NO FREEHAND REVISIONS WILL BE ACCEPTED.

47. DRAWINGS OF EXISTING CONDITIONS HAVE BEEN COMPILED FROM EXISTING DATA SUPPLIED BY THE OWNER TO THE ARCHITECT. THE ARCHITECT MAKES NO WARRANTY EITHER EXPRESSED OR IMPLIED, FOR THE ACCURACY OR COMPLETENESS OF THE EXISTING INFORMATION RECORDED. CONTRACTOR SHALL FIELD VERIFY ALL EXISTING CONDITIONS. NOTIFY ARCHITECT IN WRITING OF ANY DISCREPENCIES FOR CLARIFICATION PRIOR TO PROCEEDING WITH WORK.

48. INSTALLATION OF FIRE ALARM SYSTEM, AUTOMATIC FIRE SPRINKLER SYSTEM, AND STANDPIPE SYSTEM SHALL NOT BE STARTED UNTIL DETAIL PLANS, SPECIFICATIONS AND ENGINEERING CALCULATIONS HAVE BEEN ACCEPTED AND SIGNED BY THE ARCHITECT OR STRUCTURAL ENGINEER IN GENERAL CHARGE OF DESIGN AND THE SIGNATURE OF THE ARCHITECT OR PROFESSIONAL ENGINEER WHO HAS BEEN DELEGATED RESPONSIBILITY COVERING THE WORK SHOWN ON A PARTICULAR PLAN OR SPECIFICATION AND APPROVED BY THE LOS ANGELES FIRE DEPARTMENT. (DEFERRED APPROVAL)

49. FIRE ALARM SYSTEM SHALL BE APPROVED BY THE LOS ANGELES FIRE DEPARTMENT PRIOR TO INSTALLATION. (DEFERRED APPROVAL)

50. THE EXIT DOOR MUST OPEN OVER A LANDING NOT MORE THAN 1" BELOW THE THRESHOLD 3304(h).

51. OVERHEAD DOORS ARE NOT PERMITTED AS EXIT DOORS 3304(g).

52. CONTRACTOR SHALL OBTAIN NECESSARY PERMIT FROM THE
    STATE OF CALIFORNIA DIVISION OF INDUSTRIAL SAFETY
    PRIOR TO THE ISSUANCE OF A BUILDING OR GRADING PERMIT.
    (HSC 17922.5, EFFECTIVE 3-6-76)

53. THE CONSTRUCTION OR DEMOLITION OF ANY BUILDING
    STRUCTURE, SCAFFOLDING OR FALSEWORK MORE THAN
    THREE STORIES OR 36' IN HEIGHT REQUIRES A PERMIT FROM
    THE STATE OF CALIFORNIA DIVISION OF INDUSTRIAL SAFETY
    PRIOR TO THE ISSUANCE OF A BUILDING PERMIT. (HSC 17922.5,
    EFFECTIVE 3-6-76)

54. A PERMIT FROM THE DEPARTMENT OF PUBLIC WORKS IS
    REQUIRED FOR A PROTECTION FENCE OR CANOPY ON OR
    OVER ANY STREET OR PUBLIC SPACE: 91 33C3.2.

55. APPROVED NUMBERS OR ADDRESSES SHALL BE PROVIDED
    IN SUCH A POSITION AS TO BE PLAINLY VISIBLE AND LEGIBLE
    FROM STREET.

GENERAL CONSTRUCTION REQUIREMENTS

1. CONTRACTOR SHALL PROVIDE AN APPROVED AUTOMATIC
    FIRE SPRINKLER SYSTEM THROUGHOUT THE NEW BUILDING
    (WAREHOUSE, OFFICE, AND EXTERIOR SOFFIT AREAS),
    IN-RACK SPRINKLER SYSTEM (WAREHOUSE), AND MODIFY
    EXISITNG AUTOMATIC FIRE SPRINKLER SYSTEM IN THE
    EXISTING BUILDING REMODEL. SEE FIRE DEPARTMENT NOTES
    SHEET T-0.2 FOR ADDITIONAL REQUIREMENTS.

2. ALL SINGLE-LAYER GYPSUM BOARD WALLS CONTINUOUS
    AND CONTIGUOUS WITH DOUBLE-LAYER GYPSUM BOARD.
    WALLS SHALL MAINTAIN ONE CONTIGUOUS OUTER LAYER OF
    GYPSUM BOARD AT THE SAME FACE OF FINISH. STUDS AND
    FURRING CHANNELS SHALL BE OFFSET ACCORDINGLY.

3. CEILING SYSTEMS SHALL PROVIDE FOR LIGHTING FIXTURES
    AND AIR CONDITIONING DIFFUSERS. INDEPENDENT FRAMING
    AND ATTACHMENTS TO THE STRUCTURE SHALL BE ADEQUATE
    TO SUPPORT THE CEILING SYSTEM WHERE DUCTWORK
    INTERFERES WITH NORMAL SUSPENSION. ATTACHMENT OF
    HANGERS OR FRAMING TO DUCTWORK IS PROHIBITED.

4. DOOR OPENING NOT LOCATED BY DIMENSION SHALL BE
    CENTERED IN WALLS AS SHOWN OR LOCATED 4" FROM
    FINISH WALL TO FINISH JAMB UNLESS OTHERWISE NOTED.

5. REFER TO DOOR SCHEDULE, DETAILS, AND SPECIFICATIONS
    FOR DOOR, DOOR FRAME, AND DOOR HARDWARE
    REQUIREMENTS.

6.   LATCHING AND LOCKING DOORS THAT ARE HAND-ACTIVATED
     AND WHICH ARE IN A PATH OF TRAVEL SHALL BE OPERABLE
     WITH A SINGLE EFFORT BY LEVER TYPE HARDWARE, PANIC
     BARS, PUSH-PULL ACTIVATING BARS, OR OTHER HARDWARE
     DESIGNED TO PROVIDE PASSAGE WITHOUT REQUIRING THE
     ABILITY TO GRASP THE OPENING HARDWARE. LOCKED EXIT
     DOORS SHALL OPERATE AS ABOVE IN THE EGRESS
     DIRECTION.

7.   ALL DISSIMILAR METALLIC MATERIALS SHALL BE EFFECTIVELY
     ISOLATED FROM EACH OTHER TO PREVENT GALVANIC
     ACTION.

8.   REFER TO SPECIFICATIONS AND FINISH SCHEDULE FOR TYPE
     OF PAINT FINISHES, METAL FINISHES, CEMENT FINISHES,
     WEATHER AND SOUND SEALANTS.

9.   "NO TRENCHES OR EXCAVATIONS 5' OR MORE IN DEPTH INTO
     WHICH A PERSON IS REQUIRED TO DESCEND," OR, OBTAIN
     NECESSARY PERMIT FROM THE STATE OF CALIFORNIA
     DIVISION OF INDUSTRIAL SAFETY PRIOR TO THE ISSUANCE OF
     A BUILDING OR GRADING PERMIT.
     (HSC 17922.5, EFF. 3-6-76)

10. ALL WOOD IN CONTACT WITH MASONRY OR CONCRETE
     SHALL BE PRESSURE TREATED WITH AN APPROVED
     PRESERVATIVE.

11. ELECTRICAL OUTLET BOXES IN OPPOSITE FACES OF
     SOUND- RATED WALLS SHALL BE SEPARATED HORIZONTALLY
     BY A MINIMUM 24". BACKS AND SIDES OF BOXES TO BE
     SEALED WITH 1/8" RESILIENT SEALANT AND BACKED WITH 2"
     MINERAL FIBER INSULATION.

12. ALL RIGID CONDUIT, DUCTS, PLUMBING PIPES, AND APPLIANCE
     VENTS LOCATED IN SOUND ASSEMBLIES SHALL BE
     ISOLATED FROM THE BUILDING CONSTRUCTION BY MEANS
     OF RESILIENT SLEEVES, MOUNTS, OR 1/4" MINIMUM THICKNESS
     APPROVED RESILIENT MATERIALS.

13. APPROVED PERMANENT AND RESILIENT ACOUSTICAL
     SEALANT SHALL BE PROVIDED ALONG THE JOINT BETWEEN
     THE FLOOR AND ALL SEPARATION WALLS.

14. GLASS DOORS, ADJACENT PANELS, AND ALL GLAZED
     OPENINGS WITHIN 18 INCHES OF ADJACENT FLOOR SHALL BE
     OF GLASS APPROVED FOR IMPACT HAZARD. (71.2406.4.7)

15. WINDOWS AND OPENINGS WITHIN 12 FEET OF GROUND
     LEVEL WITH OVER 96 SQ. IN. AREA ARE DEEMED
     "ACCESSIBLE." GLAZING AND GLAZED ASSEMBLIES FOR
     "ACCESSIBLE" OPENINGS SHALL BE CERTIFIED AS MEETING

TEST PROVISION OF UBC 41-2.

16. GLAZING IN EXTERIOR DOORS OR WITHIN 40 INCHES OF ANY LOCKING MECHANISM SHALL BE TEMPERED OR BURGLAR-RESISTANT.

17. ALL INSULATION MATERIALS SHALL BE CERTIFIED BY THE MANUFACTURER AS COMPLYING WITH THE CALIFORNIA QUALITY STANDARDS FOR INSULATING MATERIALS.

18. DUCTS SHALL BE CONSTRUCTED, INSTALLED, AND INSULATED ACCORDING TO CHAPTER 10 OF THE 1991 UNIFORM MECHANICAL CODE W/ CITY OF LOS ANGELES 1992 AMENDMENTS. ALL JOINTS OF THE DUCT SYSTEM SHALL BE TIGHTLY SEALED WITH APPROVED MASTIC OR TAPE.

19. DOORS AND WINDOWS BETWEEN CONDITIONED AND UNCONDITIONED SPACES SHALL BE DESIGNED TO LIMIT AIR LEAKAGE INTO OR FROM THE BUILDING ENVELOPE.

   A. MANUFACTURED DOORS AND WINDOWS SHALL HAVE AIR INFILTRATION RATES CERTIFIED BY THE MANUFACTURER AS NOT EXCEEDING THOSE SHOWN IN TABLE 2-53J.

   B. SITE-CONSTRUCTED DOORS AND WINDOWS, EXTERIOR JOINTS, AND OPENINGS IN THE BUILDING ENVELOPE THAT ARE OBSERVABLE SOURCES OF AIR LEAKAGE SHALL BE CAULKED, GASKETED, WEATHER-STRIPPED OR OTHERWISE SEALED. (DOES NOT INCLUDE FIRE-RATED DOORS AND WINDOWS, UNFRAMED GLASS DOORS, AND EXTERIOR ELEVATOR SHAFTS. ELEVATOR SHAFT VENTILATION DAMPERS ARE ALSO NOTED IF REQUIRED.) (SEC. 2-5317(AXB)(C))

20. CABINETS AND CASEWORK ARE LOCATED ON FLOOR PLANS AND IDENTIFIED ON INTERIOR ELEVATIONS.

   A. PLASTIC LAMINATE: MODULAR CASEWORK IDENTIFIED WITH A DIGIT NUMBER (E.G., WIC 304) AND CONSTRUCTED ACCORDING TO THE SPECIFICATIONS OF WOODWORK INSTITUTE OF CALIFORNIA, MANUAL OF MILLWORK, SHALL BE CONTRACTOR FURNISHED AND CONTRACTOR INSTALLED.

   B. SPECIAL CASEWORK DESIGN TO W.I.C. SPECIFICATIONS SHALL BE PROVIDED ACCORDING TO REFERENCE NOTES AND DETAILS ON THE DRAWINGS.

21. GYPSUM BOARD DRYWALL BACKING FOR CERAMIC TILE INSTALLED IN TOILET ROOMS SHALL BE USG W/R (WATER RESISTANT) PANELS OR EQUAL.

22. A NARROW FRAME WITH A BEVELED TOP EDGE (30

DEGREES MAXIMUM BEVEL TO VERTICAL PLANE) INSTALLED AT THE BOTTOM OF A GLASS DOOR (WITH NO SIDE FRAMES) MAY BE USED IN LIEU OF PROVIDING THE REQUIRED 10-INCH UNINTERRUPTED SURFACE AT THE BOTTOM OF THE DOOR.

23. FIRE-RATED PARTITION WALLS AND FIRE-RATED OCCUPANCY SEPARATION WALLS SHALL EXTEND FROM CONCRETE FLOOR SLABS TO UNDERSIDE OF STRUCTURE ABOVE. ALL OPENINGS SHALL BE PROTECTED, AS FOLLOWS.

   A. ONE-HOUR WALLS: LABELED CLASS "C" FIRE DOOR, AND FRAME ASSEMBLY AND HARDWARE.

   B. TWO-HOUR WALLS: LABELED CLASS "B" FIRE DOOR, AND FRAME ASSEMBLY AND HARDWARE.

   C. THREE-HOUR WALLS: LABELED CLASS "A" FIRE DOOR, AND FRAME ASSEMBLY AND HARDWARE.

24. ALL PIPES, DUCTS AND BUSS DUCTS WHICH PENETRATE THE FLOOR CONSTRUCTION SHALL BE INSTALLED SO AS TO MAINTAIN THE FIRE RESISTIVE RATING AND STRUCTURAL INTEGRITY OF THE BUILDING.

25. ALL INSULATIONS NOTED ON PLANS SHALL BE NONCOMBUSTIBLE AND MAINTAIN THERMAL MOISTURE PROTECTION AS NOTED IN THE SPECIFICATION.

26. ALL ROOF COVERING SHALL BE CONSTRUCTED OF FIRE-RETARDENT MATERIAL PER UBC 1991 SECTION 3202.

27. ALL PENETRATIONS THRU FIRE-RATED WALLS AND CEILINGS SHALL BE INSTALLED WITH FIRE DAMPERS, FIRE SEAL, ETC., SO AS TO MAINTAIN THE FIRE-RESISTIVE RATING AND STRUCTURAL INTEGRITY OF WALL OR CEILING ASSEMBLY.

The following is an example of a set of general demolition notes for working drawings. These notes were written for a specific project[2] in a specific state but many of the notes would apply to any project in any location.

GENERAL DEMOLITION NOTES

1. THESE DEMOLITION PLAN DRAWINGS WERE CREATED FROM EXISTING WORKING DRAWINGS AND ARE INTENDED TO SHOW THE GENERAL CONDITIONS WHICH ARE EXPECTED TO OCCUR. VERIFY ALL CONDITIONS BEFORE PROCEEDING WITH THE DEMOLITON WORK IN ANY AREA. DEMOLITION OF DOORS, WINDOWS, CABINETRY, FINISHES, PARTITIONS, OR ANY OTHER

NONSTRUCTURAL ITEMS MAY PROCEED AS INDICATED. WHERE DISCREPANCIES INVOLVE STRUCTURAL ITEMS, REPORT SUCH DIFFERENCES TO THE ARCHITECT AND SECURE INSTRUCTIONS BEFORE PROCEEDING IN THE AFFECTED AREA.

2. THE CONTRACTOR SHALL COORDINATE WITH THE OWNER'S REPRESENTATIVE THE SALVAGE OF LIGHT FIXTURES, FURNISHINGS, DOORS, AND MISCELLANEOUS EQUIPMENT.

3. THE CONTRACTOR SHALL REMOVE EXISTING WALLS AND OTHER ASSOCIATED CONSTRUCTION AS INDICATED ON THE DEMOLITION PLANS WITH DASHED LINES.

4. REFER TO MECHANICAL AND ELECTRICAL DRAWINGS FOR ADDED DEMOLITION NOTES AND INFORMATION.

5. THE CONTRACTOR SHALL PROVIDE ALL NECESSARY BARRICADES AND OTHER FORMS OF PROTECTION AS REQUIRED TO PROTECT THE OWNER'S PERSONNEL, OTHER TENANTS AND GENERAL PUBLIC FROM INJURY DUE TO DEMOLITION WORK.

6. THE CONTRACTOR SHALL ENSURE THAT DEMOLITION WORK DOES NOT INTERFERE WITH OR PROHIBIT THE CONTINUING OCCUPATION OF ADJACENT OPERATIONS WITHIN THE STRUCTURE. THIS INCLUDES BUT IS NOT LIMITED TO THE SELECTIVE DEMOLITION OF PARTITIONS, ELECTRICAL AND MECHANICAL SYSTEMS. THE CONTRACTOR SHALL INFORM THE OWNER OF A MINIMUM OF 72 HOURS OF DEMOLITION ACTIVITIES THAT WILL AFFECT NORMAL OPERATION OF BUILDING.

7. THE CONTRACTOR SHALL REPAIR DAMAGES CAUSED TO ADJACENT FACILITIES BY DEMOLITION WORK.

8. THE CONTRACTOR SHALL REMOVE & RETURN TO OWNER ALL SHELVING BRACKETS WHERE THEY INTERFERE WITH NEW WORK.

Notes
[1]A warehouse addition. Stephen Wen + Associates Architects, Inc. Pasadena, California.

[2]An elementary school. HKT Architects, Inc. Somerville, Massachusetts.

Drawing Convention Symbols

Graphic scales:

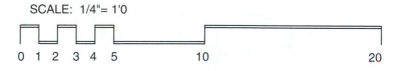

SCALE: 1/4"= 1'0

0 1 2 3 4 5   10   20

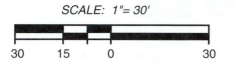

SCALE: 1"= 30'

30   15   0   30

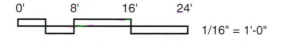

0'   8'   16'   24'

1/16" = 1'-0"

0"   3"   6"   9"   1'

1-1/2"=1'-0"

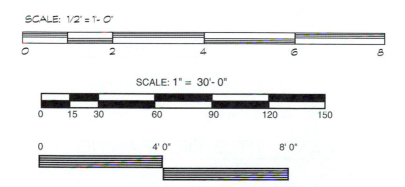

SCALE: 1/2" = 1'- 0"

0   2   4   6   8

SCALE: 1" = 30'- 0"

0   15   30   60   90   120   150

0   4' 0"   8' 0"

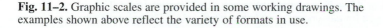

Fig. 11–2. Graphic scales are provided in some working drawings. The examples shown above reflect the variety of formats in use.

Sheet numbering:

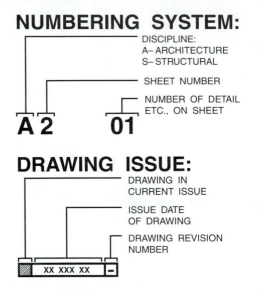

Fig. 11–3. The sheet numbering system shown above is the common format with variations generated by the use of hyphens or points (as indicated in the sheet index examples).

Drawing titles:

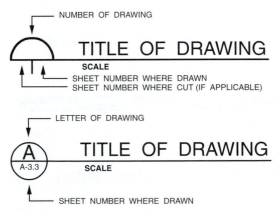

Fig. 11–4. Two methods of titling drawings are shown. The system can be used for any drawings including plans, elevations, and details.

Column grid lines:

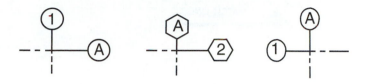

Fig. 11–5. The common grid notation symbol is a circle. Usually letters are used in one direction and numbers in the other. The direction used for letters and numbers varies.

Elevation notations (datum):

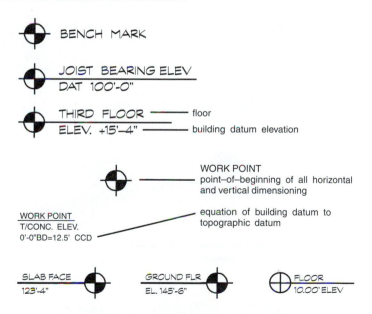

Fig. 11–6. Relative heights of key building elements are typically indicated by the same symbol with variations in the format of the datum information as shown.

Match lines:

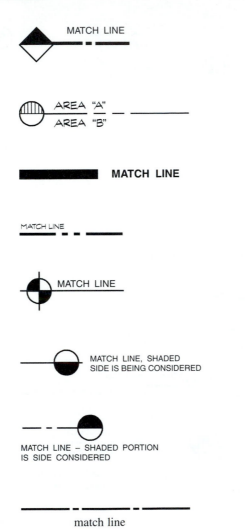

match line

Fig. 11–7. Match lines are used to indicate the edge of a drawing which continues in another drawing. A wide variety of lines and symbols are used for this purpose.

Miscellaneous site plan lines:

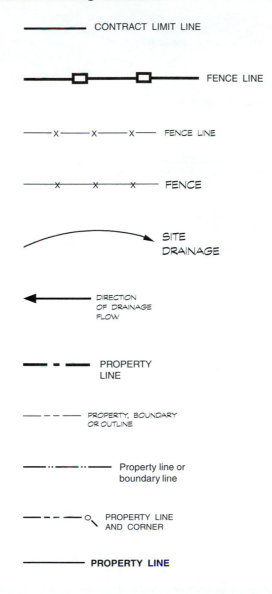

Fig. 11–8. Property line symbols vary among firms with the double-dash being slightly more common than the others.

Site contours and spot elevations:

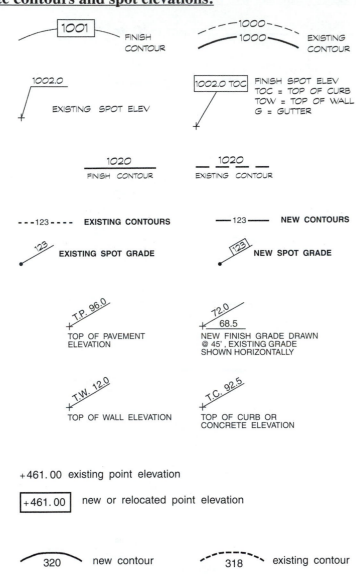

Fig. 11–9. A variety of notations for site elevations are used. In some cases the line configuration is the same but the position of the elevation number varies.

New spot elevations:

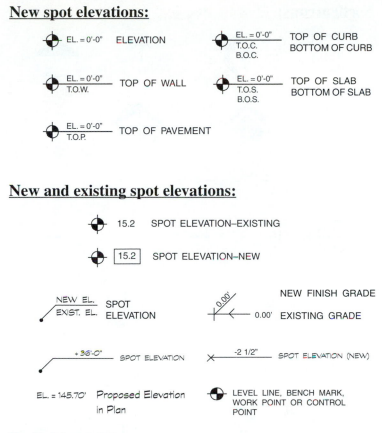

New and existing spot elevations:

Fig. 11–8 (concluded).

Test boring locations:

Fig. 11–10. Test boring notations are typically circles with a variety of shading and cross-line techniques. Usually a number accompanies the symbol to identify the boring in a schedule.

North arrows:

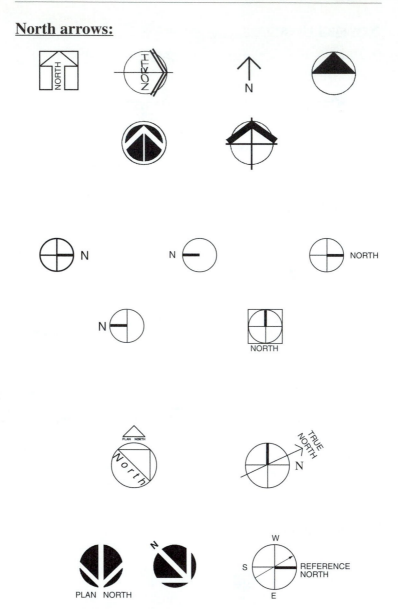

Fig. 11–11. Offices use a great variety of north arrows as indicated above. Most use the letter "N" or the word "North" with the symbol.

Room name and number:

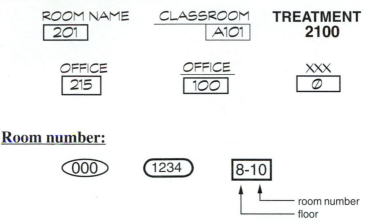

Room number:

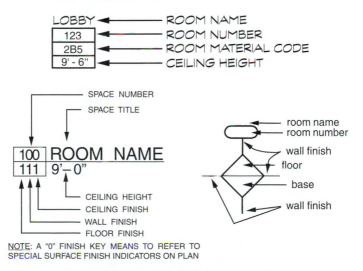

Fig. 11–12. The horizontal rectangle is the common geometric shape for room number with a variety of numbering systems and positions for room name as indicated.

Room number with finish information:

Fig. 11–13. These room name and number designations are suitable for use on plans designated for finish information.

Door numbers:

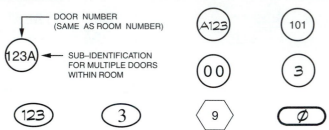

Fig. 11–14. The variation in numbering formats in the different geometric shapes reflect the difference in systems used by the firms surveyed.

Door graphics:

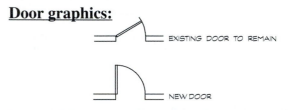

Fig. 11–15. The two door symbols are used in drawings for renovation and/or addition work where some doors in the plans are existing.

Window designations:

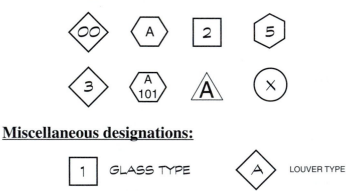

Miscellaneous designations:

Fig. 11–16. The variation in numbering formats in the different geometric shapes reflect the difference in systems used by the firms surveyed.

Paired building and wall section symbols:

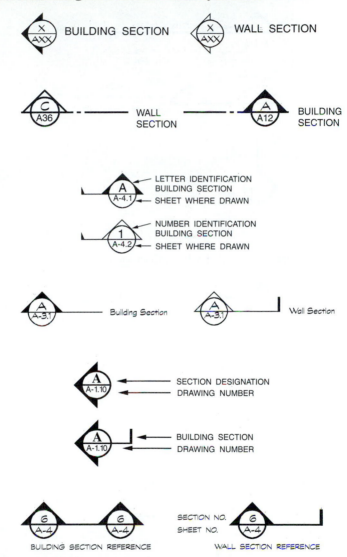

Fig. 11–17. Section cut symbols are usually shown in a legend as pairs (one for building sections and one for wall sections). The examples also include symbols serving for both purposes and a pair used for wall sections.

Multipurpose section symbols:

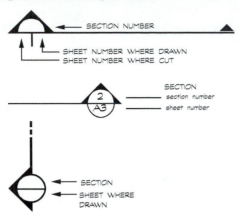

Wall section and detail section symbols:

Fig. 11–17 (concluded).

Detail section cut designations:

Fig. 11–18. Detail indications are often provided for sections and enlargements as shown above. Individual plan and detail enlargement symbols are also shown as are several individual section cut notations.

Detail enlargements and section designations:

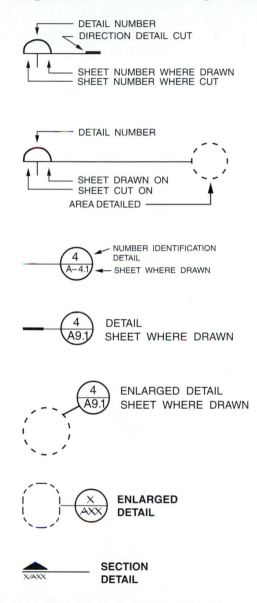

Fig. 11–18 (concluded).

Interior and exterior elevation notations:

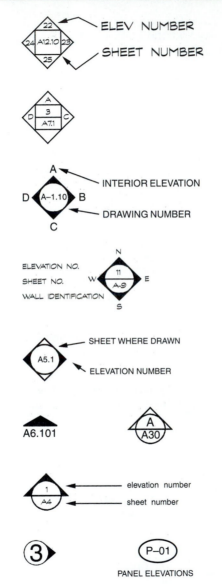

Fig. 11–19. The symbols are used in plans to indicate the identifiation and location of interior or exterior elevations.

Wall and partition types:

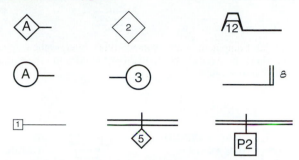

Fig. 11–20. Only two of the partition-type symbols are shown crossing walls in the plan view but when applied to the drawings, all of the symbols cross their respective walls in this format.

Finishes:

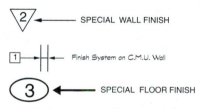

Fig. 11–21. The finish notations are usually shown on a floor plan. Their numbers correspond to those in a finish schedule.

Drains in the plan view:

Fig. 11–22. The "area drain" shown above was used to indicate a roof drain in the set of drawings where it was shown.

Equipment:

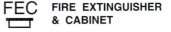

Fig. 11–23. Equipment numbers match those in equipment schedules. The legend where these are shown sometimes includes the sheet number where the schedule is located.

Fire extinguishers:

FE   **FIRE EXTINGUISHER**   FEC   **FIRE EXTINGUISHER**
○   **ON HOOK**   ▭   **& CABINET**

Fig. 11–24. The symbols appear in plan view and vary in size depending on the scale of the drawing. The size of the cabinet symbol must fit into the thickness of a wall.

Revision indications:

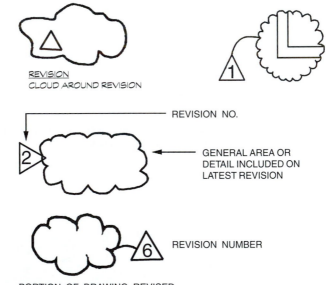

Fig. 11–25. Revision notations are fairly consistent among offices with a triangle being the geometric shape containing the revision number. A freehand "cloud" is typically used to encircle the part of the drawing that has been revised.

Miscellaneous line symbols:

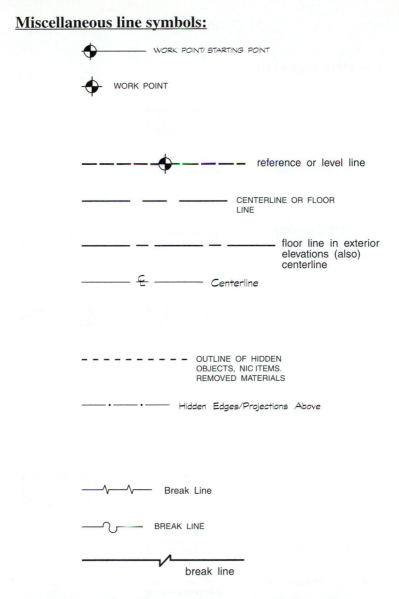

Fig. 11–26. Some variation occurs in common line symbols such as for hidden objects. Both the traditional dashed line and the alternating or single dashes with long continuous lines are used. The zig-zig segment of break lines varies considerably between offices.

Materials Symbols

Ceramic materials:

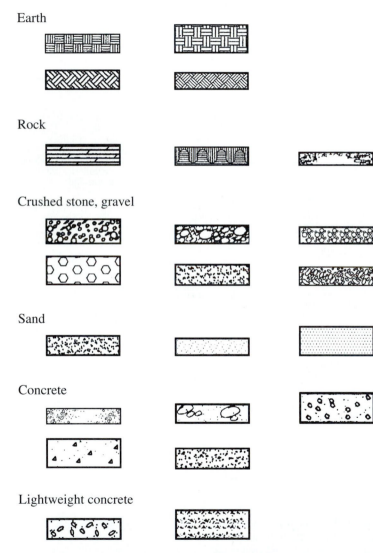

Earth

Rock

Crushed stone, gravel

Sand

Concrete

Lightweight concrete

Fig. 11–27. Materials symbols used by several architectural offices.

Precast concrete

Precast concrete plank

Cement grout

Brick

Masonry elevation

Structural tile

Glazed concrete masonry

Fig. 11–27 (continued).

<u>Ceramic materials:</u> (concluded)

Concrete masonry

Stone

Marble

(also travertine)

Granite

(elevation)

Fig. 11–27 (continued).

<u>Wood:</u>

Dimensional lumber (continuous)   Wood blocking (discontinuous)

Wood shim

Finished wood

Plywood

Microlam

Particle board

Fig. 11–27 (continued).

Metals:

Steel

Aluminum

Brass or bronze

Metal

(small scale)

Insulation:

Batt insulation

Form or sprayed insulation

Rigid insulation

Fig. 11–27 (continued).

Finish materials:

Gypsum wallboard

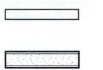

Textured ceiling paint

Plaster and lath

Plaster

Stucco

Acoustical tile or board

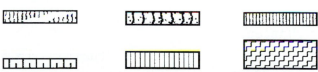

Fig. 11–27 (continued).

<u>Finish materials:</u> (continued)

Ceramic tile

(also quarry tile)   *(elevation)*   *(elevation)*

Carpet

Terrazzo

<u>Glazing:</u>

Glass

Translucent panel   Spandrel glass

<u>Miscellaneous:</u>

Plastic laminate   Bituminous concrete

Fig. 11–27 (concluded).

The drawing conventions and materials symbols were taken from working drawings produced by the following architectural firms: Ankrom Moisan Associated Architects. Portland, Oregon; C. Allen Mullins Architect. Bear Creek, Pennsylvania; Cromwell Architects Engineers. Little Rock, Arkansas; David Woodhouse Architects. Chicago, Illinois; Gossen Livingston Associates, Inc., Architecture. Wichita, Kansas; HKS, Inc., Architects, Engineers, Planners. Dallas, Texas; HKT Architects, Inc. Somerville, Massachusetts; The Hollis and Miller Group, Inc. Lee's Summit, Missouri; Overland Partners, Inc. San Antonio, Texas; PBK Architects, Inc. Houston, Dallas/Fort Worth, San Antonio, Austin, League City, Texas; Perkins Eastman Architects, P.C. New York, New York; Phillips Metsch Sweeney Moore Architects. Santa Barbara, California; Spencer Godfrey Architects. Round Rock, Texas; Stephen Wen + Associates Architects, Inc. Pasadena, California; Watkins Hamilton Ross Architects. Houston, Texas; Wilson Darnell Mann P.A., Architects. Wichita, Kansas.

Wall Types

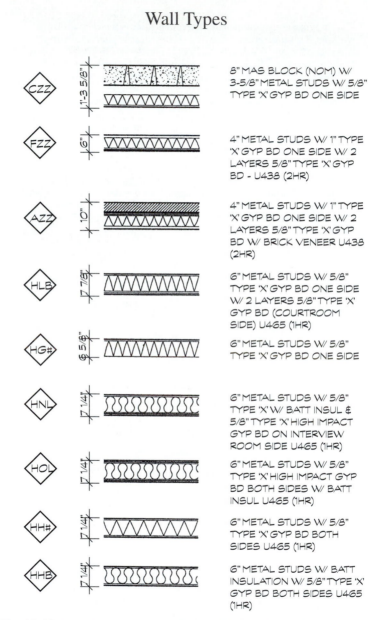

CZZ — 8" MAS BLOCK (NOM) W/ 3-5/8" METAL STUDS W/ 5/8" TYPE 'X' GYP BD ONE SIDE

FZZ — 4" METAL STUDS W/ 1" TYPE 'X' GYP BD ONE SIDE W/ 2 LAYERS 5/8" TYPE 'X' GYP BD - U438 (2HR)

AZZ — 4" METAL STUDS W/ 1" TYPE 'X' GYP BD ONE SIDE W/ 2 LAYERS 5/8" TYPE 'X' GYP BD W/ BRICK VENEER U438 (2HR)

HLB — 6" METAL STUDS W/ 5/8" TYPE 'X' GYP BD ONE SIDE W/ 2 LAYERS 5/8" TYPE 'X' GYP BD (COURTROOM SIDE) U465 (1HR)

HG# — 6" METAL STUDS W/ 5/8" TYPE 'X' GYP BD ONE SIDE

HNL — 6" METAL STUDS W/ 5/8" TYPE 'X' W/ BATT INSUL & 5/8" TYPE 'X' HIGH IMPACT GYP BD ON INTERVIEW ROOM SIDE U465 (1HR)

HOL — 6" METAL STUDS W/ 5/8" TYPE 'X' HIGH IMPACT GYP BD BOTH SIDES W/ BATT INSUL U465 (1HR)

HH# — 6" METAL STUDS W/ 5/8" TYPE 'X' GYP BD BOTH SIDES U465 (1HR)

HHB — 6" METAL STUDS W/ BATT INSULATION W/ 5/8" TYPE 'X' GYP BD BOTH SIDES U465 (1HR)

Fig. 11–28. (A police and court facility. The Hollis and Miller Group, Inc. Lee's Summit, Missouri.)

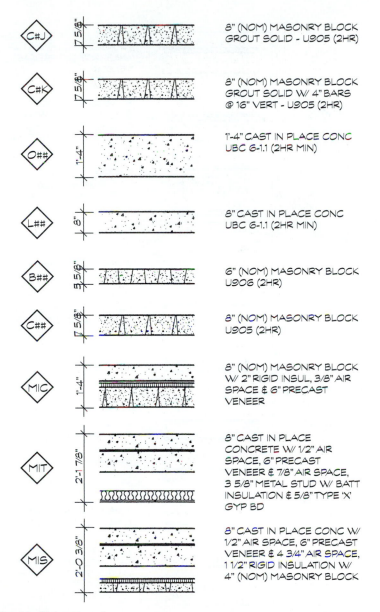

Fig. 11–28 (continued).

MIL — 1'-4" — 8" CAST IN PLACE CONC W/ 1/2" RIGID INSULATION 1/2" AIR SPACE & 6" PRECAST VENEER

 MIR — 1'-4" — 8" (NOM) MASONRY BLK GROUTED SOLID W/ 4" BAR @ 16" VERT W/ 2" RIGID INSUL, 3/8" AIR SPACE & 6" PRECAST VENEER

 MIV — 2'-0" — 1'-4" CAST IN PLACE CONC W/ 2" RIGID INSUL, 4" (NOM) MAS MLK W/ 2 3/8" AIR SPACE

 M## — 6" — 6" PRECAST PANEL UBC 6-1.1 (2HR MIN)

 MIU — 2'-1 1/2" — 1'-4" CAST IN PLACE CONC W/ 5/4" AIR SPACE, 3 5/8" METAL STUD & 5/8" TYPE 'X' GYP BD

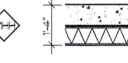 MHH — 1'-4" — 8" PRECAST CONC W/ 1/2" AIR SPACE, 6" METAL STUD W/ 1/2" SHEATHING & 5/8" TYPE 'X' GYP BD

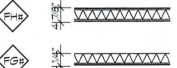 FH# — 4 7/8" — 3 5/8" METAL STUDS W/ 5/8" TYPE 'X' GYP BD BOTH SIDES U465 (1HR)

FG# — 4 1/4" — 3 5/8" METAL STUDS W/ 5/8" TYPE 'X' GYP BD ONE SIDE

FGB — 4 1/4" — 3 5/8" METAL STUDS W/ BATT INSULATION W/ 5/8" TYPE 'X' GYP BD ONE SIDE

Fig. 11–28 (continued).

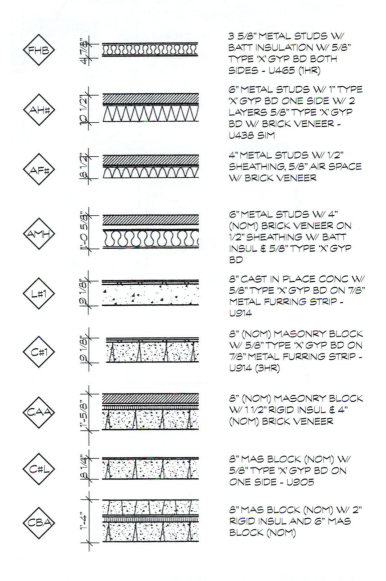

FHB — 4 7/8" — 3 5/8" METAL STUDS W/ BATT INSULATION W/ 5/8" TYPE 'X' GYP BD BOTH SIDES - U465 (1HR)

AH# — 10 1/2" — 6" METAL STUDS W/ 1" TYPE 'X' GYP BD ONE SIDE W/ 2 LAYERS 5/8" TYPE 'X' GYP BD W/ BRICK VENEER - U438 SIM

AF# — 8 1/2" — 4" METAL STUDS W/ 1/2" SHEATHING, 5/8" AIR SPACE W/ BRICK VENEER

AMH — 1'-0 5/8" — 6" METAL STUDS W/ 4" (NOM) BRICK VENEER ON 1/2" SHEATHING W/ BATT INSUL & 5/8" TYPE 'X' GYP BD

L#1 — 9 1/8" — 8" CAST IN PLACE CONC W/ 5/8" TYPE 'X' GYP BD ON 7/8" METAL FURRING STRIP - U914

C#1 — 9 1/8" — 8" (NOM) MASONRY BLOCK W/ 5/8" TYPE 'X' GYP BD ON 7/8" METAL FURRING STRIP - U914 (3HR)

CAA — 1'-5 5/8" — 8" (NOM) MASONRY BLOCK W/ 1 1/2" RIGID INSUL & 4" (NOM) BRICK VENEER

C#L — 8 1/4" — 8" MAS BLOCK (NOM) W/ 5/8" TYPE 'X' GYP BD ON ONE SIDE - U905

CBA — 1'-4" — 8" MAS BLOCK (NOM) W/ 2" RIGID INSUL AND 6" MAS BLOCK (NOM)

Fig. 11–28 (concluded).

Rennovation Notations

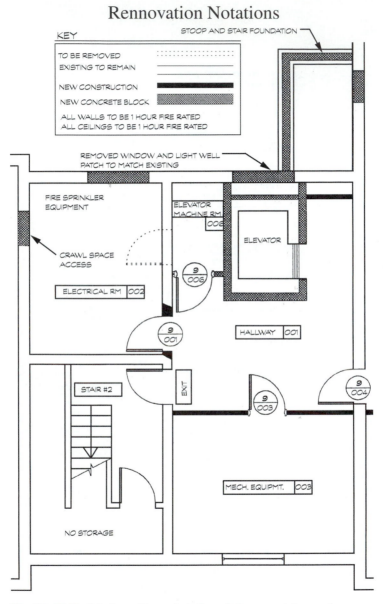

Fig. 11–29. Partial plan with symbols for existing, remaining, and new construction. Dimensions were removed for clarity. (A children's home addition. C. Allen Mullins Architect. Bear Creek, Pennsylvania.)

Code Building Data
For a Multistory Residential Building

PROJECT NAME	(-----------)													
ADDRESS	(-----------)													
LOCATION	(-----------)													
CODE	UNIFORM BUILDING CODE, 1994 ED. OREGON ED. 1996													
OCCUPANCY	A	B	E	F	H	I	M	[R]	S	U	SR			
DIVISION	[1]	2	2.1	3	4	5	6	7						
OCCUPANCY	A	B	E	F	H	I	M	R	[S]	U	SR			
DIVISION	1	2	2.1	[3]	4	5	6	7						
OCCUPANCY	A	B	E	F	H	I	[M]	R	S	U	SR			
DIVISION	1	2	2.1	3	4	5	6	7						
CONSTRUCTION	TYPE I		TYPE II		TYPE III		TYPE IV		TYPE V					
	COMBUSTIBLE				NON-COMBUSTIBLE									
	[FIRE-RESISTIVE]				1–HOUR		N	H.T.	FULLY SPRINKLERED					
SEISMIC ZONE	1	2	2b	[3]	4									
SITE SIZE	41,000 / .94 SQ. FT. / ACRES													
MAX. ALLOWABLE FLOOR AREA	29,900____ SQ. FT. / FLOOR / BUILDING													
APPLICABLE AREA INCREASE	119,600____ SQ. FT. / FLOOR / BUILDING CODE REF. : 504.2 & 505.1.2													
TOTAL PROJECT FLOOR AREA	90,700____ SQ. FT. / FLOOR / BUILDING 181,400____ SQ.FT. TOTAL ALL BUILDINGS													
MAX. ALLOWABLE HEIGHT (UBC)	12____ STORY(IES) 160_____ FEET													
PARKING MIN.	DISABLED	-------------- VEHICLE SPACES												
PROJECT	(------------)													
DESCRIPTION	Six story multifamily housing with basement level parking and													
	some street level retail.													
RESIDENTIAL	No. of Units		123											
RETAIL	Total Sq. Ft.		7,907	Sq. Ft.										
PROJECT PARKING	Floor Area		48,260	Sq. Ft./Basement										
	No. of Stalls		136	Total										
	Acessible		4	Total										
	Van Accessible		1	Total										
BUILDING AREAS	Floor Areas		48,200	Sq. Ft./Basement										
			30,400	Sq. Ft./Typical Floor										
			229,660	Sq. Ft./Total Project Incl. Basement										

Fig. 11-30. (A multistory residential building. Ankrom Moisan Associated Architects. Portland, Oregon.)

Code Building Data
For a Multistory Residential Building (concl.)

WALL 7 OPENING PROTECTION BASED ON LOCATION ON PROPERTY			
FIRE RESISTANCE OF EXT. WALLS	Non-Combustible OVER 40 FEET		
	One HOUR(S) LESS THAN 40 FEET		
	Two HOUR(S) LESS THAN 20 FEET		
PROJECT	60 FT. R.O.W.	at (--------------)	
		street front walls = NC	
	40 FT. R.O.W.	at (--------------)	
		street front walls = 1 hr. F.R.	
	60 FT. R.O.W.	at Courtyard	
		parallel walls = 1 hr. F.R.	
	30 FT. R.O.W.	at Courtyard	
		parallel walls = 2 hr. F.R.	
APPEALS	April 9, 1997	Item no. 3	
	No. 5		
OPENINGS IN EXTERIOR WALLS	PROTECTED LESS THAN 20 FEET		
	NOT PERMIT LESS THAN 3 FEET		
ZONING			
LAND USE ZONING	Exd. (CCPD)		
USE	Retail / Residential		
SETBACKS	FRONT	0 FEET	
	SIDE INTERIOR	0 FEET	
	CORNER	0 FEET	
	REAR	0 FEET	
MAX. ALLOWABLE HEIGHT (ZONING)	6 STORY(IES)	75 FEET PROJECT	
	plus BASEMENT	Z1 1/2 FEET PROJECT	
PARKING	MIN NONE VEHICLE SPACES		
	MAX NONE VEHICLE SPACES		
LANDSCAPE	MIN NONE %		

Fig. 11–30 (concluded).

Code Building Data
For a Police and Court Facility

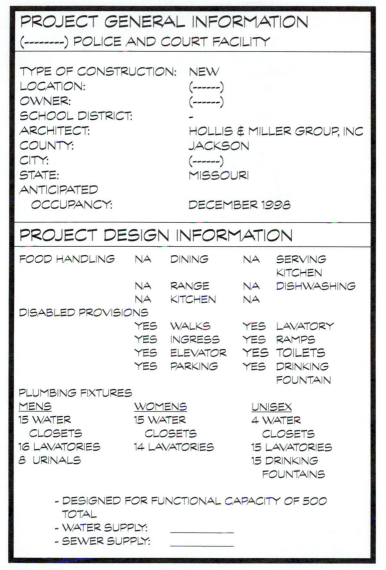

PROJECT GENERAL INFORMATION
(--------) POLICE AND COURT FACILITY

TYPE OF CONSTRUCTION: NEW
LOCATION: (------)
OWNER: (------)
SCHOOL DISTRICT: -
ARCHITECT: HOLLIS & MILLER GROUP, INC
COUNTY: JACKSON
CITY: (------)
STATE: MISSOURI
ANTICIPATED
  OCCUPANCY: DECEMBER 1998

PROJECT DESIGN INFORMATION

FOOD HANDLING   NA   DINING   NA   SERVING
                                              KITCHEN
                 NA   RANGE   NA   DISHWASHING
                 NA   KITCHEN   NA
DISABLED PROVISIONS
                 YES   WALKS   YES   LAVATORY
                 YES   INGRESS   YES   RAMPS
                 YES   ELEVATOR YES   TOILETS
                 YES   PARKING   YES   DRINKING
                                              FOUNTAIN
PLUMBING FIXTURES

MENS	WOMENS	UNISEX
15 WATER	15 WATER	4 WATER
CLOSETS	CLOSETS	CLOSETS
16 LAVATORIES	14 LAVATORIES	15 LAVATORIES
8 URINALS		15 DRINKING
		FOUNTAINS

        - DESIGNED FOR FUNCTIONAL CAPACITY OF 500
          TOTAL
        - WATER SUPPLY: _____
        - SEWER SUPPLY: _____

Fig. 11–31. (A police and court facility. The Hollis and Miller Group, Inc.
Lee's Summit, Missouri.)

Code Building Data
For a Police and Court Facility (cont.)

PROJECT GENERAL INFORMATION
BUILDING NO. 1

OCCUPANCY GROUP:	A-3
TYPE OF CONSTRUCTION:	11-N
BASIC ALLOWABLE AREA:	3,700 SQ FT
PERCENTAGE INCREASE:	300% AUTOMATIC SPRINKLER SYSTEM
TOTAL ALLOWABLE AREA:	11,100 SQ FT
ACTUAL AREA SEPARATION:	2 HR
ALLOWABLE STORIES:	2
ACTUAL STORIES	1
ALLOWABLE HEIGHT:	160'
ACTUAL HEIGHT	15'±
ALLOWABLE AREA:	15,100 SQ FT
ACTUAL AREA	524 SQ FT

FIRE RESISTIVE REQUIREMENTS

CONSTRUCTION TYPE	1-3	HOUR
EXTERIOR BEARING WALLS	4	HOUR
EXTERIOR NON-BEARING WALLS	4	HOUR
INTERIOR BEARING WALLS	2	HOUR
AREA SEPARATION WALLS	2	HOUR
CORRIDOR WALLS	1 1/2	HOUR
PERMANENT PARTITIONS	1 1/2	HOUR
HAZARDOUS LOCATIONS	2	HOUR
STRUCTURAL FRAME	2	HOUR
SHAFT ENCLOSURES	2	HOUR
FLOOR-CEILING/FLOOR	2	HOUR
ROOF-CEILING/ROOF	1	HOUR
EXTERIOR OPENINGS	1903 (b)	HOUR

Fig. 11–31. (continued).

PROJECT CODE INFORMATION
JAIL - BUILDING NO. 2

OCCUPANCY GROUP:	I-3
TYPE OF CONSTRUCTION:	11-FR
BASIC ALLOWABLE AREA:	15,100 SQ FT
PERCENTAGE INCREASE:	350% OPEN (2) SIDES / AUTOMATIC SPRINKLER SYSTEM
TOTAL ALLOWABLE AREA:	15,100 SQ FT
ACTUAL AREA SEPARATION:	2 HR
ALLOWABLE STORIES:	2
ACTUAL STORIES	1
ALLOWABLE HEIGHT:	160'
ACTUAL HEIGHT	15'±
ALLOWABLE AREA:	15,100 SQ FT
ACTUAL AREA	4,602 SQ FT

PLUMBING FIXTURES - UNISEX

COMBO LAV / WC UNIT	9
UNISEX LAV	3
UNISEX WC	3

FIRE RESISTIVE REQUIREMENTS

CONSTRUCTION TYPE	1-3	HOUR
EXTERIOR BEARING WALLS	4	HOUR
EXTERIOR NON-BEARING WALLS	4	HOUR
INTERIOR BEARING WALLS	2	HOUR
AREA SEPARATION WALLS	2	HOUR
CORRIDOR WALLS	1 1/2	HOUR
PERMANENT PARTITIONS	1 1/2	HOUR
HAZARDOUS LOCATIONS	2	HOUR
STRUCTURAL FRAME	2	HOUR
SHAFT ENCLOSURES	2	HOUR
FLOOR-CEILING/FLOOR	2	HOUR
ROOF-CEILING/ROOF	1	HOUR
EXTERIOR OPENINGS	1903 (b)	HOUR

Fig. 11–31 (continued).

Code Building Data
For a Police and Court Facility (concl.)

PROJECT CERTIFICATION

ARCHITECT: THE HOLLIS & MILLER GROUP
                              309 SOUTHWEST MARKET STREET
                              LEE'S SUMMIT, MISSOURI 64063-2315

CODE CONSULTANT:

I CERTIFY THAT THE SUBMITTED PLANS FOR THE PLANS
REFERENCED ABOVE COMPLY WITH THE REQUIREMENTS OF
THE FOLLOWING CODES:

1991	"UBC"	UNIFORM BUILDING CODE
1991	"UMC"	UNIFORM MECHANICAL CODE
1991	"UPC"	UNIFORM PLUMBING CODE
1991	"NEC"	NATIONAL ELECTRIC CODE
1990	"ADA"	AMERICANS WITH DISABILITIES ACT

FIRE PROTECTION INFORMATION

FIRE SAFETY:	YES	SPRINKLERS	YES	EXIT LIGHTS
	YES	STAND PIPES	YES	FIRE ALARMS
	YES	FIRE EXITING	YES	SMOKE DETECTORS

HEATING:	-	REMOTE CENTRAL SUPPLY
	X	BUILDING CENTRAL SUPPLY
	-	ZONED INDEPENDENT SUPPLY

SYSTEM:	X	FORCED AIR SYSTEM
	-	HOT WATER SYSTEM
	-	STEAM SYSTEM
	-	OTHER SYSTEM

FUEL SUPPLY:	X	NATURAL GAS
	-	FUEL OIL
	-	L.P. GAS
	X	ELECTRIC

Fig. 11–31 (concluded).

Code Building Data
For an Office and Factory Building

BUILDING REQUIREMENTS (1994 SBCCI)

TABLE 500
OCCUPANCY: GROUP F – FACTORY / INDUSTRIAL
CONSTRUCTION TYPE: TYPE IV, UNPROTECTED, UNSPRINKLERED
ALLOWABLE AREA: 21,000 SQ. FT.
AREA INCREASE: 100% (503.3.2) = 42,000 SQ. FT.
  1ST FLOOR =   13,800 NET SQ. FT.
  TOTAL GROSS BUILDING AREA = 13,800 SQ. FT.
ALLOWABLE HEIGHT: 55'
ACTUAL HEIGHT: 20'

OCCUPANCY CONTENT – TABLE 1003.1
  1ST FLOOR FACTORY: 13,800 SF/100 = 138 OCCUPANTS
  TOTAL BUILDING OCCUPANT CONTENT = 138 OCCUPANTS

TABLE 1004
EGRESS WIDTH REQUIRED: 138 OCC. X .2 INCHES = 27.6 INCHES
                               = 2.3 FEET
EGRESS WIDTH PROVIDED: 15 FEET (5 DOORS AT 36" EACH)

STAIRS:
REQUIRED: NONE
PROVIDED: NONE

PLUMBING REQUIREMENTS (1994 SBCCI)

TABLE 407 (407.3.2)
TOTAL OCCUPANTS: BASED ON SHIFT COUNT OF 30 PEOPLE MAX
(SEE SHIFT COUNT LETTER ON SHEET 0.2)

	MALE	FEMALE
WATERCLOSETS REQUIRED:	2	2
WATERCLOSETS PROVIDED:	2	3
URINALS PROVIDED:	1	-
LAVATORIES REQUIRED:	2	2
LAVATORIES PROVIDED:	2	2
DRINKING FOUNTAINS REQUIRED: 1		
DRINKING FOUNTAINS PROVIDED: 1		

Fig. 11–32. (An office and factory building. Spencer Godfrey Architects. Round Rock, Texas.)

Code Building Data
For an Office and Factory Building (concl.)

PARKING SYNOPSIS	
PARKING REQUIRED (PHASE ONE CONSTRUCTION): (BASED UPON INDUSTRIAL USE CLASSIFICATION WITH SHIFT COUNT OF 30 MAX.)*	
(1 PER EMPLOYEE + 2 REQ. ACCESSIBLE + 2 VISITORS) =	34 SPACES
PARKING PROVIDED: (BASED BID) =	37 SPACES
PARKING PROVIDED: (IF ALTERNATE ACCEPTED) =	59 SPACES
APPPORTIONMENT: DISABLED/HANDICAPPED PARKING REQUIRED (TX. ACCESS. REQ.) =	2 SPACES
DISABLED/HANDICAPPED PARKING PROVIDED =	2 SPACES
STANDARD PARKING SPACES (REMAINDER) (BASE BID) =	35 SPACES
TOTAL PARKING AVAILABILITY INCLUDING FUTURE = TOTAL ALLOWABLE BUILDING AREA = 42,000 SQ. FT.	71 SPACES
APPORTIONMENT: DISABLED/HANDICAPPED PARKING REQUIRED (TX. ACCESS. REQ.) =	3 SPACES
DISABLED/HANDICAPPED PARKING PROVIDED =	3 SPACES
STANDARD PARKING SPACES (REMAINDER) =	68 SPACES

* SEE SHIFT COUNT LETTER ON THIS SHEET

Fig. 11–32. (concluded).

Code Building Data
For an Elementary School Multipurpose Building

BUILDING CODE ANALYSIS - MULTIPURPOSE BUILDING

1. SEE COVERSHEET A-0.0 FOR APPLICABLE CODES
2. OCCUPANCY GROUPS: A2.1 AND B
3. TYPE OF CONSTRUCTION: TYPE V-1 HOUR
4. ALLOWABLE FLOOR AREA:
      BASIC ALLOWABLE: 10,500
      SEPARATION ON SIDES: NOT USED
      MAXIMUM ALLOWABLE: 10,500
5. ACTUAL FLOOR AREA: 3,422 SF

Mixed occupancy formula:

$$\left[\frac{\text{Area of A-2.1 occupancy}}{\text{Total allowable area for A-2.1 occupancy}}\right] + \left[\frac{\text{Area of B-2 occupancy}}{\text{Total allowable area for B occupancy}}\right] \leq 1$$

$$\frac{2,298}{10,500} + \frac{440}{14,000} = .32$$

THEREFORE OK

6. OPENING PROTECTION:
      EXTERIOR WALLS: ONE HOUR
      OPENINGS: NOT PERMITTED LESS THAN 5'-0"
                        PROTECTED LESS THAN 10'-0"
7. ALLOWABLE HEIGHT: 50'-0"
8. ACTUAL HEIGHT: 29'-0"
9. OCCUPANCY SEPARATION: 1 HOUR
10. MIXED OCCUPANCY: YES: A2.1 & B
11. OCCUPANT LOAD: 348
12. SPRINKLERS REQUIRED: NO (NOT PROVIDED)

OCCUPANT LOAD CHART

	NO.	ROOM NAME	AREA	OCC. FACTOR	OCC	EXITS
1.	101	MULTIPURPOSE RM.	2,367	7 SF/OCC	339	1 MAIIN, 2 SIDE
2.	102	STORAGE RM. EAST	212	300 SF/OCC	1	1
3.	103	STORAGE RM. WEST	192	300 SF/OCC	1	1
4.	104	KITCHEN	440	200 SF/OCC	3	1
5.	105	DRY STORAGE	64	300 SF/OCC	1	1
6.	106	JANITOR	17	100 SF/OCC	1	1
7.	107	INCLD IN "104 KITCHEN"				
8.	108	RESTROOM	56	100 SF/OCC	1	1
9.	109	MECHANICAL	56	300 SF/OCC	1	1

348

Fig. 11–33. (An elementary school multipurpose building. Phillips Metsch Sweeney Moore Architects. Santa Barbara, California.)

Working Drawing Code Information

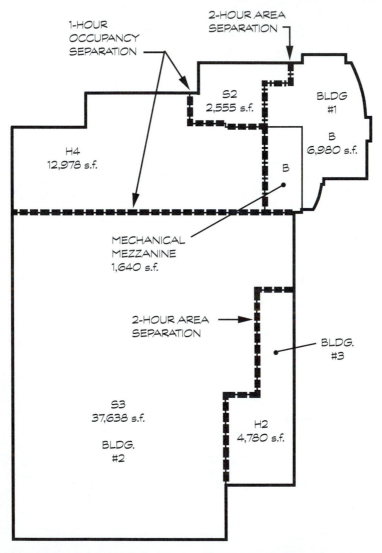

Fig. 11–34. This code information is provided near the beginning of the working drawings to facilitate a review by the building official. (An office, storage, and maintenance facility. Wilson Darnell Mann P.A. Wichita, Kansas.)

CONSTRUCTION TYPE: II-N sprinklered throughout
ALLOWABLE AREA CALCULATIONS

BUILDING #1

occupancy	allow. area	side yard increase	sprinkler increase	total allow. area	actual area
B (1st floor)	12,000	100	x3	72,000	6,980
B (2nd floor)	12,000	100	x3	72,000	1,640

BUILDING #2

occupancy	allow. area	side yard increase	sprinkler increase	total allow. area	actual area	ratio
S2	18,000	100	x3	108,000	2,555	0.024
S3	12,000	100	x3	72,000	37,633	0.52
S4	7,500	100	x3	45,000	12,978	0.29

actual allowable: .83 < 1

BUILDING #3

occupancy	allow. area	side yard increase	sprinkler increase	total allow. area	actual area
H2	3,700	50	0	5,550	4,780

Total area for all three buildings is 66,566 s.f.

Fig. 11-34 (concluded).

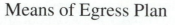

Means of Egress Plan

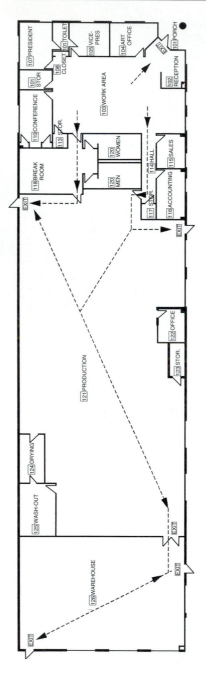

– – – – – – EXIT ROUTE LOCATION

|EXIT|

EXIT DOOR LOCATION (REFER ELEC.
DWGS. FOR EXIT SIGN LOCATION)

Fig. 11–35. Marking the means of egress paths on a code sheet in the working drawings facilitates the plan review at the building department. (An office and factory building. Spencer Godfrey Architects. Round Rock, Texas.)

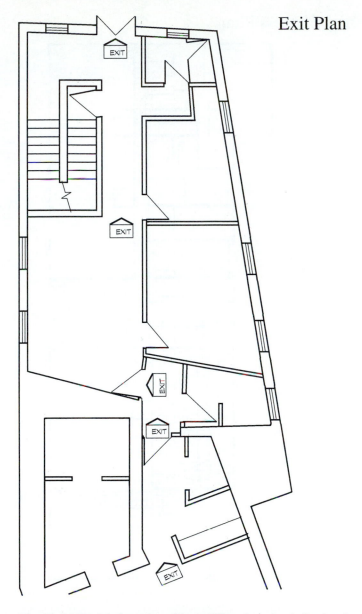

Fig. 11–36. Partial plan of an office building alteration indicating the location of the extis. (Alt Breeding Schwarz Architects, LLC. Annapolis, Maryland.)

Means of Egress Plan

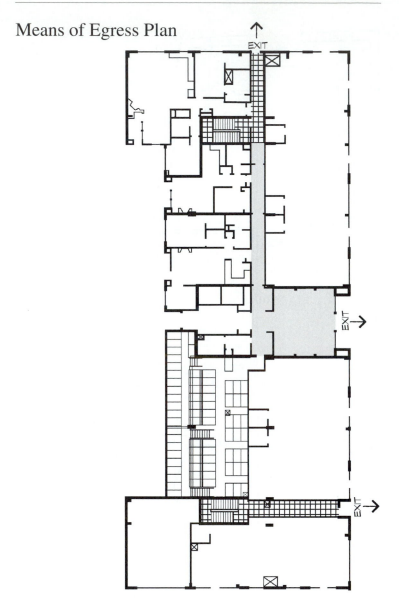

Fig. 11–37. Means of egress are shown in tones on plans provided on a code information sheet in the working drawings. (A multistory residental building. Ankrom Moisan Associated Architects. Portland, Oregon.)

Exits, Occupants, and Fire-rated Walls

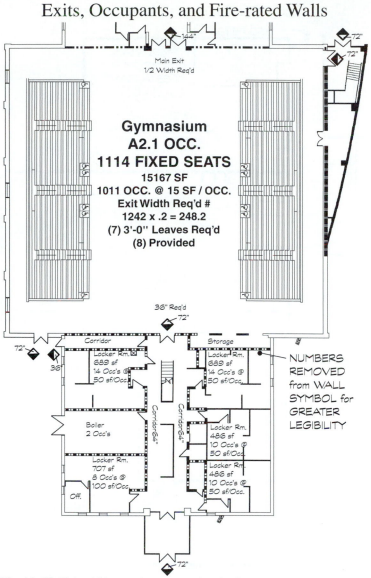

Fig. 11–38. Exit widths are shown at each exit. Occupant count and method of calculation is shown. Fire-resistance-rated walls are indicated by line symbols representing their ratings. (Partial floor plan. A university sports and fine arts complex. Gossen Livingston Associates, Inc., Architecture. Wichita, Kansas.)

Exit Occupancy and Occupants

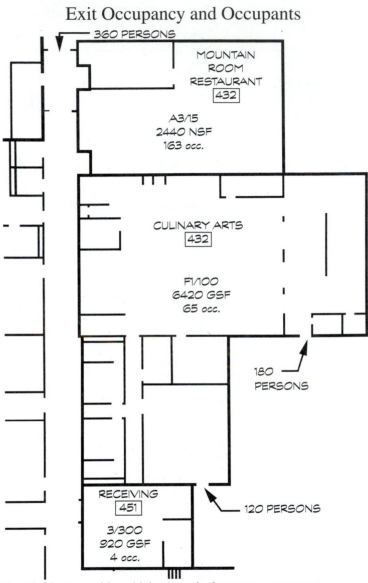

Fig. 11–39. Areas with multiple spaces in the same occupancy are bordered by dark lines (3 areas shown in the partial plan). Occupancy count and method of computation are shown in each area. Exit capacity is shown in number of people accommodated. (A vocational-technical high school. HKT Architects, Inc. Somerville, Massachusetts.)

Occupancy Plan

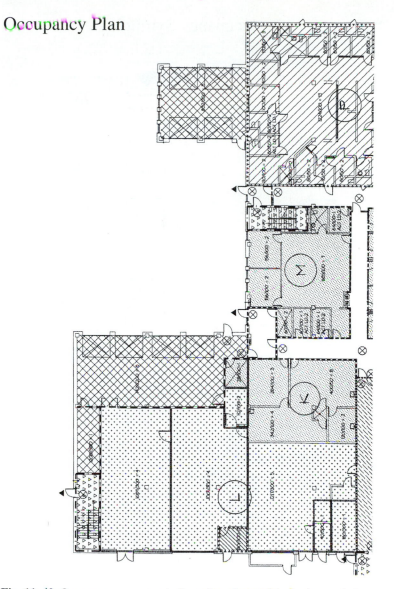

Fig. 11–40. Occupancy zones are indicated on the partial plan by symbols as shown in the legend. Each room has the occupancy calculation and total count shown. Fire-resistance ratings are indicated for walls with line symbols. (A police and court facility. The Hollis and Miller Group, Inc. Lee's Summit, Missouri.)

Occupancy Symbols

	ROOM OCCUPANT LOAD	▼	EXIT TO EXTERIOR
	BUILDING AREA	⊗	EXIT LIGHT
	(I) STORAGE W/ 45 MIN DOORS		DISTANCE TO PROPERTY LINE FROM BUILDING
	(I) HOUR SHAFT M/E		OPEN TO BELOW
	TYPE "A-3" OCCUPANCY	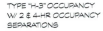	TYPE "H-3" OCCUPANCY W/ 2 & 4-HR OCCUPANCY SEPARATIONS
	TYPE "B-2" OCCUPANCY		(I) HOUR STAIRWAY W/ 60 MIN DOORS
	TYPE "I-3" OCCUPANCY W/ 2-HR OCCUPANCY SEPARATION		(I) EXITWAY W/ 20 MIN DOORS
	TYPE "B-1" OCCUPANCY W/ 1-HR OCCUPANCY SEPARATION		(I) HOUR ELEVATOR LOBBY W/ 20 MIN DOORS

Fire-resistance-rating symbols

– – – – – – –	(I) HR HORIZONTAL EXIT W/ 20 MIN DOORS
●●●●●●●●●●●●●	(I) HR ELEVATOR LOBBY W/ 20 MIN DOOR
▶●●●●●●●●●●●	(I) HR OCCUPANCY SEPARATION
▬ · ▬ · ▬ ·	(I) HR STAIR W/ 60 MIN DOORS
ⲙⲙⲙⲙⲙⲙⲙⲙⲙⲙⲙⲙⲙⲙ	(I) HR STAIR W/ 60 MIN DOORS
▽ ▽ ▽ ▽ ▽ ▽	(2) HR OCCUPANCY SEPARATION W/ 90 MIN DOOR
▬▬▬▬▬▬▬	(2) HR STORAGE W/ 90 MIN DOOR

Fig. 11–40 (concluded).

Fire-resistance-rating Line Symbols

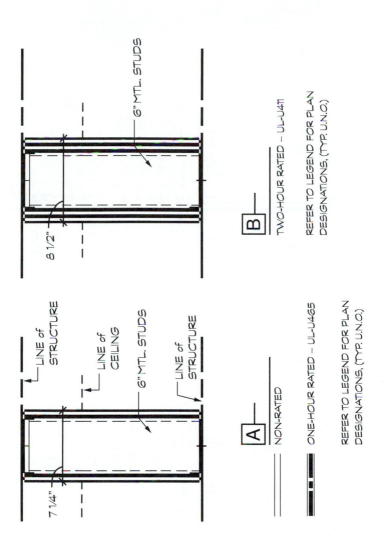

Fig. 11–41. The legends for fire-resistance-rating line symbols which appear on the code information plans are accompanied by sections of the corresponding walls. (A healthcare center. HKS, Inc., Architects, Engineers, Planners. Dallas, Texas.)

Fire-resistance-rating Line Symbols (cont.)

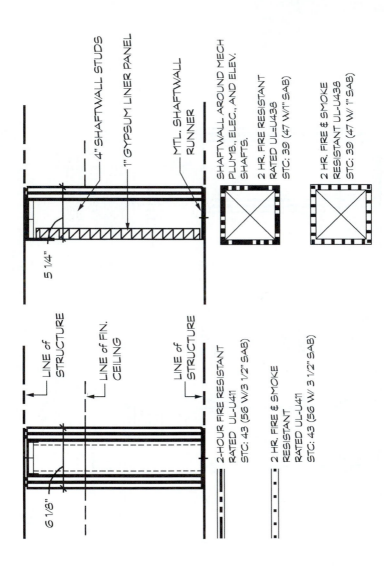

Fig. 11–41 (continued).

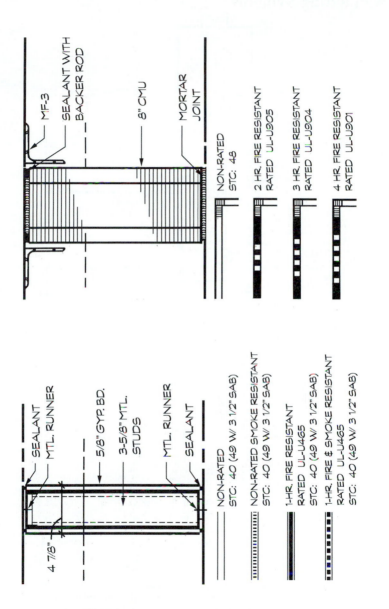

Fig. 11–41 (concluded).

Wall Rating Symbols

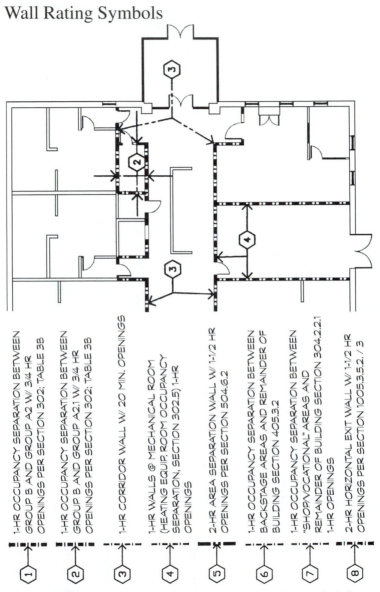

Fig. 11–42. Wall fire-resistance ratings are indicated by line symbols in the plan (partial) on the code sheet. Room names and occupancy counts have been removed for clarity. (A university sports and fine arts complex. Gossen Livingston Associates, Inc., Architecture. Wichita, Kansas.)

Wall Rating Notations

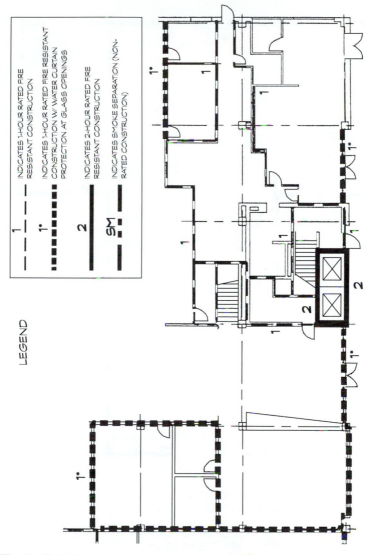

LEGEND

INDICATES 1-HOUR RATED FIRE RESISTANT CONSTRUCTION

INDICATES 1-HOUR RATED FIRE RESISTANT CONSTRUCTION W/ WATER CURTAIN PROTECTION AT GLASS OPENINGS

INDICATES 2-HOUR RATED FIRE RESISTANT CONSTRUCTION

INDICATES SMOKE SEPARATION (NON-RATED CONSTRUCTION)

Fig. 11–43. Wall rating symbols placed in a code plan (partial). Room names and numbers have been removed for clarity. (A university administration and classroom center. Perkins Eastman Architects, P.C. New York, New York.)

Emergency Lighting Symbols

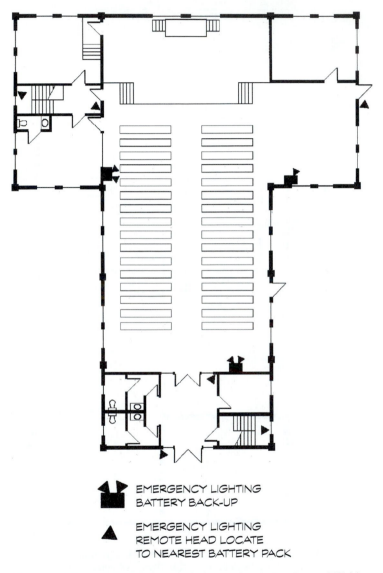

EMERGENCY LIGHTING
BATTERY BACK-UP

EMERGENCY LIGHTING
REMOTE HEAD LOCATE
TO NEAREST BATTERY PACK

Fig. 11–44. Emergency lighting symbols. (A church. Mullins and Weida, Architect and Associate. Bear Creek, Pennsylvania.)

Symbols in Plan

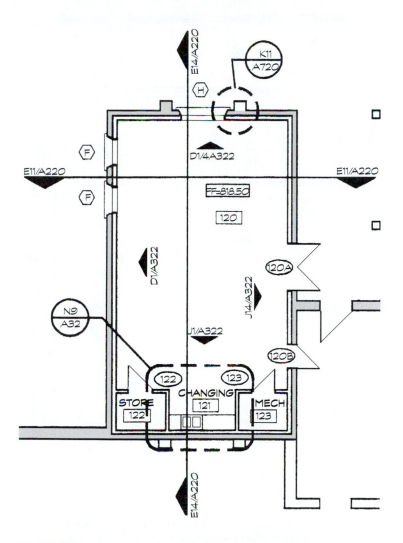

Fig. 11–45. Symbols are shown for building sections, enlarged details, interior elevations, doors, windows, room name/number, and finished floor elevation. (Partial plan. A nature center. Overland Partners, Inc. San Antonio, Texas.)

Symbols in Plan

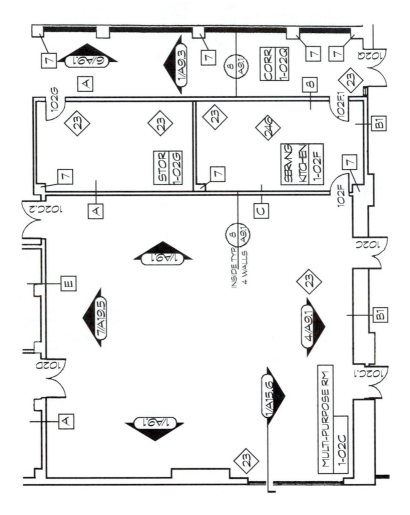

Fig. 11–46. Door numbers, wall sections, partition types, column cover details, and interior elevation indications are shown. The number in the diamond shape refers to a bulletin of information issued on a particular date which is listed in the title block of the sheet. (A university administration and classroom center. Perkins Eastman Architects, P.C. New York, New York.)

Symbols in Plan

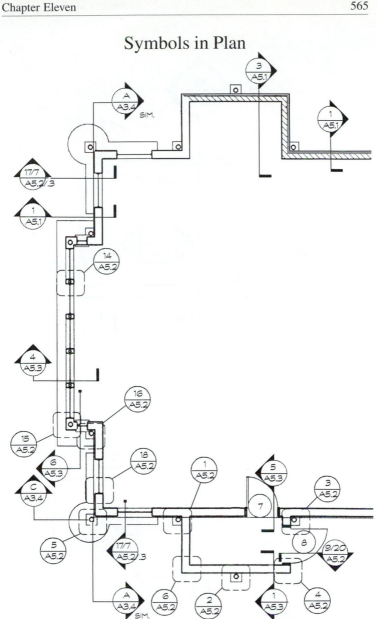

Fig. 11–47. Symbols are shown for building sections, wall sections, and enlarged details. (A park pavilion. David Woodhouse Architects. Chicago, Illinois.)

Plan Symbols

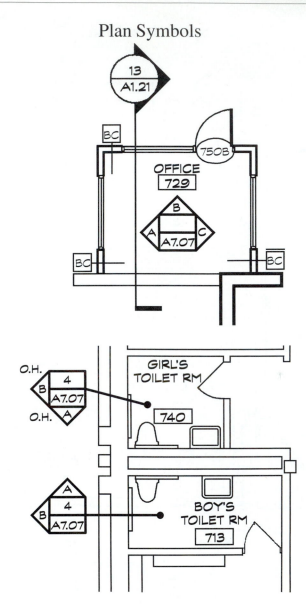

Fig. 11–48. Enlarged plans of small rooms with interior elevation symbols and a room section symbol. Wall type symbols are included as well as room number symbols and a door symbol. (A vocational-technical high school. HKT Architects, Inc. Somerville, Massachusetts.)

Symbols in Plan

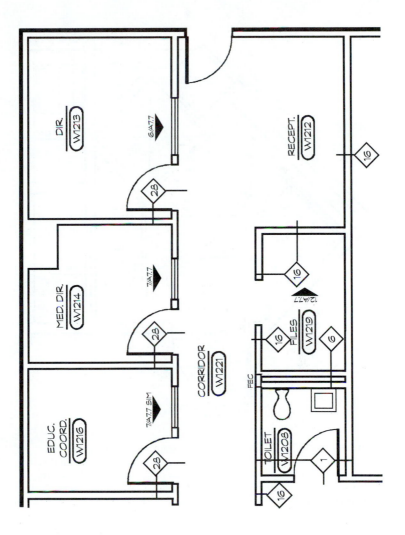

Fig. 11–49. Partition type notations, interior elevation indications, fire extinguisher cabinet, and room name/number formats are shown. (A healthcare center. Watkins Hamilton Ross Architects. Houston, Texas.)

Plan Symbols

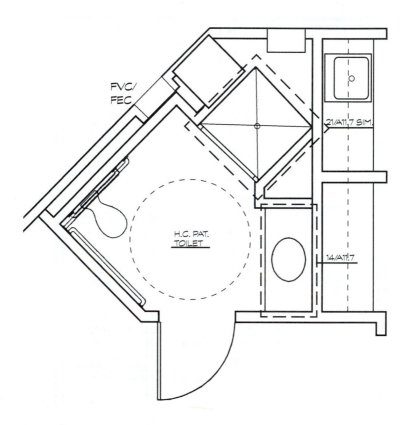

FVC/
FEC

21/A11.7 SIM.

H.C. PAT.
TOILET

14/A11.7

Fig. 11–50. The dashed circle in the toilet plan indicates that the space provides the minimum 5-foot turnaround area required for accessibility. References are indicated for enlarged details of the shower and lavatory. Dimensions have been removed from the plan. (A healthcare center. Watkins Hamilton Ross Architects. Houston, Texas.)

Plan Keynotes

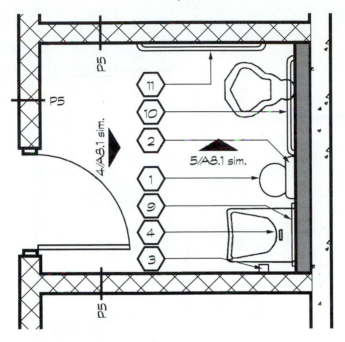

PLUMBING ACCESSORIES KEY (SEE SPECIFICATIONS)

1	TRASH RECEPTACLE	13	TOILET PAPER DISPENSER
2	WALL MOUNTED PAPER TOWEL DISPENSER	14	TOILET PARTITION
		15	URINAL PARTITION
3	SOAP DISPENSER	16	ADA COMPLIANT SHOWER
4	PIPE COVERS		SEAT
5	NAPKIN DISPENSER	17	ADA COMPLIANT SHOWER
6	NAPKIN DISPOSAL		HEAD/ASSEMBLY
7	24"W x 30" HIGH MIRROR W/ S.S. FRAME	18	ADA COMPLIANT SHOWER CONTROLS
8	36" W x 60" HIGH MIRROR W/ STAINLESS STEEL FRAME	19	12"X12"X30" LOCKERS (STACKED 2 HIGH)
9	36" x 36" MIRROR W/ STAINLESS STEEL FRAME	20	SHOWER CURTAIN & ROD
		21	TOWEL ROD
10	36" GRAB BAR	22	SOAP DISH
11	42" GRAB BAR		
12	16" X 30" GRAB BAR		

Fig. 11–51. Toilet room accessories are indicated by a keynote system in this set of drawings. Wall type indications and interior elevation references are also shown. (An office, storage, and maintenance facility. Wilson Darnell Mann P.A., Architects. Wichita, Kansas.)

Roof Plan Symbols

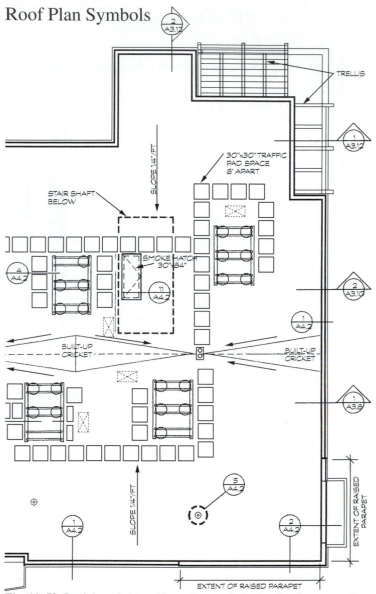

Fig. 11–52. Partial roof plan with section symbols, detail reference, and slopes. Dimension and grid lines have been removed. (A multistory residential building. Ankrom Moisan Associated Architects. Portland, Oregon.)

Roof Plan Symbols

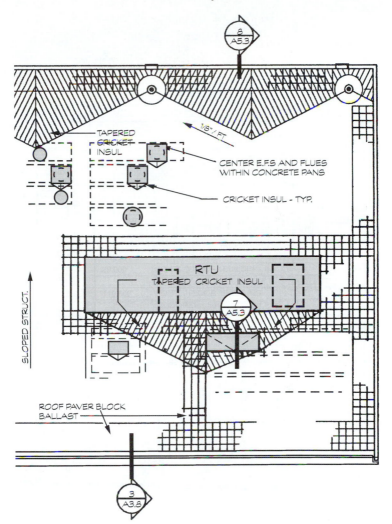

Fig. 11–53. The partial roof plan shows where crickets are constructed and indicates that the structure slopes. Wall sections and a detail section are referenced. The various devices are shown as are their relationships to the structure below where they penetrate the roof. Dimensions and some notes have been omitted for clarity. (An office and laboratory building. Gossen Livingston Associates, Inc., Architecture. Wichita, Kansas.)

Elevation Section Cuts

Fig. 11–54. Examples of a building section cut symbol, building element section cut symbols, and store front jamb cut symbols. (An office building alteration. Alt Breeding Schwarz Architects, LLC. Annapolis, Maryland.)

Elevation Section Cuts

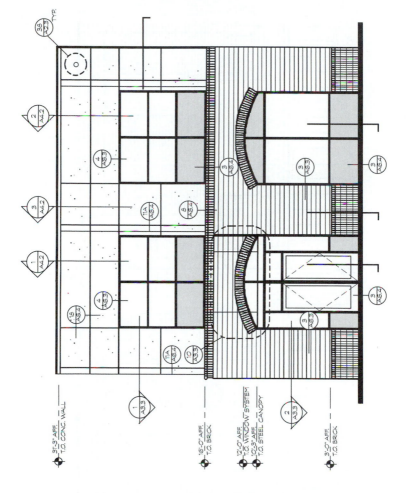

Fig. 11–55. Examples of building section cut symbols, detail section cut symbols, window section cut symbols, elevation datum symbols, and enlarged detail notation symbols in elevation. Partial elevation. (An office building. Ankrom Moisan Associated Architects. Portland, Oregon.)

Elevation Section Cuts

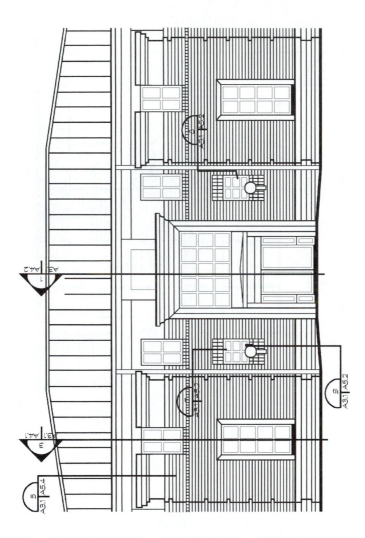

Fig. 11–56. Examples of building section cut symbols, a detail cut symbol, and window detail cut symbols. (A police department. Cromwell Architects Engineers. Little Rock, Arkansas.)

Elevation Specification Keynotes

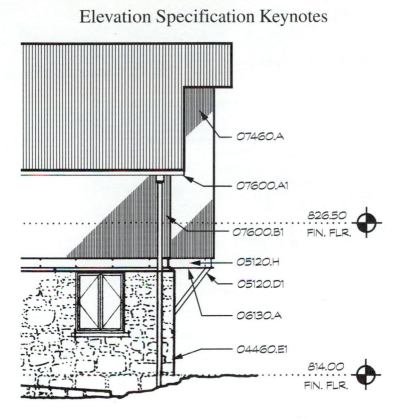

07460.A

07600.A1

826.50
07600.B1   FIN. FLR.

05120.H

05120.D1

06130.A

04460.E1

814.00
FIN. FLR.

Keynote Legend

DIV 3   Concrete
03300.B   Concrete steps

DIV 4   Masonry
04200.A   Face brick
04200.T2   Precast concrete lintel (limestone aggregate)
04200.T3   Precast concrete (limestone aggregate)

04420.A1   Cut stone sill

04460.C1   "Old Yella" limestone
             (pattern to be spec. by architect – see sheet A003)

Fig. 11–57. Partial elevation. Keynote numbers match descriptions in the specificaitons. (A nature center. Overland Partners, Inc. San Antonio, Texas.)

Elevation Specification Keynotes (concl.)

04460.E1	"Ripple" limestone
	(pattern to be spec. by architect – see sheet A003)
04460.F1	"Rust – Cork" limestone
	(pattern to be spec. by architect – see sheet A003)

<u>DIV 5</u>	<u>Metals</u>
05120.D1	Steel struts – painted – see structural
05120.H	Steel channel – painted
05120.J	Steel bracket – painted
05120.K	Steel plate
05120.L	Steel I hook
05120.M	Steel bar

05500.E1	1 1/2" dia. pipe handrail – painted
05500.R	Steel post – painted
05500.S	Steel rails w/ cables

<u>DIV 6</u>	<u>Wood and Plastics</u>
06100.R1	2"x6" cedar – smooth 4 sides – stained
06130.A	Tongue & groove wood decking

<u>DIV 7</u>	<u>Thermal & Moisture Protection</u>
07460.A	Corrugated galv. metal siding
07460.B	Galv. metal wall panels w/ pop rivets

07600.A1	Galv. metal gutter – half round
07600.B1	Galv. downspout
07600.Q1	Galv. metal trim

07610.A	Standing seam sheet metal roofing
07610.B	Corrugated galv. sheet metal roofing

<u>DIV 8</u>	<u>Doors and Windows</u>
08210.B	Wood door (red oak) w/ glass
08410.A	Aluminum storefront w/ Kynar 500 finish
	1" double glazed – tinted
08520.A	Aluminum window w/ Kynar 500 finish
	1" double glazed – tinted
08600.A	Aluminum clad wood windows w/ Kynar 500 finish
	5/8" dbl glazing

<u>DIV 9</u>	<u>Finishes</u>
09310.A	Tile sill

Fig. 11–57 (concluded).

Building Section Symbols

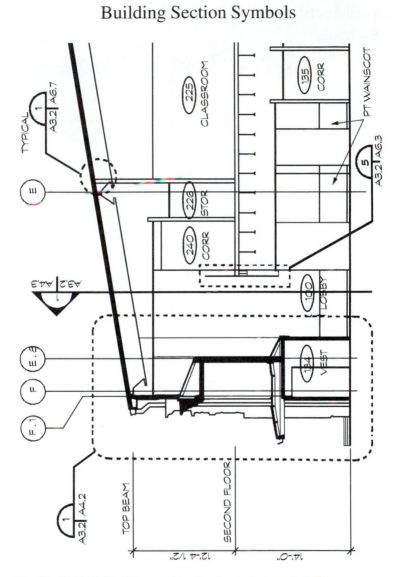

Fig. 11–58. Partial building section showing typical symbols for a building grid, a building section cut, detail references, and room numbers. This section incorporates standard dimension lines in lieu of elevation datum symbols. (A police department. Cromwell Architects Engineers, Little Rock, Arkansas.)

Wall Section Symbols

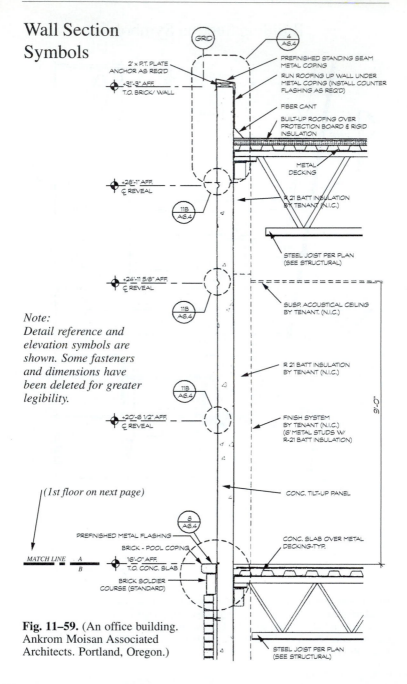

GRID

4
A6.4

2' x P.T. PLATE
ANCHOR AS REQ'D

+31'-3" AF.F.
T.O. BRICK/ WALL

PREFINISHED STANDING SEAM
METAL COPING

RUN ROOFING UP WALL UNDER
METAL COPING (INSTALL COUNTER
FLASHING AS REQ'D)

FIBER CANT

BUILT-UP ROOFING OVER
PROTECTION BOARD & RIGID
INSULATION

METAL
DECKING

+28'-1" AF.F.
C REVEAL

11B
A6.4

R 21 BATT INSULATION
BY TENANT (N.I.C.)

STEEL JOIST PER PLAN
(SEE STRUCTURAL)

+24'-11 5/8" AF.F.
C REVEAL

11B
A6.4

SUSP. ACOUSTICAL CEILING
BY TENANT. (N.I.C.)

*Note:
Detail reference and
elevation symbols are
shown. Some fasteners
and dimensions have
been deleted for greater
legibility.*

R 21 BATT INSULATION
BY TENANT (N.I.C.)

11B
A6.4

+20'-6 1/2" AF.F.
C REVEAL

FINISH SYSTEM
BY TENANT (N.I.C.)
(6' METAL STUDS W/
R-21 BATT INSULATION)

9'-0"

(1st floor on next page)

CONC. TILT-UP PANEL

8
A6.4

PREFINISHED METAL FLASHING

BRICK - POOL COPING

CONC. SLAB OVER METAL
DECKING-TYP.

MATCH LINE   A
              B

16'-0" AF.F.
T.O. CONC. SLAB

BRICK SOLDIER
COURSE (STANDARD)

Fig. 11–59. (An office building.
Ankrom Moisan Associated
Architects. Portland, Oregon.)

STEEL JOIST PER PLAN
(SEE STRUCTURAL)

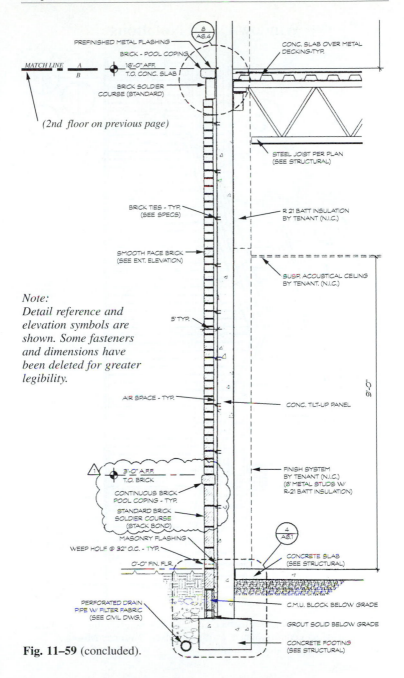

PREFINISHED METAL FLASHING

CONC. SLAB OVER METAL DECKING-TYP.

BRICK - POOL COPING

MATCH LINE   A
             B

16'-0" A.F.F.
T.O. CONC. SLAB

BRICK SOLDIER COURSE (STANDARD)

(2nd floor on previous page)

STEEL JOIST PER PLAN (SEE STRUCTURAL)

BRICK TIES - TYP. (SEE SPECS)

R 21 BATT INSULATION BY TENANT (N.I.C.)

SMOOTH FACE BRICK (SEE EXT. ELEVATION)

SUSP. ACOUSTICAL CEILING BY TENANT. (N.I.C.)

Note:
Detail reference and elevation symbols are shown. Some fasteners and dimensions have been deleted for greater legibility.

5' TYP.

AIR SPACE - TYP.

CONC. TILT-UP PANEL

9'-0"

3'-0" A.F.F.
T.O. BRICK

CONTINUOUS BRICK POOL COPING - TYP.

STANDARD BRICK SOLDIER COURSE (STACK BOND)

MASONRY FLASHING

WEEP HOLE @ 32" O.C. - TYP.

0'-0" FIN. FLR.

FINISH SYSTEM BY TENANT (N.I.C.) (6' METAL STUDS W/ R-21 BATT INSULATION)

CONCRETE SLAB (SEE STRUCTURAL)

PERFORATED DRAIN PIPE W/ FILTER FABRIC (SEE CIVIL DWG.)

C.M.U. BLOCK BELOW GRADE

GROUT SOLID BELOW GRADE

CONCRETE FOOTING (SEE STRUCTURAL)

Fig. 11–59 (concluded).

Window Detail Notations

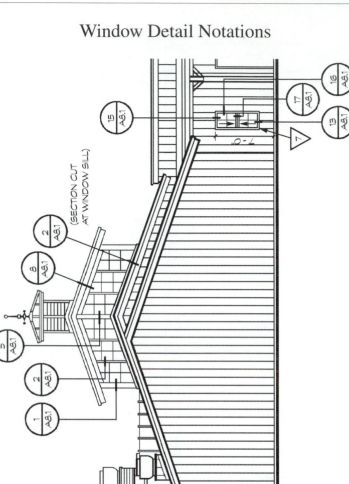

Fig. 11–60. Window detail reference cuts and key note symbols are shown. (A school district central kitchen. Phillips Metsch Sweeney Moore Architects. Santa Barbara, California.)

Window Detail Notations

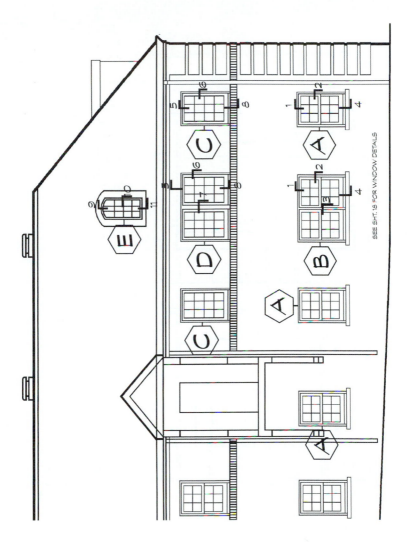

Fig. 11–61. Window type symbols and detail reference cuts are shown. (A children's home. C. Allen Mullins Architect. Bear Creek, Pennsylvania.)

Penetration Flashing

FLASHING MUST BE INSTALLED SHINGLE FASHION.

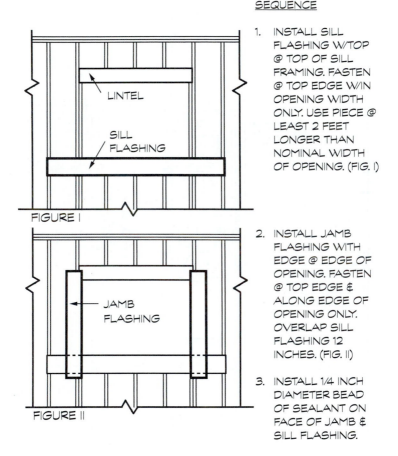

SEQUENCE

1. INSTALL SILL FLASHING W/TOP @ TOP OF SILL FRAMING. FASTEN @ TOP EDGE W/IN OPENING WIDTH ONLY. USE PIECE @ LEAST 2 FEET LONGER THAN NOMINAL WIDTH OF OPENING. (FIG. I)

2. INSTALL JAMB FLASHING WITH EDGE @ EDGE OF OPENING. FASTEN @ TOP EDGE & ALONG EDGE OF OPENING ONLY. OVERLAP SILL FLASHING 12 INCHES. (FIG. II)

3. INSTALL 1/4 INCH DIAMETER BEAD OF SEALANT ON FACE OF JAMB & SILL FLASHING.

Fig. 11–62. This set of drawings includes a series of partial elevations showing the sequence required for installing flashing at windows. (A school district central kitchen. Phillips Metsch Sweeney Moore Architects. Santa Barbara, California.)

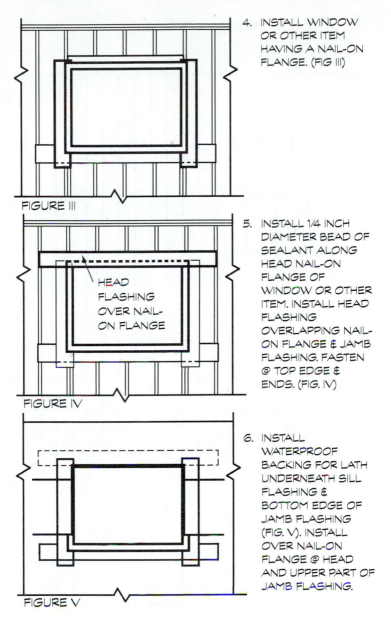

4. INSTALL WINDOW OR OTHER ITEM HAVING A NAIL-ON FLANGE. (FIG III)

FIGURE III

5. INSTALL 1/4 INCH DIAMETER BEAD OF SEALANT ALONG HEAD NAIL-ON FLANGE OF WINDOW OR OTHER ITEM. INSTALL HEAD FLASHING OVERLAPPING NAIL-ON FLANGE & JAMB FLASHING. FASTEN @ TOP EDGE & ENDS. (FIG. IV)

HEAD FLASHING OVER NAIL-ON FLANGE

FIGURE IV

6. INSTALL WATERPROOF BACKING FOR LATH UNDERNEATH SILL FLASHING & BOTTOM EDGE OF JAMB FLASHING (FIG. V). INSTALL OVER NAIL-ON FLANGE @ HEAD AND UPPER PART OF JAMB FLASHING.

FIGURE V

Fig. 11–62 (concluded).

Window Schedule

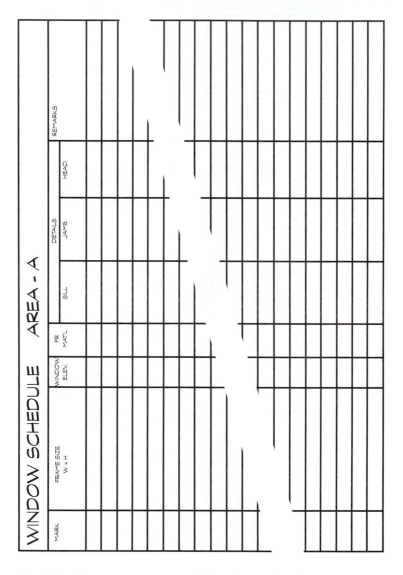

Fig. 11-63. (An elementary school. PBK Architects, Inc. Houston, Dallas/Fort Worth, San Antonio, Austin, League City, Texas.)

Door Schedule

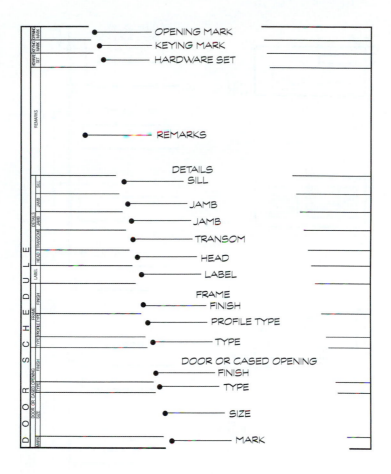

Fig. 11–64. (RTKL Associates, Inc. Dallas, Texas.)

Door Types

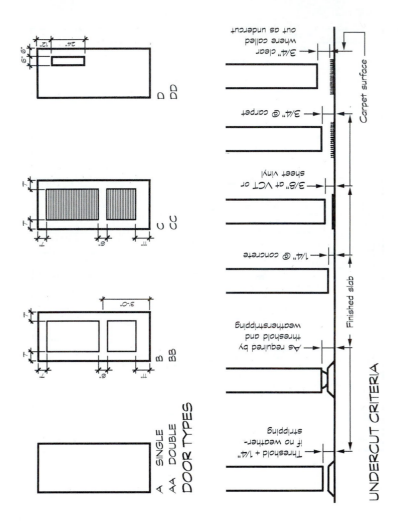

Fig. 11–65. This set of drawings includes undercut dimensions with the door types. (An elementary school multipurpose building. Phillips Metsch Sweeney Moore Architects. Santa Barbara, California.)

Standard Heights

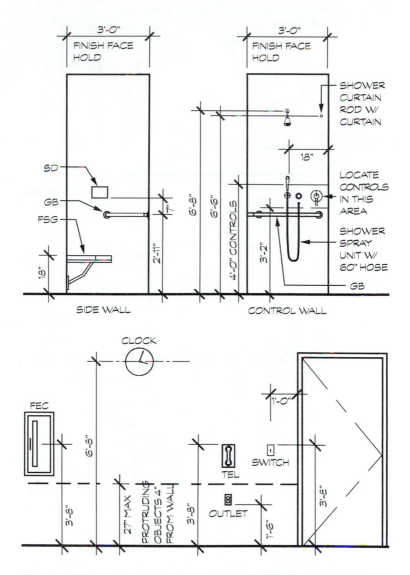

Fig. 11–66. This series of typical mounting heights appears on an interior elevation sheet. (A university sports and fine arts complex. Gossen Livingston Associates, Inc., Architecture. Wichita, Kansas.)

Standard Heights (cont.)

NOTE: ONE OF EACH PAIR, MINIMUM SHALL BE MOUNTED
AT ACCESSIBLE HEIGHT.

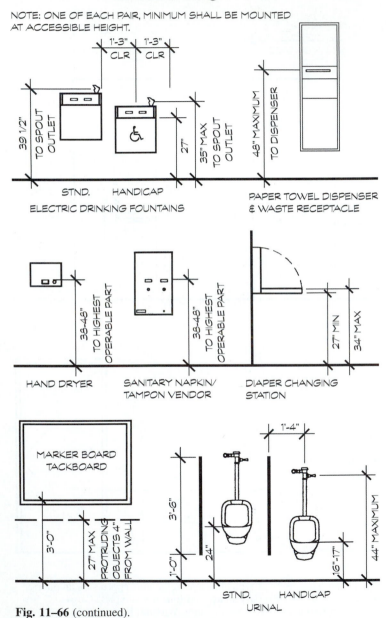

Fig. 11–66 (continued).

MOUNTING HEIGHT NOTES

1.   THESE ARE TYPICAL DIAGRAMS INTENDED TO SHOW MOUNTING HEIGHTS, DIMENSIONS, SPACIAL REQUIREMENTS, ETC., FOR BOTH HANDICAP AND NON-HANDICAP FIXTURES-ACCESSORIES.

2.   NOT ALL DEVICES, FIXTURES, ACCESSORIES, ETC., THAT ARE SHOWN IN THESE DIAGRAMS ARE APPLICABLE TO THIS PROJECT. REFER TO OTHER DRAWINGS AND SPECIFICATIONS WHICH ARE SPECIFICALLY INCLUDED UNDER THIS CONTRACT.

3.   COMPLY WITH DIMENSIONS SHOWN ON THESE DIAGRAMS UNLESS SPECIFICALLY DIMENSIONED ELSEWHERE ON THESE DRAWINGS.

4.   REFER TO 25/A7.4 FOR ADDITIONAL TYPICAL MOUNTING HEIGHTS.

ACCESSIBLE SHOWER NOTES

1.   ALL SHOWER FIXTURES AND ACCESSOREIS TO BE ADA COMPLIANT.

2.   BLOCKING IN WALL AS REQ'D FOR ALL SHOWER ACCESSORIES, TYPICAL.

3.   SHOWER STALL SIZE - 3'-0" x 3'-0", FINISH FACE TO FINISH FACE, HOLD.

Fig. 11–66 (concluded).

Interior Elevation Keynotes

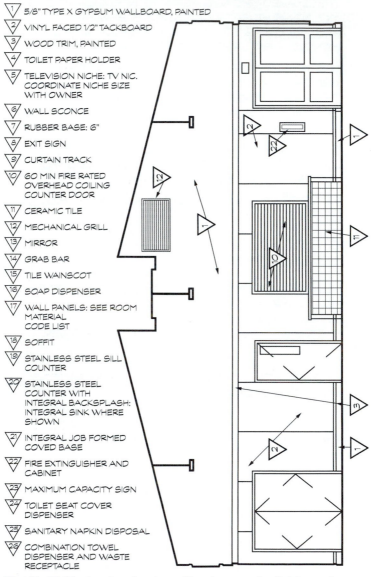

1. 5/8" TYPE X GYPSUM WALLBOARD, PAINTED
2. VINYL FACED 1/2" TACKBOARD
3. WOOD TRIM, PAINTED
4. TOILET PAPER HOLDER
5. TELEVISION NICHE: TV NIC. COORDINATE NICHE SIZE WITH OWNER
6. WALL SCONCE
7. RUBBER BASE: 6"
8. EXIT SIGN
9. CURTAIN TRACK
10. 60 MIN FIRE RATED OVERHEAD COILING COUNTER DOOR
11. CERAMIC TILE
12. MECHANICAL GRILL
13. MIRROR
14. GRAB BAR
15. TILE WAINSCOT
16. SOAP DISPENSER
17. WALL PANELS: SEE ROOM MATERIAL CODE LIST
18. SOFFIT
19. STAINLESS STEEL SILL COUNTER
20. STAINLESS STEEL COUNTER WITH INTEGRAL BACKSPLASH: INTEGRAL SINK WHERE SHOWN
21. INTEGRAL JOB FORMED COVED BASE
22. FIRE EXTINGUISHER AND CABINET
23. MAXIMUM CAPACITY SIGN
24. TOILET SEAT COVER DISPENSER
25. SANITARY NAPKIN DISPOSAL
26. COMBINATION TOWEL DISPENSER AND WASTE RECEPTACLE

Fig. 11–67. The interior elevation utilizes keynotes for finishes and devices. (An elementary school multipurpose building. Phillips Metsch Sweeney Moore Architects. Santa Barbara, California.)

Interior Elevation Symbols

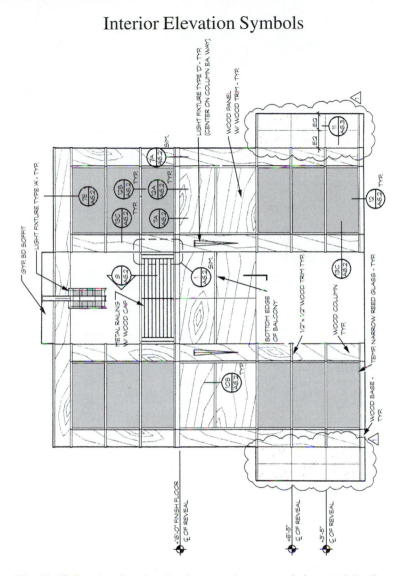

Fig. 11–68. Interior elevation showing a section cut symbol, several detail cut symbols, and an enlarged detail reference. Distance above finished floor is shown at the elevation datum symbols. The "cloud" symbols signify a change to the original drawing with the reference number in the triangle. (An office building. Ankrom Moisan Associated Architects. Portland, Oregon.)

Interior Finish Schedule

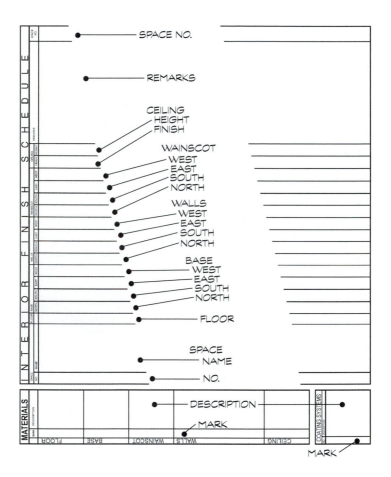

Fig. 11–69. (RTKL Associates, Inc. Dallas, Texas.)

Reflected Ceiling Plan

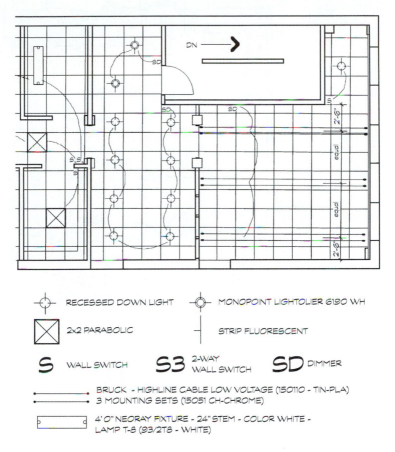

Symbol	Description		Symbol	Description
	RECESSED DOWN LIGHT			MONOPOINT LIGHTOLIER 6190 WH
	2x2 PARABOLIC			STRIP FLUORESCENT
S	WALL SWITCH	S3	2-WAY WALL SWITCH	SD DIMMER

BRUCK - HIGHLINE CABLE LOW VOLTAGE (15O11O - TIN-PLA)
3 MOUNTING SETS (15O51 CH-CHROME)

4' O" NEORAY FIXTURE - 24" STEM - COLOR WHITE - LAMP T-8 (93/2T8 - WHITE)

NOTE:
1. Coordinate ceiling registers, light fixtures, sprinkler heads, etc. with lay-in ceiling system.
2. Owner to coordinate location of receptacles, dedicated circuits, telephone jacks and general lighting fixtures, etc.
3. Coordinate decorative lighting shown on dwg with electrical plan - by others.

Fig. 11–70. A partial reflected ceiling plan is shown with symbols and ntoes. (An office building alteration. Alt Breeding Schwarz Architects, LLC. Annapolis, Maryland.)

Reflected Ceiling Plan

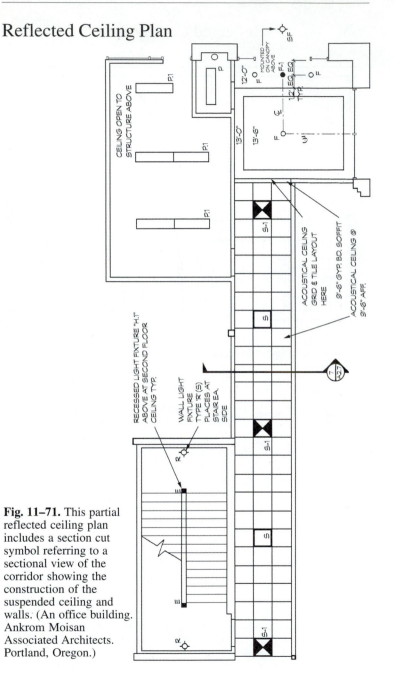

Fig. 11–71. This partial reflected ceiling plan includes a section cut symbol referring to a sectional view of the corridor showing the construction of the suspended ceiling and walls. (An office building. Ankrom Moisan Associated Architects. Portland, Oregon.)

Reflected Ceiling Plan

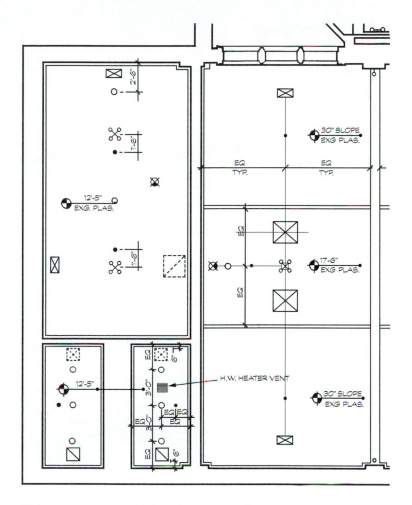

Fig. 11–72. This partial reflected ceiling plan includes HVAC and sprinkler information as well as lighting. (A city hall renovation and addition. David Woodhouse Architects. Chicago, Illinois.)

Reflected Ceiling Symbol Key

New Ceiling

Existing Ceiling (to remain U.N.O.)

Access Panel

Supply/Return Diffuser

Wall Mounted Supply/Return Diffuser

Linear Supply Return Diffuser

Recessed Incandescent Light Fixture

Recessed Low-Voltage Halogen Light Fixture

Wall Mounted Incandescent Light Fixture

Surface Mounted Incandescent Light Fixture

Suspension Mounted Incandescent Light Fixture

Exit Sign

Concealed Sprinkler Head

Pendant Sprinkler Head

Side Wall Sprinkler Head

Fig. 11–72 (continued).

Reflected Ceiling General Notes

1. Patch and refinish ceilings as required by work performed by other trades (mechanical, fire protection, etc.).

2. All new ceilings to be suspended gypsum board unless noted otherwise.

3. All ceiling heights are 8'-0" above finish floor unless noted otherwise.

4. Mechanical registers are shown on this drawing for the architectural locations only. See the Mechanical Drawings and Specifications for sizing, distribution, connections, and all other requirements.

5. Light fixtures are shown on this drawing for the Architectural locations, quantities and general fixture type only. See the Electrical Drawings for the exact fixture type and circuiting.

6. Sprinklers are shown on this drawing for the type of heads in various locations and for the general architectural character of the layout pattern. For the specific sprinkler location requirements, and sprinkler type and locations in spaces without finished ceilings and in spaces where not shown on this drawing, refer to the Fire Protection Drawings and Specifications.

7. Coordinate exact location of all ceiling items (diffusers, light fixtures, sprinklers, etc.) not dimensioned on this or other drawings in field with architect.

8. Dashed items provided under Alternate #2.

Fig. 11–72 (concluded).

Detail Sheet Layout

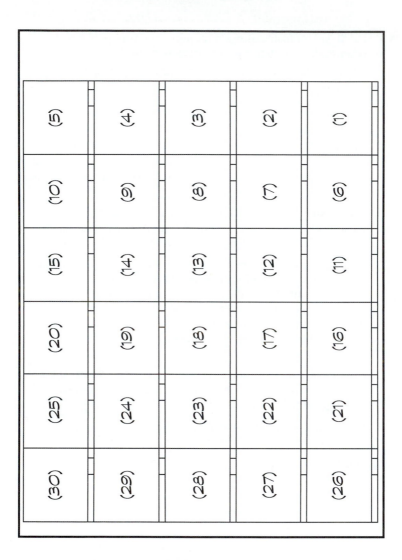

Fig. 11–73. This set of drawings has detail numbers starting at the bottom right of the sheet and proceeding up the sheet with the next set of numbers continuing to the left and proceeding up the sheet. (A warehouse addition. Stephen Wen + Associates Architects, Inc. Pasadena, California.)

Detail Sheet Layout

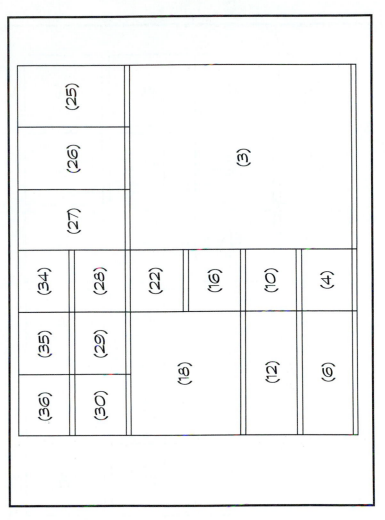

Fig. 11–74. Details in this set of drawings are numbered beginning in the lower right corner of the sheet progressing to the left. Numbers then continue across the sheet on the next higher band of modules from right to left. The numbers are based on 36 modules and where a detail takes more than one module, all numbers in the group are omitted except the one in the lower left corner of the group. (An elementary school. PBK Architects, Inc. Houston, Dallas/Fort Worth, San Antonio, Austin, League City, Texas.)

Detail Sheet Layout

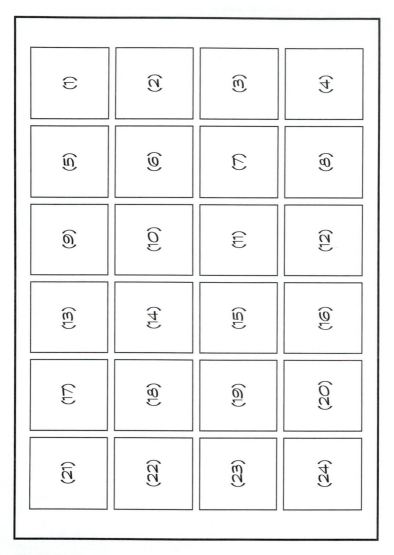

Fig. 11–75. The numbering of details in this set of drawings begins at the upper right corner and progresses downward. The same pattern continues in subsequent columns of details progressing to the left. (A children's home addition. C. Allen Mullins Architect. Bear Creek, Pennsylvania.)

Detail Sheet Layout

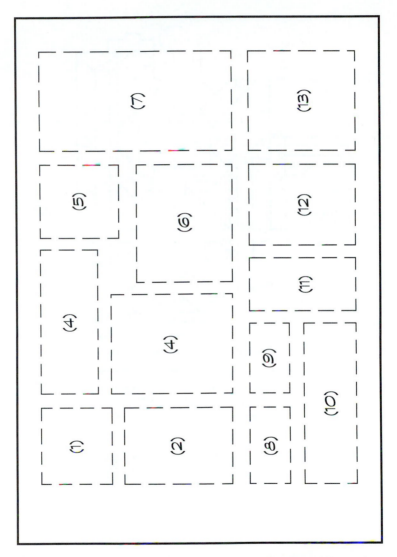

Fig. 11–76. The numbering of details in this set of drawings begins at the upper left corner and proceeds to the lower right corner in a pattern that accommodates detail sizes and configurations. (A city hall renovation and addition. David Woodhouse Architects. Chicago, Illinois.)

Keyed Horizontal Detail Notes

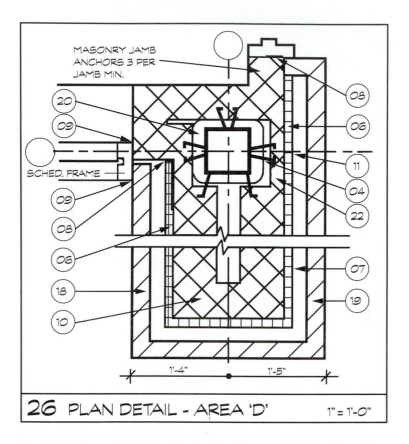

MASONRY JAMB
ANCHORS 3 PER
JAMB MIN.

SCHED. FRAME

1'-4"   1'-5"

26 PLAN DETAIL - AREA 'D'   1" = 1'-0"

Fig. 11–77. Keynotes listed on the drawing sheet are for all details on the sheet. One detail is shown. Keynotes follow. (A high school. PBK Architects, Inc. Houston, Dallas/Fort Worth, San Antonio, Austin, League City, Texas.)

(01) NOT USED ON THIS SHEET

(02) 1/2" SHEATHING BOARD

(03) BATT INSULATION

(04) FIREPROOFING (TYPICAL)

(05) NOT USED ON THIS SHEET

(06) 1 1/2" RIGID WALL INSULATION

(07) DAMPPROOFING

(08) MEMBRANE FLASHING

(09) SEALANT AND BACKER ROD 3/8" TYP.

(10) 6" CMU

(11) STEEL BEAM, JOISTS AND ANGLES, AND METAL ROOF DECK RE: STRUCTURAL

(12) TREATED WOOD BLOCKING

(13) NOT USED ON THIS SHEET

(14) NOT USED ON THIS SHEET

(15) NOT USED ON THIS SHEET

(16) NOT USED ON THIS SHEET

(17) THRU-WALL FLASHING

(18) 8" CMU

(19) KING SIZE FACE BRICK (REFER TO ALTERNATE NOS AT INTERIOR CONDITIONS)

(20) MASONRY TIES RE: TO STRUC. FOR ADDITIONAL STRUCTURAL TIES

(21) 4" CMU

(22) 2-1/4" CMU SOAP

(23) DOWNSPOUT RE: MEP

Fig. 11–77 (concluded).

Keyed Vertical Detail Notes

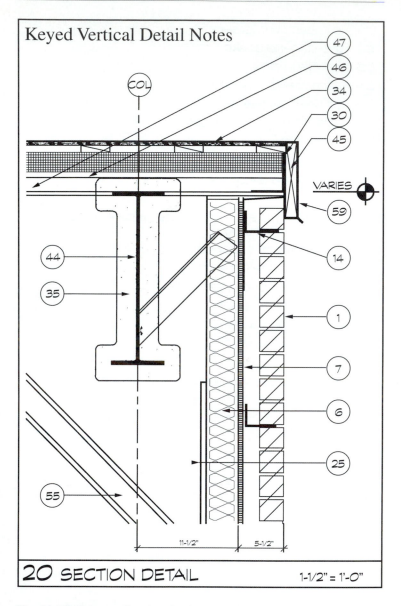

20 SECTION DETAIL   1-1/2" = 1'-0"

Fig. 11–78. Keynotes listed on the drawing sheet are for all details on the sheet. One detail is shown. Keynotes are on the following pages. (An elementary school. PBK Architects, Inc. Houston, Dallas/Fort Worth, San Antonio, Austin, League City, Texas.)

01 KING SIZE FACE BRICK

02 4" CMU

03 6" CMU

04 8" CMU

05 1 1/2" RIGID INSUL. RE: SPEC. TAPE ALL JOINTS.

06 THERMAL BATT INSUL. RE: SPEC.

07 1/2" EXT. GYP. SHEATHING

08 CONT. DAMPPROOFING

09 MEMBRANE FLASHING.

10 METAL FLASHING.

11 THRU WALL MTL. FLASHING/COUNTER FLASHING

12 3/4" TYPE 'F' REVEAL.

13 WEEP HOLES @ 30" O.C. W/ WICKCING RE: SPEC.

14 MASONRY TIE/ANCHOR AS REQ'D AT EA. WALL TYPE RE: SPEC AND STRUCT.

15 EXTERIOR CAULK RE: SPEC.

16 EXTERIOR CAULK WITH BACKER ROD RE: SPEC.

17 'C' CHANNEL WELDED TO STL ANGLE. RE: STRUCT.

18 ALUMIN. THRESHOLD SET IN FULL BED OF SEALANT.

19 CONC. BEAM & SLAB RE. STRUCT.

20 PRE-FINISHED MT. GUTTER AND DOWNSPOUT RE: SPEC.

21 TREATED WOOD BLOCKING

22 2 1/2" MTL. STUDS @ 16" O.C. 25 GAUGE RE: SPEC.

23 3 5/8" MTL. STUDS @ 16" O.C. 25 GAUGE RE:SPEC.

24 4" MTL. STUDS @ 16" O.C. 16 GAUGE RE: SPEC.

25 5/8" GYP. GD. RE: FIN. SCH.

26 SCHEDULED CEILING

27 SCHEDULED WINDOW

28 SCHEDULED DOOR AND FRAME PLAST. ON GALV. MTL. LATH RE: SPEC.

29 SUSPEND. 3/4" CEMENT STUCCO

30 STEEL ANGLE RE: STRUCT.

31 CMU BOND BEAM. RE; STRUCT.

32 BREAK METAL DRIP EDGE. FIN. TO MATCH WINDOW FRAMING SYSTEM.

33 CONT. ALUMIN. SOFFIT VENT RE: SPEC.

34 VENTD ROOF PANEL SYSTEM W/ COMPOSITION SHINGLE ROOFING RE: ROOF PLAN & SPEC.

35 FIREPROOFING AS REQ'D UL NO. AND RE: SPEC.

Fig. 11-78 (continued).

Keyed Vertical Detail Notes (concl.)

36) REINF. GLASS BLK. WALL
RE: SCHED. AND SPECS.

37) ALUMIN. CANOPY FRAME,
DECK AND SUPPORT BY
CANOPY SUPPLIER.

38) COUNTER FLASHING.

39) SCHEDULED FLOOR
FINISH.

40) SCHEDULED BASE.

41) CONT. SCRIMP TAPE.

42) SCHEDULED SUB-SILL

43) NOT USED.

44) STEEL BEM RE: STRUCT.

45) 2X TRETED WD. FACIA BD.

46) 5/8" TYPE 'X' GYP BD.

47) 1-1/2" MTL. ROOF DECK.

48) STRUCT. BAR JOIST. RE:
STRUCT.

49) RE: SITE PLAN FOR
EXTER. PAV.

50) 1-1/2" RD. ALUMIN.
HANDRAIL.

51) TUBE STL. RE: STRUCT.
DWG.

52) CAST-IN-PLACE CONC.
COL RE: S1/A4.03.

53) GALV. STEEL SUN-
SCREEN. RE: STRUCT.
DWG.

54) STEEL PLATE WELDED TO
STEEL TUBE. RE: STRUCT.
DWG.

55) 4" 16 GA. MTL STD.
BRACED AT 4'-0" O.C.

56) 6" RD. STL. TUBE. RE;
SPEC.

57) EXT. INSUL. FIN. SYS. RE:
SPECS.

58) 2 LAYERS 3/4" EXTER. GR
PLYWD.

59) PRE-FIN. MTL. FACIA W/
CONT. CLEATS.

60) 2" RD. STL. TUBE. RE:
STRUCT.

61) PRE-FIN. METAL CAP.

62) 2" HIGH CMU START.
COURSE.

63) STL. ADJ. PLATE WELDED
TO STL TUBE. RE: STRUCT.

64) EPOXY GROUT FILLER
FOR 'Z' PLATE. PROV. W/
ANCHOR BOLTS.

65) 1" PLASTER ON MTL. LATH
ON 1/2" GYP. SHEATHING.

66) VENTED SCREEN.

67) END CLOSURE.

68) DRAIN OPENING.

Fig. 11-78 (concluded).

Title Blocks

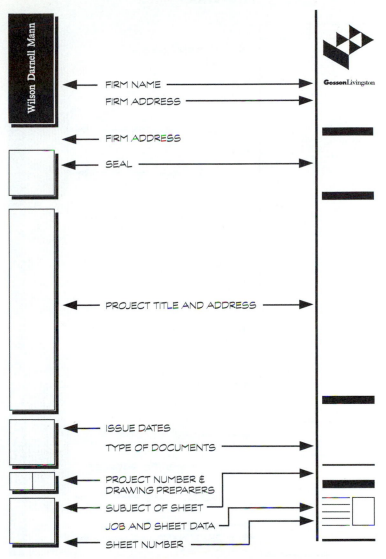

Fig. 11–79. Sample title blocks. (Wilson Darnell Mann P.A., Architects. Wichita, Kansas; Gossen Livingston Associates, Inc., Architecture. Wichita, Kansas.)

Title Blocks (concl.)

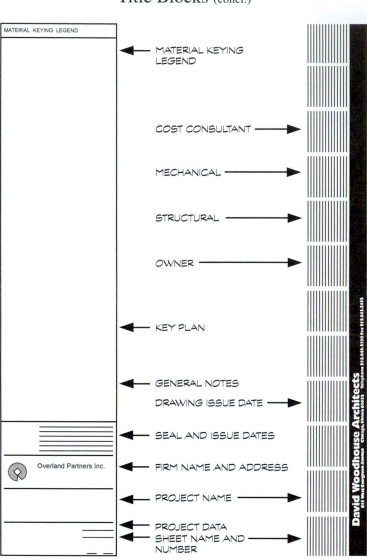

Fig. 11–79 (concluded). (Overland Partners, Inc. San Antonio, Texas; David Woodhouse Architects. Chicago, Illinois.)

12

Design-Build

In Chapter 7, a contractor observes that the rise of the design-build profession is the result of a general loss of faith by owners in the ability of architects to produce buildings in a timely manner and within the budget. It is true that the design-build process is becoming more popular although the benefits of the process might not be understood by persons who do not practice in this realm.

In this chapter, professionals in the design-build industry report that the advantages of the process are realized by the owner in terms of the faster production of the building at a better price than can be achieved in the traditional design-bid approach. They agree that this is due to having the builder and designer on the same side of the contract. It is logical in theory and practice. An example of this is that greater communication is facilitated, an achievement generally considered to benefit any type of building delivery process. Also outlined in this chapter are the responsibilities of the parties involved in the design-build process, as well as the characteristics and attitudes that are necessary to make the design-build approach successful.

Among the many aspects of design-build that are discussed here, it is noted that working drawings are not necessarily different from those prepared for bidding. All conditions still must be detailed. In the design-build method where builders and designers are on the same team, to prepare an incomplete set of working drawings is to let down a team member by shifting the cost of configuring the construction away from the designer and to the builder. Team members must consider the welfare of each other in order to overcome the adversarial relationship that typifies the bid process and is well known for having inefficienceies.

A component that can affect working drawings in a positive way is having built into the system the builder's frequent review of details and drawings so as to evaluate them for clarity and practicality. A better set of drawings in terms of completeness and economy will be the result and will benefit the work as well as the architect, builder, and owner.

Introduction to Design-Build

Eddie Scott
SGS, L.L.C.
Oklahoma City, Oklahoma

Design-build is a method of project delivery in which one organization, the design-builder, contracts with the owner to provide architectural/engineering design services as well as construction services. The design-build process merges the design and construction phases into one cohesive process. It is a combination of related but separate disciplines that allows innovation, efficiency, and teambuilding to result. During this process, creative ideas from the architectural and engineering perspectives are encouraged while construction management personnel consider budgetary constraints. It is the responsibility of both sides to provide the client with high-quality design and engineering practices for the best possible price.

There are many advantages to using the design-build process as is evidenced by its growing popularity and use in private and public sectors, including government and military construction work. Advantages to using the design-build process include:

1. Cost savings to the client.
2. Communication during design between the client and the design-build team.
3. Time saved.
4. The client receives a high-quality facility.

Cost is always a consideration and a concern for the client. The involvement of both the architect/engineer and the contractor from the beginning of the project allows the team to develop cost data much earlier in the process. This paves the way for quicker, more effective solutions to design concerns, and allows the team to aggressively pursue innovative ideas. In addition, with design-build much of the administration for both the owner and the design-builder is reduced. Many of the change orders that occur with design-bid-build projects are eliminated, resulting in a much lower price for the owner.

One of the primary advantages for owners in using design-build instead of the traditional design-bid-build is time. The design-build method can sometimes reduce the schedule to completion by as much as half. The project can be accelerated to meet critical goals by bringing the designer and constructor together, meaning that budget is considered while the design is being developed. The two perspectives can foster creative ways of solving time-sensitive issues. Since the design-build delivery process allows the design and construction phases to overlap in time, design and construction issues can be addressed more quickly, therefore, reducing the total project delivery time.

Convenience is another inherent benefit of using the design-build delivery process. With a single point of responsibility, owners avoid being caught in the middle between architect and contractor. The owners can address all questions and concerns with one point of contact. Since the architect/engineer and the contractor are working as a team, they share accountability equally.

The client also benefits from design-build in that they are able to choose from a number of design concepts during the design phase of the project. In traditional design-bid-build projects, conflicts would often arise between the design (completed by one party) and the construction (completed by another). In design-build, one party handles both aspects, therefore reducing the number of conflicts encountered during the construction phase.

All members of the design-build team share a common goal—customer satisfaction. Accomplishing this goal requires teamwork. Every team member has an opportunity to contribute during both the design and construction phases of the project. Since teamwork is the key to a successful design-build project, the way the different perspectives relate is critical. The outcome is positive when the parties working together can use their disciplines to complement each other. Under the traditional system of contracting, the two sides would be working separately, often in adversarial roles. This conflict of interest often undermines the success of the project. Design-build is intended to encourage a productive and efficient team.

A higher quality product is the result of this teamwork. Increased quality is important for the client as well as for the design-builder. Good designers working with good contractors bring out the best in not only the people involved, but in the outcome of the project as well. All parties involved in the design-build process can benefit from inherent qualities such as cost efficiency, time management, quality design and construction, convenience, and teamwork.

TECHNICAL ISSUES

In the age-old feud between architects/engineers and contractors, it would seem impossible that the two could work together as a team, with a common goal of pleasing the client. This working relationship is an essential ingredient, if a design-build firm is to be successful. The architects may feel as though the construction stifles creativity and spontaneity with budgetary constraints. At the same time, construction managers believe that designers only consider the creative aspect of the design, with no thought given to the cost required to perform the work. A firm's ability to confront and solve issues like these is an important key to becoming a successful player in the design-build arena.

The efficiency of the design-build process can be measured by factors such as time, customer satisfaction, budgetary controls, and, ultimately, the quality of the final product. If these criteria are satisfied, it can be said that the design-build process is working effectively.

CAREERS IN DESIGN-BUILD

Depending on the size of the company, the organizational structure may vary. Here is a list of some possible occupations within a design-build firm.

- President/ CEO
- Design-build Director
- Superintendent
- Safety Officer
- Account Manager
- Architect
- Mechanical Engineer
- Environmental Engineer
- Project Manager
- Project Manager Assistant
- Quality Control Officer
- Estimator
- Scheduler
- Structural Engineer
- Civil Engineer
- Electrical Engineer

Scott Guernsey Solutions (SGS, L.L.C.) was established in January 1999 in Oklahoma City, Oklahoma. In May of 1999, SGS was certified as a Small Disadvantaged Business by the U.S. Small Business Administration. With its primary focus on Design-Build contracting, SGS has assembled a highly qualified project management staff with over 100 years of combined management experience.

Teamed with C.H. Guernsey & Company as the designer of record, SGS offers clients professionalism, experience, and expertise in project design and construction. Combining the talents and resources of SGS and Guernsey created a highly qualified team of design and construction professionals, dedicated to the pursuit of design-build projects for both public and private clients across the United States.

The experience and expertise of SGS in design and construction has resulted in many successful projects ranging in cost from $150,000 to $26,000,000.

Contact Information: SGS, L.L.C., 5555 N. Grand Blvd., Suite 200, Oklahoma City, OK 73112. Phone: 405-416-8400.
Fax: 405-416-8401. Eddie Scott, President & Owner.

Productive Design-Build Practices

James L. Bauer, AIA
President
Bauer Group Architects/Ltd.
Billings, Montana

The Architect

1. Performance of architectural services should include the following:

   - Everything that is to be included must be described in the documents. Do not assume that any task is understood without a description. For example, the architect should prepare cost projections for progress of the work. Although the builder might be responsible for cost controls, this helps the builder and the owner know where they stand with regard to costs throughout the project.

   - Consultants must be managed so as to perform in a timely way and according to their agreements.

   - Specifications and/or drawings must show or convey exactly what is to be done rather than simply providing references to the tasks.

   - Overlay drawings of all disciplines with the architectural drawings and with each other to identify conflicts.

2. Cost projections must be prepared by the architect and reviewed periodically to maintain budget limitations and to confirm the builder's estimates. Realistic budgets will:

   - Allow time and costs to adequately complete items.

   - Allow overtime for problems that were not anticipated, such as the following:
     - Final costs for certain elements might exceed their budget, thus requiring budget revisions.
     - Delivery delays might occur which affect staging and scheduling.

- o Drawing production might be affected by the demands of another project.

- • Provide about 15% of the budget to address the unforeseen.

- • Provide for monthly reviews and updates of drawings to match the building team's methods, means, and sequence of construction.

3. Use the American Institute of Architect's (AIA) consultant agreement form and enforce contractual obligations where they have not been met.

4. Be prepared to field calls from many sources during document production. The primary designer is going to be the "clearing house" for questions, so budget and staff accordingly.

5. Do not tolerate members of the design-build team who request clarification of material covered in the documents. Direct initiators of such inquiries back to the documents so as to discourage unnecessary requests.

6. Eliminate unproductive activities and personnel from the process. Design-build projects do not have the resources to support costs which are not necessary to team goals.

Consultants
Participation by the consultants is of primary importance. Consultants must be:

1. Mature and willing to work with others. Significant experience contributes to maturity. Timidity is not helpful.

2. Committed to the project goals rather than their own. Consultants meeting separately with the owner or contractor to set an agenda separate from that established for the project is not workable.

3. Productive and effective rather than just efficient. The development of solutions that increase cost and delay construction is not useful, regardless of the degree of efficiency characterizing the process.

4. Available from the beginning to the end of the project, including construction. Their contracts should include services through completion of construction.

5. Able to provide design and detailing solutions early in the process. Waiting for the builder to solve problems eliminates the need for consultants, but that is not an efficient solution.

6. They must maintain a separation from the builder's subcontractors and work through the architect, if under his or her contract.

7. General guidelines for selected consultants are as follows:

    Civil
    - Site controls must be established.

    - Site field-staking must be accurate.

    - Inverts/radius, valves, manholes, etc., must be shown on the drawings.

    Structural
    - Documents must not be diagrammatic. Drawings must be to scale and clear. The availability of CAD systems renders single-line drawings unacceptable.

    - Dimensions must be tied into the architectural grids and control points. Use the outside corner of a foundation face as a control point.

    - Details must be relevant and tied to control points.

    - Structural design must be cost-conscious. Estimated cost of the structure must be based on local market conditions and within 10% of the final cost.

    - Consideration of code requirements must begin at the programming phase and continue through the project process. Code minimums must be superceded where dictated by prudent engineering practice. For example, reinforcing spaced 4'-0" o.c. each way is not necessarily required by codes in 8" concrete masonry walls. Using it in northern climates to minimize cracking, nevertheless, results in fewer problems in the long run.

    Mechanical
    - Systems must be appropriate to local conditions. Availability, installation time, and the ability to manage and operate must be considered.

- Systems must be cost-effective relative to market conditions. Ideal or state-of-the art solutions are not useful, if not cost-effective.

- Methods of code compliance must be indicated on drawings. For example, if a cooling system requires a condensate line, the engineer must show where it is located, how large it is to be, and to what it ties, instead of relying on the subcontractor to figure it out.

- Consultants must work directly for the architect or prime contractor, who should not be bypassed for decisions or instructions.

- Consultants should not change primary systems already developed. This costs others time and money.

- The quality of components must be realistic so as to be within budget limits. Systems must not be over-designed or under-designed.

- Systems must be available from more than one source to keep costs competitive. Failing to meet budget requirements impacts other team members.

Electrical
- Systems must be appropriate to local conditions. Availability, installation time, and the ability to manage and operate must be considered.

- Systems must be cost-effective relative to market conditions. Ideal or state-of-the art solutions are not useful, if not cost-effective.

- Methods of code compliance must be indicated on drawings.

- Consultants must work directly for the architect or prime contractor, who should not be bypassed for decisions or instructions.

- Consultants should not change primary systems already developed. This costs others time and money.

- The quality of components must be realistic so as to be within budget limits. Systems must not be over-designed or under-designed.

- Systems must be available from more than one source to keep costs competitive. Failing to meet budget requirements impacts other team members.

Landscape
- Systems must be practical and functional. For example, controls for irrigation systems must be simple, durable, and easily managed rather than highly computerized.

- Drawings must be accurate and highly descriptive, not diagrammatic. They should include sizes and locations of components as well as locations and methods of connection.

Construction Documents

1. Construction documents (CDs) are a derivative of the program, the design, and the design development regardless of the delivery process. The owner, designer, and builder need to be in concert by the construction documents phase. Owners who have never been involved in a design-build project might not be used to the high level of involvement required of them in the construction document phase. They need to be made aware of the necessity of their participation. This is applicable whether or not the design-build process is of the fast-track type.

2. All of the steps typical of a design-bid process need to be addressed in a design-build scenario, although the sequence may vary. The nature and scope of the working drawings are the same in both processes in order to maintain contractual compliance of those party to the project. The documents must define quantity, quality, workmanship, and time.

3. The design-build process must provide for bracketing each element of the work so that some decisions may be made after primary building elements are in place. Construction based on subsequent decisions must interface with the prior work without revision or repair. The documents, however, must indicate from the beginning the intended outcome anticipated by the owner, designer, and builder.

4. The construction documents and specifications must be cost-conscious and relative to the budget.

5. Methods of code and regulation compliance must be addressed in the documents, and not merely referenced, thus passing on the responsibility to the subcontractor. For example, solutions

to ADA requirements must be drawn and dimensioned rather than merely entering the statement, "Must meet ADA requirements" into the documents.

6. The documents require thoughtful detailing so as not to burden the building team with problems that could have been avoided. For instance, the slope on sanitary lines needs to be confirmed for proper invert elevations in the building and on the site. Also, electrical conduits need to be sized for heat build-up in them in addition to wire size. Likewise, roof drain verticals need to be offset in multistory buildings to avoid blowing out bottoms of the pipes when they bend to the horizontal.

7. The documents should define performance within specific limits while allowing the builder latitude to function within those limits. Two or three options for accomplishing goals should be possible.

8. During the production of working drawings, discussion must focus on construction issues. At this stage, it is not productive to discuss philosophical aspects of the design.

9. Code reviews are to be revised regularly and conclusions incorporated into the documents.

10. Documents must pre-empt back-tracking. Bracketing elements of work will permit construction to continue around a task until it can be accomplished without the necessity for revision at a later time.

11. Do not make changes or revisions to the construction documents unless absolutely necessary, nor without builder and owner awareness.

Teamwork
1. Personnel involved in a design-build project must be effective and be:

- Able to think quickly and be decisive.
  Once the direction for the project has been set and is in motion, pondering noneffective options is not productive.

- Knowledgeable.
  Design, cost, and construction backgrounds are necessary.

- Committed from start to finish.

All parties must remain focused on the project through its completion. They cannot be distracted by other projects or by future commitments.

2. The design-build process introduces another player in the design process, the contractor, who must be given a positive reception. This is important whether the contractor is a part of the process from the start, or joins the project at a later stage.

3. Each participant must have as his or her objective the development of a positive and rewarding experience for all involved. Individual gains of advantage at the expense of others is unacceptable.

4. Seek to contribute rather than place blame.

5. Do not bring attention to a problem without suggesting a solution.

6. Meet your responsibilities on time and within budget, and do not interfere with others as they meet theirs.

7. Work with others and do not team with those who will not work within the chain of authority.

Bauer Group Architects was formed in 1982 in Billings, Montana, by James L. Bauer, AIA. The firm's services include project assessments, facility master planning, site analysis, project management, construction management, interior design, owner representation, facility operations and maintenance consulting, cost projects, code reviews, design-build services, project budgeting, zoning assistance, consultant coordination, and traditional design services.

The firm's projects have included educational facilities, athletic and recreational facilities, institutional facilities, commercial and retail facilities, industrial facilities, churches, medical facilities, municipal facilities, residences and housing, and governmental facilities including federal, state, local, and tribal.

The Role of the Architect in the Design-Build Project

Douglas D. Gransberg, P.E., C.C.E.
Norman, Oklahoma

Background

The delivery of public and private buildings using Design-Build (DB) has been steadily increasing for more than 15 years. Proven design-build success in the private sector is encouraging public owners to utilize this innovative process. [1,2,3,4] As a result, many of the traditional relationships that exist in the Architect/Engineer/Construction community are being reforged to permit them to operate inside projects that are being delivered using alternative methods like DB. Additionally, DB is no longer a new project delivery method. It is being institutionalized on a large scale throughout the world. As a result, many designers will find themselves being drawn into DB projects due to owner pressure to compress project delivery time frames. Thus, these design professionals must be prepared to alter their business practices to accommodate the changed relationships inside a DB contract.

Design-build is a project delivery method that encompasses both project design and construction under one contract. One firm, or team, is contracted for a project in its entirety. Design-build contracts take on many different forms, but the key element is a single source of responsibility for the owner through one contract for both design and construction. There are numerous reasons why owners choose to use design-build, but the primary reason is the potential for shortened project duration.[5] Because of coordinated efforts between the designers and builders, construction can begin prior to completion of construction documents. The use of a design-build contract also has the potential to reduce the overall costs associated with design and construction. Two recent studies of more than 600 projects in the building sector have demonstrated a 30% or better increase in project delivery speed and a 6% or greater reduction in unit cost over the design-bid-build method of project delivery.[6,7]

Major changes

DB essentially alters the formation of contractual teams moving the Designer-of-Record (DoR) into a direct contractual relationship with the builder. These teams can be formed in the following four ways:

- Integrated Design-Builder: A single company with both internal design and construction assets sufficient to complete the project.

- Joint Venture: A design firm and a construction firm both take equity positions in the project, often forming a holding company to complete the project.

- Builder as Prime Contractor: The construction company consummates the DB contract with the owner and executes a subconsultant agreement with the designer.

- Designer as Prime Contractor: The design firm consummates the DB contract with the owner and executes a subcontract agreement with the builder.

Each of these structures has its own set of advantages and disadvantages. A recent study by Molenaar [8] found that builder-led DB teams were the most prevalent, occurring 54% of the time, followed by integrated design-builders at 28%, designer-led at 13%, and joint ventures at 5%. The major reason that builder-led and integrated teams happened most frequently is the requirement to have sufficient financial capacity to be able to bond a DB project.[9] As a result, most design firms wanting to work in the DB market will find themselves assuming a subconsultant relationship with a general contractor who will hold the prime contract with the owner. Thus, the traditional roles are redistributed between the players on the project.

Owner's role

The major change from the owner's perspective is that the DB contractor owns the details of design until the project is complete, and the plans and specifications are no longer part of the construction contract as they have become a deliverable out of the DB contract. Thus, the professional liability for design errors and omissions now rests with the DB contractor, and the DB contractor can change the details of design as required to meet time, cost, and quality constraints during the project. The owner no longer reviews the design for technical content. The owner's design reviews are conducted to ensure that the design conforms to the performance requirements set out in the DB Request for Proposal (RFP) and the details of the winning proposal. When the owner becomes directive or prescriptive in his or her design review comments, the owner may unintentionally assume the liability for those features of work on which the directive comments were made. This results in a split performance liability between the owner and the DB contractor. It also makes the documentation of owner design-review comments during a DB project essential for the DB contractor's DoR. This shift in professional responsibility also demands a higher level of trust and open communication between the parties to the DB contract, making true project partnering essential to success.

Architect's role with the owner
The DB Contractor's team owns the details of design throughout the period of project execution. As a result, the designer must design to both budget and schedule constraints. As most DB contracts are couched in performance terms, the designer must now be prepared to generate various design alternatives that can be priced and scheduled to ensure budget and time compliance before starting into detailed design. This is the area where a solid relationship with the general contractor is imperative. The DoR must thoroughly understand all the constraints placed on the project and must have a plan to ensure that design concepts are continuously checked against those constraints before they are approved for detailed design. Secondly, as DB is a form of performance contracting, the DoR must also thoroughly understand the owner's project performance requirements and any expectations that are not explicitly spelled out in the RFP. Add to this environment the fact that many projects are delivered using DB as a means to accelerate their completion, and one enters an environment where honest, open communication between all parties to the contract is absolutely essential.

One technique that has been used with great success to open up all the required channels of communication early and keep them open is the use of a DB charette.[10] Typically these will occur after award but before initiation of the first phase of design. The idea is to bring all the stakeholders to a single point where three essential objectives can be accomplished. First, the DB team must draw out both the owner's explicit and implicit project requirements and compare them to the design assumptions that were made during proposal preparation. Thus, before any further design development occurs, both the owner and the DB team achieve consensus on the details of the design program. Secondly, the builder must make constructability input to various design approaches and, thereby, make the DoR aware of the areas where construction economies can be accrued through the judicious selection of particular design solutions. Lastly, the group must bounce their favored alternative against the time, cost, and space constraints and adjust the design solution as required.

The remainder of the project is pretty similar to the traditional approach with one noticeable exception. Because the DB team established a firm fixed price for the project before the design was complete, the need to continuously check the project's cost as the design is developed is absolutely imperative. Thus, the DoR must plan for and schedule cost engineering reviews of designs in progress to avoid losing design effort during project execution. Additionally, the DoR should avoid showing unpriced design progress drawings to the owner. This rule pays dividends in maintaining the requisite level of trust throughout the project. The owner's greatest fear in a DB contract is that the DB team will cut corners on quality. This fear seemingly becomes reality when the owner reviews and approves an unpriced design feature only to see it changed because it failed to meet either budget or schedule constraints. This erodes the trust between the parties, and the best way to avoid this unnecessary drama is to agree at the outset to only offer design product for review after it has been priced and the schedule has been checked. If there is a reason why this cannot be done, the architect should clearly mark drawings and specifications as unpriced before delivering them for owner review.

Architect's role with the builder
As previously discussed, the architect can join the DB team in a variety of positions ranging from prime contractor to design subconsultant. In each variation, the architect's liability will be different. Obviously, liability will be greatest when the architect assumes the prime contractor role. That shifts to shared liability in the joint venture setup. This is one form that may require the most attention to the details of how the joint venture agreement is formed, as the architect might find that he or she has assumed responsibility for construction quality as well as design quality. As a result, the most common form puts the architect in the role of DoR as the primary design subconsultant.

There are several important points that must be present in the contract with the builder to allow efficient performance in this last role. First, the agreement should ensure that the DoR is contractually empowered to be the primary point for all design

effort and is given the authority to approve or disapprove any design
or extensions of design, such as shop drawings and submittals,
prepared by trade subcontractors, fabricators, and material
suppliers. Next, the DoR must be totally integrated into the DB
quality management system taking responsibility for those quality
assurance responsibilities that normally are performed on behalf of
the owner on a traditional project. Finally, the architect's
responsibility for construction administration activities is
substantially changed. The DoR performs these duties on behalf of
the DB team and will find that frequent interaction with the owner's
construction representative is essential. Depending on the pace of
the construction schedule, the architect will also find that the DoR
is required to spend a good deal more time on the project site than
on a traditional project and should budget accordingly. This often
stems from the synergy that develops with the builder's staff and
from the inclination to solve design coordination problems as
encountered in the field.

Conclusions and recommendations
Design-Build is now a fact of life in the design/construction
industry. Owners' demands for compressed delivery schedules,
combined with a fundamental shift in attitudes among design and
construction professionals, has created new opportunities for
designers and builders alike. However, to be successful, each party
to a DB contract must approach the project with a strong spirit of
teamwork, open communication, and honest business dealings. A
recent study by Arizona State University found that those who are
able to embody these values in their project delivery practices are
rewarded by earning profits that are about 3.5% higher on DB
projects than on those delivered in the traditional fashion.[11]
However, to earn those profits, the members of the DB team must
first undergo a serious change in business culture. No longer can the
parties to the project live in a legalistic, adversarial climate with
different disciplines staying in their collective technical stovepipes.
Teamwork is essential to success. To be successful in this fast-
moving arena, the architect must remember that, at its base, a DB
project is a *construction* project. The owner has contracted for a
constructed facility that must be designed before the construction
can start. Thus, managing the design effort in a fashion that
facilitates the construction effort benefits all involved in the project.

One recommendation must be made to those who are
considering joining the DB movement. Do not attempt your first
DB project without the assistance of someone with previous DB

experience. The cost of partnering with another firm with DB experience or retaining a DB consultant to facilitate the culture shift from the traditional design-bid approach will probably be trivial when compared to the potential liability that could unknowingly be incurred by inexperienced design project managers. The most successful DB teams are made up of designers and builders who have partnered strategically and have agreed to team on multiple future projects as they present themselves, rather than just for the single contract at hand.

The idea that the designer should have a direct technical and fiduciary responsibility for the construction is not counterintuitive. We only have to look back into history to see that many of the great works of architecture, like the cathedrals of Europe, were indeed DB projects. In fact, the word *architect* means "master builder," not "master designer," in Latin. Thus, the advent of DB contracting in the past two decades might be really a return to the roots of our profession.

Notes

[1] McManamy, R., Schriener, J., and Ichniowski, T. (1994). "Design-Build Goes Back to the Future," *Engrg. News Record*, 232(1), 26–28.

[2] Songer, A.D. and Molenaar, K.R. (1996). "Selecting Design–Build: Private and Public Sector Owner Attitudes," *ASCE Journal of Engineering Management*, November 1996, 12(6), 47–53.

[3] Rosenbaum, D. B. (1995). "Can't we all just get along?" *Engrg. News Record*, 235(16), 13.

[4] Yates, J.K. (1995). "Use of Design/Build in the E/C Industry," *Journal of Management in Engineering*, 11(6), 33–39.

[5] Songer, A.D. and Molenaar, K.R. (1996). "Selecting Design–Build: Private and Public Sector Owner Attitudes," *ASCE Journal of Engineering Management*, November 1996, 12(6), 47–53.

[6] Bennett, J., Pothecary, E., and Robinson, G. (1996). *Rep., Design and Building a World Class Industry: Reading Design-Build Forum*, Center for Strategic Studies in Construction, Univ. of Reading, Reading, UK.

[7] "Project Delivery Systems: CM at Risk, Design-Build, Design-Bid-Build," (1998). *Rep. RS133-1*, Construction Industry Institute, Austin, TX.

[8] Molenaar, K.R. and Songer, A.D. (1998). "Model for Public Sector Design–Build Project Selection," *Journal of Construction Engineering and Management*, 124(6), 467–479.

[9] *Ibid.*

[10] Gransberg, D.D., Koch, J., and Molenaar, K, (2000). *Design Build Contract Administration Workbook,* ASCE, Reston, Virginia.

[11] ASU.

Douglas D. Gransberg is an Associate Professor of Construction Science at the University of Oklahoma. He received both his B.S. and M.S. degrees in Civil Engineering from Oregon State University. He is a registered Professional Engineer in Oklahoma, Texas, and Oregon, and is a Certified Cost Engineer. Before moving to academia, he spent more than 20 years in the U.S. Army Corps of Engineers. In his final posting, Professor Gransberg was the Europe District's Area Engineer, stationed in Ankara, Turkey, where he pioneered the use of Design-Build to deliver facilities in remote locations. He also owns an active Design-Build consulting practice with clients such as Atkins-Benham, Frederick R. Harris, Inc., Morrison-Knudsen, International, Naval Facilities Engineering Command, the U.S. Agency for International Development, and the City of Greenville, Texas.

13

International Practice

It has become common for U.S. architectural firms to practice in foreign countries, each of which have its own procedures for securing building permits and constructing buildings. So, it is the purpose of this chapter to provide an introduction to architectural practice in several countries, giving tips for the production phase of work there, as well as other aspects of international practice. Among the topics addressed are the advantages of associating with a local architect where the building will be built, as well as issues of culture, labor, construcion, materials, and fees which should be considered. Additional research is a must for anyone contemplating practice in a foreign country.

Schneider Children's Medical Center Tel Aviv, Israel

Jerry W. Switzer, Partner
Morris/Switzer & Associates
Williston, Vermont

Foundation

In 1987, I was personally selected to design and oversee architectural services for the construction of a 224-bed, freestanding, tertiary-care children's hospital for the State of Israel. I had no previous international experience, but have since worked continuously in the healthcare design and planning fields in Israel.

The 400,000 sf Schneider Children's Medical Center of Israel took 2 years to design and 4 years to build, at a construction cost of approximately $50 million. Although the time frames were longer than would be expected in the United States, they were considerably less than usual for Israel. A comparable project in the United States would have cost about $70 million.

To point out the differences between Israel and the United States in matters architectural, one must begin with an overview of the nature of architecture within Israel.

Most of what is now built in Israel did not exist in 1948, and much of what one now sees has been built since 1967. Accordingly, the style of architecture in Israel began with and has been firmly grounded in the international school of design. Many of the notable practitioners had studied with Gropius or descended from Bauhaus influence. Although much is changing, the predominate character of buildings in Israel remains machine-like with flat industrial facades and sun screens, painted plaster, concrete or ceramic tile in grays and whites. Planning is geometric. Interchangeable box-like houses or offices rest on pilotis to capture the sea breezes. Classical, hard-surfaced, public piazzas periodically relieve the dense-pack. The impression is of modern, bristling, hard fabrications forming canyons sliced by rivers of automobiles.

Except Jerusalem.

Jerusalem is timeless. It has been built, razed, rebuilt, built over, and carved out of the same stone for over 5000 years. The stone is a soft marble of white- to rose-colored hues. By convention and later by mandate, all structures in Jerusalem are shaped of this stone. This designer immediately knew that the transcendent mission of saving children had to be expressed in the timeless stone of Jerusalem. To my knowledge, the Schneider Children's Hospital of Israel was the first major construction in Tel Aviv to be built of Jerusalem stone. Today the entire Rabin Medical Center Campus, on which the Schneider Children's Hospital is located, is being transformed with the stone, and new project after new project in the greater area of Tel Aviv is being rendered from the stone.

The first tip for working in Israel, and one that I fastidiously followed whenever an associate visited for the first time: Go up to Jerusalem. The architecture of the seacoast cities is bursting with energy. It is today; it is the future.

Jerusalem is forever.

Design
Architects in health care in Israel are designated almost along Medici principals. Each hospital campus has its own Israeli architectural firm and, for as long as the firm stays in favor, all the work will be done by the designated architect. Collaborations happen, but as would be expected, an Israeli architect must be part of the team. Certain security areas of public buildings may only be documented under separate cover by approved Israeli architects.

Major health-care projects in Israel are somewhat similar to city hospital projects in the United States. One must satisfy the users and administration of the hospital, but they are usually accountable to a larger system and not the contracting or governing entity. Most large projects will, therefore, have two clients often with conflicting requirements and agendas. The art of consensus is more difficult.

Israeli architects do not have engineers in-house. In most cases, the engineers contract directly with the owner, and, subsequently, may have considerably more autonomy than is the usual U.S. experience. My recommendation is to research and find engineers willing to be consultants to the architect, but be aware that the culture of autonomy is probably still there. The art of coordination is more difficult.

Most large projects will have a project representative working as a consultant to the owner who will act as both construction manager and project manager as we know it. A successful process depends on developing a relationship of trust, respect, and mutual reliability with such a person. If you become life-long friends, it helps.

The design process is not unlike certain U.S. experiences. There are more meetings, not fewer. Brewed coffee does not exist; instant is the coffee of choice. Israelis do not wait in lines, either to buy a ticket or to speak. Almost all speak English, as well as two or three other languages, and are very gracious about conversing in English with us monolinguists. Of course, when they want to say what they really think, they revert to Hebrew.

Codes
I was never able to find a written building code in Israel. In general, if one designs to U.S. codes, one will satisfy, if not exceed, the Israeli requirements. Codes are usually interpreted for you by a consultant who will deal directly with the various review agencies. One finds oneself trying to convince the consultant that he will be able to convince the code officials. The virtue of patience is reinforced here.

Working drawings
Drawings are metric. Just remember that 2.4 meters is 8 feet.

Specifications are in either English or Hebrew, usually both. My advice is to make the English version the record set. Translations can be fickle.

The system of bidding is based on a bill of quantities. This means that contractors are paid on what is measured as actually placed in the job, at a competitively bid unit rate. Working drawings, therefore, have a stage at which they can be released for tender without being fully complete. Tender drawings need to identify all the different types of items that will go into the job, but with only approximate quantities. This allows unit pricing to begin while the documents are being completed, but makes it difficult for architects to reach closure with a final set of documents. Architects seem to measure their lives by deadlines. Once the pressure of a deadline is removed, we are left with our own sense of sound business practice and self-directed discipline to finish the job. Hence, the problem.

Construction

Architects in the United States are careful not to stray into the field of means or methods of construction with either our drawings or specifications. In Israel, one must be precise with the details and techniques of assembly. Construction in Israel is still not an art. The workforce is changing, but it remains largely unskilled, inexperienced, interchangeable, and disengaged in the craft and traditions of construction.

Shop drawings are virtually nonexistent. The best technique is to have something built until it looks right, then repeat.

Lessons

All of my buildings have a greater sense of light since Israel.

In a multilingual, multicultural country, one is taught to make way finding more apparent and less instructional. Light- and way-finding make wonderful partners.

Making sense is much more important than making words.

An interview with Jerry Switzer

As a follow-up to Jerry Switzer's essay on practice in Israel, the following interview with Mr. Switzer was conducted by email.

TP: Is there anything you did by way of marketing to make the necessary contact resulting in your selection for the work in Israel?

JS: I was referred to the project by a children's hospital consultant with whom I had recently collaborated. The best marketing is to create solid relationships wherein others can form a sense of trust and a desire to work together again. Of course, I had to pass a test by all interested parties and then spend a week in Israel with the various stakeholders for the hospital to receive their approval.

TP: What did you do to compensate for having no experience practicing in Israel?

JS: One of the missions was to bring to Israel the best of what had been learned in the U.S. and which would apply to their system. The first week was spent visiting every major healthcare center in Israel and conducting extensive interaction with the project representative and Israeli architectural firm.

TP: Why was the time frame for construction of your project in Israel longer than it would have been in the United States but shorter than that typical in Israel?

JS: Construction productivity is low in Israel, mainly due to the untrained labor pool. As we were designing and building the Schneider Children's Hospital, my home away from home was the Tel Aviv Sheraton. On my first stay I noticed, across the street, a two-story office building under construction. At every stay thereafter, for four-plus years, I noticed progress, but at the end the building was still not finished.

We bettered the norm because of the unrelenting attention by Mr. Schneider and a project representative who could get things done. We also had two full-time architects who moved their families to Israel and virtually lived at the site during the construction period.

TP: Why was the cost of the project less in Israel than it would have been in the United States?

JS: The primary difference in cost is the cost of labor. One example is as follows:

The most common flooring material in Israel is made up of terrazzo tiles, about two inches thick, one foot square, and of any color or pattern one wishes. The tiles are hand-set on a three- to four-inch layer of sand that is lightly mixed with cement so that the natural humidity will harden the bed. The sand layer compensates for irregular concrete finishing and allows for final floor leveling. Electrical wiring and minor conduits occasionally run through the sand layer. The tiles are made of local materials, generally on a kibbutz, and set by Arab labor. The cost of such would be prohibitive in the U.S.; in Israel vinyl tile floor or carpeting would be an extra cost and placed on top of the tile flooring.

TP: Would designing in other than the dominant style in Israel be acceptable?

JS: The architects who choose to can do their own thing, and much of the recent work is truly beautiful and exhilarating.

TP: How is it that the white- to rose-colored marble has become the standard exterior material?

JS: My understanding is that it was a mandate during the British occupation and that it continues as a convention encouraged, if not enforced, by architectural review commissions.

TP: Why is it important to go to Jerusalem when first working in Israel?

JS: Whether one is religious or not, there is so much history in and around the old city of Jerusalem that it is impossible to understand or begin to gain a sense of what Israel is all about without visiting there. Every corner, every hill, every street has a different story. Until you've heard the stories, you don't know Israel.

TP: Would you clarify the Medici principal that is reminiscent to the way architects in health care are designated? Is this unique to health care?

JS: What I was referring to were the Florentine days when there was an architect or artist of the court, who served as long as favor of the court remained. And yes, I think it pertains mainly to the medical centers.

TP: What kind of security areas in public buildings may only be documented under separate cover by approved Israeli architects?

JS: Each public building must contain an area of shelter or refuge that can sustain bomb blast damage and is designated according to standards set by the defense ministry. Those technical standards are closely held, as one would expect, and can only be designed by approved architects and engineers.

The staff dining room at the children's hospital for instance, is designed as a bomb shelter.

TP: To whom, besides the users and administration of a hospital constructed in Israel, must the architect be accountable?

JS: This is complicated, and the only way to describe it is to oversimplify. But here it goes. At the time I started, 80% of the workforce in Israel belonged to a single union which forms its own HMO called, *Kupat Holim*. Kupat Holim provides health care to all its members and is reimbursed by the government. They own and operate their hospitals and clinics, and have their own doctors and staff. As a result, 80% of the health care in Israel was provided by this system. The remaining hospitals are either owned by the government or are private.

Kupat Holim is a huge corporation, with its own layers of checks and balances. An architect usually contracts with Kupat Holim, not the hospital.

TP: How does one select consulting engineers in Israel?

JS: I take my advice from the project representative/construction manager.

TP: Can you describe the metric system used?

JS: Lengths are rarely in mm. Up to 1 meter, cm are used. Meters are used after that. Within a short period, I found the ability to spatially relate to metric measures. Once one remembers that 30 cm is 1 ft, the rest comes easy. The most common scales are 1:200, 1:100, and 1:50 which are our 1/16-, 1/8-, and 1/4-inch scales, respectively.

TP: Are Hebrew notes written beside English notes on the same drawing? Who does the translation?

JS: The Hebrew version is separate. The drawings are done in Hebrew. Translations are done ad hoc on separate drawings.

TP: Can you give an example of the difference between the level of detailing required in the United States and that required for a project in Israel?

JS: One example would be window frame details. In the U.S., one indicates the general shape, type, and desired profile of a window frame, and waits for shop drawings to verify the exact dimensions as well as the flashing and mounting techniques. In Israel, information must be drawn and stipulated in the documents, and checking of a completed sample assembly is done.

TP: Can you give an example from your project of a component that was constructed as a sample several times until approved, in lieu of the U.S. method of approving shop drawings?

JS: We had perhaps a dozen different full-size precast sections built before an acceptable quality of finish and stone texture was approved. We had the first 17-m length of exposed poured-in-place foundation wall torn down and redone three times before it was accepted and served as the standard.

TP: How has a greater sense of light entered your work subsequent to the Israel project?

JS: The 60,000 sf floor-plate of Schneider Children's is penetrated by four major courtyards through four of the six levels. On those levels, there are virtually no occupied rooms which do not have outside light. Our master plans for major ambulatory care projects use courtyards to separate clinical modules, and transparency through to natural views becomes an essential ingredient. My recently completed home is separated into two houses connected by an entry link which allows three or four exposures to most of the rooms.

TP: Can you give us an example of how your appreciation of more apparent way-finding has manifested itself in your work subsequent to the Israel project?

JS: One of the four courtyards in Israel is a large space-framed enclosure formed by the joining of three buildings. The floor of the space is the main lobby, from which one can virtually look up and see all the destinations one may be going to. After that, finding one's way there and back is easy, especially on the glass-enclosed elevators that go up and down in the space.

TP: Please expand on the difference between making sense and making words.

JS: This is probably unfair and largely untrue, but I think many architects, and particularly designers, have a tendency to hide behind words to explain solution. I had a client once who started our relationship by saying he didn't like architects because they didn't talk to him, they only talked to themselves. I've always remembered that and felt that if what I'm doing cannot be explained in thoughtful, simple, plain-language terms, then there is something wrong with the solution, not the comprehension level of the client. This serves well where language differences prohibit convincing by words, but rather with sense.

Founded in 1985, Morris/Switzer & Associates has provided full architectural services for more than 500 healthcare projects, including master facility planning, hospitals, skilled nursing, assisted living, independent living, rehabilitation facilities, ambulatory care facilities, medical office buildings, as well as design-led construction services. Projects are located predominantly throughout the northeastern United States, with additional projects in Florida, Michigan, Canada, and Israel. Projects range in size from $100,000 in construction cost to over $100 million with the majority of work being between $1 million and $10 million. Dan Morris, Jerry Switzer, and Steve Mackenzie, partners and principals in the firm, came to Vermont from large national heathcare architectural firms. Combined, the partners represent more than 70 years of experience in healthcare architecture and planning, and over $2 billion in design and construction experience which is international in scope. A staff of more than 50 professionals includes architects, designers, drafters, builders, and Computer Aided Design and Drafting (CAD) operators.

Architectural Practice By Foreign Architects In India

Asheesh Bajaj
New Delhi, India

Advantages to a Local Association

In order to practice architecture in India, it is important for foreign architects to associate with local architects for the following reasons:

- The local architect has contacts in the government offices who can assist with obtaining permits, such as the building permit and who knows which people to contact regarding projects of particular scales and types.

- The local architect gives guidance regarding which design details would be less expensive to construct based on the knowledge that in India, labor is relatively low in cost.

- The local architect knows which contractor is most suitable for which type of project.

- Local construction materials are less expensive to use and the local architect knows where to acquire these materials. This is important because almost all residential and some commercial projects are conducted under a labor contract wherein the owner is responsible for providing the material.

- The local architect is able to communicate in the local language with the contractor.

- Many medium-scale projects, like commercial buildings (10,000 – 15,000 sf), and some large-scale projects are building using a "Project Manager" delivery system. Usually architectural firms provide these services as well.

     In India, project management is not a part of the contractor's standard responsibilities. There is a separate group of professionals, called project managers, who are a part of the architectural firm, or who have a consulting firm of their own. Since many projects are of a complex nature and the general contractor does not have staff with the expertise to manage such projects, the project manager becomes an important person at the site, and guides the contractor throughout the management of the project. In such a scenario, the construction manager is highly paid and the percentage of his remuneration depends on the project being completed on time and within budget.

- All projects have to be signed by a licensed architect before submitting for permits, so an association with a local architect helps this process.

Forming a Local Association

Granting a license to an architect is the sole authority of the Council of Architecture (CA). It is possible for a foreign architect to be licensed in India. In order to be licensed in India, the foreign architect has to apply to the CA. Then, depending on the foreign architect's experience, the CA will interview him or her and/or give him or her an exam. Based on the results of the exam/ interview, the CA will either grant the foreign architect the license or require him or her to take some courses by correspondence from the Indian Institute of Architects (IIA), and then reapply for a license. Also, the CA "recognizes" some universities in the United States, and readily grants licenses to graduates from these universities. A list of these universities can be obtained from the CA's office in New Delhi.

Local architects can be identified through several sources. The most reliable source is the Council of Architecture; their head office is located in New Delhi. The CA is the licensing agency for all architects in India, and has a record of all architects throughout the country. The members of the CA's council are elected by the architects all over India each year, and they are reliable guides for foreign architects in identifying local architects best suited for a particular project, e.g., health care, recreational, etc.

Another source for identifying local architects is the Indian Institute of Architects. Their office is located in Bombay City in Maharashtra State. This source is not as reliable as the CA because membership with the IIA is not mandatory for a license in India. Thus, all architects do not register with them. Other sources for identifying local architects are the municipal agencies, which issue building permits. These agencies are local to each city/ district.

The division of work between the foreign and local firms is a mutual agreement between them. There are no laws governing this relationship. In general, the foreign architect prepares the proposal, and the desired details are conveyed to the local architect in a sketchy form. The local architect is responsible for working drawings and supervision, although frequent quality checks are made by the foreign firm. Getting the working drawings done by a local architect can be beneficial as CAD draftpersons are relatively low cost in India.

Permits

There is no comprehensive code book in Indian construction practice, but each agency (e.g., the building permit issuing authority, and the fire department) have a small book of their own specifications, which is available at their respective offices in every city. These specifications are to be followed as a rule. Most Indian architects with U.S. Master's degrees in Architecture usually follow the BOCA® code, although this is not a requirement by the permit-issuing agencies.

The different permits involved in the construction of a facility are:

- A **building permit** is called a *sanctioning of plans*, and is issued by the Development Authorities of each city. For example, in New Delhi the agency is the Delhi Development Authority (DDA).

- **D Form**: This is the drainage form and the concerned authority is the Development Authority.

- **C Form:** This is the completion form for a facility and the concerned authority is the Development Authority. This form is acquired after the facility is constructed and after the as-built drawings are submitted to the authority.

- Public projects, like community halls, temples, churches etc., must be sanctioned by the local **Urban Arts Commission** of a particular city. For example, in New Delhi the agency is the Delhi Urban Arts Commission (DUAC).

- A **fire permit** must be obtained from the local fire department.

Only an architect who has a license from the Council of Architecture can apply for the above-mentioned permits.

Apart from the above-mentioned permits, other applications to be filed include electrical connections, telephone connections, and water connections.

General information

All drawings were prepared in feet-inches until 1996. Since then the industry has adopted SI units, and is now in a transition stage between the two.

In India, there is no restriction on building materials, but there is scarcity of wood. Consequently, wood is expensive and is only used in interiors for paneling, etc. The usual building materials in India are reinforced concrete, load-bearing clay brick, stone, and for industrial large-span structures, steel.

The material sizes are not documented in any reference book, and each professional gains this knowledge when he or she starts working in an office or at a site. There are, however, some construction books written by Indian authors (one of whom is Sushil Kumar), and these books include information on material sizes as a part of the construction details. Another way of getting this information is to contact the local vendors. They will send their pamphlets, which include these details.

It is important to remember that Indian construction industry is labor-intensive because the labor is cheap, and so, most of the construction is done in place. (Furniture can be fabricated to a specific design because it costs less than prefabricated or modular furniture.) Construction in India, as a whole, is more labor-intensive than it is equipment-oriented.

Asheesh Bajaj worked for a design and construction management firm in New Delhi, India, for 3 years on commercial, industrial, institutional, and residential projects, as well as corporate office interiors. His responsibilities included design development, working drawings, client contact, consultant coordination, contractor meetings, and site supervision. Mr. Bajaj holds a dual Master's degree in Construction Science and Architecture from the University of Oklahoma. His undergraduate degree, a Bachelor's in Architecture, was completed at the Institute of Environmental Design, Gujarat, India.

International Practice in Australia and the United Kingdom

Henry H. Abernathy, Jr., AIA
Principal, The Hillier Group
Princeton, New Jersey

Guidelines for Working in Australia

These suggestions are based on the Hillier Group working jointly with an Australian firm for 3 years on a major project in Sydney.

General

The Australian system is modeled after the English system of design:

- All documents are in metric units.

- Cost estimating is provided by Quantity Surveyors who also establish quantities for tendering (bidding).

- There are some basic terminology differences which also apply to the United Kingdom, amongst which are:

    Brief: The Program, or list of requirements, for the project

    Programme (program): The schedule for the project

    Lifts: Elevators

In Australia, probably 70% +/- of projects are design-build construction management projects in which the architect is contracted to the contractor. This is particularly true of the larger private projects also usually done in conjunction with a development partner.

The architect's role is to provide an independent assessment of the quality of the project, just as it is in domestic work.

A quality plan is required on almost all projects. This is a project-specific plan.

Regulatory authorities

Many buildings are "fire engineered," especially when they are multi-use and do not fit neatly into the building code. The CSIRO (Commonwealth Scientific and Research Organization), which is a national bureau providing testing and standards, is often utilized in a consulting role to provide fire engineering advice. Complex buildings which do not fit neatly into a particular building-use category may be analyzed for compliance with egress and fire safety standards by an authorized organization such as the CSIRO, who use mathematical modeling to test whether or not egress is achieved within prescribed time periods, etc. The architect proposes a compartmentation and egress plan to the CSIRO for testing, and makes modifications according to the test results. This is a more flexible, less prescriptive approach to achieve the performance requirements of fire safety.

There are also Australian Standards which are cited in the specifications for most common materials and applications. Where standards do not exist, U.S. NFPA or other standards may be used.

Planning authorities require a Development Approval, or DA, as a condition of beginning construction. Applications for Development Approval are often submitted on schematic level documents. Approval is conditioned on submission of further details as the design is developed. It is advisable to submit more, rather than less, complete documents to limit the number of conditions which must be submitted, reviewed, and approved later.

Documentation

There are some differences between Australian and U.S. working drawings. Australians generally document more structural items, particularly the "setting out" of the slab edges and penetrations through the slab. "Setting out" is simply locating the position of a component through dimensioning. A setting-out drawing for the building, for instance, ties it into the local geographic grid system and gives the grid relationships which govern the geometry of the building. Whereas in the United States, we typically describe the slab edge relationships in section, in Australia, a dimensioned plan is done by the architect.

Drawing scales are generally equivalent to U.S. scales for a particular level of design:

	Australian	Approx. U.S. equivalent
Concept Schematic	1:200	1/16" = 1'-0"
Design	1:100	1/8" = 1'-0"
Development	1:50	1/4" = 1'-0"
Construction		
Documents		
(Details & Sections)	1:20	1/2" = 1'-0"

Construction

Concrete is much more common than steel. Australia must import most of its steel and has good experience with concrete. Most products can be sourced in Australia or New Zealand though specialized interior finishes often must come from the United States or southeast Asia. Drywall is available locally. Intricately patterned carpet may be imported from New Zealand or the United States.

Guidelines for the United Kingdom

General

The UK is a metric country but still has not gotten completely away from the "imperial" system of feet, inches, square feet, etc. There are British Standards governing most materials and systems which are cited in the specifications. There is also a general acceptance of the need to conform to international quality standards. The nomenclature is similar to Australia in the use of words like brief (program), programme (schedule), etc.

There seems to be a much less aggressive stance taken with respect to extra services. There is some willingness to absorb within the fee a certain amount of what would be regarded as extra services in the United States, as long as they don't become onerous. There is also a willingness to accept contractual language that is far more broad than in the United States.

There is a requirement to name a "guarantor," or party, such as a parent company or bank, who is named on behalf of the contracting architect. The role of the guarantor is primarily to ensure performance by the architect according to the terms of the contract and to provide a backup for the architect's liability.

Regulatory process

Planning regulations vary by locality but the general phases of consent in London boroughs are:

- Outline planning consent.

  Outline planning consent is typically achieved based on submission of schematic drawings which define the bulk (area: gross and net), parking, and massing (footprint, height), general site landscaping and access to the site.

- Detailed Approval (usually details pursuant to the granting of Outline Consent).

  Detailed approval is on the design development documents which describe the site and exterior of the building in detail, including samples of façade and site materials to be used. Plans of the building are also submitted. Depending on the complexity and local conditions, acoustic surveys, "rights of light" (shadowing) surveys, environmental surveys, and traffic impact studies may have to be submitted. Technically, this phase is really the submission of "details pursuant to outline approval."

- Final Approval (when all conditions of consent have been met).

  Final approval is achieved when all of the "details pursuant", or conditions, have been submitted and agreed upon by the local authority. Some must be approved before construction can start, such as approval of the specific building envelope, and others must be approved prior to occupancy, such as details of the paving on the site.

There are special authorities which may be called into play depending on the type of project, such as English Heritage for "listed" (historically registered) buildings, the Museum of London for sites with possible archaeological significance, etc. Generally an archaeological survey would be required as a condition of planning approval. England is very archaeologically sensitized and almost every excavation in populated areas turns up something. Developers see this process as a significant risk in the construction of projects. The local fire brigade also must be a part of the review and approvals.

There are special regulations in England concerning health and safety, called Construction Design Management (CDM). This is a European Economic Community (EEC) regulation and is a criminal statute (versus a civil one). These require the relevant professional to carry out and record risk assessments for each element of the project. These assessments must identify all of the possible risks, such as falling through a skylight during construction. These become part of the tender (bid) documents. There is in addition a special position called a planning supervisor who oversees compliance by all parties with the health and safety regulations.

Documentation
The phases of design are:

Concept
Scheme Design
Detailed Design
Production Information
Construction

Documentation standards are generally similar to those in the United States. The primary CAD systems in use seem to be Autocad and MicroStation.

There is generally a higher sensitivity toward the integration of structural elements as part of the design than in the United States. Current British architecture has been heavily influenced by Richard Rogers, Norman Foster, and others who express structural elements as part of the aesthetic of the design. Elaborate trusses supporting skylights (glass roofs) window walls, and canopies are examples. The international London-based engineering firm, Ove Arup Partners, is an active participant in the design of projects in the detailing of these elements. An example is the Lloyds of London building which is an outgrowth of functional expressionism begun with the Pompidou Centre in Paris, a Rogers building.

Engineering consultants are:

	U.S. equivalent
Services engineers	Mechanical engineers
Civil engineers	Often include structural also
Public Health	Plumbing
Electrical	Electrical

Construction
Construction management is pretty well entrenched for the larger projects, as in the United States. Construction management can be utilized on projects of any size but the larger projects (more than 200,000 sf) are generally on a tight time frame in an urban or

semi-urban area requiring tight scheduling and approvals, all of which need orchestrating to meet the occupancy deadlines. This typically requires a project manager (a firm that manages the whole project) or a construction manager. This is really not different from the United States which is the model for this type of construction picked up by the British.

There is generally a good range of suppliers of products in the UK and in Europe.

The advent of the European Common Market and adoption of the Euro will decrease the currency risks currently a part of buying products in European countries. A "currency risk" is the risk of ordering a material at one price and then paying a higher price due to changes in exchange rate. This can work in reverse also, thus providing a monetary windfall. The UK is a holdout at present on full participation.

The relatively mild weather in the UK due to the tempering influence of the gulf stream allows construction year-round.

Founded in 1966 by J. Robert Hillier, FAIA, The Hillier Group
(www.hillier.com) is the third largest purely architecture firm in the
nation, with more than 175 projects (valued at more than $1.2 billion)
under construction annually. More than 400 professionals work from
offices in Princeton, New Jersey; New York City; Philadelphia;
Washington, D.C.; Scranton, Pennsylvania; Dallas, Texas; Kansas
City, Missouri; Newark, New Jersey; and London, UK. The firm has
been involved in projects of all sizes in 41 states and 23 countries,
and to date has won more than 200 state, national, and international
design awards. More than 86 percent of Hillier's annual revenues
comes from repeat clients.

The Hillier Group is a multidisciplinary architecture firm skilled in
areas of design specialization which it calls "studios." These are
either industry-focused or service-oriented and include Higher
Education, Historic Preservation, Corporate, Health Care, Hospitality,
Science and Technology, Land Planning, K-12 Public Education,
Historic Preservation, and Graphic Design. Within these areas are
both generalists and specialists with specific expertise in strategic
facilities planning, real estate analysis, land-use regulations, or the
design of libraries, laboratories, hospitals, sports facilities, retail
stores, appropriate offices, and corporate headquarters. They are
supported by technical experts in such areas as CAD (computer-aided
drafting and design), specification and documentation. The leadership
team in each studio consists of a design, administrative, technical,
and marketing lead. Hillier is thus able to combine specialized
expertise and personalized service with the technical and human
resources available to a large firm.

International Practice in Japan

Thomas L. Grassi, Architect
Dumont, New Jersey

Hiring practice

- Because Japan has a capitalistic economy (*shihon keizai*), the process of constructing public and private buildings is much like the same process in the United States.

- Private citizens have the freedom to hire an architect to design buildings as they see fit. (As in the United States, architects are generally required for the design of buildings other than one- and two-family dwellings.) The owner also selects a contractor, and, as in the United States, the contractor need not be the lowest bidder on the project because a private citizen has the right to hire any contractor.

- The process for constructing public projects, such as airports, is basically the same as for private buildings. More attention might be paid to the cost of a public project, but the client/agency is still not absolutely obliged to select the lowest bidder.

- An exclusive executive board makes the final decisions regarding the granting of government contracts. The reasons for decisions might be less clear in Japan than in the United States because the final decisions on such matters are typically made behind closed doors and no reason is ultimately given nor required.

- An architect's continuing relationship with a private client is based on the merit of their work, however, architects must go through a competitive selection procedure each time they seek government work.

Local association

- It is not necessary for a U.S. architect to associate with a Japanese architect to do work in Japan but if it is desired to associate with a Japanese architect, the process of identifying a suitable firm is much like that in the United States. Word-of-mouth advice and reputations are informal but useful in making selections. (There are several prestigious design companies in Japan which are available for consideration.)

- The division of work between a U.S. architect and a Japanese-associated architect can vary according to agreement. A U.S. firm might design a building while the associated architect might prepare the working drawings and observe construction, although this is not the only possible division of work. Because working drawings in Japan are similar in scope to those in the United States, they may be produced in the United States and then sent electronically to Japan, or they may be produced in Japan by an associated local architect. Written data on the drawings must be in Japanese. Dimensions are in the SI system.

Fees
- Fees vary with the construction cost. A typical scale is 10% of the construction cost for the planning fee, and 15% of the construction cost for the supervising fee.

Codes
- Design strategies and code requirements in Japan are similar to those in the United States, and, due to the threat of earthquakes in Japan, the codes there are especially strict regarding structures. As a result of this threat, structural design must be earthquake-resistant. For instance, beams and columns in Japan tend to be larger than those required in non-earthquake zones of the United States, and, the height of Japanese construction is restricted.

- Codes in Japan are enacted by the government, and include the building code, the city planning code, and the fire code. The first two codes may be secured from a prefectural governor's office, and the third one may be obtained from a regional fire department. These are the offices with which an architect works in order to get the various approvals required to construct a building. The codes are written in Japanese.

Building materials
- Generally, the materials which are available in Japan are similar to those in the United States, but imported materials are subject to restrictions. In particular, building materials must meet the Japanese Industrial Standard (JIS).

- In Japan, building systems and materials depend on a building's type and number of stories. Wood buildings can have no more than three stories; four- or five-story buildings are usually constructed of reinforced concrete or have a steel frame. Skyscrapers usually have a steel frame and curtain wall.

- Foundation types vary with soil conditions and building size, and are constructed of reinforced concrete, concrete piles, or steel piles. Wood piles are not used.

Construction

- One visible difference between building in Japan and the United States is the cleanliness of construction sites. Despite the size of major construction projects, the sites themselves remain impeccably clean in Japan.

- Although Japanese builders still maintain an excellent reputation for craftsmanship, many Japanese citizens are critical of the quality of technical production, which they believe is not up to the standard that it once was.

Business customs

- In Japan, there is a very distinctive way to pass business cards. (The Japanese take business cards very seriously.) They are handed to one another with two hands and with a 45-degree bow, and are received in the same way. The recipient of the card should read the card intently before placing it into his or her business card holder. (One must have a business card holder!) Business cards are never handled casually, merely glanced at, and then stuffed into a shirt pocket.

- There are two ways to bow: the casual 45-degree bow, and the formal 90-degree bow. They are performed according to the situation, the more casual bow being reserved for peers, and more immediate co-workers. The 90-degree bow is used for executive-level staff. There is some hand-shaking used in greetings, especially among the younger generation, but there is still a general sense of discomfort in doing this.

Social issues

- Despite a trend in Japan toward westernization, there remain some cultural differences with the West. For example, the Japanese rarely say "yes", or "no" with a definite tone, because it is felt that it is impolite to be so forceful. When people from the

West work in Japan and say "yes" and "no" boldly, it can cause a sense of intimidation and make trust-building a little more difficult.

- Most social customs in Japan are either significantly westernized or on their way to becoming so. Although some customs, such as the Green Tea Ceremony or Flower Arranging, remain alive, they are generally maintained by the older generation or they are perpetuated by evening cultural classes, but they are no longer a part of everyday culture.

- Before one travels to Japan, it is recommended that he or she take a course in the Japanese language or social conventions. Many books are available on these subjects and the Japanese National Tourist Organization (JNTO) (<www.jnto.go.jp>) is very helpful. Although the Japanese are generally interested in becoming westernized, being able to say a few words in Japanese and show some familiarity with their customs goes a long way toward making a good impression, and gaining trust.

Mr. Grassi is an architect and project manager in New York City. He recently spent several months living in Japan and working with the Narita Airport Authority in Tokyo. It was during that time that he became immersed in Japanese work habits, customs, and lifestyles.

A special thanks goes to Hideaki Tsuruoka, Manager of the Airport Facilities Planning Office, and architect at the Narita Airport Authority, who clarified many of the finer points of Japanese customs and business practices.

Architectural Work in the Middle East

W. Glenn Bullock, FAIA
Knoxville, Tennessee

Preparing a proposal

- When preparing a proposal for professional services, explain in detail the documents which are to be provided and when they will be furnished.

- Provide a payment schedule and require payment of 15 to 20% of the fee before beginning any services.

- Schedule the payments to be due as the phases of services are completed.

- Ask for payments by wire transfer to a local bank, or accept credit card payments.

- Because clients are always asking for more services than are provided in a proposal, specify the number of site visits, and budget extra time for travel.

- Request that a travel agent make all travel arrangements and mark up all expenses to 115% of the actual cost.

General tips

- Some clients want to meet in the evenings, and they limit the amount of work that can be done in a workday.

- Clients in the Middle East are very friendly and have a lot of exciting ideas, but people who do not like to spend a lot of time in airports, hotel rooms, and waiting for clients to meet, should not work overseas.

Part III

Acknowledgments, Appendices, and Index

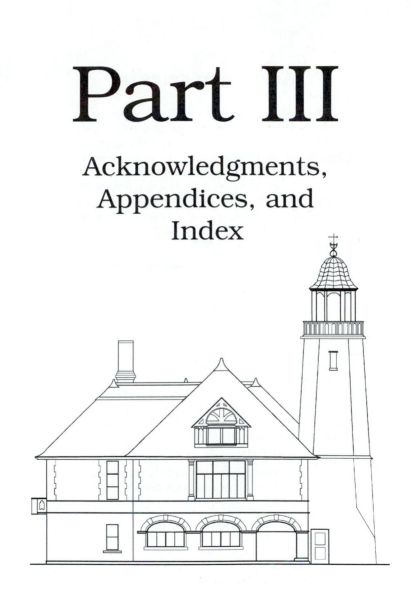

A city hall renovation and addition.
David Woodhouse Architects. Chicago, Illinois.

Acknowledgments

Over 200 people contributed to the development of this handbook and they have my gratitude for their help. First, thanks go to my wife, Jennie M. Patterson, for her significant and lengthy effort. Jennie produced the graphics for the working drawing examples and other illustrations. She edited the whole work, designed the layout, and developed the raw manuscript into a camera-ready format. She compiled the index and she kept the computers running with the necessary maintenance and software management. This handbook would not be possible without Jennie's competent and dedicated effort.

Much thanks go to my graduate assistants for their invaluable assistance. Srdan Kalajdzic, now of Anchorage, Alaska, produced charts and graphics. Rene Spineto, of Guthrie, Oklahoma, produced numerous charts. Arvind Vishnu Ram and Kevin Zhou, of Norman, Oklahoma, prepared graphics. And, Dana A. Templeton, of Norman, Oklahoma, provided administrative help. Joel K. Dietrich, AIA and James L. Kudrna have my gratitude for their assistance as Directors of the Division of Architecture at the University of Oklahoma. Their consideration of this project in their assignment of my academic work and assignment of graduate assistance was particularly helpful. I am also grateful for the continued support of the University of Oklahoma College of Architecture for my publishing efforts.

Many thanks to Yi Zhang, now of Anshen + Allen Architecture, San Francisco, California, for the use of his excellent design and computer graphics for the cover of the handbook.

A special acknowledgment goes to Randall H. Stone, AIA, Vice President of RTKL Associates, Inc., for his willingness to share RTKL's corporate CAD standards. Professionals and students alike will benefit from the generous contribution to this work. And, many thanks go to Samuel Ray Moore, Architect, Oklahoma City, Oklahoma and to John C. Womack, AIA, School of Architecture, Oklahoma State University for their help in launching this project.

I also thank the following professionals for their comments and materials provided for the content of this handbook. This group, however, bears no responsibility for my interpretation of data provided. Such responsibility is entirely my own.

Henry H. Abernathy, Jr., AIA, The Hillier Group, Princeton, NJ • **Jon R. Ackley**, V.P. of Operations, Dalmatian Fire, Inc., Indianapolis, IN, Cincinnati, OH, Columbus, OH • **Active Building Contractors, Inc.**, Pelham, AL • **James Allen**, Acme Materials & Construction, Spokane, WA • **Alt Breeding Schwarz Architects, LLC**, 209 Main Street, Annapolis, MD 21401 • **Ankrom Moisan Associated Architects**, 6720 S.W. Macadam, Portland, OR 97219 • **Jon L. Arason**, City of Annapolis, Annapolis, MD • **Associates in Design Developmen**t, 2930 E. Northern Avenue, Building A, Phoenix, AZ 85028.

Asheesh Bajaj, New Delhi, India • **Ball Architects**, 2700 N. 3rd Street, Phoenix, AZ 85004 • **Bargmann Hendrie + Archetype**, 470 Atlantic Avenue, Boston, MA 02210 • **Barnes and Associates Architects**, 221 N. Krome Avenue, Homestead, FL 33030 • **Barry Royal Wills Associates**, 8 Newbury Street, Boston, MA 02116 • **Bassetti Architects**, 1011 Western, Suite 701, Seattle, WA 98104 • **Bateman-Hall, Inc.**, Idaho Falls, ID • **James L. Bauer**, AIA, President, Bauer Group Architects/Ltd., Billings, MT • **Cathleen Baumeister**, Oklahoma City, OK • **BBL-Carlton, LLC**, Charlston, WV • **Mikel Bennett**, Norman, OK • **Brad Black**, Architect, Project Manager, City of Eugene, Eugene, OR • **Blue Sky Studio**, 1553 Platte, Denver, CO 80202 • **Charles H. Boney, Jr.**, AIA, Boney Architects, Wilmington, NC • **Jerry Bronstein**, AIA, Director of Design, International Management, Consultants, Inc., Malvern, PA 19355, Tel: 610-889-3600 • **Mark L. Brown**, Leo Brown Construction Company, Inc., 2135 South US 35, Logansport, IN 46947, Fax: 219-722-4482 • **Chris Brown**, Building Official, Grays Harbor County, Montesano, WA • **The Builders, Inc.**, Minneapolis, MN • **W. Glenn Bullock**, FAIA, 7100 Sherwood Drive, Knoxville, TN 37919 • **Dennis Burt**, President, Haussman Construction Company, Lansing, MI.

C. Allen Mullins Architect, P.O. Box 21, Bear Creek, PA 18602 • **C.R. Klewin, Inc.**, Norwich, CT • **Cameron Construction, Inc.**, Santa Fe, NM • **Robert G. Caputo**, Consolidated Fire Protection, Inc., Carlsbad, CA, Tel: 760-431-9901, Fax: 760-431-9923 • **Carl Mileff & Associates, Inc.**, Building Code Services, 5070 N. Sixth Street, Suite 103, Fresno, CA 93710, <www.cmapc.com> • **Bill Carrigee, Sr.**, CBO, City

of Bay St. Louis, P.O. Box 2550, Bay St. Louis, MS 39521-2550 •
Carter Enterprises, Inc., Cedar City, UT • **Druery E. Clark**,
AIA, CRSS Constructors, Inc., Van Nuys, CA • **CM Company,
Inc.**, Boise, ID • **Douglas Cobb**, Estimator, Greenwich Supply
Corp., 5789 Arrowhead Drive, Virginia Beach, VA 23462 •
Concord Associates, Inc., 513 Park Avenue, Baltimore, MD
21201-4537, Tel: 410-727-0200, Fax: 410-727-1267 • **James J.
Constantin**, Senior Project Architect, Rutgers, the State University
of New Jersey, Piscataway, NJ • **Contracting Corp. of Illinois**,
2326 53rd Street, P.O. Box 425, Moline, IL 61265 • **Cromwell
Architects Engineers**, 101 South Spring St., Little Rock, AR
72201 • **Martin Cuadra**, P.E., Uzun & Case Engineers, Atlanta,
GA, <www.uzuncase.com> • **Robert Curbelo**, Vice President,
Dacra Construction, Inc., Miami Beach, FL • **Ted Curtis**, AIA,
NCARB, Vice President, Capital Planning, and Facilities
Management, University of Akron, Akron, OH.

David Woodhouse Architects, 811 West Evergreen Avenue,
Chicago, IL 60622 • **Paul L. Dawes**, Building Official, City of
Natchez, P.O. Box 1185, Natchez, MS 39121-1185 • **Denis Della
Vedova, Inc.**, Albia, IA • **Devine deFlon Yeager Architects,
Inc.**, Uptown Theatre Building, Suite 300, 3700 Broadway, Kansas
City, MO 64111 • **Dickey & Burham, Inc.**, Lincoln, NE • **Joel
K. Dietrich**, AIA, Norman, OK • **Doug Wiersig Homes**, Wier-
Wright Enterprises, Inc., Huntsville, AL • **Drury Construction
Co., Inc.**, Poulsbo, WA • **Bruce H. Duschel**, BD Construction,
Inc., 4052 S. 38th St., Tacoma, WA 98409-3002 • **E.W. Burman,
Inc.**, Warwick, RI • **Christopher W. Ellis**, Associate AIA,
Associate IIDA, Norman, OK • **Karin Elmer**, Code Enforcement
Officer, Town of Amherst, P.O. Box 960, Amherst, NE 03031 •
Christopher Ewald, AIA, SSOE Studios, Toledo, OH.

Hank Falstad, AIA, Principal, Pentacore ADA Consulting,
Las Vegas, NV • **Richard R. Faubion**, Hospital Construction
Inspector, Redlands, CA • **Dan Funasaki**, Pacific Fire Protection,
Inc., Pearl City, HI 96782, Tel: 808-456-4521 ex 229, Fax: 808-
456-4654 • **G.A. Brown & Son, Inc.**, Fairmont, WV •
Todd Goertzen, Project Manager, Martel Construction, Inc., 1203
South Church, Bozeman, MT 59715, Fax: 406-586-8102 • **Aaron
J. Goodman**, Certified Building Official, Building Plans Examiner,
Building Inspector, Mount Vernon, WA • **Gossen Livingston
Associates, Inc.**, 420 South Emporia, Wichita, KS 67202 • **Todd
D. Granato**, Craffey & Co., Inc., Builders, Hanover, MA •
Douglas D. Gransberg, PE, CCE, Construction Science Division,
College of Architecture, University of Oklahoma, Norman, OK •

Thomas L. Grassi, AIA, Architect, Dumont, NJ • **Greenway Enterprises, Inc.**, P.O. Box 5553, Helena, MT 59604, Fax 406-458-6516 • **Gregory Construction Co., Inc.**, Manassas, VA • **John Griebler**, Chief Building Official, City of St. Cloud, MN • **H.V. Collins Co.**, Providence, RI • **Raymond Hamilton**, Citadel Construction, Anchorage, AK • **Harbert Roofing, Inc.**, 10274 Maddelein Lane, Palo Cedro, CA 96073 • **Brian Hecke**, Project Manager/Estimator, Player, Inc., Fayetteville, NC • **HKS, Inc.**, 1919 McKinney Avenue, Dallas, TX 75201-1753 • **HKT Architects, Inc.**, 35 Medford Street, Somerville, MA 02143 • **The Hollis and Miller Group, Inc.**, 220 NW Executuve Way, Lee's Summit, MO 64063 • **Gregg Huennekens**, United States Fire Protection, Lake Forest, IL, Tel: 847-247-4755, Fax: 847-816-0098 • **Brian Hunt**, Gail Armstrong Construction, Inc., Norman, OK • **International Architects Atelier**, 1308 Pennsylvania Avenue, Kansas City, MO 64105.

J.P. Martins & Sons Construction Corporation, Caribou, ME • **Charles G. Jeffcoat**, Director/University Architect, Office of Facilities Management, University of South Carolina, Columbia, SC • **John E. Green Co.**, Ray Brunett, Robert Jagenberg, Paul Kosnik, Highland Park, MI 48203 • **John T. Jones Construction Co.**, 2213 7th Ave. N., P.O. Box 2424, Fargo, ND 58108, Tel: 701-232-3358, Fax: 701-232-7040 • **Brian J. Johnson**, Johnson Services, Inc., 247 S. Spring Garden St., Suite 170, Carlisle, PA 17013 • **Clark Johnson**, Building Official, City of Sheridan, 55 East Grinnell, Sheridan, WY 82801 • **David Sweet**, V.P., JS Sweet Company, Inc., P.O. Box 283, Cambridge City, IN 47327-0283, Fax: 765-475-1235 • **Daniel F. Kaiser**, Senior Building Inspector, City of Carona, CA • **Pat Kelly**, Haws Corporation, Sparks, NV 89432 • **King Contracting, Inc.**, 317 Ralph Street, P.O. Box 609, Jackson, OH 45640, Tel: 740-286-2126, Fax: 740-286-5225 • **Steve Klotz**, Building Official, Laurel, MT 59044 • **Ryan Kutter**, Beers Construction Company, Chattanooga, TN.

Landmarks Design Associates, Inc., Landmark Building, Pittsburgh, PA 15219 • **League, Inc. - Design Builders**, McCook, NE • **Leigh & O'Kane LLC**, Structural Engineers, Kansas City, MO • **Doug Lind**, Lind-Exco, Inc., 1141 Deadwood Avenue, Rapid, SD 57702, Fax: 605-342-5133 • **Harwood W. Loomis**, AIA, Consulting Architect, Woodbridge, CT • **The MacMillin Co., Inc.**, Keene, NH • **G. Roger Marmor**, Sr. V.P., F.J. Murphy & Son, Inc., Springfield, IL • **Priyanka Mashelkar**, Norman, OK • **Matson, Inc.**, Little Rock, AR • **Larry L. Maxfield**, AIA, President, Construction Technologies, Leawood, KS •

James Mayer, Development Coordination, City of Scottsdale, Scottsdale, AZ • **Don McGee**, P.E., Drilling Estimator, Austin Traffic Signal Construction Co., Round Rock, TX • **Steven Meismer**, P.E., C.B.O., Plans Examiner, City of Missoula, 435 Ryman Street, Missoula, MT 59802 • **Mid America Roofing & Construction, Inc.**, 2515 W. Interstate 40, Oklahoma City, OK 73156 • **Byron Morris**, Norman, OK • **William S. Morrison**, Assistant Director, Facility Planning and Control, Division of Administration, Baton Rouge, LA.

Nevada Chapter, The Associated General Contractors of America, Inc., Reno, Nevada, Jack N. Tedford III, President, Mario Bullentini, Chairman, AIA/Design Committee, John D. Madole, Jr., Executive Director • **Andrew L. Nguyen**, Norman, OK • **Dennis G. Nolan**, Project Coordinator, Nevada State Public Works Board, Carson City, NV • **Kirk Oglesby**, City of Broomfield, Broomfield, CO • **Overland Partners, Inc.**, 5101 Broadway St., San Antonio, TX • **PBK Architects, Inc.**, 11 Greenway Plaza, Houston, TX 77046 • **Perkins Eastman Architects**, P.C., 115 Fifth Avenue, New York, NY 10003 • **Peter Nelson & Son, Inc.**, La Crosse, WI • **Phillips Metsch Sweeney Moore, Architects**, Roger A. Phillps, AIA, Principal in Charge, Marc A. Phillips, Project Architect, Santa Barbara, CA 93103 • **J. Taylor Pierson**, Building Official, City of Livingston, Livingston, MT • **John P. Plescia**, Star Roofing, 9201 North Ninth Avenue, Phoenix, AZ 85021-3113 • **Bill Prince**, City of Biloxi, P.O. Box 508, Biloxi, MS 39533-0508 • **William Prince**, BurWil Construction Company, Inc., P.O. Box 637, Bristol, TN 37621.

Richard M. Ray, P.E., Cybor Fire Protection Company, Downers Grove, IL 60515, Tel: 630-810-1161, Fax: 630-810-0685 • **William Redenius**, Captain, United States Marine Corps, Monterey, CA • **Stephen L. Reece**, Architect, Bainbridge Island, WA • **Kelly P. Reynolds**, Kelly P. Reynolds and Associates, Inc., Building Code Consultants, Chicago, IL 60656 • **Rice Enterprises, Inc.**, P.O. Box 1548, Dubois, WY 82513-1548, Fax: 307-455-3405 • **RTKL Associates, Inc.**, Dallas, TX • **Scott M. Salmon**, Tri-County Roofing and Siding Co., 312 D Turner Lane, West Chester, PA 19380 • **Hermann Schmalfeld**, Schwegman Constr. & Engrs. Inc., P.O. Box 1206, Pascagoula, MS 39568, Fax: 228-497-2148 • **SGS, L.L.C.**, Oklahoma City, OK • **Justin M. Shanley**, Chief Project Manager, Chapel Construction of New Haven, Inc., New Haven, CT • **Samantha Shotts**, Norman, OK • **Brian Sickinger**, V.P., F.J. Murphy and Son, Inc., Springfield, IL • **Kenneth Siegel**, AIA, Architect, 326 Broadway,

Bethpage, NY 11714 • **Spencer Godfrey Architects**, 1106 S. Mays, Round Rock, TX 78664 • **Ronnie L. Spooner**, Building and Zoning Official, City of Tallahassee, FL • **Stephen Wen + Associates Architects, Inc.**, 77 North Mentor Avenue, Pasadena, CA 91106 • **Sticks & Stones Architecture**, 3077 Texas Avenue, Pittsburgh, PA 15216 • **Michael Stout**, CEO, American Roofing Spec., LLC, 604 Main St., Elsmere, KY 41018, Tel: 606-342-5555 • **Glenn W. Strong**, CSI, CDT, President and CEO, Sea Hawk Enterprises, Inc., Aptos, CA • **Jerry W. Switzer**, Partner, Morris/Switzer and Associates, Williston, VT • **T & M Construction, Inc.**, St. George, UT • **W. Wintford Taylor III**, President, William Taylor & Co., Inc., Waco, TX • **Donald H. Teske**, Global Fire Protection Company, Downers Grove, IL, Tel: 708-852-5200, Fax: 630-852-5992 • **3 K Studio**, 116 Alhambra Circle, Miami, FL 33134 • **Boyd Timm**, VFP Fire Systems, South Bend, IN, Tel: 219-277-0277, Fax: 219-277-7275 • **Tomco Corp**, 500 Ala Kawa St. Deign #100 A, Honolulu, HI 96817, Fax: 808-845-1021 • **Stephen Tucker**, Architect, Worksite, Inc., Boston, MA • **Jeffrey S. Tyler**, AIA, Chief Building Official, City of Kettering, 3600 Shroyer Road, Kettering, OH 45429 • **Drew Upchurch**, Norman, OK.

David Walencewicz, P.E., P & J Sprinkler Company, Inc., Willimantic, CT, Tel: 860-456-0515, Fax: 860-423-9813 • **Bethany Waters**, Norman, OK • **Watkins Hamilton Ross Architects, Inc.**, 20 Greenway Plaza, Suite 450, Houston, TX 77046, Tel: 713-665-5665 • **Duane L. Wayman II**, Wayman Fire Protection, Inc., Wilmington, DE, Tel: 302-994-5757, Fax: 302-994-5750 • **Heather C. White**, President, COMP Corporation, 800 Maplewood Drive, Kokomo, IN 46902 • **Amy B. Williams**, Estimator, Brewer Paint and Wallpaper, Company, Inc., Rocky Mount, NC • **Wilson Darnell Mann P.A.**, 105 N. Washington, Wichita, KS 67202 • **Wink Construction Company, Inc.**, P.O. Box 8066, Evansville, IN 47716-8066, Fax: 812-477-9811 • **Barbara Wolff**, President, TL Wolff Construction, Inc., Denver, CO • **Zhu, Yun**, Shanghai, P.R. China.

Many thanks are due the following people and associations for their administrative help in launching this project:

Suzie Adams, Executive Director, AIA Fort Worth, Fort Worth, TX • **AIA Orange County**, Costa Mesa, CA • **AIA Minnesota**, Minneapolis, MN • **AIA St. Louis**, St. Louis, MO • **AIA Eastern Oklahoma**, Tulsa, OK • **AIA Wisconsin**, Madison, WI • **Wayne T. Allen**, President, Allen Consulting, Inc., Norman, OK • **Dick Anderson**, Executive Director, Associated General

Contractors of Oklahoma, Oklahoma City, OK • **Glenwood
Arnold**, Executive Vice President, Central Texas Chapter,
Associated General Contractors of America, Waco, TX • **Trudy
Aron**, CAE, Hon. AIA, Executive Director, AIA Kansas, Topeka,
KS.

Eugene W. Bayol, Jr., AIA, Executive Director, AIA Monterey
Bay, Monterey, CA • **Sheila Galbraith Bronfman**, Executive
Director, AIA Arkansas, Little Rock, AR • **Judy A.C. Edwards**,
Hon. AIA, Executive Director, AIA Connecticut, New Haven, CT
• **Anne M. Ellis**, P.E., Regional Structural Engineer, Portland
Cement Association, 9600 Clarks Crossing Road, Vienna, VA
22182 • **David W. Field**, CAE, Hon. AIA, Executive Vice
President, AIA Ohio, Columbus, OH • **Richard Fitzgerald**,
Boston Society of Architects, Boston, MA • **Sally Ann Fly**,
Executive Director, AIA Austin, Austin, TX • **Stephen P.
Gennett**, Executive Vice President, Carolinas Associated General
Contractors of America, Charlotte, NC.

Peg Hamil, AIA, Project Manager, The American Institute of
Architects, Center for Building Performance, Washington, D.C. •
Marga Rose Hancock, Hon. AIA, Executive Vice President, AIA
Seattle, Seattle, WA • **Judith W. Harvie**, Executive Director,
Maine Chapter AIA, Manchester, ME • **Jim Henley**, Director,
AIA Florida Southwest Chapter, Fort Meyers, FL • **Linda B.
Hewitt**, Executive Director, AIA Rochester, Rochester, NY •
Elizabeth J. Holmes, Executive Secretary, AIA Honolulu,
Honolulu, HI • **Melissa Hunt**, Executive Director, AIA Central
Oklahoma Chapter, Oklahoma City, OK • **Erin Kennedy**, Events
Coordinator, AIA Los Angeles, Los Angeles, CA • **Timothy D.
Kent**, CAE, Executive Vice President, AIA North Carolina,
Raleigh, NC • **Gayle E. Krueger**, CAE, Executive Director, AIA
Nebraska, Lincoln, NE • **Randy Lavigne**, Executive Director,
AIA Las Vegas, Las Vegas, NV • **Karen Lewand**, Exective
Director, AIA Baltimore, Baltimore, MD • **Bonnie Littlefield**,
Business Manager, AIA Alaska, Anchorage, AK • **Vernon Mays**,
Director of Publications, Virginia Society of the AIA, Richmond,
VA • **Evelyn B. McGrath**, Hon. AIA, Executive Director, AIA
Tampa Bay, Tampa, FL • **Alison Melton**, Executive Director, AIA
Memphis, Memphis, TN • **Lynne Merrill-Francis**, AIA
Michigan/AIA Detroit, Detroit, MI • **Jane Moya**, Program
Director, Washington D.C. Chapter/AIA, Washington, D.C. •
Martha Murphree, Hon. AIA, Executive Director, AIA Houston,
Houston, TX • **Corda Murphy**, Executive Director, AIA
Northeast Illinois, Naperville, IL.

Julienne A. Nelson, Executive Director, Washington D.C. Chapter/AIA, Washington, D.C. • **Melissa Corbin Nelson**, Executive Director, AIA Orlando, Orlando, FL • **Marigan H. O'Malley**, Assistant Director, AIA Baltimore, Baltimore, MD • **Tracy J. Owens**, Executive Assistant, AIA Central Illinois, Springfield, IL • **Kenneth W. Painter**, Executive Vice President, Austin Chapter, The Associated General Contractors of America, Austin, TX • **Carmen Perez-Garcia**, Executive Director, AIA Lower Rio Grande Valley, McAllen, TX • **Sally L. Phillips**, Executive Director, AIA East Bay, Oakland, CA • **Janet D. Pike**, Executive Director, AIA Kentucky, Frankfort, KY • **Joanne Rees**, Program Director, AIA Connecticut, New Haven, CT • **Barbara J. Rodriquez**, Hon. AIA, Executive Vice President/CEO, AIA New York State, Albany, NY • **Judith Rowe**, Program Director, AIA New York Chapter, New York, NY.

Suzanne Schwengels, Hon. AIA, CAE, Executive Vice President, AIA Iowa, Des Moines, IA • **Connie Searles**, Executive Director, AIA Idaho, Boise, ID • **Laura V. Shinn**, AIA, Chair AIA Columbus Honor Awards, AIA Columbus, Columbus, OH • **Joseph A. Simonetta**, CAE, Executive Director, AIA New Jersey, Trenton, NJ • **Alice Sinkevitch**, Executive Director, AIA Chicago, Chicago, IL • **Martha Smythe**, Hon. AIA, Executive Director, Palm Beach Chapter AIA, Wellington, FL • **Nicola Solomons**, Executive Director, AIA Los Angeles, Los Angeles, CA • **Torrey M. Stanley**, Executive Director, AIA San Antonio, San Antonio, TX • **Saundra Stevens**, Hon, AIA, Executive Director, AIA Portland, Portland, OR • **David K. Swindell**, Lieutenant Colonel, U.S. Army, Professor of Military Science, Reserve Office Training Corps, University of Oklahoma, Norman, OK • **Michael L. Tapley**, Executive Director, Alabama Council AIA, Montgomery, AL • **Dick Thevenot**, Hon. AIA, Executive Director, AIA Louisiana, Baton Rouge, LA • **Utah Chapter, The Associated General Contractors of America**, Richard J. Thorn, Executive Vice President, Salt Lake City, UT • **Erin Wells**, Assoc. Director of Communications, AIA California Council, Sacramento, CA • **Hanne N. Williams**, Executive Director, AIA Vermont, Waitsfield, VT • **Katie Wilson**, Executive Director, AIA New Hampshire, Concord, NH • **Gloria Wise**, Executive Director, AIA Dallas, Dallas, TX.

Persons who helped with this project are listed with their titles and in the locations that were current at the time of their contribution. Thanks also go to the contributors who declined acknowledgment by name for their help.

Appendix A:
Abbreviations

&	and
@	at
°	degree(s)
=	equal(s)
'	foot, feet
>	greater than
≥	greater than or equal to
"	inch(es)
<	less than
≤	less than or equal to
—	minus
%	percent
⊥	perpendicular
+	plus
+/- , ±	plus or minus
#	pounds, pounds per
sf	square foot
ACI	American Concrete Institute
ACSM	American Congress on Surveying and Mapping
ADA	Americans with Disabilities Act
ADAAG	Americans with Disabilities Act Accessibility Guidelines
A-E	architect-engineer
AFC	available for construction
AHJ	authority having jurisdiction
AIA	American Institute of Architects

AISC	American Institute of Steel Construction
ALTA	American Land Title Association
ANSI	American National Standards Institute
ASCE	American Society of Civil Engineers
BOCA®	Building Officials and Code Administrators International, Inc.
C.C.E	Certified Cost Engineer
CA	Council of Architecture
CAD	computer-aided design (drafting)
CADD	computer-aided drafting and design
CAE	Certified Association Executive
CBD	Commerce Business Daily
CBO	Certified Building Official
CCS	CertifiedConstruction Specifier
CD	construction document
CD ROM	compact disk read only memory
CDM	construction design management
CDT	Construction Document Technologist

CEO	Chief Executive Officer	Hem	hemlock
cfm	cubic feet per minute	HUD	Department of Housing and Urban Development
cm	centimeter		
CM	construction manager	HVAC	heating, ventilating, and air-conditioning
Com.	commercial		
CRSI	Concrete Reinforcing Steel Institute	I.I.A.	Indian Institute of Architects
CSI	Construction Specifications Institute	I.R.I.	Industrial Risk Insurers
		IAEI	International Association of Electrical Inspectors
CSIRO	Commonwealth Scientific and Research Organization	IAPMO	International Association of Plumbing and Mechanical Officials
DA	Development Approval		
DB	design-build	IBC	International Building Code
DDA	Delhi Development Authority	ICBO	International Conference of Building Officials
DDC	direct digital control		
DL	dead load		
DoR	designer of record	ICC	International Code Council
DOTD	Department of Transportation and Development	IIC	impact insulation class
		IIDA	International Interior Design Association
DUAC	Delhi Urban Arts Commission	JIS	Japanese Industrial Standard
DX	direct expansion		
e	eccentricity	JNTO	Japanese National Tourist Organization
EEC	European Economic Community	kips	1000 pounds
Engrg	Engineering	ksi	kips per square inch
EPDM	Ethylene Propylene Diene Monomer	kW	kilowatt(s)
		L	length of span
ESFR	early suppression, fast response	L	litre(s)
		L/s	litres per second
FAIA	Fellow of the American Institute of Architects	lb	pound(s)
		lbs/ft	pounds per lineal foot
FM	Factory Mutual	LEED	Leadership in Energy and Environmental Design
FOIC	furnished by owner and installed by contractor		
		LL	live load
ft	foot, feet	LVL	laminated veneer lumber
ga	gage		
gal.	gallons	MBH	1000 Btus per hour
GPH	gallons per hour	MDO	medium-density overlay

min.	minimum	R.C.	reinforced concrete
max.	maximum	rad.	radius
mm	milimeter	RFC	request for clarification
n/a	not applicable	RFI	request for information
NAVFACENGCOM	Naval Facilities Engineering Command	RFP	request for proposal
NFPA	National Fire Protection Association	SBCCI	Southern Building Code Congress International
NICET	National Institute for Certification in Engineering Technologies	SDI	Steel Deck Institute
		Sec.	section
		Sel.	select, selected
No.	number	sf	square foot, square feet
NRCA	National Roofing Contractors Association	SMACNA	Sheet Metal and Air Conditioning Contractors' National Association
o.c.	on center		
OBS	oriented strand board		
OSHA	Occupational Safety and Health Administration	STC	sound transmission class
		Struc.	structural
oz.	ounce	UBC	Uniform Building Code
P.E.	professional engineer		
P.T.	post-tensioned	UL	Underwriters Laboratories, Inc. ®
PDCA	Painting and Decorating Contractors of America	V	shear
		V	volt(s)
plf	pounds per lineal foot	V.P.	Vice President
psf	pounds per square foot	VAV	variable air volume
psi	pounds per square inch	W	wide flange

Appendix B:
Tables and Charts

Appendix C: RFI Forms

 KING CONTRACTING, INC.
P.O. BOX 609
317 RALPH STREET
JACKSON OH 45640
(740) 286-2126 (FAX) 286-5225

KCI RFI 074
20 October 1998

kci@zoomnet.net

REQUEST FOR INFORMATION .... RFI 074

Porter Enterprises, Inc.
239 Porter Street
P.O. Box 6855
Jackson OH 45640

(740) 555-0000
(FAX) 555-0001

(740) 555-0003 (FAX) 555-0002

Attention: Paul Porter

RE: PHASE 3 - INTERIOR BUILD OUT
PEOPLES MEDICAL CENTER
MORGAN, OHIO KCI 98-13

PLEASE ADDRESS THE FOLLOWING:

We are enclosing a copy of KCI Drawing **194** dated 10-19-98. We were drawing window head details and could not complete this detail which applies to curtainwall Types A1 and C at the west end of the First Floor Level between column lines W and T.3. Please complete the details for this situation so that the framing may be roughed in.

REFERENCE: Section B/A4-2.

COMMENTS: _____

_____

_____

_____

_____

PLEASE REPLY NOT LATER THAN 11-02-98 IF POSSIBLE.

_____
KARL L. HEINKE   PROJECT MANAGER

cc: RFI FILE

Fig. C–1. Request for information form. (Courtesy, King Contracting, Inc., 317 Ralph Street, P.O. Box 609, Jackson, OH 45640. Tel: 740-286-2126. Fax: 740-286-5225.)

JOHN T. JONES CONSTRUCTION CO.
REQUEST FOR INFORMATION

Form 2.50

TO: _____

JOB: _____
R.F.I. NO: _____
DRAWING REF: _____
SPEC REF: _____

CONTRACT NO: _____

DATE SENT: _____

INQUIRY: _____
_____
_____
_____
_____
_____
_____
_____

RESPONSE REQUIRED BY: _____

Signed: _____

JOHN T. JONES CONSTRUCTION CO.
P.O. BOX 2424
FARGO, NORTH DAKOTA 58108

- -

REPLY: _____
_____
_____
_____
_____
_____
_____

Signed: _____
Name and Date

John T. Jones Construction Co.
2213 7th Avenue North, P.O. Box 2424
Fargo, North Dakota
701-232-3358

Fig. C–2. Request for information form. (Courtesy, John T. Jones Construction Co., 2213 7th Ave., N., P.O. Box 2424, Fargo, ND 58108. Tel: 701-232-3358. Fax: 701-232-7040.)

CONCORD ASSOCIATES, INC.
513 Park Avenue
Baltimore, Md. 21201
410-727-0200 or FAX 410-727-1267

REQUEST FOR INFORMATION

No. _____

To:	Project:
From:	Area Involved:
Date:	Reference:

Problem:

Signature

Answer:

Signature   Date

Copies to:

Fig. C–3. Request for information form. (Courtesy, Concord Associates, Inc., 513 Park Avenue, Baltimore, MD 21201-4537. Tel: 410-727-0200. Fax: 410-727-1267.)

CC *GENERAL CONTRACTORS*

Contracting Corp of Illinois
PO Box 425 Moline, Illinois 61266-0425
Tel. 309-762-7391   Fax 309-762-1236

REQUEST FOR INFORMATION

To: RFI#

CC:

Information Requested   **Information Needed by** _____

Signed _____   Date _____

Response to Information Request

Signed _____   Date _____

Fig. C–4. Request for information form. (Courtesy, Contracting Corp. of Illinois, 2326 53rd Street, P.O. Box 425, Moline, IL 61265.)

TO: _____

_____

_____

FROM: _____

_____

_____

REQUEST FOR INFORMATION	
DATE	ATTENTION
RFI NO.:	
PROJECT:	

Please note requested information must be received <u>ASAP</u> to avoid delaying the project.

REQUESTED INFORMATION:

_____

_____

_____

_____

_____

_____

SIGNED _____ TITLE _____

RESPONSE:

_____

_____

_____

_____

_____

_____

SIGNED _____ TITLE _____ DATE _____

Fig. C–5. Request for information form. (Courtesy, William Prince, BurWil Construction Company, Inc., P.O. Box 637, Bristol, TN 37621.)

Index

Page numbers of figures are in italics.